THE DISPOSSESSED

I will not stand by and be silent before these terrible things. I will not forget my common humanity, the common element in the whole race. I cannot be contemporary with these events and have it said by my children that I lived through that and did nothing about it—for no reason that I could honestly offer.

WILLIAM ALLAN NEILSON
Northampton, Massachusetts, *Kristallnacht*, November 9, 1938

THE DISPOSSESSED

An Anatomy of Exile

Edited by Peter I. Rose

Foreword by Liv Ullmann

University of Massachusetts Press • Amherst & Boston
published in association with the Kahn Liberal Arts Institute,
Smith College, Northampton, Massachusetts

LC 2004018192
ISBN 1-55849-465-0 (library cloth ed.); 466-9 (paper)

Designed by Dennis Anderson
Set in Legacy Serif Book
Printed and bound by The Maple-Vail Book Manufacturing Group

Library of Congress Cataloging-in-Publication Data

The dispossessed : an anatomy of exile / edited by Peter I. Rose ;
foreword by Liv Ullmann.
      p. cm.
   Includes bibliographical references and index.
   ISBN 1-55849-466-9 (pbk. : alk. paper) — ISBN 1-55849-465-0 (library
cloth : alk. paper)
   1. Refugees. 2. Exiles. 3. Immigrants. 4. Emigration and
immigration. I. Rose, Peter Isaac, 1933–
   HV640.D58 2004
   940.53'086'914—dc22

                                                2004018192

British Library Cataloguing in Publication data are available.

Frontispiece photograph courtesy of the Smith College Archives.

The lithograph reproduced on the cover of the paperback edition of this volume by
the sculptor Jacques Lipchitz is one of eleven original lithographs and one original
serigraph by different artists published in a portfolio, *Flight*, 1971. The series, to raise
funds for the expanded work of the International Rescue Committee, was suggested
by Lipchitz and assembled by Varian Fry, rescuer of Lipchitz and many other European artists, musicians, and other political exiles in 1940. The lithograph is reproduced here courtesy of the International Rescue Committee, www.theIRC.org/
flight.

This is the inaugural volume of the Collaborations series—an occasional series of
books initiated by the Kahn Liberal Arts Institute and published by the University
of Massachusetts Press in association with the Institute.

Contents

FOREWORD

THIS VOLUME, aptly named "The Dispossessed," is about refugees and those who helped them during the turbulent twentieth century. Peter Rose and his colleagues, representing a number of academic disciplines, offer special insights into perhaps the most tragic and iconic figures of the period: the exiles, those torn from their homes because of their faith or their race or their politics or just because they were in the way of some dictator—a Stalin, a Mussolini, a Franco, a Hitler, a Mao, an Idi Amin, a Milosevic, a Duvalier, a Pinochet.

An era of inventiveness and creativity unmatched in human history, the twentieth century was also indelibly marred by wars, atrocities, gulags, and "ethnic cleansing," by the massacres of Armenians and Jews, Cambodians and Bosnians; by the transfer of populations, as between Greece and Turkey, India and Pakistan; by hundreds of thousands of refugees forced to escape from the Soviet Union and its satellites, from Nazi-dominated Europe, and, after World War II, from China and Hungary and Cuba and Chile and Haiti and South Africa and, more recently, from the various states of the former Yugoslavia. There were and continue to be conflicts in Northern Ireland, Sri Lanka, the Middle East, and many parts of Africa.

More often than not the victims of despots and demagogues, of the captains of political cadres and tribal chieftains, and of terrorists of various stripes were—and are—innocent civilians, men, women, and children. While some are fortunate enough to escape the wrath of their persecutors, finding safe havens across the border, only a relative few are able to get to a third country to start life over again. The vast majority of uprooted people are unable to escape. They, the internally displaced, are perhaps the most wretched sufferers of all.

In my experience seeing refugees at firsthand—and talking to hundreds of refugee workers (and to those who have studied both)—I have been struck not only by their often desperate situations but also by the critical roles played by those who are involved in providing relief to the dispossessed, those my friend Peter Rose has referred to as the "advocates," "caretakers," "gatekeepers," "guides," and "go-betweens," all key players in offering assistance.

Since I declare myself an advocate, it should not be surprising when I say that one of the most impressive things about the plan for this volume—and for the Smith College project, "The Anatomy of Exile," which was its incubator—was the emphasis placed on those special people who were engaged in the rescue and resettlement of refugees, especially in the dark days marked by the rise of fascism and Nazism. Not least among the groups cited is the International Rescue Committee, an organization that was created from the merging of two citizen groups, the International Relief Association, established in 1933, and the Emergency Rescue Committee, founded in 1940 by a small group of concerned citizens, writers, publicists, and six university presidents, one of whom was Smith's William Allan Neilson.

That period is especially meaningful to me because my grandfather, Professor Halfdan Ullmann, was one who gave his life trying to save Jews in Norway— and died alongside those he had helped in the first concentration camp to be opened (and the last to be closed) in Germany: Dachau. But even this special connection has not made me, my former colleagues in UNICEF, or my present ones in the International Rescue Committee immune to the suffering of others. Indeed, reflections on my own loss, the courage of those closest to me, and the proactive men and women who work in the field or behind the scenes have only heightened my resolve to continue the campaign against bigotry and injustice and to do whatever can be done to aid the dispossessed. In my travels with UNICEF and the IRC to Southeast Asia, the Middle East, and various parts of Africa, I have seen the faces of those Peter Rose calls the "Madonnas of the Refugee Camps"; in my life in the arts, I have also been privileged to know and work with those he calls the "Maestros in Exile." Whether abjectly poor or illustrious, whether northern or southern, Western, Eastern, or Middle Eastern, they have in common a desperate need for someone to give voice to their plight. This book is a fine example of responding to that desire. It is also a tribute to those who aided the dispossessed in the years from 1900 to 2000.

Those mentored by them are continuing the good work. But they need help. My help. Your help, too.

LIV ULLMANN

Acknowledgments

THIS BOOK, a tribute to the memory of William Allan Neilson, third president of Smith College, owes its origins to a unique project, "The Anatomy of Exile," sponsored by the Kahn Liberal Arts Institute at Smith during the academic year 2000–2001. The principal participants were twenty faculty and student Kahn Fellows and several Visiting Fellows who met twice a week as an ongoing colloquium. In addition, many others—artists and writers, filmmakers and foreign service officers, refugee workers and representatives of the communities all of them study or work with—came to Northampton to take part in a variety of related activities: a number of public lectures and several panel discussions, two theatrical performances, three film screenings, five concerts, and two three-day symposia (the first, in December 2000, titled "Forced Out: The Meaning of Home," and the second, in April 2001, "The Rescue and Resettlement of Refugees").

Most of the essays in this book are based on papers developed for and then presented at one of the colloquium meetings or at one of the public events. Despite the limits set by the publisher, all participants in the various programs were invited to submit essays for consideration. Most did so, and it was up to me as the volume's editor to make the difficult decisions about which manuscripts to accept for publication here. It was not easy, for each submission reflected serious research and careful reporting. Ultimately, selection depended on two criteria: the originality of the work as a contribution to the broad understanding of the concept of exile and the treatment of exiled populations; and how well it fit into a book that was conceived to be not the full "proceedings" of "The Anatomy of Exile" but rather an integrated anthology of independent essays linked to one another under several arbitrary but, I hope, logical section titles.

As the organizer of the "Anatomy of Exile" project, I acknowledge the dedication of all our Fellows, their steadfast participation in the colloquium even when faced with many competing demands, and the zeal with which they pursued their individual research projects and reported on them in "Work in Progress" sessions or in larger forums. I speak for all members of our colloquium when I thank the project coordinator, Rene Heavlow, for her assistance and support at every stage in the project and, more recently, in the preparation of the final manuscript that is now *The Dispossessed*, the first book in a new collaborative publishing venture between the University of Massachusetts Press and Smith College's Kahn Institute.

None of this could have been possible without the cooperation of two key figures: Marjorie Senechal, director of the Kahn Institute, and Bruce Wilcox, director of the University of Massachusetts Press. In addition, Bruce's colleague Carol Betsch was a tireless aid, serving the multiple roles of adviser, encourager, muse, and nudge to an often impatient volume editor.

To all of those mentioned above I say, "Mille grazie."

P. I. R.

PREFACE

Oedipus: What is the rite of purification? How shall it be done?
Creon: By banishing a man, as expiation of blood by blood.

SOPHOCLES

I always found the name false which they gave us: Emigrants.
That means those who leave their country. But we
Did not leave, of our own free will
Choosing another land. Nor did we enter
Into a land, to stay there, if possible for ever.
Merely, we fled. We are driven out, banned.
Not a home, but an exile, shall the land be that took us.

BERTOLT BRECHT

A refugee used to be a person driven to seek refuge because of some
act committed or some political opinion held . . . ; but we committed
no acts. . . . With us the meaning of the term "refugee" has changed.
Now "refugees" are those of us who have been so unfortunate as to
arrive in a new country without means and have to be helped by
Refugee Committees.

HANNAH ARENDT

HANGING ON the wall of my Smith College office is a framed
tribute to my father, Aaron Eli Rose. It bears the signatures of the members of
the Board of the American Jewish Joint Distribution Committee. The citation
describes the committee's gratitude for his extraordinary work on behalf of
the beleaguered Jews of Germany. It is dated December 31, 1936.

The Joint Distribution Committee (JDC) had been founded in 1914 to save
Jews from pogroms and was one of the first organizations to respond to a new
wave of anti-Semitism and persecution sweeping Europe.[1] Prominent among
newer agencies engaged in the same cause were the International Relief Association, founded in 1933 by Albert Einstein, and the National Refugee Service,
many of whose board members, such as Paul Baerwald, David De Sola Pool,
William Rosenwald, and Abba Hillel Silver, were also on the board of the JDC.

All three associations were almost totally dependent on the contributions of private donors and the voluntary efforts of untold numbers of concerned citizens like my father.

This book includes the stories of some of those—clergymen and social workers, journalists and political activists, philanthropists and people of modest means—who took the mandate to be one's brother's keeper to heart. But it is mainly about those whom they tried to assist, a cohort of targeted, displaced, and hounded individuals who managed to escape from Europe. Left behind were millions who would perish in the Holocaust.

At the core of the book are two sets of original essays relating to those individuals in flight from fascist regimes and Nazi domination in the 1930s and 1940s, those who worked to save them, and some of their experiences with and contributions to the societies that provided succor and asylum. Bracketing these sections are thoughtful commentaries by historians, students of literature, and social scientists addressing the general significance of being forced out, the angst of alienation, and the existential character of such an anomic condition.

While this is a collective enterprise, there is little question that my personal experiences and the memories of particular people were principal goads to the orientation of this volume and to the project from which it emerged. In fact, the seeds for what became this book were sown some seventy years ago, in 1933.

I

Among my earliest reminiscences are memories of a number of adults who came to stay with us for several weeks at a time and others who lived with us for quite a while—as long as three years—at our home on Cambridge Street in Syracuse, New York. None of our houseguests was a relative or a friend. My parents called them "refugees."

Although I was too young to understand what that meant, I somehow realized that they were very different from other adults I knew, and not just because they spoke another language with one another and with my parents, or because of the way they behaved. Rather, it was something inchoate and, seemingly, contradictory—an aura marked by a combination of self-reliance and dependence, bravado (in the sense of putting a good face on things) and fear, forced joy and profound sadness. "Melancholy" is the word I would use today.

Whatever their problems, to me the presence of our houseguests was a great boon both to my ego and to my early socialization. I vividly recall reveling in all the attention I, an only child, received from them. It isn't just that they showered me with affection; they were among my first teachers. They taught me about worlds beyond the narrow confines of central New York State. They told me about great cities like Berlin and Prague and Vienna; about wondrous places in Bavaria with high mountains where hikers could always find a restaurant miles from the nearest village; about the river Rhine with storybook castles along its palisades; and about special festivals, too. They spoke of the Oktoberfest, marked by merriment, "oompah" bands, huge sausages and even bigger steins of beer, and of Christmas festivities featuring a plump goose on the table and real candles on the tree. In broken English, they spoke of great musicians and famous writers—Remarque and Toller, Heine and Rilke and Thomas Mann. I didn't care about them. Instead I begged Alma Einstein to tell me yet another of her grisly Grimm tales and to sing me what had become my favorite children's song, the ballad of the bad fox who chased a naïve goose and the *Jaeger* (hunter) who saved the day.

As memorable as the words to stories told in heavily accented English and songs sung in animated German, and the lingering taste of Alma's anise-flavored Christmas cookies, are other, far more painful recollections: muted sobs and heavy-hearted discussions overheard through the thin walls of my bedroom, conversations that went on long into the night, usually among the refugees themselves, but sometimes with my German-speaking parents. Like *Füchse* (foxes) and *Gänse* (geese), certain words more relevant to the struggle of their human counterparts—the predators and the victims—also have stayed with me to this day. *Heimat* (home). *Verlust* (loss), *Vernichtung* (annihilation), *Elend* (misery). *Einsamkeit* (loneliness). *Exil* (exile). *Flüchtling* (refugee).

By the end of the decade, our own country was teetering on the brink of war and I was starting to come of age. I began to comprehend the true significance of each of those German words. The enormity of the circumstances that had brought Alma and Max Einstein and Walter Leipzig and the others into our lives became somewhat clearer, although I was still puzzled by why anyone would want to harm the nice people who had become so much a part of our family.

At every chance I plied them with questions. "Who is Hitler?" "Why is he against you?" "What happened to make you leave home—and the lovely mountains and big castles and . . . ?" "How did you get away?" "Don't you miss your families?" "What will happen to them?" "Will you always stay in America?"

Straightforward questions. Impertinent questions. The sort that only a child would dare to ask.

I remember the answers, too.

I was told about the noose steadily tightening around those who were Jews, or part-Jews, or, like Alma Gummeringer Einstein, Christians who were married to Jews. How they had to register with the police. How they had to go to special schools. How they had to wear yellow six-pointed stars with the word "Jude," the same word that was stamped on official documents. How they were no longer allowed to practice their professions. . . .

"But why?"

"Because . . . ," Max would stammer, in a deep, gravelly voice. "Because Hitler says that Jews are not real Germans but *Untermenschen*," a word as ugly in translation as it sounds in German. "Jews were said to be subhuman. Parasites."

Max told me that many Christian people, including lifelong friends, had turned their backs on them and joined in the discrimination.

"But why?"

"Because that was what Hitler told them to do. He said we were the enemy, 'Germany's misfortune.'" Max said that Hitler was trying to make the country *Judenfrei*, free of Jews.

I learned about roundups, deportations, concentration camps that soon became something more than places of temporary internment, and about *Kristallnacht*, but very little about the plight of the families of "our" refugees. To this day I don't know if they were reluctant to talk about it or if they simply didn't know what was going on. What little they did say about what they feared conjured awful images, pictures in my mind that were beggared by the realities unveiled six or seven years later when the full story was told.

In the course of those question-and-answer periods, often—I now realize—probing painful wounds, I also learned something about those who, like my folks, were dedicated to doing what they could to mitigate the circumstances of the persecution—which ended up being very little—and to aid the victims who managed to escape, where they were somewhat more successful.

While our government was doing next to nothing, despite the fact that many were well aware that whole communities of European Jewry were in mortal danger, the Joint Distribution Committee and several other private organizations raised and distributed millions of dollars to help people escape and facilitate their movement and resettlement. (In the early 1980s I went to Geneva to interview Simon S. Shargo, one of the highest-ranking members of the JDC's staff for over four decades. I wanted to know more about the basic mission of his agency and about its modus operandi in the 1930s and 1940s. The gentle Russian émigré startled me with his terse, emphatic response to both questions. "Our mission can be summed up in three words: *Get them out!*" Then he added, "*Get them out by any means possible.*")

Sometime in the year just before the United States entered the war, I heard my father discussing a particular rescue operation with American colleagues and several refugees gathered in our living room. He mentioned a new organization, the Emergency Rescue Committee, also known as the ERC, and the name of an "operative" who had saved several thousand scholars and writers and political figures by helping to smuggle them out of Marseilles: Varian Fry.[2]

Fry's operation lasted but a single year, 1940, and yet it became a model for others to emulate (and, many, many years later, to honor). Within a few years the ERC merged with the International Relief Association, begun in 1933 by Albert Einstein, and became the International Rescue Committee, the IRC.[3] To a growing lexicon of bureaucratic acronyms, organizational initials, and shorthand expressions—WPA, CCC, TVA, the Writer's Project, Lincoln Brigade, YPSLs (Young People's Socialist Leagues), and, of course, FDR—so widely heard in my parents' circles in the late 1930s, the ERC was added alongside the JDC.

All but one of the refugees who had come to our house was an adult and all but one was German or a German speaker. The odd man out was hardly a man. Twelve-year-old Michael Weingott was one of a number of children who had been evacuated from London shortly after the Blitz, when, ironically, a young German Jewish boy named Karl (I never learned his last name), who had come to England on the storied Kindertransport and found his refuge with the Weingotts, was sent north to Scotland.

Michael was a year and a half older than me. He was short and blond and looked just like my towheaded mother. Indeed, I confess to having had a number of startled and sometimes angry reactions when people who knew my parents had a refugee foster child living in our home would come to visit and, after being introduced to us boys, would turn to me and ask how I liked it in America. Before I could say, "Hey, he's the foreign kid, not me!" sometimes I would be asked about what happened to my family and whether I missed them, how I had gotten to America, whether I was going to stay . . .

Michael had arrived a few months before Pearl Harbor, and we were together at an afternoon matinee at a local movie theater when the manager stopped the film to inform the audience of restless kids that the Japanese had attacked the United States. The silence was stunning. So was the panic that followed. None of us knew, really, what was going on—no one except Michael. He knew what it meant to be under siege and, as a result, almost dragged me home, where he insisted we go down to the cellar and wait for the signals that would tell us what to do next.

Within a few weeks we, like those around us, settled into a new regimen, learning to cope with a bit of belt-tightening, ration cards, a renewed spirit of patriotism, and a genuine wish to be older so we could fight in the war. I have no doubt that my desire to get involved was directly related to the stories I had heard from Alma and Max and Walter and Michael and several German Jewish doctors and professors whom my father had helped to resettle in Syracuse.

Alma and Max left us first. My father had found them a new home and got Max a job as an upholsterer. Walter had gone into the U.S. Army and was assigned to the European theater. Then, late in 1944, Michael returned to England in one of the first convoys allowed to take civilians. It was about six months after D-Day.

At the end of the war, while still in Europe, Walter became romantically involved with a Dutch survivor who had discovered that a niece of hers, named Renata, had also survived. The girl had been hidden in the country by some of those people later to be known as "righteous Christians." Unable to assist her directly, Walter proposed to my parents that they adopt the child. It never dawned on them to refuse, and they immediately began the process of filing affidavits and figuring out ways to bring Renata to America.

As fate would have it, Walter married his Dutch girlfriend and, together, they decided to keep Renata in their own family. I'm sure the girl was thrilled, but I was terribly disappointed, for I was looking forward to having a Dutch sister.

In 1953 I met another Dutch war orphan, Hedy Cohen. Seventeen-year-old Hedy had lost her entire family in the Holocaust, save for her sister Betsy, with whom she had been hidden in an Amsterdam cellar by other Good Samaritans, and who had been brought to the United States in 1947 to live with relatives who were refugees from Vienna. The agency that facilitated the processing of all the paperwork and whose representative accompanied them from Amsterdam to Marseilles to board a ship for America was the Joint Distribution Committee.

Hedy didn't become my sister. Three years after I met her she became my wife.

A teacher and scholar in the field of education, Hedy is often asked to speak about her Anne Frank–like experience. When she does, she invariably stresses the critical role played by "Tante Toos," the woman to whom she and Betsy owe their lives, and others who were willing to risk everything to help innocent victims. While interested in the organizations that bring "hidden children" together, she was never a member. Still, Hedy's early biography has never been far from her mind or her sister's—or mine. As our friend Lewis A. Coser, the German-born sociologist and author of *Refugee Scholars in America*,[4] often said, "One never ceases to be a refugee."

II

Given the background just sketched out, it would not be at all unexpected to learn that, as a young sociologist, I decided early on to focus on refugees. But I didn't. Aside from encountering a number of German Jewish physicians placed in tiny hamlets by the JDC and HIAS, the Hebrew Immigrant Aid Society, where I was conducting research on isolated minorities in the late 1950s, and a growing fascination with exiled intellectuals, artists, and social scientists and their impact on our culture, as well as some familiarity with their writings and the writings about them, I did not start to concentrate on refugees until the late 1970s. In fact, I more or less backed into the subject.

Until that point in time, while my academic studies and political commitments were mainly on civil and human rights, it was not the uprooted on whom I had concentrated but the victims of discrimination in this country. Race, ethnicity, and the dilemmas of diversity were the primary subjects of my research, writing, and teaching from my entering graduate school in 1954 to the time when "the boat people" became a phrase recognized by all Americans. If there is a bridge between what I looked at from the mid-1950s to the mid-1970s and what I turned to later, it was a particular fascination with two concepts: estrangement, referring to both literal and psychological alienation, and marginality, meaning being fated to live on the edge of a dominant society as a minority. What intrigued me was the asymmetry of dominant-minority relations and the fact that the weaker party had to be able to live in, or at least understand, the rules of two worlds, while those in power were often completely ignorant of the other, relying on stereotypes and the prejudices of others. As I examined these key concepts, I became interested in what I saw as the special functions of being an "outsider-within."[5] I was struck by the fact that so many of the social critics and social scientists I knew and admired were "strangers" themselves, members of minority groups in this country or refugees. For many years I thought of writing more about this phenomenon. But I was too busy with other projects. Then, almost serendipitously, an opportunity presented itself.

Long opposed to the war in Southeast Asia and worried about what would happen in the aftermath of what was clearly a losing cause for those who supported it, I decided to look into the plight of anticommunist Vietnamese intellectuals after the fall of Saigon. I received a small study grant but, to my great disappointment, quickly learned what I should have known from the start: France got the intellectuals, and we (the United States) got the generals! I must admit that their situation was of far less interest to me, but I found myself intrigued by the question of how they managed to get out and come to the United States—and how they fared. With the sudden mass movement of thousands upon thousands of "boat people," and an international agreement that if the "countries of first asylum" (on whose shores they sought to land) would take them in temporarily, Western countries, most particularly the United States, Canada, and Australia, would provide third-country resettlement, it quickly became clear that we were facing the prospect of the largest nonwhite, non-Christian, non-English-speaking migration of refugees ever to enter America.

In the late 1970s I began conducting research on the making and implementing of U.S. refugee policy in Southeast Asia, and on the acceptance and acculturation of the refugees. The study would take me to many refugee camps overseas and many resettlement centers across this country (including those as close as nearby Amherst) and introduce me to the network of key players— the high officials of the UNHCR, the United Nations High Commission for Refugees, and the ICEM, the Intergovernmental Committee for European Migration (which became ICM, the Intergovernmental Committee for Migration and, more recently, IOM, the International Organization for Migration), in Geneva and New York; U.S. government bureaucrats in the White House and the departments of State, Justice, and Health and Human Services; directors of the agencies, field managers, and refugee workers, especially those I came to see as "advocates," "caretakers," "gatekeepers," "guides," and "go-betweens,"[6] including those who worked for the "Joint" and the International Rescue Committee.

Remembering when I first heard about such organizations, I realized I had come full circle. Back to my roots.

Once in the field, I found I was asking some of the same questions of many of the Einsteins and Leipzigs and Weingotts of the modern world (now with names like Nguyen and Tranh and Pho): "Why did you leave?" "What happened to you?" "To your family?"

Not very long after starting to look into the specifics of the rescue and resettlement of refugees from Vietnam, Laos, and Cambodia, I decided to broaden the scope of the research. I started to probe more systematically the worlds of those who had been forced to flee their homes and homelands because of their membership in particular groups and categories deemed unacceptable, or because they had a "well-founded fear of persecution," or because they were caught in the cross fire of conflicts beyond their control— people who were defined in UN protocols, and only recently in American law, as "political refugees."

Curious to know how others saw "refugees," I learned that most people in this country had two rather different impressions of such dispossessed people.

One was a poignant image of tired and poor and always troubled (and, to many, troublesome) masses of nameless persons trapped in a maelstrom of political turmoil of which they had little understanding. Their plight is summed up in the widely used portrait of the stick-thin, wan, empty-eyed mother and her dying baby in the foreground of a scene of seemingly thousands of similar mothers, an iconic figure I once referred to as the "Madonna of the Refugee Camp."[7] The second image was more exalted. It was of the exiled intellectual or scientist or artist: Ovid's descendant, or Dante's; Heinrich Heine's, or Victor Hugo's. Among my age peers and fellow academics, those who came most quickly into their mind's eye were the victims of Hitler's policies who had managed to find havens in America, members of the Frankfurt school, the Bauhaus, the Vienna Circle, who had temporarily "relocated" to the United States; or they conjured specific notables such as Albert Einstein, Enrico Fermi, Neils Bohr, Paul Lazarsfeld, Hannah Arendt, Kurt Lewin, Paul Tillich, Bertolt Brecht, Marc Chagall, Josef Albers, Lion Feuchtwanger, Billy Wilder, Marlene Dietrich, Wanda Landowska, George Szell, Bruno Walter—each an extraordinary individual, together a collectivity of maestros in exile.

What was surprising to me was how few thought very much about those who fell between the masses of bedraggled refugees and the relatively small cohort of luminaries, the many ordinary working-class and middle-class people, often lumped together by nationality or group membership or race or gender or occupation—farmers and laborers, tinkers and tailors, shopkeepers and union members and managers, bureaucrats and professionals—whose acceptability for resettlement and whose acceptance once in the host society depended on various cost-benefit analyses having to do with racial attitudes, cultural proclivities, economic conditions, the politics of rescue (meaning both international and domestic concerns), and "needs." On reflection, I realized that there was a simple explanation for the gap in understanding. Most people had little if any exposure to their plight through their primary sources—television, magazines, and newspapers.

Again I thought of those first refugees I'd known. They were neither "madonnas" nor "maestros." They were not particularly desirable to the authorities because they had no unique skills to bring to this country at a time when being a foreigner, whatever the reason for the individual's migration, meant being a competitor for scarce jobs in a depression-wracked economy.[8] I do not know how they got their visas, but they were lucky to have made it. Most people like them couldn't escape and died in the Holocaust.

"Our" Einstein, Max, had been an upholsterer in Hanover; his wife, Alma, a *hausfrau*; Walter Leipzig had started studying accounting in his hometown of Leipzig—and became an elevator operator during the first years of his exile in

America. When I first asked Michael Weingott what his father did, he said he was "in the leather trades." In fact, he sold gloves at one of the giant department stores, Selfridges or Harrods, in London; something Michael also did after returning to the United Kingdom and after a hitch in the Royal Air Force. And my wife, Hedy's, Dutch father, with the aristocratic name of Jacques Frederick Theobold Alfred Karl Cohen, had been a pastry chef on Holland-America ships that plied the Atlantic and, later, was the owner-baker of a pastry shop in Amsterdam. Jacques's Viennese-born wife, Rosa Schwarz, was a bookkeeper and bank manager. The Austrian couple who adopted Hedy and Betsy after the war, Alfred Schwarz (Rosa's brother) and Anna Trincher, were professionals: Alfred was a mechanical and electrical engineer who also had a Ph.D. in physics; Anna had spent a year training to become a physician but had been forced by financial circumstances to give it up to allow her brother to continue his medical education. She became a dress designer and had her own atelier in Vienna.

III

I began going backwards in time, studying the early days of organizations such as the JDC and the Emergency Rescue Committee, and outward, too, moving first quite hesitantly, then with increasing comfort in and out of three intersecting circles: the relatively small group of academics who study exile; the larger fraternity of the agents and agencies that provide aid and assistance to refugees; and that broad category of people, the objects of their attention and commitments, bound together by a common plight, having been forced to flee, and a shared destiny—to maintain their commonly ascribed status "even to the grave."[9]

Between 1980 and 2000 I organized a number of conferences addressing themes such as "Crisis in Cambodia: A Cry for Commitment," "The New Medina: The Rescue and Resettlement of Indochinese Refugees," "The Sociology of Exile," and "Working with Refugees," bringing together representatives of those three worlds. Some of these meetings were held on the campus of Smith College, my home base since 1960 and, owing to its distinguished third president, William Allan Neilson, one of the most important American institutions of higher learning directly involved in welcoming exiles from fascism and Nazism in the 1930s and 1940s. In the archives of the Neilson Library at Smith, I started to examine the papers of its namesake and learned that he was one of the founders of both the ERC and the IRC.

In 2000 I proposed to the director of Smith's new Kahn Liberal Arts Institute that the general subject of exile would be a most fitting subject for the sort of year-long, interdisciplinary, faculty-student projects the institute was promoting and financing. The idea was accepted and, with a cadre of twenty "fellows"—ten of them faculty members from Smith and nearby colleges and universities and ten of them undergraduates (all selected on a highly competitive basis)—and a small number of Visiting Fellows, the academic year 2000–2001 became, for us, "The Year of the Refugee." At least that is how we saw it. Increasingly, others were to see—and feel—it, too.

Our group, whose faculty ranks included several scholars who were refugees themselves and whose student members included more foreigners than Americans, was known as "The Anatomy of Exile Colloquium." We met twice weekly to discuss general themes and individual projects. We wrestled with definitions—never, I should note, satisfactorily clarifying the distinction between the often conflated words "exile" and "refugee." In addition, we sponsored a number of public events: eight lectures on topics ranging from a consideration of Ovid's exile to the then current crisis in the Sudan; five concerts, including two that featured "Music from the Ashes" of Theresienstadt and Auschwitz and one, a new cantata by Ronald Perera, that celebrated America's "Golden Door"; films on the attempts of Cambodians to reconstruct their lives in the United States and on the individuals behind the bureaucratic facade of the Immigration and Naturalization Service; two theatrical performances, both addressing the situation in the Balkans; a panel discussion, "Internally Displaced Persons and the Role of the International Community"; and two three-day symposia.

The first symposium was centered on the meaning of home for those forced to leave it; the second was on rescue and resettlement and was dedicated to the memory of President Neilson and many others at Smith College and in the immediate area who had welcomed refugee scholars and writers and artists to the campus and to homes in Northampton, Cummington, and Whately, Massachusetts.

Toward the end of a year of intensive activity, a contract was signed with the University of Massachusetts Press to publish a volume of essays based on some of the work generated by the "Anatomy of Exile" project, with a major emphasis on the 1930s and 1940s. *The Dispossessed* is the result.

The first section of the volume, "Forced Out," deals with some of the issues addressed in the first "Anatomy of Exile" symposium: visions of home, and the consequences of being forced to leave it, from the perspectives of the dispossessed. The second, "Their Brothers' Keepers," is a multi-essay case study of rescue and resettlement before and during World War II. The commentaries and analyses are arranged as if one were to use a stop-action zoom lens, starting with a broad, wide-angle perspective, and steadily zeroing in one area, the

Pioneer Valley of western Massachusetts, and then on a small number of individual refugees and their hosts. The third section, "Émigrés and Their Impacts," offers stories of several scholars, scientists, artists, and writers in exile and analyses of their experiences, personal problems, and cultural contributions. The volume ends with a special coda, the reflections of two more recent refugees, father and son, one a psychiatrist and poet, the other a sociologist who specializes in immigration.

I want to reiterate that, while the range of subjects considered in our colloquium was wide, the contributions selected for the core of this volume are intentionally limited. They are, in the main, about a particular period, a particular group of concerned activists, the people they assisted, and the contributions those reluctant migrants offered to their new communities. In some ways what is reported here is unique. In other respects there is ample evidence that certain debates about the rescue and resettlement, acceptance and acculturation of specific political refugees, their subsequent treatment, and their experiences are like leitmotifs recurring in one after another "refugee crisis" throughout the second half of the twentieth century, with people fleeing from Hungary, Cuba, Czechoslovakia, Chile, Vietnam, Laos, Cambodia, various parts of Central America, and more from South America, South Asia, Africa, and the Balkans. All these refugees were subjects of our concern and were addressed during the year-long colloquium. They are not to be forgotten. Commentaries on their situations—and on those who are internally displaced—are to be published elsewhere.

The reader will note that this book is dedicated to the memory of William Allan Neilson, Harold Oram, Miriam Davenport, Varian Fry, the members of the Joint Distribution Committee and the Emergency Rescue Committee, and all other descendants of Theseus who refused to turn their backs on the dispossessed but, instead, provided care, succor, and asylum. Among those descendants of Theseus were my parents. And among those dispossessed were some ordinary people who had an extraordinary impact on one very impressionable little boy.

PETER I. ROSE

Notes

1. See Oscar Handlin, *A Continuing Task: The American Jewish Joint Distribution Committee, 1914–1964* (New York: Random House, 1964).

2. In addition to Varian Fry's own account, *Surrender on Demand* (New York: Random House, 1945), reprinted in various editions, and Mary Jayne Gold, *Crossroads Mar-*

seilles, 1940 (New York: Doubleday), two more recent books and a film offer differing interpretations of the founding of the Emergency Rescue Committee and its activities. See Andy Marino, *A Quiet American: The Secret War of Varian Fry* (New York: St. Martin's Press, 1999); Sheila Eisenberg, *A Hero of Our Own: The Story of Varian Fry* (New York: Random House, 2001); and, on the film *Varian's War*, Peter I. Rose, "Debasing Good History with Bad Fiction," *Chronicle of Higher Education Review*, April 20, 2001, B18–19.

3. See Aaron Levenstein, *Escape to Freedom: The Story of the International Rescue Committee* (Westport, Conn.: Greenwood Press, 1983).

4. Lewis A. Coser, *Refugee Scholars in America: Their Impact and Their Experiences* (New Haven: Yale University Press, 1984).

5. See Peter I. Rose, *Nobody Knows the Trouble I've Seen: Some Reflections on the Insider-Outsider Debate* (Northampton, Mass.: Smith College, 1978).

6. For a discussion of these "types," see Peter I. Rose, *Tempest-Tost* (New York: Oxford University Press, 1997), 87–104.

7. Ibid., 44.

8. See David Wyman, *Paper Walls: America and the Refugee Crisis, 1938–1941* (Amherst: University of Massachusetts Press, 1968); Henry L. Feingold, *The Politics of Rescue: The Roosevelt Administration and the Holocaust, 1938–1945* (New Brunswick, N.J.: Rutgers University Press, 1970); and David Wyman, *The Abandonment of the Jews: America and the Holocaust, 1941–1945* (New York: Pantheon Books, 1984).

9. Antranik Zaroukian, "Let There Be Light," in *Landscape and Exile*, ed. Marguerite Guzman Bouvard (Boston: Rowan Tree Press, 1985), 185.

THE DISPOSSESSED

I

FORCED OUT

Exile is strangely compelling to think about but terrible to experience.

EDWARD SAID

Exile is the loneliness in the middle of a crowd.
Exile is the longing never to be fulfilled,
It is love unrequited, the loss never replaced.
Exile is a song that only the singer can hear.

PAUL TABORI

THERE ARE few things more devastating to the human spirit
than being forced to flee from home. Sometimes the causes of
uprooting are natural disasters; too often they are manmade.
Perhaps the cruelest type of displacement is that caused by cate-
gorical victimization, the singling out of individuals and groups
because of their ascribed positions in society. Those who fall under the large rubric "the dispossessed" have often been targeted
because of membership in a particular religious or racial or political group said to constitute a genuine or putative threat to the
established order; many are scapegoats used by those in power to
transfer onto particular individuals or vulnerable minorities
blame for their own or others' failures. Some dispossessed persons are hapless pawns in exchanges of populations between
neighboring and often hostile states; still others are innocent
bystanders caught up in the cross fire of other people's conflicts.
To this array of victims one more must be added: those who are
first viewed, then treated, as exploitable chattel or *Untermenschen*,
subhumans not fit for continued life.

The forced movement of the dispossessed is often "internal,"
that is, within the state. Familiar methods are roundups, segregation in special sectors or ghettoization, incarceration in prisons or
concentration camps, and mass extermination or genocide, often
represented today by the ugly phrase "ethnic cleansing." It should
be noted that "ethnic cleansing" is not used only as a euphemism

for causing removal, detention, and sometimes "disappearance" on one's home soil; it also refers to forced relocation, actual deportation to another country. Apart from the slave trade, which almost always involves capture and removal for financial gain, over tens of centuries most cross-border coerced migration—ethnic cleansing and other purges of particular individuals or groups— has involved two different acts, one directly initiated by those holding absolute power, the other taken by those subject to it. The first is *expulsion*, or what Sophocles, writing in *Oedipus the King*, called "purification" and "expiation through banishment." The second is *flight*, escaping to freedom.

There is clearly a difference between being ordered out and opting to flee. Yet it would be naïve to say that because banishment is involuntary, flight is ipso facto "voluntary," because the root causes of both are often closely related. The fact is that flight or escape is encouraged by those who threaten harsher treatment should those targeted remain. Twentieth-century examples abound, from the scare tactics of Turkish authorities used to encourage Armenians to get out of Turkey, to the proclamations of Nazi leaders urging their followers to ensure that the lands under their control be *Judenfrei*, "free of Jews," to the less formal but still clear messages to Arabs to leave Palestine during the Israeli War of Independence in 1948, to the worst results of the most recent balkanization in the Balkan states, the slaughter in Rwanda, the disasters in the Chechen Republic.

The expressive labels "expellees" and "escapees," for those better known as "exiles" and "refugees," are sometimes used interchangeably, even though they have very different etymological roots. Most dictionaries and encyclopedias note that the term "exile"—from *exilium*, a Latin word meaning to officially cast out or expel—refers to those who have been ostracized, then banished from their native lands. One thinks of the Exodus or the years of the Babylonian exile, or more generally of those scattered in a hundred diasporas. Refugees are described as those who flee to another country for asylum and protection in time of political upheaval or war. (Although the concept of the asylum seeker is very old, the word "refugee" itself is much more modern than "exile." It is a word rooted in French, *réfugié*. When first used in popular discourse, it referred very specifically to those known as Huguenots who favored the Calvinist communion in seventeenth-

century France and, targeted by the Catholic rulers after the revo-
cation of the Treaty of Nantes in 1685, refused to bow to the dictates of authority and chose to become expatriates, leaving their
homes and seeking sanctuary in England, the canton of Geneva,
and neighboring states.)

Many who write about exiles and refugees, including the authors of the essays in this book, are well aware of the origins of
the terms as well as their etymological differences, and still, many
tend to conflate the concepts. The principal reason lies in the single notion of coercion. No clearer example is to be found than in
the works of the Hungarian writer Paul Tabori. In the very first
section, "The Semantics of Exile," of his comprehensive tome
(and source of my subtitle) *The Anatomy of Exile: A Semantic and
Historical Study* (1972), Tabori states that "an exile is a person who
is compelled to leave his homeland," then adds, "It does not make
an essential difference whether he is expelled by physical force or
whether he makes the decision to leave [himself] without such an
immediate pressure." For Tabori, and many of our writers, what is
important is that while conceptually and linguistically separable,
the strains resulting from coerced displacement and the resulting
sense of alienation are generally indistinguishable. Those who, in
Tabori's terms, have been "compelled to leave" and those who
"choose" to flee share a common fate and a common reality. They
are alienated in the most literal sense of the word: they are strangers on foreign soil.

To be sure, some dispossessed persons are more alienated than
others. Sharing a common language with those in the host society, as well as similar cultural orientations, religious beliefs,
and/or physical traits, can often ease the strain of estrangement.
But even such mitigating factors cannot alter the fact that, advantaged or not, they all tend to share the transcendent reality of
homelessness.

It is perhaps this binding trait that makes all who are dispossessed—whether exiles or refugees—seem members of a different
species under the overall genus *migrants*, or people on the move. If
the sine qua non condition of the dispossessed is *centrifugal*—and
this is something that is reified in international law, where the
singular criterion is that individuals are categorically persecuted
or have a "well-founded fear of persecution" should they be
forced to return to their countries of origin—the prime character-

istic of immigrants is *centripetal*. They are pulled in by the promise of a better life, the key incentives being economic. It is often said that, without such a prospect of greener pastures, few guest workers or would-be immigrants would venture forth. The dispossessed generally do not have the luxury of such a choice. Most seekers of asylum never want to leave kith, kin, or country; they don't want to leave their homes, their true refuge. They don't want to wander far and stand as by the rivers of Babylon crying, "How shall we sing the Lord's song in a strange land?" or live in the limbo of being, as the Armenian writer Antranik Zaroukian says, "strangers even to [the] grave." They don't want to be haunted by memories of persecution, wrenching decisions about leaving family, friends, and familiar surroundings, the ordeal of expulsion or escape, the anomic limbo where familiar rules have been torn asunder and normal responses to stress no longer obtain, constant thoughts of those who were and what was left behind, the frustrations of existence in foreign environs, and the uncertainty of future prospects, including fading dreams of going home. But they are. And that is what distinguishes the dispossessed from all other migrants.

Elie Wiesel, Auschwitz survivor, writer, and Nobel laureate, recognizing the significance of these melancholy motifs, has written: "What has been done to the word refuge? In the beginning the word sounded beautiful. A refuge meant 'home.' It welcomed you, protected you, gave you warmth and hospitality. Then we added one single phoneme, one letter, e, and the positive term *refuge* became refugee, connoting something negative."

That negativity is related not only to the angst suffered by most uprooted people but also to the responses of those in would-be countries of asylum. The Australian writer Bruce Grant describes those who are asked to provide sanctuary, who, it turns out, are far more often apt to reflect the spirit of *xenophobia*, the fear of the stranger, than what the Greeks called *philoxenia*, or hospitality to the stranger. It is a fact of life that many, perhaps a substantial majority of people, at least in the Western world, are more inclined to build walls against what they see as encroachment rather than bridges of welcome; they are wary of the strangers at their gates—even those who have suffered persecution and undergone expatriation.

A refugee is an unwanted person. He or she makes a claim upon the humanity of others without always having much, or even anything sometimes to give in return. If, after resettlement, a refugee works hard or is lucky and successful, he may be accused of taking the work or the luck or success from someone else. If he fails or becomes resentful or unhappy, he is thought to be ungrateful and a burden to the community. A refugee is especially unwanted by officials: his papers are rarely in order, his health is often suspect and sometimes, although he claims to be fleeing from persecution, he is simply trying to get from one poor, overpopulated country to a rich underpopulated one. (*The Boat People*, 2.)

Many essays in this volume, especially those in the two largest sections, are about the 1930s and 1940s and focus on those who were forced to leave Nazi-occupied Europe, as well as those who reached out to give aid to the dispossessed.

The authors of the first set of essays all wrestle with Wiesel's question, and, indirectly, with Grant's concerns, but in many different ways. The section begins with a challenging chapter by the Norwegian scholar and English professor at the University of Bergen, Orm Øverland, who has spent a lifetime studying and writing about exiles and immigrants and their literatures. Here he focuses on the variables of departure and entry not only as actions but also as "states of mind" in the shaping of post-migration identities.

Next, Smith College political scientist and Middle East specialist Donna Robinson Divine also writes on post-migration identity and the concepts of home and homeland in Zionist ideology. Divine argues that, to Zionists, the experience of exile—the exile of an entire people—carries "burdens of reference so deeply rooted in the personality of Diaspora Jewry that nothing short of negating the Diaspora, as symbol, culture, and system of authority, could truly bring Jews back to their home."

Diasporas are common themes in writings about exile, ancient and modern. In her poignant analysis of one of the numerous twentieth-century examples of "ethnic cleansing," this one in Asia Minor, Thalia Pandiri, professor of classics at Smith College and noted translator, offers a case study of the trauma of persecution, expulsion, and resettlement. "Driven Out of Eden" reverberates with the echoing voices of Greek and Turkish refugees, their words drawn from the narratives of their lives and plight found in the archives of Athens under the title *Exodus*.

Bulgarian writer, Smith College graduate, and doctoral student in comparative literature at the University of California at Berkeley, Polina Dimova offers a most appropriate bridge to the core sections of our volume, moving from the general to the very specific. In a masterly essay she indicates how literature may capture the experience of exile as she examines one autobiographical short story written by the German Jewish writer Anna Seghers.

Then, in keeping with the syncopated rhythm of this book of analytical essays and descriptive accounts, the final contribution in this section is a lengthy excerpt from *Haven*, a firsthand report on the politics of rescue and the resettlement of some one thousand refugees from Europe to the United States in 1944. The author is the indefatigable journalist, activist, and mid-level official in the administration of Franklin Delano Roosevelt, Ruth Gruber, who helped to arrange for the transport of the refugees, accompanied them on their journey, and wrote about their experiences—and her own.

VISIONS OF HOME
Exiles and Immigrants

ORM ØVERLAND

> Perhaps a successful immigrant is an exaggerated version of the
> native. From now on, I'll be made, like a mosaic, of fragments—and my
> consciousness of them. It is only in that observing consciousness
> that I remain, after all, an immigrant.
>
> EVA HOFFMAN, *Lost in Translation*

> To be an exile is, in some ways, to be a split personality. The longer
> one lives in a foreign country, the farther away one feels from the old
> homeland, and the fonder one gets of the new one. However, the
> old country never disappears beyond the horizon, and the new one, to
> the exile, will never become the open book that it is to those who
> were born there, and can read it with no difficulty.
>
> JOSEF ŠKVORECKÝ, *Two Murders in My Double Life*

THE WORD *immigrant* speaks of entry, of going into and settling
in another country. The related words *emigrant* and *exile* are both about departure. These three words, however, are about departure and entry not only as
acts but also as states of mind. They may be used to refer to the same person
seen from different points of view, as one leaving a homeland or as one entering a new homeland, but they may also be used to distinguish between two
different mindsets, that of a person who remains emotionally and intellectually attached to a former homeland, and that of one who is preoccupied with
relating to a new homeland. These words, then, are about identities. A shared
migration may be experienced by one individual primarily as immigration and
by another primarily as emigration. Indeed, both experiences may at different
times be foremost in the mind of the same individual.

The words *emigrant* and *exile* may speak of different kinds of departure, the
one voluntary (although there may be pressing reasons behind the decision),
the other forced and enforced by the threat of violence and loss of life or
freedom. In extreme cases, such as leaving for adventure or for banishment,
the differences between emigrant and exile are clear. There may, however, be
such pressing political or economic reasons behind a decision to emigrate that
it is not always useful to distinguish too clearly between the emigrant and the

exile. Both may live in a state of longing; the exile, moreover, lives in a state of banishment. Another way of distinguishing between the mindsets of emigrant and exile is to see the former preoccupied with a homeland as it was and the latter with a homeland as it should become. One cannot, however, leave a country without entering another. By crossing borders, both emigrants and exiles are perceived as immigrants—except for the many who live, often for a long period of time, in the limbo of detention camps or various kinds of halfway institutions. Individuals may continue to identify themselves as emigrants or exiles, but in a receiving country little distinction is made among immigrants on the basis of their reasons for departure.[1]

In this essay I am concerned with expressions of post-migration identities and states of mind, and the words *emigrant* and *exile* are both used to characterize an identity focused elsewhere, on a former, even an imagined, homeland. An immigrant identity, for the purposes of this essay, is one focused on the entering and making of a new homeland.

For the individual, the difference between remaining an exile and becoming an immigrant may be one of time as well as of mentality. Eva Hoffman divides her justly celebrated memoir *Lost in Translation* into three parts—"Paradise," about her Jewish Polish childhood; "Exile," about her first years in Canada and the United States; and then, finally, "The New World"—suggesting that for her the sense of exile was a phase. As her titles for her book and its third part suggest, although something is unavoidably lost, something has also been achieved: a new world. In his foreword to his recent novel *Two Murders in My Double Life*, the Czech Canadian writer Josef Škvorecký suggests that exile is a lifelong identity, an identity that may even persist long after the home country has opened its borders. To him an exile is a divided personality who will never feel fully at home in his new country even though the old one becomes not merely distant but strange. Not only may an exile live a double life, but also he may be estranged from both of them: the loss of an old homeland is not necessarily followed by the acquisition of a new one.[2]

Øyvind Gulliksen, a Norwegian scholar of American immigration, uses the metaphor of the "double landscape" in his study of the emotional and intellectual life of immigrants.[3] He demonstrates the impact of two linguistic and cultural traditions in immigrant writing, one of memory of the former homeland and the other acquired in the process of immigration. In his fine analysis, these two traditions within one identity are not in conflict but in harmony. The ability to inhabit—intellectually and emotionally—a double landscape is an asset rather than a flaw, and the tensions of such a life are creative rather than destructive. The double landscape as a metaphor of the immigrant mind opens up an awareness of this expansive and creative potential of the experience of immigration as well as a perception of the immigrant as an actor rather than as the victim of uprootedness or transplantation, two classic metaphors for the immigrant experience.[4] Given the complex migrations of contemporary life, many of us live in multiple, palimpsest-like layered landscapes. My concern here is with the two mental landscapes before and after migration to the United States. Most of my own research has focused on immigration from Europe in the decades just before and after the turn of the twentieth century. For the exile, the first landscape held more meaning; for the immigrant, the other one took on the greater emotional and intellectual significance.

The written record may have misled historians into exaggerating the importance of memory in the daily lives of immigrants. Because the nineteenth-century migration of Europeans to the United States coincided with the widespread acquisition of literacy by ordinary men and women, it became the first mass movement of people to be recorded by so many of the participants themselves. Even the many who could not compose a letter could be helped by a more skilled family member or neighbor. Before migration, in a life where family and friends were usually within walking distance, there was little reason to communicate in writing. Migration gave both motivation to write and much to write about that was unknown to correspondents in Europe. The large mass of letters sent to Europe from American immigrants—"America letters," as they are often called—is an important source for understanding not only how immigrants experienced their transition but also what were the factual aspects of their lives. Nevertheless, like all historical documents, these texts must be read critically. For in the very act of writing the occasional letter to parents, siblings, or close friends—often late at night in poor urban or rural housing and after a long day of hard labor, perhaps when the writer was the only person awake in a room full of sleeping people—immigrants could naturally be overcome by a longing that was not characteristic of the other moments of their day and their usual preoccupation with making a home in America for themselves and their families. I have referred to this phenomenon as situational nostalgia, a nostalgia created by the very act of writing.[5] Another genre that may similarly mislead us into exaggerating immigrant nostalgia is popular verse and song. For the genre itself, with all its conventions, invites sentimentality—about being far from home or about a lost love as the case may be. This is not to say that all emigrants easily became forward-looking immigrants with little thought of their former lives. Even the most successful immigrants may on occasion be overwhelmed by the memory of a landscape, a street, a situation, or a person in the country they have left; and many, unable to make the mental transition into being an immigrant, spend their lives thinking back on life in a country whose loss they experience as exile. Expressions of exile in immigrant letters and verse, however, may mislead us about the preponderant mentality of the majority of Europeans who entered the United States. An individual's sense of being an exile or an immigrant, then, may be a question not only of development over time but also of changing moods depending on specific situations.

About three decades ago, one image of exile made a lasting impression on me. I was walking up Fifth Avenue in Manhattan and there, at a table on the sidewalk, surrounded by posters and pamphlets, sat a woman unsuccessfully trying to attract the attention of passers-by. The posters and pamphlets spoke of the harsh suppression of freedom in the Soviet Union. In my imagination this exiled woman had once suffered from this suppression in a land where even the most circumspect expression of opposition was taken seriously by all. The views promoted by her posters and pamphlets would, in that other context, certainly have cost her freedom, perhaps her life. She was now enjoying the fruits of freedom but in a context in which her expression of this freedom was not taken seriously, not even by the police, and attracted no interest from those who hurried past. Exile can be a doubly isolating experience.

This image of exile is complemented in my mind by an earlier image of immigration and of identification with a new homeland. I was leaving Yale's cathedral-like Sterling Memorial Library after a long day of graduate study. Ahead of me at the exit desk, where a guard was obliged to inspect our bags, a woman refused to open hers as a line of impatient people grew behind us. Finally she gave in, the guard peeked cursorily in her bag, and she went out through the heavy doors. As I walked after her into the dark and rainy New Haven evening, she turned around, looked up at me, and said with a heavy accent, "Imagine their doing this to me, an American citizen." She, too, had no doubt sought asylum as an exile in the United States. In her accented voice, however, I heard expressed a vision of a new home, a vision that has been shared by many generations of immigrants to the United States.

THE HISTORIAN would be well advised not to draw clear distinctions between emigrants and exiles, voluntary and involuntary immigrants. At the time of the first U.S. Census in 1790, the culturally and politically dominant British Americans made up approximately 48 percent of the population of the new republic. Africa had once been the home of about 20 percent.[6] Abduction and enslavement are certainly more apt terms than emigration to describe the departure of Africans for America in the seventeenth and eighteenth centuries. Yet, if these African Americans are not included in the study of immigration history, our account of the population of the colonial period is skewed. Moreover, to study the influx of European peasants into the cities of the northern

United States at the turn of the twentieth century without also considering the influx of rural African Americans into the same cities would be to miss important aspects of what was happening. Even though the latter group did not cross national borders in their migration, the cultural and social adjustments required of both groups are surely comparable. Finally, a third point: to neglect the involuntary migration of Africans as part of the history of American immigration would lead to strange discontinuities in the study of twentieth-and twenty-first-century immigration from the Caribbean and from Africa. We should also recognize that the difference between voluntary and involuntary migration is not always clear-cut. The Irish who were taken from poorhouses to emigrant ships in the mid-nineteenth century with little or no understanding of their destination cannot in any meaningful way be characterized as voluntary emigrants. One factor that may throw light on the suffering of *their* middle passage is that the owners of these ships were paid for the number of passengers taken on board rather than for the number that arrived in America.

The German '48ers—refugees from the upheavals of 1848—left as political exiles, but many created meaningful roles for themselves as Americans and were in their American behavior indistinguishable from those whose departure from Europe had been voluntary. Thus the individual response to the experience of immigration may eventually become more important than the different motivations for departure of the emigrant and the exile. But motivation may also have a more lasting impact. In immigrant families of the nineteenth century, the decision to emigrate need not have involved all family members. Typically, the decision would rest with the male head of the family, and as a consequence, one spouse could have the forward-looking mentality of the immigrant while the other could be consumed by the longing typical of exile. The difference between exile and immigration, then, may be a question not only of time and mentality, nor of political versus economic motivation, but also of gender.[7] Until recently, the immigrant of immigration history has been male.

The distinction between exiles and immigrants remains problematic when we consider two apparently contrasting kinds of expressions of belonging that were common among three immigrant groups in the United States at the turn of the twentieth century: Irish, Poles, and Jews. One is an expression of belonging in the country from which they had experienced exile and the other is about belonging in the United States, the country they had chosen as theirs but which insisted on regarding them as foreigners; one focuses on the re-creation of a former homeland and the other expresses a desire to make a new one.

It is difficult to speak with accuracy about popular thought and emotion in the past since most people have left little record of their emotional and intellectual lives. When we speak of immigrant expression—in spite of all the preserved immigrant letters—we speak primarily of those who have left behind a published record, those we may call the immigrant elite. As has been observed by so many, however, from the American sociologist Horace Kallen in 1915 to the Swedish historian Dag Blanck in 1997, the immigrant leadership of writers, journalists, clergy, teachers, professionals, businessmen, and politicians played an essential role in voicing and shaping the attitudes of the immigrant rank and file through newspapers and other publications, churches, parochial schools, picnics and entertainments, festivals and celebrations, and local as well as national ethnic associations.[8] Consequently, immigrant expression, though unavoidably shaped by an elite, was shared by many.

In his important book *Special Sorrows: The Diasporic Imagination of Irish, Polish, and Jewish Immigrants in the United States* (1995), Matthew Frye Jacobson suggests that the word *exile* "conveys those aspects of the immigrant experience most often eclipsed by American mythologies of 'golden door' opportunity: the outlook of those who left the old country only reluctantly; the feelings of loss of those who experienced the flight from the Old World as a form of political banishment and whose first and enduring devotion was to the land and the people they left behind." In the United States, he argues, many Irish, Poles, and Jews experienced themselves as exiles rather than as immigrants; their imagination focused on the land they had left rather than on the one they had come to. A qualification may be necessary. While the Irish and Poles remained engaged in Irish and Polish nationalism, that is, in the future status of the land they had left, the Jews who have interested Jacobson were engaged not so much in their home regions in the Russian and Austro-Hungarian empires as in two ideologies that in different ways were expressions of Jewish nationalism: Zionism and socialist labor nationalism (the endeavor to have the Jews recognized as a nation like Germany or France within the international labor movement).[9]

A fine historian, the late Carl Chrislock, observed that "the vicissitudes of an overseas homeland have often encouraged ethnic group consciousness within the United States."[10] Consequently, some brief notes on the Old World contexts of these three groups may be helpful. The political and economic situation of Ireland in the mid-nineteenth century created a sense of banishment among Irish immigrants and a corresponding perception in Ireland of emigrants as exiles. Not only did Irish Americans engage in Irish nationalist causes, but also nationalists in Ireland looked (and still look) to their countrymen in exile for aid and support. As for the Poles, after the unsuccessful nationalistic uprising in the Russian-ruled part of present-day Poland in 1863, political independence was regarded as an unrealistic goal. Most promoters of Polish nationalism stressed the preservation and cultivation of "Polskość," or Polishness, rather than the struggle for political independence. With a concept of nationhood that was not limited to statehood, the importance of Poles who lived outside the three parts of Poland under Prussian, Austrian, and Russian rule was recognized in the concept of a "fourth partition," Polonia, which designated all Poles in exile. Finally, to a greater degree than most other European immigrants, Jews from eastern Europe arrived in the United States with a sense of ethnic identity created by their minority status and the discriminatory practices in the regions where they had lived.[11] Their sense of apartness was fueled by the prejudices of both Gentile Americans and, paradoxically, assimilated Jewish Americans. Neither Zionism nor Jewish labor nationalism was the product of emigration to the United States, but both kinds of Yiddish nationalism were embraced by large numbers of Jewish immigrants. (Jacobson prefers to speak of "Yiddish" rather than "Jewish" nationalism, a distinction to which I will return.)

Literary expressions of the eagerness to do battle for the cause of independence abound, as do songs and stories about the excellence of the nationalities concerned. Some of the texts Jacobson considers also illustrate how the glorification of the new and the old homelands could merge in one expression, as when the Polish American poet Teofila Samolinska wrote in praise of the United States in 1870: "Here one is free to fight for the Fatherland; / Here the cruelty of tyrants will not reach us, / Here the scars inflicted on us will fade." Similarly, in the Irish American John Brennan's novel *Erin Mor: The Story of Irish Republicanism* (1892), we are told that "Andy Dillon's sweetest consolation in exile was the contemplation of a 'Greater Ireland.' His liberty-loving soul yearned to gaze upon his exiled race in its trans-Atlantic home, where free institutions, unlimited opportunities, and equality before the law afforded ample scope for the exercise of the 'cloudy and lightning genius of the Gael.'"[12] Not only is the vision of a free Poland or Ireland kept alive by the liberal institutions of the United States, but also it is a shared love of freedom that explains why Poles and Irish as well as Jews are at home in America. In other words, it is their native affinity for American democratic traditions that makes both their exile and their immigration meaningful.

Most nineteenth-century immigrants did not have much awareness of their nationality before arriving in the United States; they had local or regional rather than national identities. This does not mean that immigrants coming through Castle Garden or Ellis Island did not know that they came from Norway or Italy. Nevertheless, nationality would not have been central to the identity of people who had rarely associated with foreigners, with other people who were not of their own nationality. The experience of migration created a new awareness of a shared difference from others and a need for a more comprehensive ethnic identification than that of village and region. An early comment on the development of a new ethnic identity among immigrants in the United States is Horace Kallen's seminal 1915 essay "Democracy versus the Melting-Pot." Here he explains that "it is the shock of confrontation with other ethnic groups and the natural feeling of aliency reënforced by social discrimination and economic exploitation that generate in them an intenser group-consciousness." Two factors in this process were the ethnic enclaves, the coming together with "kin and friends who have gone before," and the immigrant's encounters with the Anglo-American, who dealt "with him as a lower and outlandish creature." Thus the immigrant who arrived "totally un-conscious of his nationality... must inevitably become conscious of it."[13] Such consciousness of an ethnic identity would develop at varying speeds and through a variety of stages. Consequently, immigrants from the same country and even from the same region could have different identities with both time and individual mentality as determining factors. An Italian immigrant could of course perceive herself as an Italian emigrant, but she was as likely to identify herself primarily as an emigrant from a specific region or even place.[14] Those who experienced exile, then, did not necessarily experience exile from a nation-state.

For one individual to have both an ethnic identity and an American identity may appear contradictory, but both were products of the experience of immi-gration, and they were complementary rather than opposed to each other. For immigration led not, of course, primarily to the development of an Old World national identity but rather to the development of a New World ethnic one. With variations in time and intensity, most immigrants who did not return to their homeland came to identify themselves with the United States while re-taining and cultivating an ethnic identity that certainly had Old World origins but was created through a New World experience. In 1862 an immigrant in Iowa wrote to his son in Norway asking him to send a Norwegian flag for celebration of the Fourth of July, which, he wrote, was celebrated here as was the Seventeenth of May (the Norwegian Constitution Day) in Bergen.[15] This harmonious interplay of two identities, one American and one ethnic, illus-trates what the historian Jon Gjerde has called the complementary identity of European immigrants.[16] For this Norwegian immigrant it was natural to cele-brate the enjoyment of American freedom with a Norwegian flag. We have no record of what his Yankee neighbors thought of this. It would be nice if they took it in the spirit in which it was done. When Americans celebrate their ethnicities, as on Columbus Day or Saint Patrick's Day, it is a confirmation of their American identity.

The history of Lithuanian Americans was closely tied to that of Polish Americans. In Europe both nationalities were subjected to Russian rule and both were made to feel the repercussions of the 1863 uprising. In the United States they tended to congregate in working-class areas of the same industrial cities and mining towns and experience similar conflicts within the Catholic Church.[17] As in the Polish American community, many leaders among the Lithuanian immigrants saw themselves as exiles rather than as Americans in the making. Their organizational and journalistic endeavors were primarily motivated by their vision of an independent Lithuania. As the historian Gary Hartman has argued, however, Lithuanian American nationalism was "not only about restoring Lithuania's sovereignty" but also about validating "the Lithuanian-American community itself."[18] Strengthening the immigrants' identities as Lithuanians also meant strengthening their sense of being a special kind of Americans: Lithuanian Americans. Similarly, the various nationalist endeavors of the Irish, Poles, and east European Jews were also expressions of a developing identity as Americans. I would therefore suggest that the insights of Matthew Jacobson into the expressions of a nationalism in exile in these three groups may not show us the entire range of their attachments and loyalties, nor of their sense of home. As in other European immigrant groups, arguments were made and stories were told to demonstrate that Irish, Poles, and Jews had special rights to be American because they were Irish, Poles, and Jews.

This is the burden of my recent book *Immigrant Minds, American Identities: Making the United States Home, 1870–1930*. In insisting that they had a right to be at home in America, where they were considered foreigners, European immigrants in the decades just before and after 1900 developed arguments in which accounts of American history that placed fellow nationals in prominent roles were central.[19] This history telling was filiopietistic, but no more so than the account of the United States developed by the dominant Whig school of American history, which described the nation as a purely Anglo-Saxon creation.[20] The story of America that the children of immigrants were taught at school excluded non-English participants. To the extent that immigrants were mentioned at all, they were discussed as a problem for the nation. As one widely used textbook asked, "Can we assimilate and mold into citizenship the millions who are coming to our shores, or will they remain an ever-increasing body of aliens, an undigested and indigestible element in our body politic, and a constant menace to our free institutions?"[21] Immigrant leaders recognized that the negative self-image created by such views and attitudes in the dominant Anglo-American culture was a problem for immigrant communities and for a positive development of American identities.

Immigrants responded to the Anglo-Saxon version of American history by creating equally filiopietistic historical narratives that demonstrated the important role of Americans of origins other than British. I have called such narratives homemaking myths because they were part of a homemaking argument: they were told in order to argue that members of a particular immigrant group had a unique right to a home in America. These homemaking myths may be categorized in three genres: myths of foundation (stories that demonstrate, "We were here first" or "We were among the first"), myths of sacrifice (stories that demonstrate, "We have given our blood"), and myths of a close ideological relationship (stories that demonstrate, "We were American to begin with" or "We were American before we came to America"). The first kind of story, then, argued that a particular group was one of the charter groups of the nation, the second that it had saved the nation in time of need, and the third that it had contributed significantly to the Americanism of America.

It is essential to the arguments of these stories that it is because of and not despite one's ethnicity or nationality that one has a privileged right to be recognized as American. These stories should be called myths rather than history not because they are not factual accounts of the past but because they have a mythic function in the present, making the newly arrived immigrants active participants in the American past and demonstrating that America is now their rightful home. Typically, the use of the first-person plural pronoun rather than the third-person singular in the narration of such stories includes speaker and audience in the deeds of past heroes. It is not simply that Kazimierz Pulaski died fighting for American independence but that we Poles have given our blood for America and thereby made it ours.

For a full discussion of homemaking myths, I must refer to my *Immigrant Minds, American Identities*. These stories and the homemaking arguments they supported were pervasive in all European immigrant groups, including those in which expressions of exile were pervasive. Expressions of exile and expressions of an American home could be presented to the same audiences of Irish and Polish Americans without creating a sense of conflict.

The uses and functions of homemaking myths may be illustrated by a newspaper report of the visit of the Polish statesman and pianist Ignacy Paderewski to Detroit in 1918. Speaking to a large convention of Polish Americans, he told them that "the Poles in America do not need any Americanization. It is superfluous to explain to them the ideals of America," because they already had these ideals because they were Poles. His audience would have appreciated this not because it was a new idea but because it was what they had been told many times by other leaders. The historian Victor Greene has noted a speaker at the celebration of Polish Day at the Columbian Exposition in Chicago in 1893 who "reminded his listeners of the close ideological tie between the Declaration of Independence and the Polish Constitution, a link that would be described often." This particular speaker represented the Polish National Alliance, one of the organizations in which expressions of exile were strong. Here, however, he was arguing that Poles were natural Americans.[22]

Polish Americans also had myths of foundation, but their most often told homemaking myth was one of sacrifice, with the Revolutionary War heroes Pulaski and Tadeusz Kościuszko at the center. After many years of dedicated work as well as squabbles, Polish Americans succeeded in raising a monument to Kościuszko in Chicago in 1904. The messages read at the unveiling ceremony are emblematic of the dual nature of immigrant identities. One was from the president of the United States. The others came from a divided Poland, from Lwów, Kraków, Warsaw, and Poznan.[23] It would be misleading to separate the importance of the recognition from the president of the United States, which was their home, and the importance of the recognition of their endeavors for the Old World national cause signaled by the telegrams from a disunited Poland from which they were exiled. In Kościuszko, Polish Americans had an American hero who legitimized their claim to a home in the United States and who also served as a symbol of hope for a united independent Poland. Similarly, Irish Americans could insist both that the shared experience of wars with the English had made Americans of the Irish even before they stepped off the ship and that the United States was a natural base for exiled Irish nationalists.

The Jews who argued that America was the natural home of Jews may not have been the same as those who argued for a Jewish home in Palestine, South Africa, or Brazil, or for the recognition of Jews as a nation within the international labor movement, but their audiences certainly overlapped. The main Jewish myth of foundation, the Jewish *Mayflower* story, was the account of the *St. Catarina*'s arrival in New Amsterdam in 1655 carrying Jews who had first tried to establish themselves in Latin America. At one of the events celebrating the 250th anniversary of this landing, in 1905, speakers drew parallels between the arrivals of the Pilgrims and the Jews, both seeking liberty, and characterized the Jews as one of the charter peoples of the United States. Like other ethnic groups, Jews had their stories of blood sacrifice, especially with reference to the Civil War, but the myth most often referred to is of a close ideological relationship. In a sermon published in 1854, the rabbi and editor Isaac Mayer Wise explained that "the principles of the constitution of the United

States are copied from the words of Moses and the prophets." Fifty years later, the Chicago rabbi Emil G. Hirsch echoed Wise: "Judaism and fundamental Americanism are one." Hirsch often spoke of Judaism and Americanism as inseparable, as when he insisted: "We cannot be good Jews and not be good Americans. And we cannot be good Americans and not live up to the spirit and teachings of our race and religion." On the occasion when Hirsch spoke, the anniversary of the *St. Caterina*, the *Chicago Record Herald* noted that "the walls of the temple were covered with American flags. A large crowd breathed affirmative response to the sentiment that because of their Judaism American Jews are better Americans."[24]

The same argument was made for virtually all European immigrant groups in this period: it was precisely because they were German or Polish or Finnish that an immigrant group could lay claim to being the best Americans.[25] In this context it is not always possible to distinguish between arguments for an American identity and endeavors on behalf of an Old World nationality. Expressions of exile and of making America home were not necessarily in conflict and may more usefully be placed on a scale where at one extreme are expressions of exile that show no interest in the United States and at the other is an Anglo-American nationalism that does not recognize the place of ethnicities within the nation. My account of immigrants making the United States their home and Jacobson's account of immigrants as exiles are complementary rather than contradictory.

I CONCLUDE with some reflections on Lithuanians and Lithuanian Americans as an instance of a culture in which the experience of exile has become central to the national identity in ways that have affected both homeland attitudes to emigrants and the cultural loyalties of many Lithuanian Americans. After a long history as part of the Russian Empire, the three Baltic nations had a brief history as independent republics between the two great European wars of the twentieth century.[26] They became independent again in 1991, having in the meantime gone through two periods of organized attempts to change the composition of their population, the first efficiently doing away with much of their Jewish and Gypsy populations, the second more protracted and perhaps less efficient, yet decimating the relative sizes of the populations of Estonians, Latvians, and Lithuanians respectively.

The first large emigration from Lithuania came in the decades just before and after 1900. Many of these immigrants were Jews; most were ethnic Lithuanians. In either case they were subjects of the Russian tsar. In the United States, Lithuanians were more marginalized than most other immigrant groups in that their nationality was not officially recognized until 1910, when the U.S. Bureau of the Census for the first time registered them as Lithuanians rather than as Russians or Poles. In the Lithuanian American homemaking story, Tadeusz Kościuszko became Tadas Kosciuska, "the great Lithuanian hero of the American Revolution."[27] But such was the competitive nature of the identity politics of American immigrant groups that Polish and Lithuanian Americans may be said to have been separated by a common culture hero. Lithuanian Americans did not participate in the unveiling of the Kościuszko monument in Humboldt Park in Chicago in 1904 or in the unveiling of a memorial for the same hero in Washington, D.C., in 1910. The Chicago newspaper *Lietuva* actually urged Lithuanians to boycott the Washington celebrations, for even though there was reason to be proud that "a son of Lithuania is recognized as a hero and a pillar of liberty," it was more important to keep in mind that, as a headline declared on April 23, 1909, "The Poles Are Eternal Enemies of Lithuanians." For much of this first period, exile endeavors in support of an independent Lithuania were, as Gary Hartman observes, inseparable from immigrant endeavors to create and strengthen a Lithuanian American identity.

One consequence of the failed uprising in 1863 was a ban on the use of the Latin alphabet in Lithuanian publications for four decades (1864–1904). In effect, this meant a ban on publications in the Lithuanian language. Thus the printed language itself was exiled for much of the period of mass emigration, and East Prussia (now the Russian enclave of Kaliningrad) and Chicago became centers of Lithuanian publishing, the former because of its convenient proximity, the other because of its large number of Lithuanian immigrants.[28] The first American newspaper in the Lithuanian language, *Gazieta Lietuwiszka*, was founded in New York a few years before the ban on the language, in 1859. The editorial in the first issue illustrates how the expressions of exiled nationalism and of pride in being American were complementary:

> All of us had grieving hearts when we left our birthplace perhaps forever. Even today we all wait for our homeland to be free of the tar in which it has been drowned for over a hundred years. Enough of our brothers died in wars and at home, persecuted for their religion. We in America, however, are free, therefore we can provide for ourselves in such a way that we will be equal to all other nations. . . . [We] will be able to send home to our brothers publications from so far away and boast that in America nobody prohibits us to print or to read whatever is useful.[29]

That Chicago was a center of Lithuanian culture at the turn of the century may be illustrated by the publication there of the first Lithuanian-English and English-Lithuanian dictionaries. Encyclopedias are often central to nation building, and Chicago was the home of the first Lithuanian encyclopedia project, which, however, was not completed.[30] For a full appreciation of the many Lithuanian newspapers, journals, and other publication efforts in the United States during the first period of immigration, it should be remembered that a majority of Lithuanian immigrants were illiterate in their own language.[31]

In the second major period of Lithuanian emigration, beginning with the upheavals at the end of the Second World War, Lithuanians in the United States were almost exclusively refugees and exiles. Both because there had been virtually no immigration since the First World War, and because of the cultural and social differences between the earlier immigrants and the later ones, there was little organizational and cultural continuity between the immigrant populations created by these two periods. An illustration of the cultural difference between the two migrations is the completion of a Lithuanian encyclopedia in thirty-six volumes in the 1950s and 1960s. This achievement was followed up with a six-volume edition in English.[32] Such an effort can be explained only by a patriotic dedication to the language, history, and literature of the homeland nourished by the experience of exile.

One effect of the Lithuanian history of exile since the late nineteenth century is that exile itself has become central to the national experience and, consequently, exiled Lithuanians have played central roles in the literary and intellectual history of their native country. Both that the nation has included its exiles and that many of the exiled have retained their Lithuanian identity may be seen in the impact that returned emigrants have had on politics, business, the media, and education in post-Soviet Lithuania. A common experience of emigration from most European countries, however, is that the cultural elites of the home country have shown little interest in the cultural endeavors of emigrant societies, and that emigrants who have returned are regarded as outsiders.

In the United States immigrant writers may have been well known within their immigrant group, but they were as unrecognized by the English-speaking public as they were in their former homeland. William Dean Howells, who wanted to help Abraham Cahan, a Jewish immigrant from Russia, find a publisher for his first novel, *Yekl, a Tale of the New York Ghetto* (1896), was discouraged when Cahan told him that it was being published in Yiddish, but then he realized, "It means the book hasn't been published."[33] Immigrants remain foreigners in the eyes of the inhabitants of the countries to which they have come, while emigrants are quickly forgotten, and their literary expressions go unnoticed in the culture from which they have departed. Most American immigrant writers are not recognized in their former homelands. In Russia, Abraham Cahan is not considered a Russian writer. In Lithuania, however, exile has become an inextricable aspect of the national identity. A 1970 study of Lithuanian literature is titled *Perfection of Exile: Fourteen Contemporary Lithuanian Writers*, suggesting that there are circumstances in which exile may be not just a nationalist virtue but a source of creativity. In a recent anthology of Lithuanian literature in English translation, published in Vilnius, almost half the space is given to what the editor labels "émigré" poetry and prose, mainly by writers who have resided in the United States, suggesting that Lithuania has a culture in which exile may be a positive factor for inclusion in the literary canon.[34] This inclusion of exile may extend to readers as well as writers, as when the exile scholar Rimvydas Šilbajoris, in an introduction to the 1979 anthology *Lithuanian Writers in the West*, writes of the poet Jonas Maironis (1862–1932) that his "patriotic verse . . . still echoes in the hearts of the people, both at home and in exile."[35]

It may be necessary, however, to consider some of the political and ideological aspects of the selection processes involved in creating literary canons before we draw any sweeping conclusions on the basis of how Lithuanians today perceive their history. There is remarkably little interest in Lithuania at the present time in studying the culture of Lithuanian Americans at the turn of the twentieth century. This may of course be because little of lasting interest was then being created in Chicago, Philadelphia, and other cities with concentrations of Lithuanian immigrants. It may also be, however, because of the peasant origins and working-class status of the majority of these immigrants and their tendency to support socialist and labor causes, which may—if historical differences are disregarded—be seen to relate them to the communist ideology of the Soviet period.[36] Similarly, the canonizing of the post–World War II literature of exile may in part be a function of an endeavor to de-canonize the literature of the Soviet period. Yet it also seems only likely that the constraints of a vulgarized and prescriptive Marxist criticism and an imposed aesthetics of socialist realism may have been less conducive to good literature than the pressures of exile, and that the main motivation for changing the canon thus may be aesthetic. In *Perfection of Exile*, Šilbajoris writes of the division of Lithuanian literature "into two separately functioning entities, one of them being the literature of exile, and the other the literature of Soviet Lithuania." He does not dismiss the latter, but observes that the two literatures are so different that it is difficult to discuss them in the same context.[37] We may have to leave it to a post-post-liberation generation of Lithuanian critics to sort out the relations between exile and home in both the tsarist and Soviet periods of Lithuanian history. Nevertheless, and with due consideration of these caveats, this brief survey of the importance of exile in Lithuanian culture suggests that there may be literary cultures in which exile does not mean separation from home but is, rather, an extension of home.

EXPRESSIONS OF exile and immigration are as varying as are the experiences and understandings of exile and home. Although the circumstances of departure may be traumatic, the eventual outcome of migration is not necessarily tragic for the individual. There is always the loss of an old homeland, but there is also often the acquisition of a new one. The multilayered intellectual and emotional landscapes of the individuals involved in migrations may be a source of new understanding and creativity. For most emigrants, the journey of emigration eventually becomes a journey of immigration. For some, however, exile remains the defining element of their lives. When the sense of home includes those who are in exile, then exile itself may also be a home. Or perhaps, if our migrations make us, as Eva Hoffman suggests, a composite of fragments, a mosaic, and we may be defined by how conscious we are of these fragments, it may be that in our "observing consciousness" we remain natives, immigrants, and exiles. I am certainly not alone in claiming to have been—at different times as well as simultaneously—conscious of all three states.

Notes

Jay Martin read an early version of this article and gave invaluable advice. I am also grateful for the opportunity to discuss that early version with my colleagues in the Department of English at the University of Bergen and to Peter Rose for the invitation to present it at one of the sessions of the Kahn Institute Project "The Anatomy of Exile" at Smith College in 2000.

1. As the sociologists Alejandro Portes and Rubén G. Rumbaut have observed in *Immigrant America: A Portrait*, 2d ed. (Berkeley: University of California Press, 1996), 23, however, for some would-be immigrants their status, whether as legal immigrants, returnees, or illegal immigrants, may depend on whether they succeed in being classified as refugees, and this is "not a matter of personal choice, but of governmental decision based on a combination of legal guidelines and political expediency."

2. Eva Hoffman, *Lost in Translation: A Life in a New Language* (New York: Penguin, 1989); Josef Škvorecký, "Before the Story Begins," in *Two Murders in My Double Life* (New York: Farrar, Straus and Giroux, 2001). W. G. Sebald, *The Emigrants*, trans. Michael Hulse (New York: New Directions, 1977), is a poignant literary meditation on the meaning of emigration and exile in the lives of some twentieth-century Europeans.

3. Øyvind Gulliksen, "Double Landscapes, Midwestern Texts: Studies in Norwegian-American Literature" (Ph.D. diss., University of Bergen, 1999).

4. These two metaphors are taken from the titles of two justly admired accounts of immigration to the United States: Oscar Handlin, *The Uprooted* (Boston: Little, Brown,

1951), and John Bodnar, *The Transplanted: A History of Immigrants in Urban America* (Bloomington: Indiana University Press, 1987).

5. Orm Øverland, *Immigrant Minds, American Identities: Making the United States Home, 1870–1930* (Urbana: University of Illinois Press, 2000), 26–27.

6. Roger Daniels, *Coming to America: A History of Immigration and Ethnicity in American Life* (New York: Harper Perennial, 1991), 68. Native Americans were not included in the census.

7. This gendered difference in the experience of immigration has not been carefully studied by historians but has been explored in fiction by immigrants. See Abraham Cahan, *Yekl, a Tale of the New York Ghetto* (New York: D. Appleton, 1896); Ole Edvart Rölvaag, *Giants in the Earth* (New York: Harper and Row, 1927); and Henry Roth, *Call It Sleep* (New York: Cooper Square Publishers, 1934).

8. Horace M. Kallen, *Culture and Democracy in the United States* (1915; reprint, New Brunswick, N.J.: Transaction, 1998), 97–98; Dag Blanck, *Becoming Swedish-American: The Construction of an Ethnic Identity in the Augustana Synod* (Uppsala: Acta Universitatis Upsaliensis, 1997), passim. For discussions of the representativeness and impact of immigrant leaders, see John Higham, "Leadership," in *Harvard Encyclopedia of American Ethnic Groups*, ed. Stephan Thernstrom (Cambridge: Harvard University Press, 1980), 642–47; idem, *Ethnic Leadership in America* (Baltimore: Johns Hopkins University Press, 1978); Victor Greene, *American Ethnic Leaders, 1800–1910: Marginality and Identity* (Baltimore: Johns Hopkins University Press, 1987); and Øverland, *Immigrant Minds*, 28–41.

9. Matthew Frye Jacobson, *Special Sorrows: The Diasporic Imagination of Irish, Polish, and Jewish Immigrants in the United States* (Cambridge: Harvard University Press, 1995), 1–3.

10. Carl H. Chrislock, intro. to *Cultural Pluralism versus Assimilation*, ed. Odd S. Lovoll (Northfield, Minn.: Norwegian-American Historical Association, 1977), 14.

11. There is irony in applying the fairly recent term *ethnicity* to the Jews since, in the Bible, the Greek *ethnikos* is the word used to translate the Hebrew *goyim*, that is, "non-Jews" or "Gentiles." Exile, living in the Diaspora, has been central to being Jewish since biblical times.

12. Jacobson, *Special Sorrows*, 121, 128. In a brief essay I cannot possibly illustrate the Old World nationalism of these three groups with an adequate sample of the wide range of expressions of exile discussed by Jacobson nor do justice to his convincing argument. Readers would be well advised to consult *Special Sorrows* themselves.

13. Kallen, *Culture and Democracy*, 86–87, 94. This often repeated view may need to be qualified by an awareness of how many immigrants came from multiethnic regions, even villages. Russian Jews were, as noted, made acutely aware of their ethnicity. Romanians, Germans, Hungarians, Jews, and Gypsies sharing the same villages but not the same churches in nineteenth-century Transylvania were surely acutely aware of difference even though they may not have had developed concepts of nationality, being subjects of an empire rather than citizens of a nation.

14. See, for instance, Marie Hall Ets, *Rosa: The Life of an Italian Immigrant* (Madison: University of Wisconsin Press, 1999).

15. Orm Øverland and Steinar Kjærheim, *Fra Amerika til Norge*, vol. 2, *Norske utvandrerbrev, 1858–1868* (Oslo: Solum, 1992), 209.

16. Jon Gjerde, *The Minds of the West: Ethnocultural Evolution in the Rural Middle West, 1830–1917* (Chapel Hill: University of North Carolina Press, 1997), 8, 60, 63.

17. Victor Greene, *For God and Country: The Rise of Polish and Lithuanian Ethnic Consciousness in America, 1860–1910* (Madison: University of Wisconsin Press, 1975).

18. Gary Hartman, "Building the Ideal Immigrant: Reconciling Lithuanianism and 100 Percent Americanism to Create a Respectable Nationalist Movement, 1870–1922," *American Ethnic History* 18 (Fall 1998): 37.

19. In order to understand immigrant filiopietistic rhetoric, it is essential to appreciate that immigrants were repulsed by the country they were trying to enter. Immigrant leaders were not so much beating their breasts as they were knocking on doors. American dictionaries do not note that the word *foreigner* had the meaning "an American of an origin other than English" in the period discussed here. In the early-twentieth-century Chronicles of America series, the volume on immigration and race by Samuel P. Orth was titled *Our Foreigners* (New Haven: Yale University Press, 1921). The subtitle, *A Chronicle of Americans in the Making*, is misleading. Some might, according to Orth, be able to adapt fully to American values, but many would always remain outsiders. The author deplores the fact that "even Americans do not at once think of the negro as a foreigner," and explains that "the negro, however, is racially the most distinctly foreign element in America" (45–46). Orth dismisses the notion that "mere citizenship" makes an American, "for there are millions of American citizens of foreign birth or parentage who, though they are Americans, are clearly not of any American stock" (22). While a majority of publications, popular and scholarly, propagated this exclusive view of the American, there were others that used terms such as "comrades," "neighbors," and "friends." Examples from Episcopal Church publications are *Neighbors: Studies in Immigration from the Standpoint of the Episcopal Church* (New York: Domestic and Foreign Missionary Society, 1919); Leila Allen Dimcock, *Comrades from Other Lands: What They Are Doing for Us and What We Are Doing for Them* (New York, 1913), a book for children sponsored by the Council of Women for Home Missions; and Thomas Burgess, Charles Kendall Gilbert, and Charles Thorley Bridgeman, *Foreigners or Friends, a Handbook: The Churchman's Approach to the Foreign-Born and Their Children* (New York: Department of Missions and Church Extension, 1921).

20. Nina Baym, "Early Histories of American Literature: A Chapter in the Institution of New England," in *The American Literary History Reader*, ed. Gordon Hutner (New York: Oxford University Press, 1995), discusses the rise of the Whig school and the teaching of American history as a response to immigration.

21. Quoted in Frances Fitzgerald, *America Revised: History Schoolbooks in the Twentieth Century* (New York: Random House, 1980), 78.

22. For information about the Paderewski visit and the account of Polish Day in 1893, I am indebted to Victor Greene, *For God and Country* and *American Ethnic Leaders*.

23. These Polish American illustrations are from my *Immigrant Minds*, 95, 127, and 133. An account of the unveiling of the Kościuszko monument appears in *Narod Polski*,

September 14, 1904, and is among the many excerpts translated in the valuable Works Progress Administration project *The Chicago Foreign Language Press Survey*.

24. Øverland, *Immigrant Minds*, 20, 77, and 129.

25. "We have often heard that the Norwegian immigrant, in comparison with other immigrant groups, makes a good American. . . . What people say and write in this regard is right. However, it would be even more true if they changed the tense of the verb. The Norwegian doesn't *become* a good American. He *is* one already before he emigrates. He was one already in the saga age!" Ole E. Rölvaag, *Concerning Our Heritage*, trans. Solveig Zempel (Northfield, Minn.: Norwegian-American Historical Association, 1998), 110.

26. The Republic of Lithuania was broken up. A large section of the present country, including the capital, Vilnius, was made part of the new Poland.

27. Reported in the Chicago Lithuanian newspaper *Sandara*, October 10, 1930. The newspaper wrote his name Tad Koscinsko. The hero claimed by both countries was born in present-day Lithuania. For accounts of the strife between Polish and Lithuanian Americans from the earliest years of immigration, see Antanas Kučas, *Lithuanians in America* (Boston: Encyclopedia Lithuania Press, 1975).

28. "Books in Latin letters were printed in East Prussia and brought across the border with the help of a well-organized underground network composed of selfless patriots as well as professional smugglers interested in the material rewards of this enterprise." Rimvydas Šilbajoris, *Perfection of Exile: Fourteen Contemporary Lithuanian Writers* (Norman: University of Oklahoma Press, 1970), 8.

29. Quoted in David Fainhauz, *Lithuanians in Multi-ethnic Chicago until World War II* (Chicago: Lithuanian Library Press and Loyola University Press, 1977), 162.

30. Ibid., 170–71. As so often in immigrant cultures, books and newspapers were parts of the same business. Thus the publisher of these dictionaries and many other books was also the publisher of the newspaper *Lietuva*. Kučas, *Lithuanians in America*, 200.

31. Fainhauz, *Lithuanians*, 21, reports that "53% of the Lithuanian immigrants who came to America between 1899 and 1914 were illiterate."

32. Kučas, *Lithuanians in America*, 202. This book, translated from Lithuanian, is itself a product of the Encyclopedia Lituanica (EL) Press in Boston

33. Jules Chametzky, "Our Decentralized Literature: A Consideration of Regional, Ethnic, Racial, and Sexual Factors," *Jahrbuch für Amerikastudien* 17 (1972): 64. When working with the Norwegian American Ole Edvart Rölvaag in 1926 on the translation of *Giants in the Earth*, the Anglo-American writer and journalist Lincoln Colcord wrote to his publisher, Harper and Brothers, of the many books Rölvaag had already published, in Norwegian, in Minneapolis: "There is a formidable background to the present picture, and a body of work already in existence sufficient to make or break a literary reputation. He tells me that never before in his life has he been met on just this ground, or felt himself in touch with the publishing profession in America." Implied, of course, is Colcord's assumption that publishers in languages other than English did not count as members of "the publishing profession in America." Letter dated March 9, 1926, in

the O. E. Rölvaag Papers, Norwegian-American Historical Association, Saint Olaf College, Northfield, Minn.

34. Šilbajoris, *Perfection of Exile*; Laima Sruoginis, ed., *Lithuania in Her Own Words: An Anthology of Contemporary Lithuanian Writing* (Vilnius: Tyto Alba, 1997). It may be objected, however, that this recognition is given only to ethnic Lithuanians and not to those with other languages. Thus Abraham Cahan, who wrote in Yiddish, may, strictly speaking, be considered a Lithuanian emigrant, having come from Vilna, now the capital city Vilnius. His nationality is further complicated by the fact that he thought of himself as Russian and that Russian remained his preferred language. See Konrad Bercovici, *Around the World in New York* (1924; reprint, New York: D. Appleton-Century, 1938), 83.

35. Alina Skrupskelis, ed., *Lithuanian Writers in the West: An Anthology* (Chicago: Lithuanian Library Press and Loyola University Press, 1979), 16. We should keep in mind, as Šilbajoris reminds us in his introduction to this anthology, that writers may be more inclined to a sense of prolonged exile than immigrants who are less sensitive to the importance of language: "The writers ... tended to regard the normalization of life abroad as more of an illusion than it seemed to many other Lithuanians whose imagination turned rather quickly to finding ways and means of establishing themselves in the new lands" (18). By generalizing uncritically on the basis of literary expression alone, we may run the risk of romanticizing the exile culture.

36. The little that Antanas Kučas, in his filiopietistic *Lithuanians in America*, writes about Lithuanian American involvement in labor unions and in socialist and communist organizations is prejudiced and dismissive. His sympathies are clearly with those whose allegiance was not only to Lithuania but to Catholicism as well.

37. Šilbajoris, *Perfection of Exile*, 21–22.

NEXT YEAR IN JERUSALEM
Exiled in the Homeland

DONNA ROBINSON DIVINE

No IDEA is more fundamental to the Zionist sense of mission than the ingathering of the Jews in the land of Israel and the ending of their exile. The determination to end Jewish exile in all its dimensions is thoroughly embedded in the documentary record of Zionist history, particularly during the period of British rule in Palestine (1918–1948), the years so critical to the struggle for Jewish sovereignty. Zionists did not simply describe Jewish life in the Diaspora as exile, they judged it and expressed that judgment so starkly that they rendered this return to the ancient homeland the religious equivalent of blessing the Torah. In the Zionist view, immigration to the land of Israel constituted an absolute rejection of exile, and conversely, emigration from Palestine was denounced as betrayal and a dereliction of a sacred duty.

But to conclude that the ending of exile simply required a change of domicile and physical contact with the land of Israel would be far too simple. For the term "exile" carried burdens of reference so deeply rooted in the personality of Diaspora Jewry that nothing short of negating the Diaspora, as symbol, culture, and system of authority, could truly bring Jews back to their home. The word "home" gathered its political and emotional resonance as an antidote to exile rather than as a term with its own absolute and independent essence. Zionist discourse in Palestine focused far more often on displacement and exile than on belonging and home. Rather than project a clear vision of home, Palestine's Zionist leaders continually looked backward and organized the ways in which they thought and talked about the Jewish society being formed in Palestine in reference to exile and to the very societies and cultures they rejected and denounced. Exile, in fact, took on much of its modern connotation in the process of the reshaping of Jewish society in Palestine. Intending to generate a unified Jewish culture in the land of Israel, Zionist discourse, partly because of its preoccupation—some might say, obsession—with exile, more often than not exposed many of its own cultural contradictions and fault lines.

Although the idea of rejecting the Diaspora may have been a consistent theme in Zionist ideology, it did not provide a unifying point for generating a common set of policies or priorities. Even as a component of Zionist ideology, the approaches to exile were complex, and Zionist activists oriented them-

27

selves in a variety of ways to this principle.[1] No matter how committed Zionists were to rejecting the Diaspora, those born in exile could not but bring to their activities an experience reflective of their society. Their notions of how to end exile often drew their momentum from the very culture that marginalized them and that they claimed to be rejecting.

Exile was so central to Zionist political language in Palestine that to focus on the usage of the term is more than a semantic exercise. The building of a Jewish state is a tale of debates, disagreements, and struggles, not a narrative of linear progress toward a preordained goal. What is important is not so much the determination of a single definition of exile as a recognition of the multiple purposes to which the idea of exile was put and how grounded these were in the diverse and ever-changing social experiences of Palestine's Jews. Since exile embodies not a single idea but a complex of values, the attempt to define its multiple meanings and usages is simultaneously an exercise in intellectual as well as social and cultural history.

In standard Zionist historiography, exile is central to the assessment and description of the developing Jewish national home in Palestine. The devaluation of the Diaspora experience and the unquestioned presumption of exile and home as antinomies are typically invoked as explanations for the triumph of the Zionist cause and the establishment in 1948 of a Jewish state. Even as recent scholarship has challenged the tendency to take as given any of the Zionist assumptions about nation building, the belief in the radical differences between Jewish communities in the Diaspora and in Palestine has proved relatively resilient. Consider *Zionism and the Creation of a New Society*, the most successful synthesis in English of the new research. In attesting to the importance of the Diaspora-homeland link as the site of crucial interacting developments, Ben Halpern and Jehuda Reinharz observe that political developments in Palestine's Jewish community did not correspond to the simple story of opposition between homeland and Diaspora woven by Zionist ideologies:

> Zionism determined the eventual shape of Israel's institutions through two separate, and sometimes opposed, channels: the diaspora movement and the immigrant settlers. The direct activity of the world movement in Palestine was controlled for a long time by a consensus based on values that arose and developed in the diaspora. Zionist immigrants originally shared similar values and often adhered to ideologies and factional organizations that were rooted in the diaspora, but they developed new ideas and grew to be an independent force as they faced the specific problems of life in Palestine.[2]

While recognizing that the framework for developing the Jewish national home in Palestine cut across international boundaries, Halpern and Reinharz still accord privilege to a set of values and centralizing strategies as both hegemonic and decisive for Zionism's successful state and nation building enterprises. Although they acknowledge the diversity of Zionist interests and ideologies, they continue to consider exile as comprising a set of attributes informed by geography and the condition of Jewish powerlessness. Thus, while contemporary discussions of Palestine's Jewish community contain less certainty about the political dynamics engendered by economic or ideological developments, they have not made the supposed polarities between exile and home more urgent subjects of scholarly investigation. This is astonishing, given that the negation of the Diaspora has insinuated itself into a wide range of contemporary debates on Israeli society and on its capacity to accommodate cultural diversity. For their part, students of Zionist history continue in one way or another to equate Palestine's Jewish community with returning home.

In this essay I respond to this omission by taking stock of exile as a critical element in Zionist discourse.[3] My approach represents not so much a conscious effort to present a new model of Zionist political development as an exercise in generating alternative ways of conceptualizing the Jewish nation-building experiences in Palestine. I use exile (*galut* in Hebrew) as the controlling metaphor for examining Zionist discourse in Palestine during the British Mandate because in this period, nation- and state-building processes intersected, giving the idea of exile its broadest application and strongest currency.

While Zionist leaders insisted, in rather straightforward fashion, that immigration to Palestine amounted to renouncing exile, they also proclaimed that not all Zionists in Palestine had truly crossed the homeland's threshold. The imagined consensus on restoring an ancient homeland was belied not only by the limited numbers of Palestine's Jews actually participating in nationalist self-governing institutions—about one-third—but also by the very rhetoric of the presumed cultural mainstream. In the context of the British Mandate, exile became a way of ordering the experience of specific immigrants, of shaping their outlook on the world, and of rationalizing their place and identity in the new context. But the term's usage was also powerfully attached to vested interests of various stripes. An understanding of exile that emphasizes its diffuse and divergent attributes and the variability of its relationship to Zionist political forces also allows a deeper appreciation of the contradictions embedded in the emerging Jewish nationalist culture and community.

In this essay I focus, first and foremost, on Labor Zionist discourse precisely because of the movement's preeminence. By confining my discussion to the dominant ideologies, I recognize that I am ignoring many other reasons why Palestine's Zionist immigrants felt ill at ease in Zion. Age, gender, class, family, country of origin, political affiliation all affected the prospects for successful integration and, presumably, for achieving satisfaction. But because most of the immigrants I examine were part of the Labor Zionist social and political orbit before they came to Palestine, their experiences expose the human strains and divisions encountered in building the new society and permit a more accurate reckoning of its political culture.

The assumption that cultural and physical survival warranted the establishment of a Jewish national home not only generated controversies for the World Zionist Organization and its branches over how to set priorities but also proved a troubling touchstone as a program of social change for the Zionists who came to live in the land of Israel. Insofar as the creation of a Jewish national home in Palestine supposed a radical transformation of Jewish culture and society, it could not become a refuge for the Jewish masses threatened by poverty and violence but not yet prepared for dramatic social change. A thorough negation of the Diaspora would demand that Zionists limit the flow of people to Palestine in order to control the course of nation building. No wonder that negating the Diaspora, seemingly an ideal congruent with the hopes and dreams of all Zionists, proved repeatedly to be a locus of serious political controversy as well as a reflection of contradictory Zionist impulses.

How to translate the principle of returning to the homeland into an actual immigration policy often provoked political disputes and crises over the criteria established for distributing immigration certificates because certain categories of people were ignored or left behind. But while Great Britain defined the legal framework of immigration generally in accordance with economic goals and political considerations, the Zionist movement exercised considerable influence—though not absolute dominance—over recruiting and selecting the men and women who actually came to live in Palestine. Notwithstanding a consciousness of economic constraints or a profound commitment to social change, Zionists had to structure their immigration stances in the hope of fulfilling their demographic as well as their political objectives.

The Zionist assertion that immigration meant victory over the fragmentation wrought by the dispersal of the Jewish people thus bore an ambiguous relationship to the political, economic, and cultural pressures unfolding for Palestine's Jewish community. The claims of Palestine's Zionist leaders to be representing something that transcended the bounds of their political interests and differences were constantly being undermined by the myriad ways in which these claims were understood and deployed. Expressions of national loyalties seemed less a reflection of a shared identity than a desperate attempt to bypass or ignore communal differences. The differences between exile and home that suffused public discourse and seeped into every aspect of Yishuv culture did not provide a point of unity in the Zionist nation-building project, as the conventional scholarly wisdom suggests, so much as it did a marking of its sometimes unacknowledged ruptures.[4]

What I propose is that we understand exile as a thoroughly flexible concept not framed by either geographic boundaries or a demonstrated faith in the Zionist mission. Rather, exile was a cultural resource for justifying political power and for rationalizing a particular allocation of resources. To be sure, the vectors of exile could run in opposite directions. But several features of the word are noteworthy for the specificity of their context. The first thing one notes about the usage of the word "exile" was its contribution to the creation of a binary view of the world in which everything outside the national home was depicted as brutal and as the antithesis of the supposedly harmonious Zionist society being established in Palestine. Zionists asserted that the land of Israel, the creation of Jewish farmers, collective agricultural settlements, militias, and people who engaged in and valued productive labor, constituted a stark difference from the degraded conditions in which Jews living in countries not their own were mired. Although the claims of uniqueness were problematic, the principle of difference became fundamental to legitimizing the Zionist enterprise.

A second and closely related feature of exile was its political application. Exile entered the vocabulary when political and social dissent within Palestine's Zionist community intensified. Particularly for Labor Zionists, the more immigrants streamed into cities instead of onto the land, preferring to open small businesses rather than work as laborers, the more evidence leaders found of exile's traces in the land of Israel. Confronting what in their view was a severely limited capacity for national redemption and simultaneously for popular support, Labor Zionist leaders redefined the meaning of exile, suggesting that its effects might be mitigated by the correct kind of political affiliation and action.

Third, exile was incorporated into debates over economic priorities as the availability of resources expanded but was still insufficient to meet the demands of all factions. Zionist leaders had to justify allocation policies that were designed to relieve the developing economy of burdens it could ill afford to carry but were distinctly at odds with their ideological principles. Questions about the justice of the economic order or the relations between immigrant groups described in many other places in the language of class equality or ethnic justice tended to be examined in the Yishuv in the context of the presumed dichotomy between exile and home. Finally, exile as a theme in Hebrew literature during this period sometimes referred to a place of turmoil and conflict, and at other times to the sources of familiar customs and family harmony. Because it was a distinguishing feature of Zionist public discourse, the dichotomy between exile and home was seized on as a trope justifying power but also as a metaphor of dissent.

Definition and Experiences of Exile and Home

Those who drew up plans to colonize Palestine were often either determined to produce an entirely new Jewish society or convinced that only a new kind of economic and social dynamic could produce factors critical to the development of a national home. In November 1919, Chaim Weizmann wrote to Herbert Samuel that "building the national home will depend on bringing 100,000 not 1,000,000 creative and productive Jews to Palestine." The tragedy, he went on to observe, was that "those 100,000 Jews do not yet exist."[5] If the idea of returning to a Jewish homeland promised deliverance from the communal and political disharmonies that structured the world of their childhood and of their parents, whom they considered trapped in an earlier era and by a rigid value system, it also presented its own problems. Consciousness of community, often acquired in the densely populated towns or cities of eastern Europe and nurtured through a vibrant associational life, was strained by the encounter with Palestine's relatively small Jewish population. The demographic relationship of the immigrants to the much larger population of Arabs growing in numbers through the seemingly natural life cycles of high fertility rates and longer life spans could not help but raise questions about Zionism's long-term prospects. Additionally, Arab rebellions and attacks reminded Palestine's Jews that their claims were contested and that their political objectives would be vigorously opposed. Prompted by the 1929 violence, Shai Agnon seized on one of the most hated artifacts of the Jewish Diaspora as a possible source of refuge: "From the days of the disturbances, Jews have changed their daily interactions with Arabs. Now the relations are such that we don't hate and we don't love but what I want is not to see them. I think we need to build a gigantic ghetto of a half-million Jews in the land of Israel, and if not, we are, God forbid, lost."[6]

Still, for many Zionists in eastern Europe, particularly after World War I, immigration held the promise of a Jewish national home as an instrument of liberation from the economic, political, social, and cultural patterns of the Diaspora.[7] Immigrants to Palestine had more than a passing acquaintance with imagining change as increasing numbers acquired their Zionist consciousness through their affiliation with youth movements and passionate involvement in their many activities. Zionists seem to have had what they described as intense experiences of autonomy and creativity in the context of these Diaspora activities.

Before leaving the lands of their birth, young Zionists had already established and participated in organizations that unleashed challenges to the inherited structures of their Diaspora hometowns. Influenced by European youth movements, these Zionist organizations "created a world of [their] . . . own . . . in contrast to adult society which they perceived as a sham" and decisively reoriented participants away from full inclusion within the cultures and societies represented by their parents.[8] Zionist youth movements flourished in Europe and created in many of its towns and cities a space proclaimed free from the constraints of local authority, structures, and norms. In setting out to reclaim their national rights, these young men and women Zionists projected their activities as a profile of opposition to the dominant Jewish culture and as agents of social change.

Some young activists undoubtedly intended their rhetoric to generate the structural possibilities for opposition to mainstream Zionism, but the Zionist youth movements enjoyed the benefits of official sponsorship and had multiple ties to the World Zionist Organization and to its political party constituents. For that reason, youth movements had access to a wide array of resources—most significantly, to immigration certificates—distributed through the offices of the Zionist Organization, or later through the Jewish Agency. Thus, while the sense of transformative change and total autonomy was real, Zionists were much freer to imagine what an independent Jewish society might become than they were to produce it.

For the World Zionist Organization as well as for the youth movements, the nationalist cause embraced both romantic ideals and pragmatic calculations. If some participated only out of idealism, others out of economic grievances, the combination was profoundly powerful, and the nationalist stamp it impressed on youth movement activities was nonetheless marked. As Pinhas Lavon, leader of the Gordonia movement, observed, there was a pretentiousness about youth movement assertions of autonomy.[9] Exaggerating the degree of their autonomy in Europe, youth movement members and activists nevertheless faced an even more powerful test of the affinities between their romantic visions of home, on the one hand, and their calculations about how to make a homeland, on the other, after they came to live in Palestine.

Although the vision of agricultural labor as the sole way to achieve true spiritual freedom and autonomy remained central to their public rhetoric, it did not necessarily inform their choices of employment once these youth movement graduates settled in Palestine. Most gravitated to cities and not to what they saw as the agricultural hinterland, even as their ideology urged them to settle the frontier. The largest of the youth movements—he-Halutz—rallied its members under the slogan of "productive labor" first and foremost on the land, but according to one authority, "approximately 70 percent and perhaps more, of the membership that had settled in Eretz Israel left the movement."[10]

When they founded or joined kibbutzim, youth movement activists encountered all sorts of obstacles in trying to sustain their ideals. Labor needs and market forces demanded all sorts of compromises. Above all, the hope for a new era of freedom that had stirred these Zionists as young men and women diminished as they aged, particularly when they began to consider the implications of absolute liberty for their own children. Agricultural labor had represented a choice for the graduates of youth movements, but as they married and became parents, they offered no comparable range of options to their children. Schools without grades and degrees were founded on kibbutzim precisely to foreclose opportunities for employment outside the agricultural communities for children born and raised on the land. If one generation had chosen freedom and work on the land, the next generation, nurtured in the Jewish national home, was, in Rousseau's words, "forced to be free."[11]

Although the struggle for a Jewish state and for defining the meaning of homeland forced Zionists to move through some rather conventional channels, it also took them down many surprising paths. With regard to even radical innovations, the drawing of clear ideological markers between exile and home was not always the natural outcome of a national consensus. For example, embracing Hebrew as the rightful language of the Jewish people offered a clear boundary between those building a national home and those living elsewhere, but this cultural solidarity was forged in the midst of many more contradictory norms and impulses than implied by official Zionist rhetoric.

The ironies of a nationalist identity based on Hebrew are evident when one considers that Yiddish, the spoken language of European Jewry, had had a far more powerful impact than Hebrew on preserving Jewish cultural distinctiveness. For the Zionists, selecting Hebrew as the national language was to move against the nationalist and populist tide in Europe. As S. Daniel Breslauer has observed, "The connection between the Jewish struggle for rights and the use of Hebrew was not intuitively obvious."[12] Hebraists started as a fringe element of the Zionist movement, and only after a struggle and the backing of the British mandatory government was the language secured, as Michael Berkowitz puts it, "as the movement's standard."[13] That the birth of Hebrew as the national language did not automatically mean the death of Yiddish is best reflected in the novels of the early labor Zionist writer Yosef Haim Brenner, set in Palestine. The vernacular of the stories is clearly a mixture of Hebrew, Yiddish, and Arabic.

The insistence of Zionism on renewal and growth only within the context of a Jewish national home was constantly challenged also by its own official reckoning of the movement's achievements. No matter how many immigrants arrived, Zionist leaders expressed considerable disappointment with the extent of the social changes they introduced into Palestine. Either the acres of land purchased were insufficient or the number of genuine pioneers working on farms too few. The observations of Menachem Ussishkin, director of the Jewish National Fund (the land-purchasing agency of the Zionist movement), as late as 1940 confirm this pattern of Zionist self-criticism:

> I am entitled to speak about the sin that the nation of Israel has committed with regard to redemption of the land in our homeland. For the sixty years since the beginning of the Hibbat Zion movement, for the forty-two years since the founding of the Zionist Organization, for the twenty-two years since the Balfour Declaration, few of the nation's leaders have ceased crying out and warning: the most important factor in guaranteeing our future is to redeem and continue redeeming the land of Palestine through all possible ways and means. And what effect has their cry had? . . . [a] ghetto is being created in our land."[14]

Justice, Fairness, and Equality

Negating the Diaspora as a platform for social change in Palestine also meant that public discussions of economic justice and equality would revolve around the presumed differences between home and exile. No matter how many ideological markers could be drawn between home and exile, at the very least, home had to mean that basic needs could be met if Zionist ideas were to reflect more than utopian fantasies. How could Zionism prove its worth to Jews who barely eked out a subsistence living when employed, and then only intermittently, and who had to contend with inadequate housing and sometimes even the possibility of starvation?

Although immigration and the commitment to participate in the building of a Jewish national home in Palestine were supposed to, in Ben Gurion's words, "guide the young and energetic Jew to a life of labour . . . [and] to the true origin of mankind, to physical and mental health and to the essence of all that is good in man,"[15] periods of rapidly increased immigration, particularly from 1924 to 1925 and from 1932 to 1935, swelled the bottom ranks of the labor force and intensified poverty.

Many Zionists experienced their own immigration to Palestine and the process of finding employment not as an enhancement of their power to shape their world but rather as a loss of control over their lives. Aware that the popular Zionist conviction argued that involvement in the national project increased individual power over the future and intensified collective responsibility for the fate of other immigrants, the immigrants were deeply unsettled by the difficulties they encountered, and their reactions took on special critical power. Grievances included low wages, irregular employment, and the discretionary and unfair distribution of benefits by the all-powerful labor organization the Histadrut. Iris Gracier's descriptions of the workers' housing projects in Tel Aviv illustrate the grounds for this dissatisfaction. "The construction of several hundred housing units certainly did not offer any solution to the housing crisis besetting the urban working class in Palestine," because, as she emphasizes, "the housing complexes . . . demanded a substantial sum from the residents . . . [and] only someone who had a permanent job and a reasonably high income could acquire an apartment."[16]

The periodic and deep depressions of the 1920s and 1930s, coupled with the pervasive insecurity of employment even in flush times, meant that much of the working class remained desperately poor and that the security associated with the Zionist visions of home lay well beyond their reach. The near collapse of the economy between 1925 and 1927 and the severe depressions a decade later sharpened the distinctions between the favored pioneers and the often disgruntled and uncooperative urban workers. Immigrants were not all equal strangers in a foreign land because many had cultivated useful political or personal contacts for purposes of forwarding their ambitions and securing jobs. Those without such contacts could be truly alone as employment opportunities were far from evenhandedly dispersed.

The unfairness of these practices struck many Zionist idealists, caught between their belief in socialism and their belief in nationalism or between their commitment to equality and the necessity of cooperating with the bureaucratic strictures of state building.[17] For these reasons, many wage laborers were increasingly attracted to dissenting factions within the dominant Labor Party and to critiques of Histadrut wage policies and disciplinary practices. These political and economic conflicts structured the issues around which the Zionist discourse on exile took its bearings. Even as the national homeland in Palestine became larger and more developed, signs of exile were presumably found everywhere. The fierce partisanship that flared up over bitterly contested economic priorities and political principles fed an invective of conflict fueled by a rhetoric of exile, which equated political dissent with heresy. Exile became not only the watchword for defining radical opposition but also the touchstone for delegitimizing it. "The individual worker has not become a partner in anything with the pioneer," insisted Berl Katznelson, agitated and frightened by the threats of the workers' branch in Tel Aviv to secede and join the opposition. Dov Ben-Yeruham, a true workers' leader, led the opposition group in the Tel Aviv branch, which at the end of the 1930s constituted a majority there. Katznelson and the Labor Zionist establishment considered Ben-Yeruham irresponsible, vulgar, and prone to demagoguery and often dismissed him as "the leader of the Tel Aviv branch of Mapai whose members, terrible to say, still sometimes spoke Yiddish."[18]

Expecting affirmation and celebration, Palestine's Jewish workers actually often encountered a criticism magnified with a disdain they could not have anticipated. Rather than being lauded as exemplars of Zionist idealism, some became representative figures of all that threatened or corrupted the newly forming Jewish civilization in Palestine. Yitzhak Shenhar, railroad worker, agricultural laborer, writer, and symbol and spokesman for the socialist Zionist cohort of immigrants arriving after the conclusion of the First World War, captures this experience of disintegration in his novel *One of a Thousand*, as he classifies the deep social cleavages in Palestine during the 1920s and 1930s in accordance with the Zionist discourse on exile:

> Ehrlich felt that his face was turning green, like those wretched plants in their clay pots. Who says, he asked himself, that the class divisions in this country are employers, workers and the in-between people? It's a lie. The three classes here are the sabras, the new immigrants and the refugees. Right here, on this little balcony, are the three classes in miniature, and only a deaf man can fail to hear the fanfares of battle. A mental class war. And, too, woe to the loser, woe.[19]

Labor Zionists were not alone in perpetuating their conflicting definitions of the transformed Jewish society they aimed to create. Their major opponents, the Revisionists, were no more successful than Labor Zionists in propagating a coherent set of values or goals for the future Jewish state.[20] Having turned Vladimir Jabotinsky into an iconic representative of their movement, Revisionists never endorsed all of his policy proposals. United by their opposition to what they called the overly weak and ghetto-like tactics adopted by the World Zionist Organization leadership, Revisionists were equally scornful of socialist policies as demonstrating insufficient nationalist conviction and commitment. While Jabotinsky, as Revisionist leader, wrote about the need to set up a Jewish army with the belief in its centrality for social discipline and as a necessary symbol of political sovereignty, not all Revisionists agreed. One important branch of the Revisionist youth movement, Beitar, mobilized its members around the idea of working the land even as Jabotinsky and other Revisionist leaders attributed equal value to all occupations. Jabotinsky's stress on the immediate mobilization of a mass Jewish immigration only introduced additional confusing rhetorical tropes about how to create the truly liberated Jewish society. Those who continued to raise the issue of land settlement found themselves subject to charges of undermining the national cause.

And at Revisionism's radical edge, the invective was sustained by those who endorsed the idea of military training not as a means of instilling new qualities of mind and soul, as Jabotinsky had advocated, but rather as the only way to produce an absolute militancy sufficient for statehood. While the fervor aroused by the issue of establishing a Jewish army did not split the movement, it certainly allowed Revisionists to construe their differences as implicit challenges to one another and to their commitment to creating a new Jewish society.

Although offering fierce opposition to Labor Zionism, Revisionist activities sprang from a similar urgency to reform the Jewish people and eliminate the consequences of centuries of subordination and dispersion. But whether triggered by Zionism's political right or its left, the imperatives of that process of change engendered such deep divisions and challenged so many assumptions about social harmony and national unity inherited from Zionist political culture that those enveloped in its rhetoric—Palestine's Jewish immigrants—could not help but feel a deep sense of unease.

Thus the Zionist effort to constitute a public realm expressive of the common values shared by Palestine's Jews resulted in a discourse more concerned with the struggle to erase the traces of exile, which seemed to be everywhere in the country, than with the effort to assure immigrants that through their presence and initiative, the Jewish homeland was being created. Because this Zionist discourse on exile was at the center of a deliberate effort to nourish a public morality appropriate to the newly evolving forms of society and government in the country, it informed Palestine's Jewish culture, and in so doing mirrored both the accomplishments and shortcomings of Zionists in moving beyond their Diaspora past.

Education and Culture

In Palestine's educational system, according to Eliezer Schweid, the issue of exile "invalidated any positive view of the continuous historical heritage of the Jews" because the schools selected for their curricula only those texts that described the Jewish Diaspora as sapped of vitality.[21] Interestingly, even though politics was thrust into every aspect of Palestine's Zionist cultural life, Hebrew literature itself constituted a remarkable outpouring of commentary on the complexities of both exile and home. Nurith Gertz has astutely and correctly observed that the best of the writers understood exile as a source of Jewish creativity even as they endorsed Zionism. Gertz acknowledges, however, that many of the most popular novels adhered to the Zionist narrative about the defects of exile, and, as Yael Zerubavel notes, settlement on the land was depicted as "a progression from chaos to order, from wild nature to civiliza-tion, from a personal and a national struggle to redemption."[22]

But when the poetry or prose self-consciously promoted a particular Zion-ist vision, it could not always avoid disclosing a strong sense of displacement and discomfort. "O Kinneret, my Kinneret—Were you there, or did I dream a dream?" writes the pioneer poet Rachel in a poem that, as Sidra DeKoven Ezrahi argues, "has become over the years so embalmed in the sentimental culture as to vitiate its subversive implications," for the reference to a dream hints at the possibility of "a radical skepticism at the heart of the central Zionist enterprise of settling the land."[23]

The literary critic Dan Miron has posited that Hebrew poetry and prose instilled into Palestine's Jewish community a notion of a common identity and served as an important element in fulfilling the Zionist national mission.[24] Culture can sometimes seem like a substitute for politics, a way of posing only imaginary solutions to real problems, but under other circumstances culture can become a rehearsal for politics, trying out values and beliefs permissible in art but forbidden in social life. Most often, culture exists as a form of politics, as a means of reshaping individual and collective practice for specified interests, and as long as individuals perceive their interests as unfulfilled, cul-ture retains an oppositional potential. Fredric Jameson argues that the domi-nant culture can only presume to ease the disorienting anxieties arising from disconnecting from the past by calling attention to them in the first place, thereby running the risk of reopening the very ruptures it seeks to close.[25]

Jews did not simply immigrate to the land of Israel; they returned home. It was a sanctified act presumably in fulfillment of a collective vision. But lan-guage itself could not totally eradicate all signs that as much as the return to the land of Israel seemed a blessed move, it was a painful experience of mem-ory about who or what was left behind. That exile was a central component of Zionist discourse in Palestine had particular causes as well as general implica-tions, but certainly the facts of human psychology—that people cling to mem-ories—were of fundamental importance.

Zionists could leave the lands of their birth but could not discard habits of mind and of body expressive of their displacement and subordination. It is not surprising, then, that along with their move to the land of Israel in fulfill-ment of Zionist ideals, many Jews found themselves similarly estranged from the place their ideology insisted was their true home.[26] Sidra DeKoven Ezrahi describes this kind of alienation as a mark of Jewish distinctiveness. "There is a specific poetics of exile," she writes, "that emerges in modern Jewish culture not only from the experience of mass displacement but from the struggle with an inherited construction of homecoming that was essentially ahistorical."[27]

Ezrahi suggests that a classical Jewish literary tradition born in exile, no matter its political transformations and achievements, could not provide the conceptual resources for a clear and comprehensible description of home. Despite rhetorical assertions to the contrary, Jews carry traces of exile wherever they live. Similarly, in comments on Yosef Haim Brenner's classic *Breakdown and Bereavement*, Gershon Shaked notes that the theme of exile gave the novel its enduring quality. Shaked observes that "the worlds of Jerusalem, Jaffa, and Tiberius depicted in the novel are filled with ideologically and religiously motivated immigrants, uprooted from their familiar environments and unable to find satisfaction, or even proper employment, in a community that everywhere disappoints and defeats them."[28]

Of course, no fixed set of categories can fully capture how the act of immigrating to the land of Israel was actually experienced and interpreted by individuals. To judge by their literary and political discourses, Zionists held seemingly contradictory definitions of both exile and home. But just as Benedict Anderson holds that a nation is more than a political entity, and is rather an imagined community, Zionist discourse frequently suggested that while Jewish immigrants in Palestine lived in their national homeland, they did not necessarily fully belong to its new society. For the most ardent of Zionists, then, returning home could easily give rise to discomfort and a consciousness of marginality. Ironically, the very Zionist leaders who claimed that Jews could live full and free lives only in their own nation and called on Jews to "ascend to the land of Israel" also insisted that even in Palestine, Jews were still, in Haim Brenner's words, "children of the ghetto." Hearing these words, Palestine's Jewish immigrants could only be reminded of exile and of their own alienation in their national homeland.

ZIONISM'S FOUNDERS constantly repeated the mantra that Jews harbored uniform impulses and held to universal goals, but ironically this self-conscious insistence on the existence of national unity exacerbated the very tensions and divisions they were designed to ignore, deny, or delegitimize. National identity may well have been built on a publicly enunciated appreciation of the Jewish people's diversity and an explicit recognition of the positive qualities of exile. But this kind of honesty about the realities of Jewish life did not inform Zionist discourse or politics. And because diversity can be ignored, denied, delegitimized, but not quickly or totally erased, Zionist culture left those aspects that did not conform to the dominant ideology pushed to the margins, ever ready to be invoked on behalf of radical challenges or dissent or to be infused, perhaps unself-consciously, into people's personal lives and individual mores. Not surprisingly, the Zionist narrative of homecoming remained full of contradictions and conflicts. For Palestine's Jewish immigrants, the very pervasiveness of the dichotomy between exile and home turned their search for employment into a struggle for survival rather than a quest for independence. That Jewish immigrants to Palestine encountered a reality different from their expectations is not particularly noteworthy. But that many were told that their very actions weakened the pursuit of Zionist goals and the sustenance of the national purpose had to be a profoundly shocking experience and one for which they were absolutely unprepared.

Notes

1. Shalom Ratzaby, "The Polemic about the 'Negation of the Diaspora' in the 1930s and Its Roots," *Journal of Israeli History* 16, no. 1 (Spring 1995): 19–38. Ratzaby writes: "The idea of 'Negation of the Diaspora' [*shililat hagolah*] in Jewish national thought emerged when Diaspora or Exile was no longer conceived of in *a priori* metaphysical terms, but rather as a social and historical phenomenon. Thinkers of modern Jewish nationalism probed the roots of the new perception of Exile searching for an understanding that could serve as a basis for social change. This new perception of Exile was based on three premises: First, Exile has no purpose and serves no mission. Second, Exile is a negative phenomenon that causes suffering for the Jewish people, places the Jewish nation in existential peril, and distorts the nation's way of life thereby causing harm to the authentic creative potential of the nation and its individuals. Third, the existence of a Diaspora is untenable in the age of modern nationalism. . . . [T]he logical conclusion was that Exile could not be repaired within its own context and that to endure as a nation, the Jewish People must return to its homeland and establish a state" (19). See also Arnold M. Eisen, *Galut Modern Jewish Reflection on Homelessness and Homecoming* (Bloomington: Indiana University Press, 1986).

2. Ben Halpern and Jehuda Reinharz, *Zionism and the Creation of a New Society* (New York: Oxford University Press, 1998), 46.

3. This essay does not address any of the biblical narratives incorporated into the Zionist discourse. From Eden to Egypt and Babylonia, the notion of exile as punishment for sin has also served as a source of Zionist reflection on the lessons of life in the Diaspora.

4. For the conventional wisdom, see Ben Halpern, *The Idea of the Jewish State* (Cambridge: Harvard University Press, 1969); Dan Horowitz and Moshe Lissak, *The Origins of the Israeli Polity: Palestine under the Mandate* (Chicago: University of Chicago Press, 1977); Gideon Shimoni, *The Zionist Ideology* (Hanover: Brandeis University Press, 1995); and in Hebrew, Oz Almog, *The Sabra: A Profile* (Tel Aviv: Am Oved, 1997).

5. Yigal Elam, "Political History," in *The History of the Jewish Community in Eretz-Israel since 1882*, ed. Moshe Lissak, pt. 1 (Jerusalem: Mossad Bialik, 1989), 139–222, 180–81.

6. Quoted in Pinhas Ofer, "The Crystallization of Mandate Administration and the Establishment of Fundamental Principles Governing the Jewish National Home, 1922–1931," ibid., 325.

7. Yael Zerubavel, "Revisiting the Pioneer Past: Continuity and Change in Hebrew

Settlement Narratives," *Hebrew Studies* 41 (2000): 209–24. Zerubavel writes: "The pioneer period thus marked the new nation's emergence as a major phenomenon that transformed Jewish history. The common references to Zionist settlers as "pioneers" [*haluzim*], "founders [*miyasdim*], and the "first generation" [*dor harishonim*] reflected and reinforced their role as opening a new historical era" (211).

8. Eyal Kafkafi, "Changes in Ideology during Two Generations of a Zionist Youth Movement," *Journal of Israeli History* 17, no. 3 (Autumn 1996): 283.

9. Ibid., 285–86.

10. Israel Oppenheim, "Hehalutz in Poland between the Two World Wars," in *Essential Papers on Zionism*, ed. Jehuda Reinharz and Anita Shapira (New York: New York University Press, 1996), 266, n. 42.

11. Moshe Reches, "Education in the Kibbutz," in *Education in an Emerging Society*, ed. Walter Ackerman (Jerusalem: Van Leer Institute, 1985); Yehuda Riemer, "Interaction between Youth Movements and Kibbutz: The Case of Kfar Blum," *Journal of Israeli History* 17, no. 2 (1996): 167–77; Eyal Kafkafi, *Truth or Faith: Yitzhak Tabenkin as Mentor of Hakibbutz Hameuhad* (Jerusalem: Yad Itzhak Ben Zvi, 1992).

12. S. Daniel Breslauer, "Language as a Human Right: The Ideology of Eastern European Zionists in the Early Twentieth Century," *Hebrew Studies* 36 (1995): 56.

13. Michael Berkowitz, *Zionist Culture and Western European Jewry before the First World War* (Chapel Hill: University of North Carolina Press, 1993), 46.

14. Ruth Kark, "Land-God-Man: Concepts of Land Ownership," in *Ideology and Landscape in Historical Perspective*, ed. Alan R. H. Baker and Gideon Biger (Cambridge: Cambridge University Press, 1992), 77–78.

15. Zeev Tzahor, "David Ben Gurion's Attitude toward the Diaspora," *Judaism* 32, no. 1 (Winter 1983): 10.

16. Iris Gracier, "Social Architecture in Palestine: Conceptions in Working-Class Housing, 1920–1938," in *The Land That Became Israel*, ed. Ruth Kark (New Haven: Yale University Press, 1989), 304–5.

17. David De Vries, *Idealism and Bureaucracy in 1920s Palestine: The Origins of "Red Haifa"* (Tel Aviv: Hakibbutz Hameuchad, 1999) [in Hebrew].

18. Zeev Sternhell, *The Founding Myths of Israel* (Princeton: Princeton University Press, 1998), 145.

19. Gershon Shaked, *Modern Hebrew Fiction* (Bloomington: Indiana University Press, 2000), 274–75.

20. For this section on Revisionism, I have relied on Esther Stein-Ashkenazy, *Betar in Eretz-Israel, 1925–1947* (Jerusalem: Jabotinsky Institute, 1997), pt. 1, chaps. 1–6. See also Shimoni, *Zionist Ideology*, 236–68.

21. Eliezer Schweid, "The Rejection of the Diaspora in Zionist Thought: Two Approaches," in Reinharz and Shapira, *Essential Papers on Zionism*, 136.

22. Zerubavel, "Revisiting," 211.

23. Sidra DeKoven Ezrahi, "Our Homeland, the Text . . . Our Text, the Homeland: Exile and Homecoming in the Jewish Imagination," *Ariel* 31 (1992): 477.

24. Dan Miron, "From Creators and Builders to Homeless," *Igara* 12 (1985–86): 71–

135 [in Hebrew]. See also Dan Miron, "H. N. Bialik and the Quest for Ethical Identity," *Hebrew Studies* 41 (2000): 189–208.

25. George Lipshutz, *Time Passages: Collective Memory and American Culture* (Minneapolis: University of Minnesota Press, 1990), 16–17.

26. David Patterson, *A Phoenix in Fetters: Studies in Nineteenth- and Early-Twentieth-Century Hebrew Fiction* (Savage, Md.: Rowman and Littlefield, 1988), 150: "The exponents of nationalism had viewed the land so consistently through a rose-colored monocle, which allowed little shift in perspective, that physical contact with the country would seem to imply only two possibilities. Either the vision would have to shatter against the harsh reality of Palestine, or an attempt would have to be made to make the land conform to the vision of Eretz Yisrael."

27. Ezrahi, "Our Homeland," 467.

28. Shaked, *Modern Hebrew Fiction,* 51.

DRIVEN OUT OF EDEN

Voices from the Asia Minor Catastrophe

THALIA PANDIRI

IF ONE LOOKS for a common denominator, all refugees resemble one another. They are marked—often for generations—by the traumatic experience of persecution, war, expulsion from their homeland, economic hardship and discrimination in the land where they resettle, and culture shock under even the most benign conditions of resettlement. Yet the particular circumstances of every group are unique. For Greece, the "Asia Minor Catastrophe" is the refugee event par excellence, and it has left a lasting imprint on the history of the Greek people both in Greece and in the diaspora.

In the summer of 1922, Smyrna (Izmir), the most prosperous and internationally important port of Asia Minor/Turkey, was burned to the ground. Smyrna was a largely Greek city, and had been for a long time: for centuries it had been known popularly as "the city of infidels" because it was home to so few Muslims. The destruction of Smyrna marked unforgettably the defeat of the Greek army and also the end of the Ottoman government, which had ruled for close to five centuries. Mustapha Kemal's Nationalist Party had won, and was recognized by the Entente powers (Britain, France, and Russia) even before the end of the Greco-Turkish War.[1] On January 30, 1923, the Convention for the Compulsory Exchange of Greek and Turkish populations was signed in Lausanne after months of negotiations; it would go into effect with the Treaty of Peace signed in Lausanne on July 23 and ratified in August 1923. There had been voluntary exchanges of minority populations earlier, but the *compulsory* exchange of minority populations was unprecedented. All Greeks resident in Turkey except those who could prove established residence in Constantinople before October 30, 1918, were to be expelled from Turkey and "repatriated" to Greece; all Turks resident in Greece except those who could prove established residence in western Thrace at the signing of the Treaty of Bucharest in 1913 would be expelled and "returned" to Turkey. Provisions were agreed upon to cover reparations, indemnification, the orderly transfer of movable property, and the deportation of the "exchangeable" populations, with no right of return.[2]

The Turkish minority in Greece had not been subject to persecution, and Greeks living in areas remote from the fighting had escaped the worst of the atrocities and hardships suffered by those inhabiting areas where military operations had been concentrated (especially Smyrna and nearby coastal cities, towns, and villages). On both sides, those whose communities had not been destroyed were the most reluctant to be displaced. They also suffered the fewest hardships, since they did not leave until the ratification of the Lausanne peace treaty and the establishment of a Mixed Commission to supervise their departure. In some areas of Turkey, Greek and Armenian refugees did not leave until 1925.

Origins of the Asia Minor Catastrophe

Greeks had been living in Asia Minor since at least the eighth century B.C.E., when the Greek colonies in Ionia were among the most prosperous in the region. Greek settlements in Asia Minor were a natural outgrowth of the commercial relations and affiliation that had flourished between the Greek islands and the Asian continent ever since Minoan times. The epic poet Homer was an Ionian; Sappho's brother, from Lesbos, lived as a wealthy merchant in Sardis, and we know from Sappho's poetry that Lydian girls were among her pupils; the historian Herodotus was from Halicarnassus; the scientist-philosopher Thales was a Milesian. These are a very few examples, but the list is almost inexhaustible. The prosperity of the Ionian cities, and their strategic position, attracted the expanding Persian Empire in the early fifth century, and the capture of Miletus in 494 B.C.E. was greeted by Athenians as a tragedy so devastating for the Athenian *polis* that when the dramatist Phrynichus presented a play titled *The Capture of Miletus*, the Athenians banned the play and imposed a heavy fine on him, as Herodotus reports (*Histories* 6.21). The Persians went on to invade Greece, were defeated at Marathon and Salamis, and retreated; Asia Minor, particularly Ionia and Anatolia, remained essentially Greek. In short, long before the Roman Empire (which allowed Greek language and culture to flourish without interruption), before the Byzantine Empire, long before the fall of Constantinople to the Ottoman Turks in 1453, Asia Minor was for the Greeks a homeland and part of a larger Greek identity.

The fall of Constantinople gave rise to irredentism on the part of the Greeks, and in the nineteenth century the struggles for independence from the Ottoman Empire fostered the dream of a free Greece that would be not a small nation-state but a territory as large as the Byzantine Empire. This irredentist aspiration came to be known during the protracted War of Independence as "I Megali Idea" (The Great Idea). By no means universally espoused either by "free" Greeks who lived within the new Greek nation-state or by diaspora Greeks, it was persistent enough to fuel the catastrophic behavior of the Greek government under Prime Minister Eleftherios Venizelos after World

War I. The waning power of the Ottoman Empire promoted a feeding frenzy among the Great Powers on both sides of the Great War. Squabbles (and deals) among Britain, France, Italy (induced to enter the war by territorial promises that included Smyrna), and Russia continued throughout the war years. They involved territorial claims, commercial concessions, and the exploitation of mineral deposits and other natural resources. Both the small state of "free" Greece and the troubled Ottoman Empire were chess pieces to be exchanged among the more powerful players. Although Turkey entered the war on the side of Germany, relinquishing its neutrality was not an easy choice, nor was it a forgone conclusion that it would ally itself against Britain. The nationalist Young Turks had in fact made overtures to Britain but were not taken seriously as a force to be reckoned with. They turned to Germany. At the invitation of the Young Turks, Germany sent a military mission early in 1914, headed by General Liman von Sanders. German officers, technicians, and instructors arrived by the hundreds. Even so, Turkey did not enter the war on the side of the Central Powers until 1915, when the swift victory anticipated by the Germans failed to materialize. Greece entered the war on the side of the Entente even later, toward the end of 1917, when the pro-British prime minister, Venizelos, had been restored to power through the intervention of Britain and France.[3]

With the defeat of the Central Powers (Germany, Turkey, Austro-Hungary, and Bulgaria), national boundaries and spheres of influence were once again on the bargaining table. "The Eastern Question," the division of the spoils in the Balkans and the eastern Mediterranean among the Great Powers (the Austro-Hungarian Empire, Russia, Britain, Germany, Italy, and France) was nothing new, nor were the effects of international politics on the different ethnic groups in the area. Throughout the nineteenth century, wars and armed struggles in quick succession, whether revolts or invasions, had resulted in constantly shifting borders and (noncompulsory) population migrations in and out of areas as the political situation fluctuated and various ethnic groups sought relative safety and economic security.[4]

Despite the vicissitudes that influenced the lives of all who inhabited that part of the world, however, Asia Minor Greeks continued to enjoy prosperity and considerable freedom. The sacred law of Islam provided protection to the *ahl al-kitab* peoples (those who believed in the Sacred Book, i.e., Christians and Jews). Greeks in particular—as a large minority that included wealthy merchants, skilled artisans, large farmers, and a well-educated elite who played an important role in local government and in the large state bureaucracy—enjoyed a considerable measure not only of religious freedom but also of local autonomy.[5] In return they paid a tribute to the Ottoman government (the *haraç* levied on non-Muslims). They lived in harmony with their Turkish neighbors, with whom they had commercial relations: Greeks employed Turks, most often as agricultural laborers and apprentices; Turks employed Greeks, most often as clerks and farm laborers.[6]

Greeks and Turks also enjoyed close social relations, as narrative after narrative stresses. Marriage between Christians and Jews was relatively rare, but there are numerous accounts of men and particularly of women who converted to Islam and married Turks. There are also numerous accounts of turcophone Greeks—both boys and girls—whom powerful Turks offered to adopt and marry to a family member or friend, wishing to save them from persecution and expulsion. "Going Turkish," a literal translation of the Greek verb for choosing to live as a Muslim Turk, was predicated on religious conversion; the majority of Greeks resisted renouncing Christianity and chose expulsion over Islam. This information comes from refugees interviewed in Greece; those Greeks who stayed in Turkey are represented only when they are mentioned in passing. But we do hear of women who chose to convert and marry a Turk even though their families remained Christian. Some made the choice under the pressure of persecution, but by no means all. A woman from Anakou (Turkish Enegi, seventy kilometers southwest of Caesarea) speaks of a Greek girl, Marigo, who left the village with others but turned back: "She was in love with a Turk, and she was pregnant." Another ten or more women from a nearby village, and quite a few from another, also turned back and married Turks (B147). About one woman, we hear only her name—Barbara—and the fact that she "went Turkish." We hear about a priest's daughter who had married a Turk against her family's wishes and whose father refused to take her back when she was widowed (B30–31). One refugee narrative, from which excerpts appear at the end of this essay, gives us a glimpse of a powerful Bey who clearly cares about his Greek wife and his exasperating mother-in-law, and whose unwillingness to shelter Greek women and children seems to this reader due not to hard-heartedness or intrinsic prejudice but to his justifiable fear that his house would be attacked by a Turkish mob as the house of a "Greek-lover."

Despite some troubles during the period of the Russo-Turkish wars of the 1870s, and although a few Asia Minor Greeks enlisted in the Greek army in 1897 to support the secession of Crete from the Ottoman Empire, the first serious uneasiness mentioned repeatedly in the refugee narratives I have examined coincides with the rise of the Young Turks' Committee of Union and Progress, the Constitution of 1908, and the deposition of the sultan in 1909.[7] Even then, informants stress that their relations with Turkish neighbors in their own hometowns are close and good. The Balkan Wars (1912–14) resulted in more movements of populations and changing borders, but persecution of minority populations escalated and became systematic when Turkey entered the First World War on the side of Germany. General von Sanders promoted a genocidal policy that resulted in the massacre of much of the Armenian population in 1915, and he encouraged the persecution of the Greek population whose expulsion and eradication he presented as necessary for the creation of a strong modern state. Many Greeks left their homes during World War I, going either into internal exile or to Greece as they fled from concerted persecution and from massacres, especially in the area around Constantinople, Gallipoli, and the Black Sea. They refer to this period as "First Persecution." It was not their intent to leave home permanently, and most returned when Turkey was defeated in 1918. First-person accounts tell repeatedly of Greeks finding their homes and property intact when they returned, often guarded by their friends and neighbors, the Turks with whom they had lived for generations.

Ironically, the real trouble came with the victory of the Entente powers. The Ottoman Empire had been defeated, but the Young Turks who had gained military and political strength during the war refused to abide by the extremely damaging terms of the Armistice. "Irregulars," partisans who failed to disarm, augmented by armed brigand and terrorist groups, took to the mountains as terms of peace continued to be hammered out.[8] As they had done during the war itself, the victorious Entente continued to squabble and cut secret deals, each party fighting and conniving to secure territorial claims, commercial concessions, and the exploitation of mineral and petroleum deposits. The terms of the Treaty of Sèvres (which was finally signed on August 10, 1920) ceded Smyrna to Greece. The defeat of Turkey, the symbolic as well as very real economic value of Smyrna for Greece, aroused popular sentiment in Greece; the promise of "taking back Smyrna" fueled the irredentist dream of recapturing the Byzantine Empire.

This expansionist policy was promoted by the Orthodox Church and by nationalists clustered around Venizelos, whose own motives may have been more complex. Britain came to an agreement with the Venizelos government that Greece would send troops to enforce the terms of the Armistice, as they had been revised in the Treaty of Sèvres. Britain would offer support, although Greece would lead the invasion. Italy and France were reluctant to see Greece in such a role, but they were more reluctant not to keep an eye on Britain, and they agreed to halfhearted participation.

In May 1919 the Greek army landed in Smyrna. In June of that same year, several largely Greek towns (Pergamos, Aidini, Ayvalik) were attacked and burned by the terrorists, who plundered, raped, and slaughtered indiscriminately. At the same time that these "irregulars," often under the leadership of notorious warlords and brigand chieftains, were terrorizing Turks as well as minority populations, Mustapha Kemal's nationalist (Young Turk) forces were clashing with the regular Ottoman army. Kemal's movement was a force to be reckoned with, and Greece's "allies," who had promised military and financial support of the operation, turned their attention to securing their own interests in the region, negotiating severally and secretly with Kemal. Support evaporated; Italy, France, and Britain declared "strict neutrality" in this "Greco-Turkish" war. Even while being undermined and held back by a British strategy that allowed Kemal to consolidate his resources and manpower, the Greek army was victorious as it marched toward Ankara, although by this time the "neutral" countries were (unofficially) selling arms to Kemal.[9] The Greek army was defeated in August 1922 at Afion Karahissar, and on October 11, 1922, an armistice was signed at Moudania. The retreat of the Greek army left Greek communities exposed not only to the pursuing Turkish soldiers but also to bands of terrorists under the leadership of local warlords, or groups of common criminals who took advantage of the situation to extort, pillage, rape, and murder. The local Greek population was not warned of the retreat; in repeated instances the retreating army even deliberately lied about being on the run as it passed through villages. As they retreated, Greek soldiers set fire to Greek as well as Turkish villages.[10] The systematic burning of Smyrna by Turkish soldiers and mobs had begun on September 9 and lasted for days. Neighborhoods of Armenians and Greeks were pillaged and burned and their inhabitants robbed, tortured, raped, and led off to slaughter. Refugees from other towns gathered in Smyrna hoping to escape. As they were trapped on a narrow street between the conflagration and the harbor where "neutral" foreign ships were stationed to "observe," many perished.[11] Not just in Smyrna but generally along or near the coast, the devastation caused by war and terrorism and the persecution of a fleeing refugee population were brutal realities before the compulsory exchange was mandated by the Lausanne agreement early in 1923 and largely completed by the end of 1924, with the last Greek and Armenian refugees leaving Turkey in 1925.

The Impact of "Repatriation" on the Refugees and on Greece

The reverberations of the Catastrophe had a lasting effect on every aspect of Greek life and culture. Refugees had begun to trickle into free Greece earlier, but the flood of desperate refugees between 1922 and 1924 overwhelmed a small country ill prepared to receive such an influx. Fleeing genocidal massacres, the vast majority of refugees arrived with only the rags on their backs, after suffering the loss of their homes, their loved ones, in some cases their sanity. Many were sick with typhus. They were lice-ridden and desperate. The country was singularly unprepared to meet their basic needs for food and shelter, let alone medical care and employment. They were housed in school buildings, abandoned warehouses, refugee camps, shantytowns in malarial swamps. A shack was a luxury: many had only a makeshift tent; others had not even that much shelter, and no sanitation. In some areas, lodging for refugees was requisitioned in private homes, and those forced to take in these unwelcome lodgers were resentful.[12] The refugees, forced into exile by the Lausanne agreement, had been "repatriated" to a Greek Orthodox state. For many it was an alien as well as an unwelcoming place, but there could be no illusion that this was a temporary asylum, or that they could ever return home. The burning of Smyrna was symbolic of the definitive loss of Asia Minor. The expulsion of the surviving Greeks to what was supposed to be a national homeland marked the end of a Greek presence in the area that had prospered for millennia, even under Persian, Roman, and Ottoman rule.

To this day, in Greek "the Catastrophe" denotes only one event: the burning of Smyrna and the ensuing "Expulsion." Similarly familiar, self-explanatory, and resonant is " '22," shorthand for everything that happened leading up to the burning of Smyrna and all that ensued. Even today, when Greece is teeming with economic and political refugees from Albania, the former Yugoslavia, Poland, the Black Sea region and northern Epirus, the Sudan, Ethiopia, and Pakistan—to name only some—the noun "refugee" unqualified by an adjective means only "Asia Minor refugee," and even the adjective "refugee" denotes something pertaining to the Asia Minor refugees, unless there is further delimiting specification.[13]

The flood of refugees that overwhelmed Greece in the 1920s had a pervasive and lasting impact on the economy, language, and culture of the new "fatherland." Asia Minor Greeks brought with them their rich hybrid culture, their "Turkish" music, cuisine, customs, and language. The *rebetika* sung to the accompaniment of the *bouzouki*, with their Middle Eastern melodies and their lyrics full of Turkish words and place-names, moved quickly from the refugee settlements and the wineshops and opium dens of dangerous slums into mainstream society, coming to dominate popular music by the end of the 1950s and very soon afterward to inspire serious composers such as Manos Hadzidakis and Mikis Theodorakis, who also set to music the verse of poets such as Kostis Varnalis, Yannis Ritsos, and the Nobel Prizewinners Yiorgos (George) Seferis and Odysseas Elytis. The music and dance that anyone familiar with *Zorba the Greek* thinks of as typically Greek is that of Asia Minor refugees; even the name of Kazantzakis's protagonist, Zorba, like so many

Greek names, is a Turkish word, meaning something like "macho man," someone you don't mess with. Many of the refugees were Greek-speaking or bilingual, although quite a number (particularly from areas such as Cappadocia) were wholly turcophone; but all were familiar with Turkish words and expressions, which rapidly became part of mainstream Greek, both spoken and, eventually, literary. Many prominent writers in Greece were Asia Minor refugees; best known to a non-Greek audience is probably Seferis. The prolific and often translated novelist Ilias Venezis was also from Asia Minor. As an adolescent, Venezis was a prisoner in a forced labor camp in the interior of Turkey, and in 1931 he published a memoir about his experience, *Number 31328*.[14]

Despite—or perhaps because of—the suffering and poverty that characterized the life of a great many of the refugees in Greece not only immediately after their arrival but also during the economic and political crises of the 1930s, the invasion of Greece by the Axis, a brutal German occupation, and the ensuing bloody civil war that ravaged Greece until the early 1950s, the refugees retained their cultural identity as a group while doing their best to put down roots and work their way out of poverty. Many had been successful farmers, experienced merchants, skilled craftsmen, internationally educated and multilingual intellectuals. From these socioeconomic strata, even those who had not been able to save or transfer property eventually improved their lot and became productive and not infrequently influential members of their new country both on the local level and in national politics. But even those who hired themselves out as farm workers, found jobs in factories, scrubbed floors, or made lace and sold it for a pittance managed to secure a better life for their children if not for themselves. Typically, Asia Minor refugees remained proud of their heritage even though they were reviled by "Old Greeks" as *tourkosporoi*, "Turkish spawn." As soon as they could, they formed new communities, civic "brotherhoods" and organizations based on their region, city, or village of origin in Asia Minor. These community and cultural organizations still abound throughout Greece, and even in the diaspora, and continue to be important not only as social groups but also in sponsoring cultural events and fostering serious research and publication.

The cataclysmic loss of a homeland reverberated in poetry and fiction as well as in fields such as ethnography, ethnomusicology, sociology, linguistics, and lexicography. There is a vast bibliography of literary and scholarly works on Greek Asia Minor, and scholarly journals dedicated to research on individual geographical areas have preserved and studied its geography, folklore, dialects, music, regional customs, and superstitions. The refugees arrived in large numbers, at the same time, and often settled initially in large communities. (One instance of many: fifty thousand refugees settled in the Kokkinia neighborhood near Piraeus.) They tended to cluster in groups from the same town or area in Asia Minor and retained their local identity and culture. They provided an ideal database for scholars: collecting material in the field from the first-generation refugees preserved information about a rich and varied culture; following the members of a refugee community through several generations has allowed sociologists to document the refugee experience from the first traumatic years through successful resettlement to the assimilation of a third and fourth generation.

More indicative of the importance of the Catastrophe for Greece than the attention paid to it directly, however, is the way in which both subsequent and prior events are viewed through the lens of an experience (like the Holocaust) which informs the way all other events and experiences are conceptualized.[15] For instance, the Albanian campaign in 1940, when the Greek army defeated Mussolini's invading troops on the Albanian border, is linked in literary and political writings to the Asia Minor disaster and the foreign policy of the Great Powers. So too is the CIA-backed putsch of April 21, 1967, along with the brutal seven-year-long military dictatorship that ensued, and the 1974 invasion of Cyprus by that same military government. The Asia Minor experience may act as a subtext linking ancient history and mythology to World War II, to the Greek civil war that followed it, and to the brutal military dictatorship of the colonels. Itself a powerful symbol, it provides a framework for Nikos Kazantzakis's *Christ Recrucified* (completed in 1948 in the aftermath of World War II and as Greece was reeling from civil strife), a novel that is not historical but— like so much of Kazantzakis's work—symbolic and philosophical. The story of this modern Christ is set in an Anatolian village sometime between the Russian Revolution and the Asia Minor disaster. Similar phenomena occur in popular music. The song "Vromiko psomi" (Dirty Bread) by Dionissis Savvopoulos, a popular songwriter, composer, and singer hailed in the 1970s by serious critics as the most original and important poetic voice of the decade, enjoyed enormous popular success. The singer views the terror and oppression of the junta from the perspective of a refugee father who came to Greece from Smyrna in '22. Another song, "I mana tou Alexandrou" (Alexander's Mother), first recorded in 1979 by the internationally successful singer Yiorgos Dalaras (to music by the internationally recognized composer Yiannis Markopoulos), was popular in the post-junta years and has been reissued on a best-selling CD. The song is ostensibly about ancient Macedonia and Alexander the Great, but it is the timeless lament of a Macedonian mother whose only son has gone to Asia Minor to fight, be betrayed, and die alone.

Survivors' Narratives and the Center for Asia Minor Studies

I grew up with the lore of the "Catastrophe," not just as a Greek but as the child of an Asia Minor refugee. My father was from a town outside Gallipoli (Greek Kallipolis, "the fair city"; Turkish Gelibolu). He often told stories about his hometown and his childhood on the farm as the twelfth son of an Orthodox priest who was also a farmer. He was completely bilingual in Greek and Turkish, and had studied Turkish in school before Kemal's reforms substituted the Latin alphabet for Arabic script. To the end of his life my father read Turkish literature, kept up his calligraphy as a hobby, worked on compiling a Turkish-Greek dictionary, and spoke Turkish both with Greek friends from Asia Minor and with new Turkish friends whenever he could, whether in Greece or in the United States. Like the majority of refugees, he talked mainly of the peaceful, hardworking, culturally rich life his family had enjoyed before the "persecution." Consistently, he blamed Greek nationalism and religious intolerance more than he blamed the Turkish government and Islam, and never extended his criticism of official Turkish policy to individual Turks or the Turkish people. About the events surrounding exile he was far more reticent, and what I learned of the hardships his family had endured as refugees in Greece I gleaned incidentally. My aunt and her family were so poor that they could not buy a "twist" of salt to put on the porridge they received as charity in the shantytown outside Volos where they initially settled. All that my father had left from the prosperous home his family had owned for generations was a blanket woven by his mother (I remember it: red, full of holes that had been carefully mended over the years), his father's pocket watch, and a few photographs. Particularly with their children, refugees avoided talking about the horrors, just as Holocaust survivors, parents of friends I met in New York, did not speak of what they had endured to their own children in the decades immediately following the events. Although they were nostalgic about the lost homeland, their concern was survival in daunting circumstances, and later the struggle to make their children and grandchildren prosperous, assimilated citizens of the new country, proud of their heritage but unmarked by the tragedy that drove the refugees into Greece. A friend's father escaped from Smyrna in 1922 as the city burned. He was only five years old, and he had lost his family in the conflagration and the stampede. My friend knows only that somehow he was swept along in a crowd of fleeing refugees; someone lifted him onto a boat. No other details were forthcoming: whenever his children questioned him, he would say, "Let it go, let it go . . . I don't want to remember, I can't."[16]

My own interest in the Asia Minor disaster and its impact on Greek literature and culture led me to seek out narratives of survivors, to look for a broader range of data than what I knew from reading fiction, poetry, history, and what I had gleaned anecdotally from relatives and family friends. I was particularly interested in accounts recorded closer to the events, not in the memories of the few now very aged survivors I could still interview, nor in second- and thirdhand accounts. Fortunately, there is a treasure trove of archival material in the Center for Asia Minor Studies in Athens. Founded in 1930 by Melpo Logotheti Merlier, a musicologist from Asia Minor and the wife of the director of the French Institute in Athens (Octave Merlier), the center began to conduct serious research under her supervision on the music, language, and culture of Asia Minor, beginning in the 1930s with turcophone Cappadocia.[17] Well-trained scholars (some of them fluent in Turkish as well as Greek and able to interview Turkish speakers and record and translate their narratives) interviewed informants in refugee settlements throughout Greece, and compiled the largest archive (roughly 145,000 pages) of oral history in Greece. Some 2,163 settlements inhabited by Greeks were identified in Asia Minor; based on the evidence of 5,051 informants who had resettled in Greece, research was conducted on 1,375 of those settlements. The accounts are catalogued by geographical region (in Asia Minor) and provide a wealth of detailed information on local geography, religious life, superstitions and folk traditions, dialects, relations with Turks and other minority populations, administration, and daily life. The material can be studied at the Center. Most of it is as yet unpublished and in handwritten form. I have had the opportunity to read a significant amount of it, and I have been granted permission to translate material published by the Center, selections from narratives collected in two volumes on the *Exodos*. Although these excerpted accounts represent a small segment of the archival material (261 narratives), I have been able to ascertain that they are representative, covering a wide range of diverse settlements and, within those settlements, diverse socioeconomic classes.

Plain to see are both the commonality of forced flight and exile and the diversity of individual experience, varying not only from village to village but also within each village between the rich and the poor. Not surprisingly, inhabitants of certain cities and towns (particularly on the west coast), where both the Greek and the Turkish armies concentrated their efforts, were far more likely to suffer atrocities. Urban areas experienced the troubles differently from rural villages with a tight-knit local population of Greeks and Turks (and sometimes Jews, Armenians, and Circassians) who had lived together in harmony for generations. Those Greeks who spoke Turkish fluently were more easily able to "pass" and avoid persecution. Those with close ties to their Turkish neighbors and associates speak of being protected from both the sultan's and Kemal's forces, and whenever possible from the marauding bands of warlords and their "irregulars" who terrorized Turks and minority populations alike. Inevitably, wealth and influential connections made both flight and resettlement easier for some than for the majority of refugees.

Expulsion and Compulsory Exchange

The voices of the Greek refugees, and in their narratives those also of their Turkish friends and of the Turkish refugees forced to leave their own homes in Greece, make it impossible not to reflect on what "homeland" means, who is a "brother" and who a "foreigner." The "repatriation" of Greeks and Turks alike served, among other things, to make both Turkey and Greece more homogeneous nation-states. An Islamic Turkish state was the express objective of Kemal's Nationalist Party; an ethnically and religiously homogeneous nation-state was arguably, though not overtly, Venizelos's objective as well.[18] Whatever the politicians' rhetoric, neither those Greeks who had lived for many generations in what was to become a Turkish republic nor those Turks who had lived for generations in what had become a Turkish republic nor those Turks who had lived for generations in what had become Free Greece felt that they were coming home. For the majority of Greeks, Asia Minor was their ancestral home, and the Turks who had lived with them for generations considered them brothers, while they saw the Turkish refugees from Greece as foreigners.

In integrated villages that had not been touched seriously by the war, Greeks and Turks alike were shocked and outraged when they heard about the compulsory exchange. (The Turkish term is *mübadele,* and it also means "barter.") They protest: "What's this business?! You can trade donkeys and oxen, but not people!" (B238). Another narrator reveals the resistance of Greeks and their Turkish fellow villagers at Tenei (Turkish Yesilburç or Enegi, in the region of Nigdi) to take the expulsion of the Greeks as an ineluctable order: "After the Destruction, we found out there would be an Exchange.... That's what the Powers had decided. We didn't like the idea at all. Who wants to abandon his fatherland, his property, everything good, to go into exile?... We didn't want to believe it. When we asked the Turks, they told us not to worry, they would take care of things so we could stay. And it was true, as I found out since I was the president of the town council, they *were* trying to pull some strings in Ankara. They loved us, and wanted us to stay. They petitioned the Ankara government three times. The first two, they got no answer; the third time, Ismet Inönü ... said nothing could be done because the Exchange Agreement had been signed" (B249).[19]

"It was August of 1924 when the terrible news of the Exchange reached our ears. There was mourning and lamentation all through the village, as soon as we heard the order of the Turkish government that doomed us to being uprooted. We were never asked, just as if we were herds of sheep. It was unethical, tragic, how we let the fruits of centuries worth of toil and struggle be dissipated and lost. How we abandoned our schools, our churches, our culture, the bones of our ancestors. . . . But nothing was to be done, unless we were to convert to Islam" (B287).

Even when they saw coastal refugees who had been sent into internal exile, turcophone Greeks in the interior did not imagine that they too would eventually be forced to leave their homes: "Two years before the Exchange, Greek refugees came to Gelveri [ancient Nazianzos] from Denizli and Nazli, near Smyrna. They told us the Turks had exiled them, and that later they would expel all the Greeks" (B9).

A poor and uneducated informant from Tsarikli, recorded in 1959, gives us a variation on the theme, suggesting how gullible and vulnerable to "Greek patriotism" some of the peasants were who had been living in rural isolation and hardworking poverty: "It was the summer of 1923. 'You know, there's going to be an Exchange!' 'What's that?' 'Well, we Christians will go to Greece and Turks will come from Greece to take our place.' Then we were bombarded with propaganda: 'You find wealth in the streets, in Greece! We'll live like rich folks! They have so many grapes, they feed them to their goats! They irrigate their fields with wine!' Even so, we left with a chill in our hearts. It's not easy to leave your native soil, your property, earned and tended with sweat and toil since your great-grandfather's time. We were tricked. We've lived to regret coming here. It's good, you could argue, that we have freedom here. What good is freedom if my belly is empty?" (B255). "That was the Exchange. We thought we were headed for heaven but we came here to hell" (B31; recorded in 1954). "It would have been better if the Exchange hadn't happened. Our life back home was a thousand times better" (B24). And again: "We left paradise and came to hell" (B321).[20]

Narrative after narrative recreates conversations between Greek and Turkish neighbors, the sadness of parting, the sense of kinship between old neighbors despite their different religions. We see the way Turkish refugees from Greece are received by Asia Minor Turks as "foreigners." We hear echoes in these Greek refugee narratives of the Turkish refugees who also experienced displacement, loss, and hardships: they too were strangers in a strange land just as their Greek counterparts were soon to be.[21] In integrated villages, Turkish neighbors were as sad to see their old Greek friends leave to be replaced by Turks from Greece as the Asia Minor Greeks were to leave. "The Turks in our parts were good people. They gave us no trouble, and the war over Smyrna didn't change their behavior at all. A war was going on, but we weren't affected at all" (B48). Turkish friends plead: "Stay here. Don't go to Greece—you'll suffer! You'll have to work too hard there, for too little food. The only good thing about that place is that a widow can marry three times" (B19). "Some Turks who had come back from Greece, where they had been prisoners of war, kept saying: 'Don't go to Greece. They're all bastards there. You won't fare well. They're all swindlers'" (B25). "Some Turks had fought in Greece during the Balkan wars and had been POWs so they knew the place, and they gave us advice: Don't go there, it's a narrow land, the people there are full of lice. There are no sheep there with broad tails: they've got dog-tailed sheep there" (B62). "The local Turks ... couldn't stomach the Turkish refugees, and they protected us from them. One day I was standing in the street, and a Turkish refugee across the way aimed at me with his slingshot and hit me in the head with a rock. A local Turk immediately came out of his shop and beat him up" (B25).

In another town (Karaçaören, also in the area of Caesarea) the local police instituted a curfew for the Turkish refugees and protected the local Greeks (B78). "As we were leaving, our Turkish neighbors brought us gifts, bulgur, honey, clotted cream. They embraced us, weeping: 'Don't go there. We live like brothers here, we are brothers from the same womb/earth'" (B30). "The local Turks were sorry to see us go. There was an *aga* [a high official of the empire] of Caesarea, Imam Zade Mehmet Bey, he was called, and as he looked at the Turkish refugees from Serres, gathered in front of the church, poor, miserable wretches, he shook his head and said: 'We have exchanged gold for iron. By Allah, we will really miss you.' The Turkish refugees had arrived a month before we left. They were all poor peasants. . . . The local Turks didn't care for them. In general, Turkish refugees were not welcome in Caesarea" (B40; this narrative was given wholly in Turkish in 1959). "As we were passing [as refugees] through the plain of Melendiz, Turks from the neighboring towns would come to meet us; they were crying, begging us: 'Don't leave. Stay here with us.' They gave us a refreshing yoghurt drink and put fresh cheese in our satchels for the road" (B21). "'Greek sisters, don't go there. You won't find a better place than our village. You'll go there, and they [the Turkish refugees] will come here and we won't be able to get along with them.' . . . The Exchange was a curse" (B9). To the duet of local Turks and Greeks is added a third voice, that of the Turkish refugees for whom Greece was a lost home. "A few days before we left [in 1924] Turkish refugees came, from somewhere in Greece. They were all crying because they had been sent to our village. 'We left all the good things we had behind, and we came here to suffer'" (B59).

A Greek refugee who was eleven years old when she left her hometown, Sarmousakli (Turkish Bunyan or Hamidije), near the city of Caesarea, re-counts: "Before we left, Turkish refugees arrived from Greece. A bundle of cloth on their heads, and a lot of filth. They would go to the town spring and we'd see them there. They ripped the doors and windows off our houses and burned them. It was they who filled us with despair about Greece. They would tell us: 'On the boat you'll only be able to look out through a hole; they'll put you in jail where you're going, you'll die.' . . . These Turks spoke very little Turkish [as opposed to the turcophone Greeks of the informant's town]. They weren't religious people. They didn't even fast for Ramadan. One of them was summoned to court and reprimanded for not observing Ramadan. His re-sponse was: 'We had freedom in Greece, we paid no attention to fasts and things of that sort, life was better in Greece.' They punished him. . . . The Turks in Hamidije hated these people because they were not pious. They lamented losing us: 'We're losing our own kind; who's going to buy our butter?'" (B104).

The voices are interwoven in a communal lament, whether they are blend-ing in harmony or raised in contradiction and recriminations. "Meanwhile, Turkish refugees had arrived from Kozani. They were bad folks, wolves, they'd stab you as soon as say good morning. The local Turks couldn't stand them" (B80). "A month before we left, Turkish refugees came from Macedonia. They were really crude peasants. We [women] were afraid and gathered in houses where there were still some men. The local Turks didn't receive them well, they wanted nothing to do with them" (B87). "There was a good *hodja* in our village [Kermira]. He wept as we were leaving: 'Ach, ach, Venizelos tricked us with his politics. They've taken away our neighbors who were like diamonds and put in their place rusty old iron. A single tree doesn't make a garden; it yields no sweetness. You need many different fruit trees to make a garden'" (B91; in this narrative as in others, utterances by Turks are repeated in Turkish). "The Turks who came to our village were from Macedonia. They wore a tall fez and baggy pants. It was the first time we had ever seen such a costume. There were two or three vacant houses, that's where they went to stay. You know what they ate? Corn! They'd make cornmeal, and make a kind of pie with corn on top and corn on the bottom, and in the middle something that looked like a nettle. They kept asking for broad beans. Their Turkish was strange, we couldn't understand them" (B118). "These Turks didn't know wheat. They wanted to grow corn, to eat corn" (B129). "At Ulukisla [where there was a train station] we ran into Turkish refugees who were coming from Greece, going toward Neapolis [Nebsehir]. They asked us where we were going. 'To Greece.' 'Where in Greece?' 'We don't know.' 'Go to Kozani—the corn there grows so high.' And they would ask my mother, 'Auntie, is there corn where you come from?'" (B140). "When the Turkish refugees came, they called us 'neighbor.' We were all in the same situation. We just took it lying down, they said, we didn't put up a fight, and they were sorry now. Many of the young men begged Christians to list them as family members so they could be deported and return to Greece" (B147).

Resettlement: "We were driven out of Eden and came here to Hell"

The Turks who came to Turkey from Greece were not received with enthusiasm, but the vast majority of Greek refugees experienced far worse conditions when they were "repatriated" to Greece. Under five hundred thousand Turks were resettled in communities in Turkey vacated by roughly six times as many Greeks; the million and a half refugees who made it to Greece were (conservatively) about a third of the Greek minority population living in Turkey before the massacres, the forced marches, and the labor camps. Arriving Greek refugees found not only that the homes and land previously owned by Turks were far too few, but also that there was very little provision for absorbing and resettling the flood of destitute, ill, and traumatized refugees. To be sure, those relative few with wealth and connections were able to leave Turkey with far fewer difficulties and to build a new life with some degree to ease: some tell of renting good lodgings before buying land, building a house, and setting up a business. In one instance, after moving from a tent camp in Piraeus to an old fortress on Corfu and then to some warehouses, refugees from a village in the region of Caesarea along with others from neighboring villages went to Yiannina; there one of their number managed to surmount bureaucratic and other obstacles and secure an expanse of marshy land for the refugees; they built a village which they named "New Caesarea" (B65–66).

For most, however, the arrival in Greece was little better than the voyage in filthy boats without food and water, people crammed together like animals; many who had endured persecution and captivity were ill with dysentery and typhus, teeming with lice; some had lost their sanity or were so overwhelmed by despair after the atrocities they had endured and witnessed and the loss of their loved ones that they threw themselves overboard to perish at sea. Once they reached a Greek port, ships were quarantined and for weeks denied permission to dock; ships were shunted from port to port, particularly as locations such as Chios that were closer to Turkey were saturated with refugees.[22] Chios in particular, as one of the closest Greek ports, opposite Smyrna, was soon flooded with refugees: "We got to Chios, which was the nearest Greek port. They didn't give us a warm welcome. I have to admit, a *lot* of refugees had landed there. They wouldn't even give us a drop of water to drink. In two, three days we got back on the boat and left for Thessaloniki" (A107). "When the Chians saw that the boat was full of refugees, they got their donkeys and put them inside their houses, so as not to take in any refugees and save them" (A23). But Nikolaos Papanikolaou from Sançak also saw the Chians' position: "When we got to Chios, there were more of us than of them. We suffered, but Chios suffered a lot too" (A76).

Another close port was Mytilene (Lesbos). "The boat brought us to Mytilene. The whole town shuttered all the windows and bolted the doors against us; they wouldn't take us in. The folks who got there first stayed in the churches. We spent eight days outside, under the trees. Then another boat came and took us to Piraeus. They didn't let us disembark, they were shouting that Athens was too crowded. So they took us on to Patra. They didn't want us to disembark there either, but then the men [the refugees, doubtless with the collusion of the crew] grabbed some planks and made it off the boat anyway. They went and got the police, and the police took charge of everyone" (A65). Although we hear also of kind people and attempts, spontaneous or organized, to help the refugees, generally no one wanted them, and no one had the wherewithal to receive them. Piraeus, the port of Athens, received hundreds of thousands of refugees; they were kept sometimes for weeks in a makeshift compound surrounded by barbed wire. Because of the heavy lice infestation, refugees were shorn, a particular disgrace for the rural women, who prided themselves on their long hair and for whom a shaved head was the mark of being convicted as a whore or an adulteress; we hear of quite a few such women who committed suicide in their humiliation.

Some locations were wild and insalubrious, and the early years were devastating even if eventually villages were built and the land was tamed. A Turkish landowner had turned over one-fifth of his grazing land outside Kavala to the Ministry of Agriculture and left the rest for the refugees. About two thousand mountain villagers from the Gelveri (Greek Karvali, ancient Nazianzos) arrived in an area outside Kavala in northern Greece, only to find a malarial swamp full of thickets and brambles in a location so isolated that at night jackals came to the camp to dig up the newly buried corpses of those who had died of illness. For three years their only shelter against the bitter cold winters consisted of flimsy makeshift tents. Half of the two thousand refugees who settled there were dead within three years; others became disheartened and left. In 1926 those who had survived and stuck it out began to build their village, New Karvali (A14). Even those who secured housing constructed by the state for refugees near a city had to fight to secure shelter. Saroula Skyfti came as a young girl from a small village fifteen kilometers northwest of Magnesia and thirty-nine kilometers northeast of Smyrna, and did finally manage to secure such a structure; had she been less spunky and less lucky, she would not have succeeded in getting or retaining her little portion of a construction site.

Gradually, everyone managed to secure some form of housing and to make a living, but refugee communities remained poor for decades. They were in outlying rural areas, in shantytowns and urban slums. Poor urban refugees were targeted as "subversives" and "communists" during the Nazi occupation and the bitter civil war that followed it, and subject to raids and even to the burning of entire neighborhoods, first by the SS and its Greek collaborators, then by the police and right-wing groups, often the same people who had collaborated with Hitler's occupying forces. When the colonels came to power in 1967 after a CIA-backed coup and ruled for seven years, the same communities were targeted by the same reactionary groups, from whom were drawn the torturers of the dreaded security police. Ironically, in more recent decades many of those refugees and their descendants relegated to the most unpromising locations have fared particularly well. Barren coastal land, remote and impossible to farm, became prime beachfront real estate once the boom in foreign and domestic tourism gained momentum in the 1970s. As cities throughout Greece experienced vast population increases and began to expand in all possible directions, neighborhoods that were once remote and what had once been isolated villages came to form part of an enlarged city center, or turned into desirable suburbs, or—where there were suitable expanses of undeveloped land—attracted large international corporations. Primitive one-room hovels have long since been razed and replaced by villas and luxury high-rises.

Such a happy ending was unimaginable for the refugees of the 1920s, whose narratives are shaped by suffering and loss. Each survivor has a different story to tell, but all are variations on the same theme, the story of all refugees, be they Palestinian, Somali, Ethiopian, Jewish, Bosnian Muslim, Serbian, Croatian, Cambodian, Haitian, Rwandan, Afghan . . . the list goes on, seemingly endless. We must listen to their narratives and strive to bring about a world in which no one will need to tell or listen to new variations on the same tragic story. I wrest hope from the narratives that say, "We lived like brothers."

Notes

Almost all the refugee narratives excerpted here are drawn from material in the archives of the Center for Asia Minor Studies (CAMS) in Athens; direct quotations are from selected narratives published in two volumes: *Exodos A: Martyries apo tis eparchies ton dytikon paralion tes Mikras Asias* (Testimonies from Provinces on the West Coast of Asia Minor) (Athens: Center for Asia Minor Studies, 1980) and *Exodos B: Martyries apo tis eparchies tes Kentrikes kai Notias Mikras Asias* (Testimonies from the Provinces of Central and Southern Asia Minor) (Athens: Center for Asia Minor Studies, 1982). All translations are mine. References to these volumes are cited in the text by volume letter and page number, e.g., B64. I thank the Center for Asia Minor Studies for making my archival work possible and for permission to publish my translations of these narratives; I also thank the Kahn Institute and Smith College for supporting my research.

1. The first official recognition of Kemal's government by France came in January 1920, with the defeat of French troops in Cilicia; France negotiated a separate armistice with Kemal, ceding Cilicia to Turkey, along with manpower and materiel, and securing commercial and mineral rights. In his confidential telegrams, however, Kemal describes meetings with emissaries from Greece's "allies" and the supposedly neutral United States as early as August 2, 1919. Woodrow Wilson had sent high-ranking military officers to meet with him, and they had assured him of support and friendship; behind the scenes, French and British emissaries were also making diplomatic overtures, with the British reminding Kemal that Britain had a long history of friendship with Turkey. In a confidential telegram to Pasha Abdul Kerim (September 28, 1919), Kemal reports that the nationalist movement has the support of Italy, France, the United States, and Britain. Meeting with Kemal in Sebasteia, the British again stressed that Britain had been friendly to Turkey for fifty years, pointed out that they had withdrawn occupying troops from Merzifun, and promised to withdraw troops from Amisos. Kemal goes on to say that that promise had been fulfilled. Furthermore, the British promised to remain "neutral" and not interfere to the detriment of the nationalist movement, which they recognized as a justified and legitimate popular movement. Italy, France, and Britain continued to made overtures to Kemal in 1920 and 1921 while declaring their "neutrality" in the Greco-Turkish conflict. March 1921 saw an agreement signed in Rome between Italy and Turkey; Italy withdrew its forces as a sign of goodwill and undertook to return Smyrna and Thrace to Turkey. Kemal exploited competition among the Entente powers, while Greece persisted in a campaign that was being sabotaged by its supposed allies. Furthermore, Greece refused any rapprochement with Russia, while Kemal astutely concluded a separate agreement with Lenin on March 16, 1921. Documentation in Dido Soteriou, *I Mikrasiatike Katastrophe kai I strategike tou imperialismou stin Anatolike Mesogeio* (Athens: Kedros, 1975), 33–84.

2. For a detailed discussion of the population exchanges in the Balkans, Greece, and Turkey, see Stephen P. Ladas, *The Exchange of Minorities: Bulgaria, Greece, and Turkey* (New York: Macmillan, 1932). For a more recent analysis with a broader focus, more easily accessible documentary evidence, and extensive bibliography, see Harry J. Psomiades, *The Eastern Question: The Last Phase, a Study in Greek-Turkish Diplomacy* (Thessaloniki: Institute for Balkan Studies, 1968). The texts of the Lausanne agreements appear as appendixes. For a brief summary of events and incisive analysis, see John A. Petropoulos, "The Compulsory Exchange of Populations: Greek-Turkish Peacemaking, 1922–1930," *Byzantine and Modern Greek Studies* 2 (1976): 135–60.

3. For a succinct analysis of Greek domestic politics in relation to foreign policy in the eastern Mediterranean and the Balkans, see Theodore A. Couloumbis, John A. Petropoulos, and Harry J. Psomiades, *Foreign Interference in Greek Politics: An Historical Perspective* (New York: Pella Publishing, 1976); on Venizelos in this period, see esp. 38–41. The case of Eleftherios Venizelos is worth considering briefly because it underscores the inextricability of Greek domestic politics from the foreign policy of major foreign powers. Venizelos had served as prime minister from 1910 to 1915 and had undertaken a reorganization of the Greek army and navy through a French military mission and a British naval mission. As early as 1914, he wanted Greece to enter the war but could not prevail against King Constantine's policy of neutrality. To protest the king's opposition to his war policy, Venizelos resigned—twice—in 1915. The second time, his party boycotted the December elections and so gave the British and French (who had already landed in Thessaloniki in October) a pretext to intervene as guarantors of the constitution. In June 1916 the Entente demanded a new Greek government, the dissolution of parliament, and demobilization of the Greek army. By October 1916, Venizelos established a rival government in Thessaloniki; less than two months later, the British and French contingents landed near Athens, recognized the Venizelos government, and blockaded royalist Greece. Many died of starvation as a result of the blockade, among them my mother's older sister. In June 1917 the Entente forced Constantine to abdicate in favor of his second son, and Venizelos returned to Athens in triumph. Greece then formally entered the war against the Central Powers and played a major role in the Macedonian campaign in the fall of 1918.

4. The history of the Balkans and the eastern Mediterranean is complex, and no event should be viewed out of context, without regard to past history. The details of nationalist movements and imperial policy among all the players, with the resulting dizzying fluctuations of hegemony and shifting borders, cannot be addressed here. We should remember, however, that for many centuries it was never clear what constituted a homeland or what state or ethnicity could lay claim to the allegiance of such a diverse population. William Miller's study *The Ottoman Empire and its Successors, 1801–1927*, with an appendix 1927–1936 (Cambridge: Cambridge University Press, 1936) is still well worth reading, even if the occasional lack of political correctness and the style seem dated.

5. Population figures are approximate and contested, but Turkish census statistics in 1912 suggest that Greeks constituted 19.6 percent of a total population of slightly over 10,000; Turks constituted 71.3 percent; and Armenians, Bulgarians, Jews, Europeans, and Roma 9.1 percent. These figures appear in a detailed analysis of changing population statistics between 1900 and 1925, with figures drawn from a variety of sources including the League of Nations, in the introductory chapter of *Exodos A*.

6. Eleftherios Iosifidis came from Zile, a mountain town forty-six kilometers south-southwest of Caesarea. In 1924, when they first heard about the Exchange, there were 51 Greek households, 224 individuals, who spoke only Turkish and no Greek. There were about 2,250 Turks. When he was interviewed in 1962 in a settlement near Athens, he said that he still corresponded with the son of the Turkish landowner whose fieldhand he had been; his Turkish age-mate had been a good friend and treated him well, and in

his letters kept inviting Iosifidis to return to the town as his guest (B61). Anecdotes abound that illustrate the close ties between employers and employees on both sides. My aunt returned to her hometown of Lampsakos as a tourist, with her children and grandchildren, in 1990. Serendipitously, one of the first people they ran into was an old Turk who had been her father's apprentice. He remembered her as a little girl, spoke with warmth and nostalgia about the days when they had all lived in harmony, and took my relatives to meet his daughter and her family.

7. The Young Turks met in Thessaloniki and demanded that the Constitution of 1876, which the sultan had approved and rescinded a year later in 1877, be put into effect. After some domestic battles, the reformists prevailed and the sultan was deposed, although the sultanate was not abolished. Kemal did not declare his party a de facto government until April 23, 1920, at the Grand National Assembly in Ankara; the last sultan fled from Constantinople/Istanbul in 1922.

8. Narratives in Greek consistently mention the atrocities committed by Tsetes, the hellenized form of Turkish çete, defined in the Redhouse dictionary as "1. armed band (of irregulars, partisans, guerrillas, bandits, brigands); 2. gang (usually one engaged in illegal activities)." The first irregulars may have been nationalist soldiers who refused to disarm when Turkey was defeated in 1918, but their numbers were soon augmented by terrorist gangs commanded by brigand chiefs, or "warlords," as we have more recently come to call them in countries such as Somalia and Afghanistan. There were also other criminals who took advantage of chaotic conditions not unlike those prevailing in Afghanistan today. A report from Kandahar (January 15, 2002) indicated that the police force formed to keep order was composed of seven hundred illiterate former "freedom fighters," gunmen with no police training. Only seventy of them had uniforms, making it even easier for thugs to pose as police in order to rob, torture, and kill civilians.

The Tsetes are almost always distinguished from both Ottoman and Kemalist soldiers, although occasionally narrators speak of such groups commanded by a regular Kemalist officer. They were feared by Greeks (and other minority groups) and Turks (see B413, for instance). The Tsetes were kept out of Vekse (nineteen kilometers northeast of Caesarea) by a gully. The mixed population consisted of sixty-eight turcophone Greeks and about three hundred Turks. Father Isaac, a priest, says that all the inhabitants in the village enjoyed "real freedom" because it was protected by a wealthy and enlightened Turk (B 54). In an unpublished narrative from the Adapazar region (Center for Asia Minor Studies archive, folder Exodos I 44.1, 89–90) we find that in 1919–20 Turkish local authorities told three hundred attacking rebels to leave the village alone, and when they refused, Greeks and Armenians put up armed resistance and the attacking band left. Numerous villages formed (mixed) militias or civil defense groups with Turks, Greeks, and Armenians working together to keep out attackers. In Pergamos the civil defense militia seems to have been composed largely of Greek partisans; the informant who was the leader of the group had served in the Turkish army, which he deserted; he had also served in the Greek army as a volunteer (A139).

The Tsetes are not a unified group; rival warlords clash with one another (A173).

One such feuding pair are the "good" Demertzis (who does not persecute minorities) and the notoriously cruel Yürük Ali (A178; Yürük = a Turkish nomad). Particularly feared was Ghiaour (*gâvur*) Ali, who was responsible for the horrendous massacres and gratuitous atrocities in the Ortaköy region in 1920 (*gâvur* = a non-Muslim, or Christian; by extension it means obstinate, intransigent, merciless, fanatical, cruel). Kyriaki Das-kalaki, from Houdi (Büyük Saracli) in the Geyve-Ortaköy area, saw him as a child when he came with his men to raid her village. She describes him: "He was swarthy, his face covered with hair. He wore a turban on his head, and his chest was covered with bullets. He had hand grenades in his belt, and pistols. Even in his boots, he had knives and pistols" (A329).

9. See note 1 and, for further documentary evidence, the introduction to *Exodos A.*

10. One comment, "We had no news whatsoever in Pergamos [Turkish Bergama] that the Greek army was retreating" (A138), strikes a familiar note. Refugee narratives are complemented and corroborated by a unique document, the diary of Charalambos Pleziotes, a typical young soldier with no schooling past the fourth grade. A native of Smyrna, he began basic training on April 4, 1920, and a month later he left for the front. His last entry is dated October 9, 1921. The diary was given to the archives of the Center for Asia Minor Studies (CAMS) in 1980 by a nephew of the diary's author and published in 1991 as Charalambos Pleziotes, *Anamneseis tou Metopou: 1920–1921, Mikra Asia–Thrake* (Memories from the Front: 1920–1921, Asia Minor–Thrace) (Athens: Center for Asia Minor Studies, 1991).

Pleziotes is no ideologue, and no martyr. He is preoccupied with getting enough decent food, getting a serviceable pair of boots, curing his earaches, diarrhea, stomach problems, and blistered bloody feet, having a cigarette with a buddy, getting a letter from home. But he is also a sensitive observer, and his disgust with the war, and with the exploits of the "Liberation Army" as well as with those of Turkish soldiers and "irregulars," increases as the campaign progresses. From the beginning, he comments on the soldiers' pilfering ("liberating," he says ironically) cheese, animals, fruit, butter, and other goods from villages they enter in order to "disarm" those Turks who have not already abandoned their homes. On July 12, 1920, for instance, his entry reads: "We were ordered to search and found chickens, eggs, cheese and other goodies. We gave the enemy no quarter! In ten minutes we had devoured the opposition" (5). By September 20, when his company entered Nikaia, his tone is more serious. For seventy-five days Tsetes had blockaded the Greek quarter of Nikaia before leading all the Greeks out of the town and slaughtering them. By the time the Greek army came to Nikaia, most of the Turkish inhabitants had fled. "The soldiers scattered in all directions and looted houses and shops; all but a few of the Turkish inhabitants had already left. No Greek had survived the slaughter that took place a few days ago. . . . Some of us went for a stroll outside the town to see the slaughtered Christians; there were heads strewn all over the road, hands, feet, other things of that sort, enough to make you lose your mind just looking at it all. Further along there were three wells, all full to the top with corpses. Finally, a cave with about 400 corpses piled up in it, victims of all ages, killed in all kinds of ways. We didn't stop there at all, we felt dizzy and we were suffocating.

We went on immediately to the Greek quarter; what a horrific wasteland! We went to the church of Saint Sophia, an old Byzantine church, but you couldn't tell if it was a house of worship or a hay barn" (79). He goes on to describe the systematic vandalism that had destroyed the church. Before leaving three days later, the Greek soldiers set fire to the town. "Afterwards we found a vantage point where we could sit and admire our handiwork, like Nero when he burned Rome" (81). The genocidal atrocities of the "irregulars" are without parallel, but Pleziotes has no illusions about what Greek soldiers can do. On October 18, 1920, his company entered Yeni-sehir to find that other soldiers had gotten there first and looted all the stores. He goes to sleep, and wakes (with diarrhea, as usual) in the middle of the night to see "a riot outside, the soldiers were rushing in all directions as if they were possessed by the devil, brandishing candles and lanterns, breaking into stores and houses, you could hear the Turkish women screaming and crying, but no one cared about that. Strange things were going on. I went out with my buddy Pezaros to see what was happening. What we saw is indescribable—the only thing missing was a full-fledged massacre" (96).

By the end of December, Pleziotes had become increasingly depressed about what the war had done to the people; both Greeks and Turks were forced to flee as one army or another advanced. "On the road we saw the villagers fleeing, on both sides of us. Old men, old women, young women, children, with everything they could carry on their backs; they were pale and beaten down by terror and grief. In the afternoon we got to Biledjik, and the inhabitants there were all running around in a panic, like crazy people, and they were all looking at us, an expression in their eyes I can't interpret with certainty: Were they sorry for us because we were leaving? Did they hate us? Were they pleading with us to protect them? I don't know. Ever since we passed the first village, my heart had gotten really heavy, I walk with my head down because I can't look anyone in the eye, I don't want to raise my eyes and see anyone. Meanwhile, the lieutenant gave orders that all the inhabitants should stay put in their villages, and those who had left should turn back, because they had nothing to fear!! In the evening we got to Peldos and bivouacked, another abandoned village, the people are fleeing. . . . Well now, what's their problem, isn't the Greek army taking good care of them? After all, they've been liberated from the Turkish yoke, what more could they possibly want? Poor people! They were living well enough, in peace . . . and out of the blue their Greek brethren show up as Angels of Deliverance and Liberators!! I dread to think what's going to happen in two or three days to all those villages in the Liberated Zone; God only knows" (135–36; December 29, 1920). Two days later the Greek army blew up the Köprü-hissar bridge once the last soldier had made it across. "On the other side quite a few of the villagers who were following us were left stranded. Children had managed to cross with us but their mothers were left behind; some guy's wife had made it across, someone else's husband, things of that sort, the fruits of Freedom!! And Civilization!! This glorious campaign happened so we could destroy quite a few villages and many thousands of people who had been minding their own business" (137).

Abandoning Greek civilians was a policy that seems to have had its source in Aristidis Stergiadis, the Greek high commissioner, who is quoted as saying, "Better they should all stay there and be massacred by Kemal than come to Athens and turn every-thing upside down" (cited in introduction to *Exodos A*, οζ n. 2). The order from on high to the Greek army was: "Save troops. Abandon civilians" (A240). Polyvios Narliotis saw the telegram sent to the Greek officer stationed in Kutsukuyu, a village of about two hundred Greeks and considerably fewer Turks, on the coastal road between Çannakale and Adrammyti, thirty-six kilometers west-southwest of Adramytti and twenty-seven kilometers north-northwest of Ayvalik.

11. Accounts of the burning of Smyrna are virtually without number. Interesting because of its source is the eyewitness account, with photographs, in George Horton, *The Blight of Asia* (New York: Bobbs-Merrill, 1926), 126–67. Horton was U.S. consul general in Smyrna in 1922, and had been a consular official in the Near East (including Greece and Turkey) for decades. "One of the keenest impressions which I brought away with me from Smyrna was a feeling of shame that I belonged to the human race," said Horton, not least because the Allied and American battleships that filled the harbor did nothing to stop the slaughter, rape, and plunder going on before them (153). Refugee narratives refer repeatedly to the "neutral observers" who made no effort to stop the slaughter of refugees trapped between the burning city and the narrow strip along the harbor; the particularly odious behavior of French crews is singled out more than once. "The behavior of the French was reprehensible. When people managed to climb up, they would throw them back into the water, especially if it was a young man who managed to climb on board. As they saw people swimming toward the ship, they poured scalding water on them to keep them from climbing up" (A38; Anna Karabet-sou, from Nymphaio/Nif). Like other informants, she says that Italian crews were more humane. Theodoros Loukides (A127) describes the nightmarish scene in Smyrna and how the crew on Allied ships beat the refugees with clubs and threw scalding water on them if they tried to climb aboard to escape the bullets aimed at them by the Turkish "irregulars" as they swam toward the ships in the harbor. President Panagiotes Kanel-lopoulos, in a letter to the writer Ilias Venezis published in *Nea Estia* 92 (Christmas 1972): 24, speaks of the callous "neutrality" and the merciless treatment of fleeing refugees, with the exception of two commercial freighters, one Italian and the other Japanese, and notes that all the diplomats in the area with the exception of Horton remained "neutral." Horton himself documents the overtly pro-Turkish utterances and behavior of his American colleagues.

12. *Prosfygike Ellada/Refugee Greece: Photographs from the Archives of the Center for Asia Minor Studies* (Athens: CAMS, 1992), a bilingual publication with a brief history of the flight and resettlement of Asia Minor refugees, includes selected narratives and a wealth of rare photographs both from Asia Minor and from refugee communities in which fieldworkers interviewed informants during the first few decades after the Expulsion. For readers of Greek, the edited volume of papers from a conference on refugee settle-ments held in Athens in April 1997 is worth consulting: *O Xerizomos kai I Alli Patrida: oi prosfygoupoleis stin Ellada* (Athens: Etaireia Spoudon Neoellinikou Politismou kai Geni-kes Paideias, 1997). Papers address social, economic, and cultural topics.

13. The term is applied not only to those who were forced to flee but also to their

descendants. I was reminded of this recently in Athens. My cousin's wife, a woman in her early forties from "Old Greece," was ranting about some "dirty refugees" who had come to her office at the Ministry of Finance. They were two older men, sons of Asia Minor refugees, who had come to see her about some land their parents had received as indemnification and which they had inherited. Suddenly she stopped in mid-tirade: "I forgot, you're part of that tribe too, just like my husband—but you're different, after all you've been living in the United States, you don't have quite the same mentality."

14. Venezis was almost eighteen when he was arrested in October 1922 in his home-town of Ayvalik and sent as a prisoner to the interior of Turkey to join a forced labor "battalion." Men of military age were arrested; depending on the region and the whim of the Turkish authorities, the limits were often stretched on both ends of the normal age range of eighteen to forty to encompass all males between the ages of fourteen and seventy. Agape Venezi-Molyviati, the author's sister, describes his arrest in an issue of the journal *Aiolika Grammata* 2, no. 11 (1972): 504–9. His memoir is a powerful literary work as well as a historical document, although Venezis differentiates it from his many novels: "This is a true chronicle, so I don't feel it belongs to me the way my novels do that draw on creative imagination. No art is more difficult than that of describing events you've lived through." From his aphorisms and meditations, *Ek Batheon/De Profundis*, cited in the journal *Nea Estia* 92 (December 1972): 31.

15. Particularly useful for readers of English is Thomas Doulis, *Disaster and Fiction: Modern Greek Fiction and the Asia Minor Disaster of 1922* (Berkeley: University of California Press, 1977). This is an astute and sensitive study and also a monument of thorough research. Doulis demonstrates his command of even obscure literary and critical texts in Greek, including articles and interviews in the popular press.

16. In their (unpublished) notebooks, fieldworkers often note that an informant has interrupted his or her narrative, overcome by tears. Adult children or the spouse of an older narrator with a heart condition may cut short the interview, or try to. One such fieldworker's note is published (*Exodos B* 65). Forty years after the events, in 1962, Eleftherios Iosifidis was so moved by digging up old memories that "he interrupted his narrative for a moment. My questions went unanswered. He looked at the ground; when he spoke, his voice was weak: 'Where did you come from to reopen this old wound, reminding me of the past!'" Venezis, speaking about his captivity memoir (no. 31328) decades after it was first published, said that for years he could not bear to pick up the book and "dig around in that old wound." Cited in *Nea Estia* 92 (Christmas 1972): 31.

17. *Refugee Greece* includes a history of the Center and its research, and some bibli-ography; see also *65 Chronia Epistemonikes Prosforas* (Athens: CAMS, 1996), a retrospective volume celebrating the sixty-fifth anniversary of the founding of the Center for Asia Minor Studies; includes bibliography, photographs and illustrations, and critical articles.

18. John A. Petropoulos, "The Compulsory Exchange of Populations: Greek-Turkish Peacemaking, 1922–1930," *Byzantine and Modern Greek Studies* 2 (1976): 135–60, argues very convincingly that Venizelos actually attained his objective at Lausanne, to secure a

nation-state with defensible borders and a homogeneous population. Like Kemal, Venizelos was concerned with stability in domestic politics.

19. Local Turks in Aksaray as well, a town 132 kilometers southwest of Caesarea, petitioned the Ankara government to allow those Greeks who had not departed by 1924 to choose not to be exchanged and to stay on in their village. The *mutasarrif* (provincial governor), who was well educated and friendly to Greeks, had helped all those who had chosen to leave before the Exchange obtain the right legal papers, sell their property, and leave in comfort. All the Greeks in the village were turcophone. In 1924 only 203 Greeks remained, and 6,000 Turks (B5-6). Quite a few towns made attempts to keep clear of the war, to resist ethnic enmity. Nikolaos Papanikoloaou from Sançak (seventy kilometers northwest of Smyrna, with 500 turcophone Greeks) volunteered in the Greek army in 1921. Once the Greeks were defeated and he was retreating, he passed through the mixed village of Ambarseki. "There we saw a group of Turks and Greeks, living like brothers. 'What are you guys doing here?' we aked. 'We've taken an oath of brotherhood and we've decided to stay.' 'Bad idea,' we told them. 'All of Asia Minor has been emptied out. After the things that have happened, there's no way you can stay friends.' We found the same situation in [the next village] Saipi" (B75).

20. These narratives were all recorded in the 1950s, when most refugees were living in very poor settlements and neighborhoods.

21. Greeks in Smyrna were sophisticated and well traveled, but the inhabitants of remote rural areas—particularly the women—had never left their villages; they experienced even the journey to the coast, where they would be put on ships and taken to Greece, as travel into an almost surrealistically unfamiliar world. They speak of seeing the sea for the first time: "a big plain that looks like the sky" (B176), "green fields" (B26), "what an infinite plain" (B64). They had never seen a train before, and thought of it as a "black devil" (B263); they called out to one another, "Come take a look at this big black thing that's stretching out like *masticha* [the resin of the mastic tree, which can be made into chewing gum and pulled like taffy] and it carries people!" (B20). Never having seen a motor car before, they cannot fathom what sort of thing it is (B24); when representatives of the Mixed Commission on Refugees show up in a car, they wonder, "How can this four-wheeled cart move without any oxen, without a horse!" (B64). Bicycles, too, puzzle a number of informants; someone's sister-in-law had once seen a bicycle and was able to report that she had been told what the thing was called: "the devil's boat" (B24).

22. Both to be allowed to land initially and to find a place to settle, refugees traveled all over Greece. Typical itineraries are: Rhodes-Piraeus-Corfu; Piraeus-Volos-Farsala-Corfu-Bulgarian border; Piraeus-Volos-Velestino-Kavala-Alexandroupolis-Bulgarian border; Piraeus-Crete-Thessaly-Thebes-Kaisariani (near Athens in 1926, in Athens now).

Exile, Creativity, and Memory
Reflections on "The Excursion of the Dead Girls"

POLINA DIMOVA

THE SHORT STORY "The Excursion of the Dead Girls" by the German Jewish writer Anna Seghers, written during Seghers's years of exile in Mexico, presents us with a model exile text. In its autobiographical tone, the story perfectly blends its subject matter, which concerns exilic existence, with narrative technique, which expresses exile on the formal level by enacting nostalgic mental returns to the past. The issues that the story raises concern the ways in which one transforms the experience of exile into a piece of writing, in which nostalgic memory relates to exile and exile stimulates creativity.

By examining a variety of theoretical approaches to realism in relation to exile, I aim to show the inadequacy of some formal achievements of nineteenth-century realism, such as unified plot and narrative consistency, for rendering faithfully exilic experience. Whereas homebound authors promote the principles of unity and action, which reflect a sense of belonging, Seghers's narrative conveys a sense of stasis, fragmentation, and discontinuity, which evokes the exile's ruptured existence and nostalgic preoccupation with the past. Seghers's short story seeks serenity and reconciliation in its return to the past so as to counteract the disruption of loss, trauma, and the anguish of exilic experience. Additionally, by frustrating narrative action and unity, Seghers's text exposes the adversities of exile and the horrendous aftermath of the war that has caused it.

Seghers's narrative achieves its resonance by using memory as its thematic and structural principle. We shall see that, although exile writers realize the futility of their attempts to reassemble a past preserved only as partial, confused, and distorted recollections, they must rely on their faulty memory as their only resort to reclaim fractions of an idyllic past and home. By exploring the dynamics of memory in exilic texts, I differentiate between nostalgic memory and performative memory, which suggest respectively the recuperation of and the recuperation from (recovery from) the past. That is, the memory of homesickness laments the irrevocably lost past and is determined to recuperate it, while the memory of social duty and creativity helps the exiled writers transcend the experience of exile and recover from nostalgia, as they realize their moral and aesthetic obligation to recreate the past in writing.

Appreciating the importance of Seghers's personal experiences for her short story "The Excursion of the Dead Girls" necessitates a brief account of her life. Born Netty Reiling in 1900, Anna Seghers grew up in Mainz in an atmosphere of cultural refinement and learning.[1] She received a broad liberal arts education at Heidelberg, where she studied art, sinology, philology, and history. An intellectual of leftist convictions, she became a member of the Communist Party of Germany in 1928. During the same period, Seghers made her literary debut and received the Kleist Prize for young writers. When the National Socialists came to power in 1933, their regime triply denounced Seghers—for her communist affiliation, her Jewish background, and her efforts as a female author. The same year, after being arrested and then released, Seghers fled to France.

Seghers's literary work during her French period includes *The Way through February* (1935), *The Seventh Cross* (1942), and *Transit* (1944). In these novels, Seghers resorts to modernist techniques, such as frequent shifts in setting and narrative voice, stream of consciousness, and multiple plot. Thus, she embraces the concept of a more open-ended, freer realism, which she articulated in her theoretical positions on literature in the late 1930s. She explores her ideas of realism in greatest detail in her most experimental short story, "The Excursion of the Dead Girls" (1946), which she conceived in Mexico, the next station of her exile after the advance of the German army to southern France.

Exilic Realism: Fragmentation and the Frustration of Narrative

Toward the end of the debates over realism in the late 1930s, Anna Seghers and the Hungarian-born literary critic and Marxist philosopher Georg Lukács initiated an exchange of letters to share and elucidate their views about the nature of realism in literature.[2] In this correspondence Lukács and Seghers broach and discuss questions about literary realism as respectively universal and belonging to a particular historical period, and about the artistic process that can render reality as drawing on one's immediate basic experience and on methods for transforming such experience. Although they both emerged from virtually the same background of Marxist literary theory, they interpreted differently the primarily Hegelian concept of reality as "totality" composed of essential relationships that can be grasped only when one overcomes the immediate present.[3]

In his theoretical essay "Narrate or Describe?" Lukács insists on realism's rendering the idealistic totality and transcendental wholeness of human life in literature by means of unified plot and coherent consecutive narrative, as, for instance, in the works of the great nineteenth-century realists.[4] He adopts the idealistic notion of the inner logic, organization, and order of life beyond the immediate present and institutes it as the overarching formal principle of realist literature, naming it "narration." This so-called method of narration Lukács juxtaposes with the mode of description, which renders the banality of the immediate reality. The lack of selection of the descriptive method results in the obliteration of the unified plot and its action, well-defined climaxes, and sense of direction and presents us with a chaotic medley of unrelated detail. The method of description obstructs the action essential for the mode of narration, fails to convey the essential relations of fundamental reality, and engenders monotony and tedium in the reader.

In contrast to Lukács, who prefers the mode of narration, Anna Seghers favors the method of description in her writings, allowing for an open-ended, fragmentary realism.[5] She questions Lukács's prescriptive discussion of realism, which defines a unified methodology for literary creation. In her view, methods represent only one stage of the creative process. To illustrate her theoretical position on the artistic rendition of reality, she adopts Tolstoy's two-stage model of artistic creation: the first stage of the creative process manifests itself in the artist's immediate and unconscious reception of reality; then, after acquiring this new experience of reality, the artist brings back to consciousness the unknown experience and makes it known again through artistic methods. Seghers designates this conversion of experience into literature by the application of realist methods a process of artistic synthesis. She believed that Lukács had violated this synthesis of experience and methods by favoring theory over immediate personal experience in the creative process. In her letters to Lukács, Seghers argues also that realism could be a historically and geographically changing variable. She articulates her "splinter" theory, which allows for diversity and change in realism.[6] The "splinters" break the wholeness of the old reality and realism but, at the same time, honestly represent a fragment of the present world and indicate the beginning of "an age of transition," the passage from the past into the present. The splinters signal that art advances, that there is new basic experience to be expressed, which reflects the reality of the new epoch.[7]

In her story "The Excursion of the Dead Girls," Seghers implements her ideas of artistic creation. She inscribes her basic experience of exile in the plot and renders through it the fragmenting reality of war and exile. Formally, the story's intricate multiple-plot scheme palpably defies wholeness and action to evoke the experience of loss, separation, and death. Thus Seghers defies Lukács's formal conventions of narration, such as the well-contrived unified plot promoting action and the consistency of time and narrative voice, and resorts to the descriptive mode he denounces as decadent.

The first plot strand of Seghers's story develops in Mexico; it frames the text with the narrator's recounting of her trip from a Mexican inn to the white wall of a deserted ranch that had drawn her attention earlier. When she reaches the wall, however, the narrator passes into a completely different time and place. By a sudden leap of the narrator's memory from the experience of reality to the experience of the past, Seghers thwarts the rising action of the plot of her journey to the white wall and fragments the spatial consistency, temporal totality, and chronological order of her story. She moves the narrative from the present moment back into the past of the narrator's childhood and, at the same time, from Mexico to Germany and the river Rhine. Thus, Seghers delineates an imaginary coordinate system of exile in space and time with travel and memory as its axes. Relinquishing her first plot strand and returning to it only near the end, she frustrates the reader's expectations of a story situated in a Mexican setting and deconstructs the story's potential for adventure and action, present in the plot's conventional spatial shift from "the village into the wilderness."[8]

Seghers uses a similar ploy in handling her second plot strand, which tells of a school excursion along the Rhine but nevertheless fails to organize a consistent unified story, as she ruptures the story line and refuses to carry out the potential for action that the journey motif promises. The author frequently punctuates her narrative of the excursion with physical descriptions of the narrator's school friends, acquaintances, classmates, and teachers which evolve into digressive subplot reflections about the life they have led since then. In this way, Seghers suppresses and breaks up the excursion plot by subduing it to description.

Seghers's maneuvering of different plot strands and her tendency to describe rather than narrate is, however, not an end in itself. The reasons for her approach lie in her basic personal experience of exile and the Second World War. Seghers actually inscribes in her text the travels—from Mainz to Berlin, from Paris and the south of France to Mexico—that she had experienced in her own life before she wrote "The Excursion of the Dead Girls." In this way she implements her theory of the two-stage model of artistic creation and affirms in practice her views on literary realism; her spatial movement, experience of loss, and separation from home inform the ruptures in her narrative.

Still, Seghers does not just replicate her personal experience in writing but transforms it so as to make sense of her life and the experience in general of people during war (in the excursion subplot) and exile (in the frame plot). She does not arbitrarily assign importance to the formal devices, her methods. Seghers rather incorporates and contextualizes them within the historical time of fascism, bringing forward her ideas of historically and geographically changing realism. Through the use of the descriptive mode, she makes fascism's indiscriminate violence patent and demonstrates its chaotic nature. Thus, Seghers defines war and, more subtly, exilic reality as fragmentary, inverting the normal order of events and confusing the logic of time and space.

Seghers explores the essential relationships that underlie fascism, war, and exile by subverting the Lukácsean narrative mode and indicates that the present fundamental reality manifests itself not in totality but in chaos and irrationality. The author imbues her text with sporadic incidental interactions between her characters, which do not develop along with the development of the story and are virtually smothered by its plot. The narrator's encounter with a Mexican innkeeper, for example, does not prefigure any further examination of his personality or the development of a relationship between them. The innkeeper's initial interest in the narrator's "fantastic origin," as he interprets her Europeanness, subsides into his indifference toward the narrator at the end of the story (39, 51–52). All manifestations of positive feelings and love in the excursion plot are consistently thwarted, fail to develop, and resolve into their negative opposites—aversion, betrayal, and death—in the secondary plots, which reveal the subsequent lives of the characters. Thus, the details that Seghers gives about her characters turn out to dismantle rather than contribute to the development plot. They appear inessential and frustrate the expected unraveling of the subplots. For instance, Otto Fersenius's untimely death during the First World War breaks off the ideal love between him and Marianne. Additionally, Marianne betrays her best friend, Leni (41, 49), and Nora's gestures of appreciation of and affection for her favorite teacher, Miss Sichel, are later transformed into derision and aversion (42). Even the narrator's literal and metaphorical return home fails at the end of the excursion plot, when, because of her fatigue, she cannot climb "the stairs towards [her] mother" (51).

Seghers further develops the sense of frustration and lack of fulfillment in her short story through the pervasive use of the death motif. The symptomatic title, "The Excursion of the Dead Girls," underscores war's sinister aftermath of death and formulates the motif, which resounds throughout the text. In "The Excursion," almost all the characters meet their demise during the First or Second World War. Even the narrator, who is one of the few survivors, seems to be symbolically dead because she is in exile, dislocated, torn apart from her country, and incapable of returning home. The war also reverses the natural order that associates youth with life and age with death. The teacher Reiss is "the older teacher of the boys' class" and is called "the ancient one." Because of the lack of logic and the unnaturalness of the war, he, in spite of his age, survives all his students: "Contrary to the way it usually happens, that teacher experienced the dying away of his young students in the following and then in the present war, in black-white-red and then in the swastika regiments. He survived it all unharmed. For he gradually became too old not only for battles but also for making ambivalent remarks which could have meant arrest or concentration camp" (47). Here the depleted physical energy and the dulled mind turn out to be the only human qualities that can preserve one's life, as Nazism has annulled the law of the survival of the fittest, whether intellectually or physically superior. Similarly, Sophie, who was once a pupil of Miss Sichel's, dies in the teacher's arms "all shriveled up and old," "like a sister of the same age" (47). Here again we witness an inversion of the natural order, as Sophie seems to have undergone an accelerated aging. Yielding to age and the pain of having twenty years of her life crossed out, she turns gray, her physical appearance changes, and she dies before her much older former teacher.

Seghers's narrative technique subverts the story's action by accommodating death in the plot so as to effect lack of cohesion in the narration. Achieved through the death motif, the fragmentation and discontinuity between the excursion plot and the biographical subplots, between the Mexican plot and the middle section of the short story, surface as another narrative element to express the chaotic, irrational nature of war and exile, which causes reality to fall apart. Although the short story does not follow Lukács's criteria for good writing, that is, the narrative mode, it manages to capture the new reality which the war has wrought.

Memory as Theme and Structural Principle

To reinforce the sense of irrationality in her short story, Seghers creates an unreliable narrator whose memory wavers, who shifts in time and space, does not know all the answers that life poses, and cannot account for everything that happens in her story, which sometimes seems spun out of impossibilities. For instance, we sense this inexplicable state of reality in the way the narrator presents the development of Marianne and Leni's friendship into Marianne's subsequent betrayal of Leni: "Everything seemed impossible now that they told and wrote me later about them. If Marianne held the seesaw so carefully for Leni and if she pulled the straw out of her hair with so much friendliness, if she put her arm around Leni's neck, it would be impossible later on, she would refuse in harsh words to help Leni like a friend in need. She could not have brought herself to answer as she did" (41), she thinks. "How could later a betrayal, a delusion infiltrate her thoughts"? (49).

The only clues to untangling the impossibilities underlying the narrative present themselves in the lapses of memory typical of the story. While Nora's "thin memory" emerges as a valid and explicit means of accounting for her future distaste for her teacher, Marianne, who "did not even want to remember Leni when [she was] begging for her help" (44), betrays her best friend by the deliberate act of forgetting, the conscious refusal to remember. The memory motif also recurs in the narrator's sudden returns to the past, to long-forgotten people and names, including her own old name, Netty, which "remained lost" among all the good and bad names friends and enemies have given her. Thus, in addition to shedding light on the reasons for the rambling quality of the text, the properties of the narrator's memory also structure the plot, such as it is.

The narrator's vulnerable, unreliable memory reveals itself as the over-arching organizational principle of the story, which supplants the motif of the journey as the driving force of the narrative. Seghers thwarts the journey's potential for action only to transfer its momentum to memory. In the framing plot line, the narrator undertakes her trip to the white wall, which eventually grants her a mnemonic passage to her past and home: "The yearning for strange and eccentric undertakings that earlier used to cause me restlessness had long been satisfied to the point of weariness. There was only one undertaking left able to inspire me: my trip home" (39).

The narrator's "idle curiosity" about the ranch with the white wall is "just a remnant of [an] old desire to travel" (39). Through the years of endless traveling and exile, the narrator's long-standing fascination with travel disintegrates into a dysfunctional habit. Her over-fulfilled wanderlust has reached the point of excess and satiety and figures in the text as an implicit metaphor for exile. Moreover, the narrator attaches a negative sign to the concept of journey, develops a retroactive perspective, and nurtures a nostalgic desire for the homeland that can be fulfilled only through an act of memory. This negation of the trip motif determines the discontinuous, serene, almost static flow of Seghers's narrative of memories and defies Lukács's mode of narration with its demand for action. It also subverts the preconceived notions of realism established by homebound authors whose characters long to travel, and gives us a new perspective on reality—that of an exile who is determined to reclaim her homeland.

Nostalgic Memory, Performative Memory

In his essay "Less Than One," the Russian exile poet Joseph Brodsky theorizes about memory in relation to realism. In terms evoking Lukács's descriptive mode, he posits memory in the center of the realistic narrative:

Memory, I think, is a substitute for the tail that we lost for good in the happy process of evolution. It directs our movements, including migration. Apart from that there is something clearly atavistic in the very process of recollection, if only such process never is linear. . . . [M]emory coils, recoils, digresses to all sides, just as a tail does; so should one's narrative, even at the risk of sounding inconsequential and boring. Boredom, after all, is the most frequent feature of existence, and one wonders why it fared so poorly in the nineteenth-century prose that strived so much for realism.[9]

Through the prism of exile experience, Brodsky hails the narrative of memories in this wonderful poetic theory of realism. Digressing, inconsequential, causing boredom, it emerges as more faithful to reality than unified and thus contrived nineteenth-century fiction. Brodsky insists on the importance of memory in exile literature and depicts the exile writer as an atavistic creature whose existence is directed by the past. Thus, the writer becomes "a retrospective and retroactive being,"[10] in the same way that the narrator of "The Excursion," determined to reclaim her past, shows distaste for any future enterprise. Informed by nostalgia, both Seghers's narrative and Brodsky's essay are built on rambling memories of the homeland, regardless of the positive, negative, or very often ambiguous feelings that the authors feel for their countries. This suggests a certain literary kinship between them because of their common fate. Owing to loss and the traumatic experience of dislocation, exile writers come to perceive that the apparent continuum of human existence is constructed out of the arbitrary and inconsequential details retained by one's memory.

Brodsky's reflections disclose a profound understanding of the deficient nature of human memory. His realization that "memory betrays everybody, especially those whom we knew best[;] [i]t is an ally of oblivion, it is an ally of death,"[11] signals the loss of continuity and totality in life once the most basic parameters of human identity—home, family, and language—have been alienated from a person. In another autobiographical essay, "In a Room and a Half," Brodsky assembles shreds of his earlier Russian existence, claiming overtly his narrative's fragmentary quality. He organizes it in forty-five sections representing isolated memories of his parents and childhood complemented by philosophical reflections on memory. In doing so he produces a narrative that defies the organically unified plot as an artistic necessity. In this essay, he also resists his mind's attempts "to produce a cumulative generalized image of [his] parents" because his memories of them lack continuity, and the impulse to reconstruct their figures would render them incomplete and inaccurate.[12]

Likewise, Seghers's narrator experiences a similar estrangement from the memory of her mother. On her return home from the school excursion, she approaches her house with apprehension, seeing her own street as if she knew that it was to be destroyed. She captures at first the image of her mother as she used to be—"young" and "cheerful." But the vision soon fails her, in a metaphor for her vulnerable memory, and she reexperiences the traumatic anguish of loss: "The gray blue fog of fatigue enveloped everything. . . . I forced myself up the stairs toward my mother; the staircase, not clearly visible, because of the haze, seemed unreachably high to me, unconquerably steep. . . . Perhaps my mother had already gone into the hall. . . . Only as a very small child had I felt a similar anxiety that fate could prevent me from seeing her again" (51). Enveloped in the haze of oblivion, the narrator's memory falters and fails to recollect the union with her mother. Unable to experience the motherly embrace, the narrator is transported back from the past into her present exile reality.

To understand this leap of memory away from the image of the mother and the subsequent return from the past, I recall Brodsky's interpretation of the deficiency of memory: "The shorter your memory, the longer your life, says a proverb. Alternatively, the longer your future, the shorter your memory. That's one way of determining one's prospects for longevity."[13] In this sense, the failure of memory means a return to life for Seghers's ailing narrator; it enacts a shift of focus from a preoccupation with the past to a concern for and moral obligation toward the future. Merging with the dead mother could only result in the narrator's succumbing to her sickness and fatigue, emphasized throughout the story—that is, in metaphorical death due to fixation on the past. Deficiency of memory guarantees survival, a perverse example of which we saw in Nora's and Marianne's provisional survival owing to their refusal to remember Miss Sichel and Leni. The failure of the narrator's memory, however, signifies a recuperation from her past, a recovery from "months of illness that [have] caught up with" the exiled narrator after she apparently escaped the dangers of war (39). Still, her ailing memory is fraught with poignant remembrances of the death and destruction of war, whose gravity draws the narrator, too, to her utter surrender and demise as her legs fail her and she imagines breaking down from exhaustion on the stairs leading toward her mother.

Miraculously, the narrator revives as her memory stumbles, and the familiar sounds of Netty's household transmute into the sounds of her Mexican surroundings. This recovery from the excruciating memory of loss of home, of native land, family, and friends, is possible only after nostalgic memory's reclamation of the past has run its course. In her homesick remembering, Netty realizes her moral responsibility to "remember forever the most minute details" of the school outing and "not to commit a sin of omission" (43); she receives an assignment from Miss Sichel to write a composition about the excursion (48). Thus, the narrator's lapse of memory indicates the turning of her perspective toward the future, which demands that she fulfill her moral and creative duty; we witness the emergence of her performative memory as writing. Despite her lingering weariness after her return to the present, the narrator is now invigorated with a new proactive spirit. She walks "more briskly" and wishes "to return to the mountains" as soon as she catches her breath (51, 52). After the narrator comes back to the inn still contemplating her experience of nostalgic memory, she wonders about her future life, about how she should go on "today and tomorrow." She remembers her teacher's assignment given in appreciation of her love for writing; she has "to describe carefully the school excursion" (52) in a composition, which she has yet to write: "I intended to do the assignment right away, tomorrow or even this evening, after my weariness had gone away" (52).

The hopeful realization of the narrator's moral task to remember in writing helps her recover from her ailing nostalgic memory and move on with her life in the future. The text suggests this new optimistic orientation in its emphasis on the adverb "tomorrow" and the presentation of her new energized self near the end of the story. In the recreation of nostalgic memory in writing, a doubling of memory occurs as the simultaneous mournful inhabiting of the past and its hopeful projection into the future, as loss and reclamation: "This one day of the excursion seemed to have taken away everything and given it back to me at the same time" (49). The loss and salvage of the past seem to clash but in fact reconcile in the ambivalent resonance of nostalgic memory, which folds back on itself to constitute creative memory.[14] From an atavistic capacity, memory turns into a constructive, future-oriented power with a social and aesthetic function: memory as resistance and as creativity.

Social and Creative Aspects of Performative Memory

The narrator in "The Excursion" espouses the "higher duty" of fighting fascism.[15] "Our main enemy is fascism. . . . [W]e combat the expression of fascism in art,"[16] claims Seghers in her theoretical views about the social function of art. In view of this political positioning of literature, the motif of memory functions on two levels in the text. On the one hand, the vulnerability of memory represents the dysfunctional national memory that pertains to fascism and war. They obliterate the people's recollection of national unity, ethnic tolerance, and the constructive coexistence of different convictions, which is possible in the excursion plot and generally during times of peace. On the other hand, recollection surfaces as a form of resistance. The conscious act of remembering through creativity aims at recreating, explaining, and condemning the new fascist reality; it is an act of opposition. From a very different political position, Brodsky also believes that "deficient memory serves the interest of the state," of totalitarian Russia, which doomed him to banishment. He tries to oppose and denounce the state by "remembering even mere details, fragments."[17]

Seghers and Brodsky recognize the deficiency and futility of memory containing only "details, not the whole picture,"[18] but they put their creativity at the service of their failing memory—which is also associated with death and sickness—so as to prevent history from repeating the mistakes of the past. In this sense, the retroactive orientation of Seghers's and Brodsky's writings does not just aim to defy an idealist vision of literature, as seen, for instance, in Lukács's theories. Nor does it just capture the experience of exiles and their nostalgic longing for a lost homeland and past, which can result in mere sorrowful lamentation and compulsive remembering that endeavor to counteract trauma. In fact, both exile writers strive to represent and make sense of the historical circumstances that brought about their banishment so as to demystify the pernicious political ideologies at the core of their suffering. Seghers wants to expose the atrocities of National Socialism as well as the destruction of the two World Wars and thus evokes them and condemns them in the narrative frustration, the death, and the reversal of natural order in her text. Brodsky, by contrast, aims to expose the attempts of Soviet propaganda at total uniformity, conformism, and subjugation in the centralized state and conjures up its workings in his use of the theme of repetition in "Less Than One." For both authors, it is the experience of exile and its subsequent remembering in writing that creates their voice of moral authority. The double layering of nostalgic and performative memory validates their moral pronouncements, which are informed by wisdom and historical insight. Their hindsight ensures their foresight.

Similarly, past and future merge to produce not only the social aspect of memory but also the creative aspect. The memory-driven trip home inspires Seghers's narrator to write; her nostalgia facilitates her creativity. Thus, the association between inspiration and the loss of home posits for us the relationship between literary creativity and homesickness. Caused and continuously amplified by exile, nostalgia appears as the driving force behind the leap in time and space that structures Seghers's short story. In her essay "The New Nomads," Eva Hoffman observes and delineates a similar relationship between artistic creation and exile:

> The distancing from the past, combined with the sense of loss and yearning, can be wonderful stimulus to writing. Joyce Carol Oates, in a striking formulation,

has written that "for most novelists, the art of writing might be defined as the use to which we put our homesickness. So powerful is the instinct to memorialize in prose—one's region, one's family, one's past—that many writers, shorn of such subjects, would be rendered paralyzed and mute." In exile, the impulse to memorialize is magnified. . . . For this reason, . . . exile can be a great impetus to thought and creativity.[19]

In "The Excursion of the Dead Girls," two specific episodes framing the plot of the narrator's recollections of home and past stand as metaphors for the correlation between exile, memory, and creativity. The exploration of the white wall, which has reawakened the character's "old desire to travel," confirms her belief that any trip, any undertaking, points at and makes sense for her only as a trip home. Granting the narrator a passage to her homeland, to long-forgotten events and beloved people, the white wall acts as a catalyzing and inspiring empty screen onto which she can project her memories.[20] At the end of the story, the narrator refers directly to the act of literary creation binding together her capacity to remember with the need to express her memories. She pledges to complete the assignment with which her teacher, Miss Sichel, has entrusted her: to recollect and recreate the experience of home once again. By means of the frame these two instances establish, the text creates the sense of infinite commemoration of home. The journey to the white wall that the narrator undertakes is transformed into the memory of home, which in turn, after the narrator relives the past, demands of her in the voice of Miss Sichel the solemn promise that she will revivify the past in fiction. These two episodes—the passage to the past and the pledge to recreate it—refer back and forth to each other. Insofar as "The Excursion of the Dead Girls" is the completed composition for the German class,[21] it remains yet to be completed and will always anticipate its new rendition of home. Much in accord with Eva Hoffman's idea that exile magnifies the need for creativity and memorializing, Seghers's exile and traumatic, hypertrophic memory, conditioned by loss, serve as an incentive to her creative act.

As Hoffman demonstrates in "The New Nomads," the interplay between loss and gain marks the experience of an exile writer and makes his or her text idiosyncratic.[22] The imagination of the creative memory, which lovingly and attentively evokes the images of homeland, friends, and parents in Seghers's story, draws on the lamenting disposition of the exile's nostalgic memory. Although Seghers's short story inhabits the past, near the end of the text the narrator's memory stumbles, after which she returns to reality, her gaze fixed on the future. In the last analysis, the narrator's failing memory grants her the chance to transcend her exile and past by transforming them into literature.

We are accustomed to thinking of exile as a devastating experience causing physical deprivation, separation from loved ones, the loss of home, language, a sense of security, and belonging. Yet Hoffman's essay poses a provocative question about the nature of literary exile, "Is it then all pain and no gain?" and asserts, "Of course not."[23] Hoffman suggests that the experience of exile contains an irresolvable ambiguity between pain and gain, between the sense of loss not only as a cause for nostalgia but also as "a wonderful stimulus to writing," to creativity.[24] The double memory—nostalgic and optimistic—the exilic homesickness and hopeful creativity, as well as the exile's preoccupation with and transcendence of the past all reveal the Janus face of literary exile. In the compensatory oscillation between preservation and creation of the past, anguish bears the most exquisite and marvelous fruit.

Likewise, Anna Seghers created her best literary works during her years of exile: *The Seventh Cross, Transit,* and "The Excursion of the Dead Girls."[25] These remained unsurpassed by her later fiction. Still, exile continued to shape Seghers's literary career after her return to Germany, where she settled in East Berlin in 1947. In the postwar years Seghers drew literary inspiration from her experiences in Mexico and rendered her cultural encounters in short story collections such as *Caribbean Stories* (1962) and *Three Women from Haiti* (1980). Interestingly, while in exile Seghers reinvented her homeland, whereas the cultural encounters of her exile years began to inform her writings only after her return home. Thus, exile establishes a double perspective in Seghers's work, in which the past directs her fiction retroactively. This salient feature of exile literature once again underscores the intimate relationship of exile, memory, and creativity in Seghers's work.

Notes

I thank Gertraud Gutzmann, without whose help and guidance this essay would not have been possible. I am also grateful to Thalia Pandiri, the Kahn Institute fellows from the "Anatomy of Exile" project, my co-teacher Lital Levy, and the students from our reading and composition class "Exile, Displacement, and the Literary Imagination."

1. Gertraud Gutzmann, "Anna Seghers," in *Contemporary German Fiction Writers: Dictionary of Literary Biography*, vol. 69, ed. Wolfgang D. Elfe and James Hardin (Detroit: Bruccoli Clark Layman, 1988), 297–310. This biographical overview, as well as the one in the concluding paragraph, draws entirely on Gutzmann's essay.

2. Georg Lukács, "A Correspondence with Anna Seghers [1938–39]," in *Essays on Realism*, ed. Rodney Livingstone, trans. David Fernbach (Cambridge: MIT Press, 1981), 167–97.

3. Terry Eagleton, "Lukács and Literary Form," in *Marxism and Literary Criticism* (Berkeley: University of California Press, 1976), 27–31.

4. Georg Lukács, "Narrate or Describe?" in *Writer and Critic*, trans. Arthur Kahn (New York: Grosset and Dunlap, 1970), 118–42.

5. Lukács, "Correspondence with Seghers," 167–75, 185–97.

6. Ibid., 187.

7. Ibid.

8. Anna Seghers, "The Excursion of the Dead Girls," in *German Women Writers of the Twentieth Century*, ed. and trans. Elisabeth Rütschi Herrmann and Edna Huttenmaier Spitz (New York: Pergamon Press, 1978), 39. Further references are cited in the text.

9. Iosif Brodsky, "Less Than One," in *Less Than One: Selected Essays* (New York: Farrar Straus Giroux, 1986), 30.

10. Iosif Brodsky, "The Condition We Call Exile," in *On Grief and Reason: Essays* (New York: Farrar Straus Giroux, 1995), 27.

11. Iosif Brodsky, "In a Room and a Half," in *Less Than One*, 492.

12. Ibid., 492.

13. Ibid., 493.

14. Paul de Man, "Wordsworth and Hölderlin," in *The Rhetoric of Romanticism* (New York: Columbia University Press, 1984), 47–65. The structure of my idea is inspired by de Man's essay, which talks about the folding of the poetic act upon itself in the doubling of act and interpretation in Wordsworth's and Hölderlin's poetry.

15. Gertraud Gutzmann, "Literary Antifascism: Anna Seghers's Exile Writings, 1936–1949," in *Facing Fascism and Confronting the Past: German Women Writers from Weimar to the Present*, ed. Elke P. Frederiksen and Martha Kaarsberg Wallach (Albany: State University of New York Press, 2000), 92–93.

16. Lukács, "Correspondence with Seghers," 187.

17. Brodsky, "In a Room and a Half," 494.

18. Ibid.

19. Eva Hoffman, "The New Nomads," in *Letters of Transit*, ed. André Aciman (New York: New Press and New York Public Library, 1999), 51.

20. Gutzmann, "Literary Antifascism," 93.

21. Ibid., 91.

22. Hoffman, "New Nomads," 50.

23. Ibid.

24. Hoffman, "New Nomads," 51.

25. Gutzmann, "Anna Seghers," 309.

A FORTUNATE FEW

Politics, Perseverance, and the Rescue of
One Thousand Refugees, 1944

RUTH GRUBER

EDITOR'S NOTE

The account presented here is the exception to the rule that all essays in this volume be original. It is a reprint, or, better stated, a lengthy set of excerpts, from an extraordinary book, *Haven*, written many years ago by an extraordinary woman—a journalist, photographer, government representative, and champion of refugees. Despite the fact that she is over ninety years of age, Ruth Gruber is still active and still pleased to speak about her lifetime of experiences, including being the youngest Ph.D. in the history of the University of Cologne, the first journalist to fly into the Soviet Arctic and report about conditions there, and an eyewitness to the voyage of the *Exodus*, about which she has written extensively. In April 2001 she came to Smith College to talk about an earlier rescue of what turned out to be the only group of refugees from Nazism to be brought to the United States under government auspices during World War II.

When I heard her retell the story of the rescue and the camp (which I had visited with my mother in 1945 when we had gone to visit one of the refugees, a relative), I decided that it had to be included in this book about the dispossessed. Unable to write a new paper (her lecture had been a remarkable "oral" report delivered without a single note), I exercised an editor's prerogative and asked if she would give me permission to reprint a part of *Haven*, and she agreed. What follows are several selected chapters and smaller sections from the beginning of Ruth Gruber's insider views of the voyage of the damned on their way to America aboard the troopship *Henry Gibbins* and some briefer commentaries about refugee camp life at the former Fort Ontario in Oswego, New York.

Foreword

THIS IS a true story.

Few people are aware, and those who knew have largely forgotten, that nearly one thousand refugees were brought to the United States as guests of President Franklin Delano Roosevelt during World War II.

Transported on an army troopship, with wounded soldiers from Anzio and Cassino, hunted at sea by Nazi planes and U-boats, brought to haven in Oswego, New York, they were to know the exquisite relief of freedom from bombings and terror.

They were refugees from eighteen countries Hitler had overrun, who tried to rebuild their lives inside an internment camp on American soil.

As a special assistant to Harold L. Ickes, secretary of the interior, I was sent by our government to escort them from war-torn Italy and to help resettle them at Fort Ontario, a former army camp on Lake Ontario.

Thus I became both a witness and a participant. I experienced their joys and pain, rejoicing in their marriages and love affairs, sharing pride in their children, mourning those who died by their own hand or by acts of God.

Stowed away in the bottom of filing cabinets were more than forty notebooks that I had filled during the eighteen months my life was interwoven with theirs. These notebooks, together with copies of the reports, letters, and documents I had prepared for the government, were the major source for the events recorded in my book, *Haven*. Invaluable, too, were the diaries that Cabinet members frequently kept, made public by their heirs. Recently the Ickes family opened Secretary Ickes's secret diaries to the world, and I spent fascinated hours in the Library of Congress discovering the personal, often intimate details of his years in office, his battles, both epic and small, and his discussion of the assignments he gave me.

In Hyde Park, I dug into the voluminous diaries of Secretary of the Treasury Henry Morgenthau Jr. and the papers of Eleanor and Franklin Roosevelt, all of whom played character roles, sometimes large than life-size, on the Oswego stage.

Luck was with me. In the National Archives I uncovered the confidential log of the *Henry Gibbins*, the liberty ship on which I sailed with the refugees, and succeeded in persuading the government to declassify it.

The Struggle in Washington

The words leaped at me from the *Washington Post*.

"'I have decided,' President Franklin Delano Roosevelt announced, 'that approximately 1,000 refugees should be immediately brought from Italy to this country.'"

One thousand refugees.

Europe was burning. It was June 1944, the middle of the war.

For years, refugees knocking on the doors of American consulates abroad had been told: "You cannot enter America. *The quotas are filled.*"

While the quotas remained untouchable, like tablets of stone, millions died.

Suddenly, one thousand refugees were to be brought in *outside* the quotas, by order of the president himself. Until now I had felt helpless, frustrated, enraged. Noble speeches were made each day about saving refugees before they were swept into the fire. But the deeds belied the words. Our doors had been slammed shut. Now, suddenly, there was hope.

At my breakfast table, air-conditioned against Washington's summer heat, I continued to devour the article. The thousand refugees, I read, would be selected by the War Refugee Board, transported to America by the army, and housed in a "temporary haven," a former army camp called Fort Ontario, in Oswego, New York. The camp would be administered by the War Relocation Authority of the Department of the Interior. Only a few months before, the president had placed WRA, soon to be disbanded, under Harold L. Ickes, the secretary of the interior. I was Ickes's special assistant, his field representative for Alaska.

Ickes would know what lay behind this sudden humanitarian gesture.

At E Street I jumped out of a cab and looked up at the handsome gray stone Interior building, with its great bronze doors and modern columns. Interior—the vast grab-bag department of Indians, parks, reclamation, public works, petroleum, mines, fish and wildlife, Alaska, Puerto Rico, Hawaii, the Philippines—would now be in charge of Europe's refugees, too.

In my office, I telephoned Ickes's appointments secretary and arranged a meeting for 11:55.

Ickes sat behind a huge desk littered with papers. His head was lowered as I began the long walk across the huge blue-carpeted office. He was writing with the thick scratchy pen I had seen him use countless times.

"Sit down," he said briefly, and continued to write.

I sat in the armchair at the side of his desk. Behind him was a long table carefully stacked with books, newspapers, magazines. *The Nation* and the *New Republic*, to which he frequently contributed, were on top.

He finished his writing and buzzed for his secretary, who took the papers and disappeared.

Now he turned his full attention to me. "Yes?" he asked quizzically. "I understand it's urgent."

"It's about the thousand refugees that President Roosevelt is inviting to America."

He nodded. "The president sent me a copy of his cablegram to Robert Murphy in Algiers announcing it."

"Mr. Secretary," I said, "it's what we've been fighting for all these years. To open the doors. Save lives. Circumvent the holy quotas. What's behind it? How did it happen?"

That's all we need, to have a young woman from our department shot down by a Nazi plane."

I wanted to tell him that I had been in the Aleutians when they were invaded, that I was a fatalist, that I would die when my number was up. Instead, I said, "It's a danger I'm prepared to face."

"Do you realize you'll be dealing with a thousand people—with men as well as women and children? Don't you see that after what they have gone through, they would have more respect for a man? They would pay much more attention to a man than they would to a woman."

In a corner of my mind I thought: Maybe there is validity in his arguments. Maybe refugees would have more respect for a man who was old and wise and experienced. I pushed the thought away, opened my purse, and pulled out copies of the president's message to Congress and the cablegram he had sent to Ambassador Murphy in Algiers. I had underlined some of the president's phrases. I read them now to Dillon Myer: "'... the Nazis are determined to complete their program of mass extermination ... we have made clear our determination to punish all participants in these acts of savagery. In the name of humanity ...'

"'In the name of humanity,'" I repeated the words. "Mr. Myer, what have age or sex to do with humanity?"

He stood up abruptly. "It's not up to me. I can't make the decision. I must speak with John Pehle; he's executive director of the War Refuge Board. I'll call you back soon after I've talked with Pehle."

Two hours later, my office phone rang,

"I've talked with Pehle." Myer's voice seemed a shade less cold. "He did some checking himself in Interior. You got some pretty good recommendations. Pehle agrees that you can go."

"Thank you, Mr. Myer," I breathed into the phone.

"You know, of course, I'm sending my own man over, Ralph Stauber. He'll be getting the statistics we need, where the people came from, et cetera."

I listened silently.

"You are Ickes's personal representative. But you can help us gain insight into the makeup of the people so that we can develop policies. You must make it clear to them that they are coming here to live inside a camp, where they will have food, a place to live in, and enough to keep them warm."

"What about leaving the camp?" I asked. "What if they have relatives? Will they be able to visit them? Will they be able to go outside to work?"

"That's a policy decision to be made later, in thirty or sixty days after they arrive. Be very careful. *Don't make any promises we can't fulfill.* We don't want to raise their hopes too high. That happened in our other camps."

The other camps were the internment and relocation camps where over

100,000 Japanese Americans were incarcerated under Myer's administration. After Pearl Harbor, after the "Day of Infamy" on December 7, 1941, the country had exploded with hysteria against the Japanese. Innocent men, women, and children were pulled up from their homes, businessmen from their shops, farmers from their land. In one of his darkest hours, the president, describing them as "potential fifth columnists," ordered the Japanese Americans segregated in isolated camps. They were fenced in with barbed wire, patrolled by soldiers. To run the camps, Roosevelt created a special agency, the War Relocation Authority (WRA); headed by Milton Eisenhower, who recommended Dillon Myer as his successor when he resigned. Two years later, in February 1944, the president ordered WRA transferred to Interior.

"This is something I distinctly do not want," Ickes recorded his reaction to his new responsibility in his secret diary. "But I told the president that I would take it and do the best that I could." . . .

ICKES LOOKED UP as I approached his desk. "Myer has agreed," he said. "I can tell from your face."

"The War Refugee Board gave me the OK," I said triumphantly, and told him that Myer had admonished me to keep the mission secret and promise the refugees nothing.

"That's not bad advice," Ickes said. "But I don't want them to hamstring you. You're to feel free to do what you want, go where you want, see what you want, and report to me. I'm giving you full rein."

That was what I needed to hear. "Mr. Secretary, this is going to be the most important assignment you've ever given me—maybe the most important thing I've done in my life."

"I'm sure you'll do an excellent job. Myer is lucky to be getting you. You can reassure those refugees, make them feel better than some official just doing his routine duty. I know that this whole thing, saving refugees, means a lot to you, as it does to me. You're going to be my eyes and ears. I'm depending on you."

That evening I called my parents in Brooklyn. "I'm going to Europe," I said.

"What?" my mother screamed into the phone. "Are you crazy? Every day I read how they sink ships and shoot down airplanes. And my daughter has to go to Europe to get her head shot off."

"Mom, don't worry."

" 'Don't worry,' she says to me. It's enough your brother Irving is in the army and I pray to God every night that he should come home safe. He has to go to war, he's a captain. But you're no soldier. What do you have to go for? What kind of *mishegaas* got into you now?"

"I can't tell you, Mom. It's a secret. But it's very important."

"Important. It's always important. Ever since you were a little girl you started running. Do I know where you went? Germany. Siberia. Alaska. I never knew if you were alive. What normal girl goes to Siberia and Alaska? Now she has to go to Europe."

"I'll be all right, Mom. Don't worry."

My father, on the extension phone, said quietly, "Will you come home to say good-bye?"

I could see his handsome face, the wide-set eyes, the tall, sturdy body, the father who always had faith in me.

"I'd love to come home before I go abroad, Pop," I said, "but I won't have time. I've got to go through a whole process of briefings before I go."

"Then I'll come to Washington to see you off," my mother announced.

The Concern

I spent the next weeks in a maze of bureaucratic briefings.

The refugees were even now being selected in southern Italy. I had to reach them before their convoy sailed.

I was completely bureaucratized. At the War Relocation Authority, where my official travel orders had to be drawn up. At the State Department, waiting interminably for a special passport. At the Public Health Service, where a battery of doctors pummeled, stethoscoped, x-rayed, and bled me and, with ominously prophetic voices, handed me a card with my blood type, "in case you're shot down and need a transfusion."

Typhus, typhoid, tetanus, smallpox, and plague were shot into my arms, my buttocks, my stomach. I reacted with high fever and was told to stay in bed. I refused, hoping to speed up the briefings. It was useless. The bureaucracy in Washington moved on slow, interminable wheels, each agency guarding its own authority, feeding on its own red tape.

Marking time, I occupied myself trying to discover why Roosevelt was acting now, after all these years of a closed-door policy. I spent hours in the Library of Congress reading newspapers, and evenings talking with my friends in government, asking the question, "Why are the quotas being circumvented now?" In restaurants and in the privacy of our apartments we told one another: "It's Congress and the State Department who bar refugees. Roosevelt can't act alone. He can't have his New Deal labeled the 'Jew Deal.'"

There were other factors, too, we reminded ourselves. Long before Hitler, Europe was an anti-Semitic continent. In America the quota system, under the fittingly racist title "National Origins Quota," had become law in the early

1920s, largely to bar Orientals and immigrants from eastern Europe, many of them Jews.

Changes in the quota were unthinkable. The labor unions were opposed, fearing that refugees would take their jobs. The isolationists in Congress were riding high. All this left the American Jewish community, with scarcely 3 percent of the population, powerless to save the Jews of Europe.

"Trust Roosevelt," one faction exhorted us. "Roosevelt saved us from a communist takeover during the Great Depression. Now he will save the world from Hitler. Don't make waves. Silent diplomacy is the safest route to rescue Jews."

"No. Silence is the enemy." A small group denounced silent diplomacy. Their leader was Peter Bergson, a young Palestinian. Only an aroused public opinion, he insisted, could save refugees.

Ben Hecht, the brilliant playwright and journalist, wrote full-page ads with venom in his pen. One of his ads, a long ballad, carried the refrain

> Hang and burn, but be quiet, Jews,
> The world is busy with other news.

Even the Zionists, united in one goal, to open Palestine, were divided on whether this was the time to fight for a Jewish state.

In the end, it was clear that only the president himself had power to break the ironclad quotas and to begin rescuing Jews. Who had reached him?

"It was the cables," a friend in Treasury told me one day.

"What cables?"

"The ones that told everything—how Jews were being murdered."

"Why didn't we know about them?"

He shrugged and was silent.

"You mean, they were suppressed?"

"For two years."

Two years in which we were kept in darkness. Two years when public opinion might have galvanized our leaders into action.

Only now can I put together the pieces of the story that would lead from those suppressed cables to FDR's belated announcement, then to a shipboard odyssey and a haven in America while war and Holocaust raged in Europe.

In the summer of 1942 a German industrialist, visiting Switzerland on business, brought shocking news. Hitler was planning to exterminate all the Jews of Europe with a new device—prussic acid, the deadly compound of Zyklon-B gas. The news was delivered to Gerhart Riegner, a thirty-one-year-old refugee from Berlin working for the World Jewish Congress in Switzerland.

Riegner, whom I was to meet two years later in Geneva, told me: "At first I wouldn't believe it. Deportation of Jews—this we knew. Killing Jews, torturing them, shooting them in graves—this we knew." His eyes clouded over. "But this was a whole, total, embracing plan. It was *Vernichtung*."

Vernichtung. Annihilation.

"I had to verify it," he said. "I had to find out: Were the Germans capable of total *Vernichtung*?"

Fair-skinned, blue-eyed, Riegner looked and sounded like the students I had known in Germany.

Riegner had promised the industrialist he would never reveal his name. He kept his promise, even though research has now pointed to Eduard Schulte, a banker and industrialist from Upper Silesia, who loathed the Nazis. With friends in high places in the Nazi government, Schulte was able to alert the Allies to Hitler's plans for annihilating Jews.

"I needed eight days to investigate the German industrialist and to convince myself. Finally convinced, I wrote a cable and took it to the American and British consuls, asking them to transmit it in code. In America it was to be sent to Rabbi Stephen S. Wise, who was president of the American Jewish Congress and was my boss in America. In Britain it was sent to Sydney Silverman, a member of Parliament and chairman of the British section of the World Jewish Congress."

The cable, dated August 8, 1942, read:

RECEIVED ALARMING REPORT THAT IN FÜHRER'S HEADQUARTERS PLAN DISCUSSED AND UNDER CONSIDERATION ACCORDING TO WHICH ALL JEWS IN COUNTRIES OC-CUPIED OR CONTROLLED BY GERMANY NUMBERING 3½–4 MILLION [excluding Jews in the Soviet Union] SHOULD AFTER DEPORTATION AND CONCENTRATION IN EAST BE EXTERMINATED AT ONE BLOW TO RESOLVE ONCE FOR ALL THE JEWISH QUESTION IN EUROPE STOP ACTION REPORTED PLANNED FOR AUTUMN METHODS UNDER DIS-CUSSION INCLUDING PRUSSIC ACID STOP WE TRANSMIT INFORMATION WITH ALL NECESSARY RESERVATION AS EXACTITUDE CANNOT BE CONFIRMED STOP INFORMANT STATED TO HAVE CLOSE CONNECTIONS WITH HIGHEST GERMAN AUTHORITIES AND HIS REPORTS GENERALLY SPEAKING RELIABLE

RIEGNER

The cable was never delivered to Rabbi Wise. The State Department decided that the information was "unsubstantiated" and summarized the report as "a wild rumor inspired by Jewish fears." Undersecretary of State Sumner Welles, one of the few State Department officials considered friendly to Jews, signed the order to suppress the cable.

Three weeks later, Riegner was informed that Wise still knew nothing. "I went through the worst period of my life," Riegner told me. "There I was in my office looking out at the lake and Mont Blanc, and there was such peace in those snow-capped mountains. And the Jews were trapped in Europe."

Fortunately, the British did not suppress the cable to Silverman, in which

Riegner had carefully inserted the words "Inform and consult New York." Silverman sent a copy of the August 1942 cable to Rabbi Wise by ordinary Western Union.

In New York, Rabbi Wise read the cable over and over. He knew Riegner well. He knew how cautious he was. It had to be true.

He rushed to Washington to see Sumner Welles. Had Welles seen this cable? Did he know these facts? Welles, of course, had seen the original cable weeks before. Now he prevailed on Wise to keep the cable secret until State Department representatives in Switzerland could confirm Riegner's charges.

Finally, in November, Welles telephoned Wise: "Come to Washington immediately."

Welles showed the rabbi documents and affidavits from his own men in Switzerland confirming everything Riegner had reported. He could no longer hold Wise to his promise of secrecy. "You're free now to release the information."

Wise released the terrible information. But three months had already elapsed. No one knew if the Nazis had begun their *Vernichtung*.

On January 21, 1943, Leland Harrison, our minister in Bern, ordered another cable from Riegner to Rabbi Wise coded and transmitted through the State Department.

It was Cable 482, a file number that was to become famous. In four horror-filled pages Riegner described the terror that had been decimating Jews in two lands: in Poland, where the Germans had been killing 6,000 Jews each day, and in Romania, where 130,000 Jews had been deported to Transnistria in the Romanian-occupied Ukraine. The clothes had been ripped off the refugees' backs; everything they owned was stolen. Of the 130,000 deported to the Transnistrian "reservation" for Jews, 60,000 had already died and 70,000 were starving to death.

Welles himself forwarded Cable 482 to Rabbi Wise. Wise immediately began arranging for a Stop Hitler Now mass rally to be held at Madison Square Garden in New York on March 1, 1943.

On February 10, 1943, the State Department sent an unusual message to Minister Harrison in Switzerland. It was Cable 354, and it opened by referring to Riegner's Cable 482:

YOUR 482, JANUARY 21. IT IS SUGGESTED THAT IN THE FUTURE, REPORTS SUBMITTED TO YOU FOR TRANSMISSION TO PRIVATE PERSONS IN THE UNITED STATES SHOULD NOT BE ACCEPTED UNLESS EXTRA-ORDINARY CIRCUMSTANCES MAKE SUCH ACTION ADVISABLE. IT IS FELT THAT BY SENDING SUCH PRIVATE MESSAGES WHICH CIRCUM-VENT NEUTRAL COUNTRIES' CENSORSHIP WE RISK THE POSSIBILITY THAT NEUTRAL COUNTRIES MIGHT FIND IT NECESSARY TO TAKE STEPS TO CURTAIL OR ABOLISH OUR OFFICIAL SECRET MEANS OF COMMUNICATION.

In the strangulated language of diplomacy this meant, "Stop sending any more messages about Nazi atrocities."

Sumner Welles again signed the cable. In Welles's defense, many people, including Henry Morgenthau Jr., the secretary of the treasury, believed that he was too busy to inquire what "482" referred to.

For Harrison and Riegner in Switzerland, Welles's cable was an enigma. Only two months earlier the Allies had announced that Nazis would be punished as war criminals for their atrocities against Jews. America would need all the eyewitness accounts from Riegner to build its case against war criminals. Why now this order from the State Department to stop all information? And why specifically the order to stop further cables disclosing Nazi atrocities, when hundreds of commercial cables for private businesses were being transmitted?

Fortunately, the cable to cease and desist was sent too late to halt the Stop Hitler Now rally.

It was a blustery first day of March 1943 in New York. The streets around Madison Square Garden were clogged with thousands of people. The Garden held 21,000 people, but at least 75,000 more were outside, unable to enter.

We kept one another warm, no longer strangers. We belonged together, a wall of Americans—Jews and Christians—shouting with one voice, "Stop Hitler now!"

We listened to the loudspeakers as leaders pleaded with the Allied governments to act swiftly, before it was too late.

"The world can no longer believe that the ghastly facts are unknown and unconfirmed," Dr. Chaim Weizman, the eloquent leader of the Jewish Agency, the shadow Jewish government in Palestine, declared. "At this moment expressions of sympathy without accompanying attempts to launch *acts of rescue* become a hollow mockery in the ears of the dying.

"The democracies have a clear duty before them." Weizmann's voice rang through the night air. "Let them negotiate with Germany through the neutral countries concerning the possible release of the Jews in the occupied countries."

Negotiate with Germany through the neutral countries to release the Jews in occupied countries. Sweden was neutral. Switzerland was neutral. In fact, Switzerland was far more. It was a giant ear, the listening post for diplomats, provocateurs, spies, mysterious travelers. It was in Switzerland that Riegner was getting much of his information from German travelers.

"Let havens be designated," Weizmann went on, "in the vast territories of the United Nations[1] which would give sanctuary to those fleeing from imminent murder."

Havens! The word became symbolic in my mind. America had been one great big haven since its birth. We could have hundreds of havens. If only we opened our doors.

Weizmann was pleading for a haven in Palestine. "The Jewish community of Palestine will welcome with joy and thanksgiving all delivered from Nazi hands."

A man near me shouted, "Tell it to Churchill!"

But Britain, with a mandate from the world to turn Palestine into a homeland for Jews, was even now sending crucially needed warships to the Palestine coast, not to fight the Nazis but to prevent the Jews from entering.

We heard Cardinal Hinsely, the Roman Catholic archbishop of Westminster, denouncing both England's Foreign Office and our State Department: "We need cold deeds, and speedy deeds, not the *rhetoric* behind which governments are still hiding."

The air grew colder. More people kept thronging the streets around us, pushing, shouting, shoving, while the police sought to keep some semblance of order.

Now, at last, the voice we were waiting for swept over us. The president was talking from Washington. I could see the patrician face, the strong jaw exuding optimism and strength. The night air grew warm again, embraced by his words.

"The Nazis will not succeed in exterminating their victims . . ." He's talking now about the Jews, I told myself, he's going to tell us how he'll save them.

"The American people will hold the perpetrators of these crimes to strict accountability in a day of reckoning which will surely come."

Was that it? Were we to wait until the war ended? Why couldn't he act now? Open havens in the empty valleys, the hilltops, the deserts of America?

This was March 1943. Our soldiers were battling in North Africa. The Russians had driven the German Sixth Army back from Stalingrad, but Hitler still controlled most of Europe. I knew the argument; it was implicit in the president's words: First we must win the war. Then we will take care of the refugees.

But how many, I thought in despair, would still be alive?

"We have adopted a resolution," Rabbi Wise's voice rolled though the loudspeakers like the music of an organ, "a resolution which we will forward to Secretary of State Cordell Hull to protest against the continuing failure to act against the strange indifference to the fate of 5 million human beings."

I clutched my arms, shivering in anger and frustration. We were 75,000 people—and all we could do was send a protest to Cordell Hull.

No havens were opened. The doors to America and Palestine remained tightly sealed.

As the clamor in the country to save refugees grew into a groundswell, the State Department called a conference in Bermuda specifically to discuss rescue. The conference opened on the day the Nazis launched their final attack on the Warsaw Ghetto. It was also the week of Passover.

The Bermuda conference was a fiasco. "Palliatives," the *New York Times* described it, "designed to assuage the conscience of the reluctant rescuers rather than to aid the victims."

Not one country offered to take in a single refugee.

Months passed. Hundreds of thousands of Jews were murdered. And still no havens were opened.

Then, late in 1943, the suppressed cables were discovered.

The World Jewish Congress in Switzerland had cabled Washington that they could ransom the lives of thousands of Jews in Romania and France. They could raise the money themselves; they knew the officials to be bribed; all they needed was the license to send the dollars abroad.

Both Treasury and State had to approve the license. Treasury agreed to issue the license immediately. State did nothing. Half a year was lost.

Outraged, Secretary of the Treasury Morgenthau called in Josiah E. DuBois Jr., a young assistant general counsel working with Treasury's Foreign Funds Control. "I want you to investigate the whole thing. Get to the bottom of it."

Joe DuBois was a large canvas of a man with a generous spirit, disheveled eyebrows, and tousled hair. He was a young man on fire. He went through all the files to dig up correspondence with State. He found a copy of the cable to the State Department, dated April 20, 1943, from Minister Leland Harrison in Bern, which opened by referring to Cable 354 (the cable of suppression). He telephoned the State Department: "Please send over a copy of your Cable 354."

"Sorry," he was told. "This cable does not relate to Treasury. Only a few people have seen it even in State. We cannot furnish it to Treasury."

"Knowing the State Department as I did," Joe told me later, "I became very suspicious. If State said it was none of our business, I was pretty sure it *was* our business. I decided I had to see it."

Joe knew the head of Foreign Funds Control at the State Department, Donald Hiss. He telephoned Hiss asking for a copy of Cable 354. Briefly he told Hiss of Morgenthau's determination to get the license issued so that the rescue from France and Romania could begin.

Hiss, sympathetic, promised to look for the mysterious cable.

Several times Joe called Hiss's office, only to be told, "Joe, I'm having a hard time getting that cable."

Finally, in desperation, Joe called Hiss at home; the cable was still missing.

On the morning of December 18, Hiss's secretary called Joe's secretary: "Please ask Mr. DuBois to be at our office at 2:30 this afternoon." No reason. No explanation.

Before 2:30 Joe was in Hiss's office. On the desk were two cables. "I've been warned," Hiss confided to Joe, "that under no circumstances should these cables be shown to Treasury. If anyone finds out that I'm showing them to you, I might lose my job."

Courageous and fearless himself, Joe knew that Hiss was risking his career to save thousands of lives.

"I can't let them out of my office, Joe," Hiss said. "I can't even give you copies."

Joe read of the terror in Poland and Romania since 1941. "Can I copy these cables?" he asked.

Hiss nodded silently.

Joe pulled several small slips of paper from his pocket and copied the full text of the cable of suppression and made notes of the longer horror cable.

Back in his office, he dictated a "memorandum for the files" and marked it confidential. For the first time it told the full story of the cables, "so shocking and so tragic that it is difficult to believe."

"I am physically ill," Morgenthau said when he read the memorandum. He then asked Randolph E. Paul, his counsel, to prepare a complete background paper describing the State Department's delays, subterfuges, and suppression.

Paul turned the writing over to Joe DuBois. With the help of Paul and John Pehle, head of Foreign Funds Control at Treasury—both, like Joe, non-Jews— he began working on the report. He dictated drafts to his secretary during the day and worked evenings at home writing. He spent Christmas morning with his wife and family, then went back to his desk and continued writing. Finally, on January 13, 1944, he submitted his report to Morgenthau. Though it was signed "R.E.P." (Randolph E. Paul), Joe had written it from his guts. He called it "Report to the Secretary on the Acquiescence of This Government in the Murder of the Jews."

It began with an impassioned denunciation of the State Department. "One of the greatest crimes in history, the slaughter of the Jewish people in Europe, is continuing unabated." Officials in the State Department

> have not only failed to use the Governmental machinery at their disposal to rescue Jews from Hitler, but have even gone so far as to use this Governmental machinery to *prevent* the rescue of these Jews.
>
> They have not only failed to cooperate with private organizations in the efforts of these organizations to work out individual programs of their own, but have taken steps designed to prevent these programs from being put into effect.
>
> They not only have failed to facilitate the obtaining of information concerning Hitler's plans to exterminate the Jews of Europe but in their official capacity have gone so far as to surreptitiously attempt to stop the obtaining of information concerning the murder of the Jewish population in Europe.

They have tried to cover up their guilt by:
(a) concealment and misrepresentation;
(b) the giving of false and misleading explanations for their failures to act and their attempts to prevent action; and
(c) the issuance of false and misleading statements concerning the "action" which they have taken to date.

DuBois pointed the finger directly at Breckinridge Long, the assistant secretary of state who was in charge of the Visa Division, which decided who could enter the United States—in effect, choosing who would live and who would die.

Breckinridge Long, in DuBois's report, was the archvillain in our government's "acquiescence in the murder of Jews." The report quoted a speech by Congressman Emanuel Celler of Brooklyn. "Frankly, Breckinridge Long, in my humble opinion," Celler had told Congress, "is the least sympathetic to refugees in all the State Department. I attribute to him the tragic bottleneck in the granting of visas. . . . It takes months and months to grant a visa, and then it usually applies to a corpse."

Congressman Celler blasted the misleading and fraudulent statements Long had made in testimony before the House Committee on Foreign Affairs. "We have taken into this country," Long had told the committee, "since the beginning of the Hitler regime [1933] and the persecution of the Jews until today, approximately 580,000 refugees. The whole thing has been under the quota—except the generous gesture we made of visitors' and transit visas during an awful period."

Celler nailed that lie:

> In the first place these 580,000 refugees were in the main ordinary quota immigrants coming in from all countries. The majority were not Jews. His statement drips with sympathy for the persecuted Jews, but the tears he sheds are crocodile. I would like to ask him how many Jews were admitted during the last three years in comparison with the number seeking entrance to preserve life and dignity. . . . One gets the impression from Long's statement that the United States has gone out of its way to help refugees fleeing death at the hands of the Nazis. I deny this. On the contrary, the State Department has turned its back on the time-honored principle of granting havens to refugees. The tempest-tossed get little comfort from men like Breckinridge Long. . . . Long says that the door to the oppressed is open but that it "has been carefully screened." What he should have said is "barlocked and bolted." By the act of 1924, we are permitted to admit approximately 150,000 immigrants each year. During the last fiscal year only 23,725 came as immigrants. Of these, only 4,750 were Jews fleeing Nazi persecution.

If men of the temperament and philosophy of Long continue in control of immigration administration, we may as well take down that plaque from the Statue of Liberty and black out the "lamp beside the golden door."

Morgenthau read DuBois's eighteen-page report with mounting rage. He changed the title to the simpler "Personal Report to the President" and cut the document to nine pages, but kept most of its evidence and accusations, even adding his own charges:

> There is a growing number of responsible people and organizations today who have ceased to view our failure as the product of simple incompetence on the part of those officials in the State Department charged with handling this problem. They see plain anti-Semitism motivating the actions of these State Department officials and, rightly or wrongly, it will require little more in the way of proof for this suspicion to explode into nasty scandal.

On a rainy Sunday morning on January 16, 1944, Morgenthau went to the White House with his young assistant John Pehle. Morgenthau had easy access to the president, who called him affectionately "Henny-Penny." On this Sunday morning, Morgenthau was no Henny-Penny. He had become a committed, anguished, passionate Jew. The suppressed cables had touched ancient roots. He told his friend the president that if these cables became public, the whole world would know of the anti-Semitism in his State Department. The scandal, he said, could reach into the White House itself.

Six days later Roosevelt created the War Refugee Board (WRB), composed of the secretaries of state, treasury, and war—Hull, Morgenthau, and Henry Stimson. Of the three, neither Hull at State nor Stimson of the army was enthusiastic.

Rescuing Jews was withdrawn from the sabotaging hands of Breckinridge Long and given to the War Refugee Board. Pehle, a slim, circumspect thirty-five-year-old lawyer, became its executive director. Cables would no longer be suppressed. Ships would be leased in Sweden to smuggle refugees out of the Balkans. Ira Hirschmann, an executive of Bloomingdale's department store in New York, would be sent to Istanbul to rescue, if he could, the sixty thousand still alive in the Romanian concentration camp of Transnistria. Raoul Wallenberg, a young Swede from a distinguished family, would be sent to Hungary and single-handedly save seventy or eighty thousand.

But time was running out for nearly a million Jews in Hungary and another eight hundred thousand in Romania. Letters flooded the White House. "Mr. President," a man in Los Angeles who signed himself "Not a Jew" pleaded, "do all you can to save the Jewish people of Europe. Establish rescue centers for temporary detention and care until we've knocked the Hell out of Hitler."

On March 6, 1944, Joe DuBois drafted a memorandum for the president urgently recommending temporary havens of refuge. Under his proposal the refugees would be treated "in effect as prisoners of war," for whom no quotas were required.

Peter Bergson and the young Palestinians who worked closely with the War Refugee Board began a massive propaganda campaign to establish temporary havens. "In the eleventh hour of the reign of death," they suggested, let "twenty-five square miles of rescue camps be set aside in five temporary mercy reservations in Palestine, Turkey, North Africa and some of our own abandoned military training camps in the United States." One of their full-page ads carried the headline "25 SQUARE MILES OR . . . 2,000,000 LIVES: Which Shall It Be?"

But bringing refugees into the United States outside the quotas was the political roadblock. How would the isolationists in Congress react? Samuel Grafton, the widely read columnist for the *New York Post*, offered a brilliant solution: Free ports! Why not, he asked in his column of April 5, 1944, "have a system of free ports for refugees fleeing the Hitler terror?"

> Obviously we need a place where we can put refugees down, without making financial decisions about them, a place where they can be stored and processed, so to speak, without creating legal and political problems. . . . Of course, I am a little ashamed to find myself pandering to anti-refugee prejudices even to the extent of saying yes, pile the legal disabilities on them, give them no rights, store them like corn, herd them like cattle—but the need is so sharp, the time is so short, our current example to the world is so bad, that it is necessary to settle for whatever can be done.

In a cordial meeting in the White House, Pehle recommended that an executive order be issued establishing a free port as a temporary haven in the United States. Roosevelt seemed receptive, though he told Pehle he preferred the term "emergency refugee shelter" to Grafton's "free port." The word "emergency" would show that it was temporary, and "shelter" was "honest," since little more than shelter would be offered the refugees. Pehle, who had expected to rescue unlimited numbers, was startled when Roosevelt ended their meeting with the promise to consider opening one camp to rescue one thousand people.

"Roosevelt was a politician first," Joe DuBois told me later, "and then a humanitarian."

Still, one camp for one thousand could be the beginning. If the isolationists in Congress lay quiescent, then perhaps more camps could be opened and more refugees saved. At least, this was what others and I hoped.

At a Cabinet meeting on May 24, Morgenthau introduced the resolution, drafted by WRB, proposing that one thousand refugees be brought from Italy to the United States. He admitted to the Cabinet members that the president was still "a little afraid."

Only Ickes expressed complete support. Ickes was now the honorary chairman of Bergson's "Emergency Committee to Save the Jewish People of Europe." Even Attorney General Francis Biddle opposed the resolution on legal grounds, though it was known that he loathed Breckinridge Long's policies on refugees.

In Europe, the trains roared toward Auschwitz. The Nazis occupied Hungary toward the end of March 1944. On April 27, 1944, the first transports of Jews were shipped from Hungary. Scarcely three months later, Adolf Eichmann had already packed 520,000 into cattle cars headed for the gas chambers.

On June 6, General Eisenhower issued his order of the day: "Soldiers, sailors and airmen of the Allied Expeditionary Force! You are about to embark upon the great Crusade... the eyes of the world are upon you." The invasion of Normandy began. At the same time, seven members of the House introduced resolutions urging Roosevelt to open "free ports."

The time, at last, was right. On June 12 the president sent the formal message to Congress—the message I had read in the press—that one thousand refugees would be brought to a safe haven in Oswego, New York.

On Friday, July 14, Ickes called me to his office.

"The Army just phoned," he said. "You're leaving tomorrow. Are you ready?"

"I've been ready for weeks. The longest weeks of my life."

He swiveled his chair, turning full-face toward me. "You're going to be made a general. A simulated general."

"Me? A general?"

"You'll be flying in a military plane. If you're shot down and the Nazis capture you as a civilian, they can kill you as a spy. But as a general, according to the Geneva Convention, you have to be given shelter and food and kept alive."

I laughed at the idea of my being a general.

"I'm coming in to work tomorrow," Ickes said. "Come see me before you take off." . . .

Searching for Life

The Naples sun streamed into the barren office, turning particles of dust into diamond sparkles, as Max Perlman came around the small wooden desk to greet me.

"What a stroke of luck to find you in Naples," I said.

I had learned that Max was one of the team that had selected the refugees. They had first been selected by Leonard Ackerman of the War Refugee Board, who, working day and night until he was no longer able to "go on playing God," had asked Max to help. Max was a natural, a representative of the Joint Distribution Committee in Italy. The JDC was the overseas arm of the American Jewish community, financing rescues through the underground, paying off officials to save Jews in Romania and Hungary, and sending men like Max to rescue and feed homeless Jews.

"I was only a small part of the team," Max said. "Captain Lewis Korn became head of the group after Len Ackerman took ill; you'll meet Lew, he's already aboard the ship. Trying to select some of those thousand refugees for America was the toughest assignment of my life. Word of that invitation from the president spread like a brushfire. Day and night, people were knocking on the doors of all the offices taking applications in Naples, Bari, Rome. Women and men weeping, people fainting from emotion, parents holding their children up in the air so we'd notice them. It was a lousy job, Ruth. We were all playing God to a group of desperate people. Three thousand applied."

"Three thousand!" I cried. "It would be so easy to bring three thousand into America!"

I remembered Joe DuBois's comment on the number of refugees. "It was the president himself," he told me, "who fixed the figure at one thousand. He's a politician first and then a humanitarian."

Max leaned forward. "There's this tiny village in the mountains called Campagnia where Jews had been hiding out. I went up there by truck with Captain Moscovitz—he's with the Palestinian Jewish unit of the British army. When the refugees saw our truck with the blue and white Star of David painted on both sides, they began embracing the two of us; they couldn't believe it—Jewish officers, one from America, one from Palestine.

"We went on to an old monastery built in the Middle Ages—the Fascists had turned it into an internment camp for about a hundred fifty refugee Jews. Some of them looked eighty; they were in their forties. I told them of the president's invitation to come to America. You can't imagine the excitement. Some of the men made whole speeches telling me how many years they had been dreaming about going to America. Others just wept openly."

His voice, usually a rich tenor, suddenly cracked. "They filled out the applications and then bombarded me with questions. 'When will we know if we're accepted? When will the transport leave for America?' I felt awful, leaving them with such anxiety. I couldn't tell them if they'd be accepted or not. These men were all alone; they had seen their entire families wiped out."

His voice broke again. "Ruth, the pain in their faces is still with me."

My own throat went dry.

"But then there were things to make you happy. The best part for me was arranging the trucks to transport the people from Bari to the ship. I decided not to use British army trucks, even though the British offered them to us. It's a long trip from Bari to Naples—five or six hours, crossing the mountains. I figured these people had been through so much that British military trucks might frighten them. I went back to my Palestinian friends, Major Bar Shmorak, a kibbutznik, and Captain Moscovitz, and asked them to lend us their trucks with the Star of David. Picture the sight. Refugees crossing Italy in a convoy of trucks with the Star of David painted on their sides, heading for a ship to America."

I stood up in the bare office, walked behind the desk, and kissed Max's cheek. "I think these refugees will never forget what you did. Nor will I."

In Hungary, Jews were being selected for death. In southern Italy, a precious few were being selected for life....

THE GI DRIVER took me to a launch where a young navy lieutenant in white uniform helped me jump in his motorboat. Soon we were chugging past wall-to-wall ships. Even the sun seemed to be searching for space in the harbor to cast silver shafts of light.

"There's your convoy." The lieutenant pointed to a flotilla of cruisers, troopships, cargo ships, some sleek and elegant, some dowdy, but all riding high as if they controlled the water. They were anchored in the Bay of Naples, waiting like soldiers to begin a parade of war.

How many thousands, I wondered, are aboard those navy escort vessels—soldiers, sailors, gunners armed to the teeth? My nerves tightened with the sense of danger and the awesome beauty of this seawall of war.

"You'll be picking up more escorts in the Med," the navy officer was saying. "The Med is a bad spot with U-boats. Bombers."

I hardly listened. "Which is the ship with refugees?"

"Over there. It's an army transport, the *Henry Gibbins*."

The ship, rigged with graceful steel cables, lifeboats, elevated tubs with gun emplacements, dwarfed our launch. Its decks were lined with people staring down at us, some waving.

The lieutenant stood up to signal the crew on the *Henry Gibbins*, who dropped a rope ladder down the side. A sailor in the launch held the ladder as I reached for the first rung. Suddenly the lieutenant stared at the white suit, the gloves, the big red hat as if he were seeing them for the first time.

"You can't climb the Jacob's ladder in that outfit. Not with a thousand refugees and a thousand wounded soldiers watching."

He ordered one of the sailors to go below. "Take off your pants and hand them up to me."

The lieutenant gave me the sailor's pants. I pulled them over my skirt, handed him my hat, and once more began climbing the ropes. The ladder swung and pitched against the hull; I clutched each rung so tightly I could feel the rope digging into my skin. The water below looked menacing. Finally, near the top of the ladder, a sailor leaned over, placed his hands under my armpits, and lifted me onto the main deck. The refugees crushed around me.

"It's Eleanor Roosevelt," a man shouted.

I laughed with relief.

Waves of bodies crowded around me, men in tattered shorts, naked to the waist, women in ragged and rumpled skirts and blouses, sad-eyed children in torn sandals or without shoes. Some of the people had cloth and newspapers tied around their feet. Several stared at me as if they were seeing an apparition. . . .

I PROWLED the ship to find Ralph Stauber, the man whom Dillon Myer had sent as his representative. I found him in the wardroom, a chunky man with heavy eyebrows, thin, well-shaped lips, and rounded shoulders. He was in a white short-sleeved shirt, drinking coffee and writing on a long sheet of paper. The wardroom was filled with army and navy officers talking across the wooden tables welded into the deck.

Stauber tried to rise.

"Don't get up." I put my hand out. "I'm glad to meet you."

He settled back, his manner correct. "Well, you made it. For a while it looked as if the convoy would sail without you."

Later I learned that someone in the State Department in Naples had sent a cable to Ickes that I had missed the ship.

"Am I interrupting you?" I asked Stauber, obviously a man of paper and statistics. Even the yellow pencil he held tightly seemed an integral part of his fingers.

"It's okay. I'm working up a statistical table on the number of refugees, the countries they came from, their sex, religion, and so forth. Would you like a breakdown?"

I nodded.

"Number of refugees, nine hundred and eighty-two."

"I thought the president invited a thousand."

Three thousand applied.

"That's all that came aboard. I'll start with religion. Most people think all refugees are Jews. The greatest number on the ship, to be sure, are Jews, but this is by no means a Jewish project." His yellow pencil pointed to the figures.

"Eight hundred and seventy-four are Jewish, seventy-three are Roman Catholic, twenty-eight are Greek Orthodox, and seven are Protestant."

Roosevelt had cautioned that the camp should not be known as a Jewish camp; he wanted refugees from all denominations.

"Here's the breakdown by sex: 525 male, 457 female. Lots of children and old people—the range is from an infant to an eighty-year-old man, Isaac Cohen from Salonika, Greece."

"And the countries they've come from?"

"Eighteen different countries." . . .

[UP ON DECK, waiting for the ship to set sail, I spoke with some of the refugees.]

"I would like [the Americans] to know who you are, what kind of people you are. What you've gone through to survive.

"You'll find out soon enough." Otto Presser spoke up. He was a smallish man, full of gestures that reminded me of Eddie Cantor. "We're all kinds of people. Big and little, some once rich, some not so rich, and now all the same: poor."

The people smiled at Presser, who was obviously a popular figure. Later I learned that he had been a song-and-dance man in Vienna.

"I want to spend as much time as I can with you," I said. "People in America are just beginning to learn what Hitler has done to you. You will be the first group of refugees the people of the United States will see."

They were listening intently now. "You are the living witnesses. Through you, through the experiences you tell me, I can report to Ickes, and he can tell the people of America what has been happening and surely is still going on now."

They sat in silence on the hatch-combing, staring far off into the sea. A few wiped their eyes.

"You're a woman," one of the men said. "How can I tell you the things they did to me—the dirty, filthy, obscene things?"

"Forget, if you can, that I am a woman. It's your story, it's your experiences that are important, not how they affect me. Maybe if the world learns what you suffered, maybe we'll be able to rescue more people."

Tuck, the boatswain, a grizzly old tar with a rubbery face, followed by a few deckhands, made his way through the milling refugees toward the bow. We heard the clang of metal on metal and watched the huge chain come up through the hawse pipe to the anchor windlass.

"We're sailing!" some of the refugees shouted.

We rushed to the rails. Some of the people hugged and kissed one another, some held up their babies to wave good-bye to the Italian shore. Several wept.

The convoy was moving; ships were steaming white foam. Naples lay behind us, golden in the afternoon sun, as warships maneuvered around us in formation, ensigns flying. The Mediterranean opened wide and blue and fraught with danger. . . .

Asylum

Thursday morning, August 3, our dark ship began to glow like a plain woman who becomes beautiful on her wedding day. Excitement built up in every corner, among the refugees, the wounded soldiers, the officers, the sailors giving the ship new spit and polish.

"Today," we told one another, "today's the day. Today we reach New York."

Only the weather was not cooperating.

Except for a few days, most of the voyage had been in warm, golden sunlight. Now we had storm warnings; a hurricane was moving toward us in the Atlantic.

By midafternoon the rain had stopped, but the sky remained ominously overcast, so that we saw almost no land until we moved into the bay. Suddenly she emerged, the green mythic figure. The Statue of Liberty. The thousand refugees waved at her joyously, tearfully, as if she were a granite mother welcoming them to the new homeland.

"The greatest day of my life," a bearded old man wept.

"Mine too," I said.

The people moved aside to let Rabbi Mossco Tzechoval come toward me. He could have stepped out of a Rembrandt painting, with a black beard framing his chalk-white face.

"With your permission, I would like to conduct a service now, while we are passing the Statue of Liberty."

"Of course."

The people grew silent. The rabbi knelt and kissed the iron deck. Then he rose and pronounced the Shehehiyanu. We joined him in the ancient Hebrew prayer, giving thanks that we had survived to this day.

The people listened, their eyes glued to the statue, as he spoke.

"We must never believe the things the Nazis say about us—that we brought evil upon the earth. We did not bring evil upon the earth. Wherever we wandered, we brought the blessings of the Torah. The countries that have tried to destroy us have brought evil upon themselves."

His eyes swept across the silent faces on the deck. "As we enter America, remember we are one people. We must speak with one voice, with one heart. We must not live with hatred. We must live with love."

He held his palms outstretched, the thumbs joining, as if he were touching our heads in the benediction. "May God bless you and keep you and make his countenance to shine upon you and bring you peace. And may God bless this new land."

"Amen," we sang in unison. . . .

Sailors tossed our lines out at Pier 84. The sign over the green-painted shed read, "Hamburg-America Line." We had escaped the Germans only to come home to the pier they had once owned.

Wounded soldiers were carried down the gangplank on stretchers and lifted into the waiting ambulances. Behind the stretcher cases came men in wheelchairs, pushed by their buddies, then the soldiers on crutches, ambulatory men, the airmen, the Red Cross workers, doctors and nurses, all hurrying to make connections and get home.

Only the refugees did not leave.

The officers of the Second Service Command, in summer uniform, came aboard with new orders. "Tell the refugees," they told me, "they are to spend the night aboard the ship. Tomorrow morning we begin the disinfestation and processing."

No one complained. The people stood on the deck, fascinated by the New York skyline and the frenzied activity on the dock.

LIGHT WAS gently streaking the sky as the people began to stir and wake and peer excitedly through open windows at America's villages, towns, and graceful dairy farms.

The train pounded toward Syracuse, then rolled north on a branch line to Oswego until, at exactly 7:30, the iron wheels ground to a halt at a railroad siding.

An MP waved his white gloves to the right. "We're at the camp. No one is to leave until we give the order."

The people on the far side of the train rushed across the aisle to gape through the windows for their first glimpse of Fort Ontario.

"A fence! Another fence!" a man gasped. His words, chilling, plunged through the train. For there, stretching as far as we could see, was a tall hurricane fence of chain links, topped with three rows of barbed wire.

Artur Hirt reached forward, rattling my shoulders. "How could you do this? In the free America! It's another concentration camp!"

The train grew ominously silent. "It's an old army post." I tried to dispel some of the fear. "All army camps in America have fences."

I knew my words had no effect. The silence persisted, awkward, nervous, disbelieving.

"The fence doesn't bother me one bit," Kitty Kaufman, a young Austrian traveling with her Yugoslav husband and young daughter, spoke up. "If you ask me, I feel safer behind a fence. Even in America."

The fence, I realized with a start, was a psychological symbol for refugees. For most of the people, the fence meant a prison, a concentration camp, a locked door, an end to freedom. To Kitty, the fence meant security. Her enemy could not enter.

A burst of activity temporarily deflected the anger and dismay of most of the people. There had been no food on the night coach. Milk and cookies were being handed up through the open windows, and children were eagerly munching and drinking, when the army announced we could begin leaving the train.

The people gathered their hand baggage. I held little Joachim Bass's hand and climbed down the steep steps, suddenly aware that dozens of Oswego's citizens were watching us from the roof of a factory that made tanks.

More townspeople were hurrying out of modest wooden houses lining the street along one side of the fence. Reporters from New York, Chicago, Syracuse, Rochester, and the local *Oswego Palladium-Times* swarmed around us. Photographers snapped their shutters, movie cameras rolled, catching the weary and frightened eyes of the elderly, the tentative smiles of teenagers, the lost look of children still without shoes, a violinist clutching his fiddle in a broken case, the knapsacks and torn boxes tied with rope in which many carried their most precious possessions, the flotsam and jetsam of the war, wearing their cardboard tags: "U.S. Army—Casual Baggage."

We struggled into the camp through a side gate at the railroad spur. It was a huge encampment of eighty acres that stretched from the town to the shores of Lake Ontario. A grassy oval parade ground filled the center of the camp, framed on one side by white wooden barracks in which the refugees were to be housed, and on the other, terraced up a small hill, by red brick Georgian houses with freshly painted white columns, the officers' quarters, where the director and part of the staff would live.

Beyond the brick houses was a gray stone rampart and a stone arch leading into the two-hundred-year-old fort itself. And, sitting behind a small table just inside the fence, military intelligence officers began the registration and identification, checking the people against a master list.

Multilingual translators flanked the officers; they wore armbands with the word *Dolmetscher*—"translator"—printed in red ink. They had been sent to the camp by private Jewish and Christian agencies to help the government though these hectic days.

I listened carefully as the army officers began the screening. Would a few, like Artur Hirt, explode again? They had been screened when they were first selected in Italy, to keep out potential fifth columnists or spies. They had been screened again in Aversa, the insane asylum. Some had dropped out during the screening—one reason why we had 982 instead of a thousand. Now they were being screened a third time. The questioning was sympathetic, benign. Name. Nationality. Country of origin. Name of spouse—if any. Names of children—if any. Profession—if any. Some were asked if they had firsthand information, photos, documents that could help our army win the war faster. The screening became a two-way street, with the people offering eagerly to answer any questions to bring victory even one day closer.

"I'm Joe Smart." A small, slender man in an open-necked white shirt extended his hand to me. The director of the camp, he had open clear eyes and a serious face with deep ridges from his nose to his chin. At forty-three he had already had a colorful career, seven years as special agent in the FBI, regional director managing New Deal resettlement projects, regional director of half of the ten Japanese American relocation centers, and assistant national director of the WRA. He had been working in Peru with the Institute of Inter-American Affairs when Dillon Myer, his former boss, telephoned asking him to take the job in Oswego. Now he was shaking hands, telling those who seemed terrified that perhaps they had come to another concentration camp, "Whenever there is a knock on your door, it will be a friendly one."

Ravenously hungry—we had eaten little all the day before—we were led to the white barracks mess halls, where long tables were stacked with pitchers of steaming hot coffee, bottles of rich, cold milk, giant boxes of cornflakes, loaves of white bread, jars of peanut butter, and bowls overflowing with hard-boiled eggs.

[One woman], her mouth stuffed with one egg, reached into the bowl for another. "We never got fed like this in Gurs."

Customs inspection on the parade ground was fast and cursory. Some of the customs men were misty-eyed as they looked into torn suitcases that held nothing but newspapers, or family photos wrapped in frayed underwear or rags. A customs agent who found only one torn shirt in a battered bag copied the man's name from his tag, spent his lunch hour in a shop, and bought the man a pair of pants, a shirt, and a jacket.

By midmorning there was an explosion of euphoria that caught me up in it. I accompanied some of the people to their homes in the two-story white wooden barracks.

"Such efficiency. Only America can do this." Olga Maurer stared at the entrance of her apartment. Her name and the names of her whole family were fixed on the door. "I feel already it's mine. My first apartment."

A tiny woman in her mid-fifties raced down the steps of her barrack near Lake Ontario. "Fräulein Ruth!" Elsa Neumann flung her arms around my waist. "This is more beautiful than anything in Europe. I have a villa by the sea." She sped off to share the news of her villa with others.

The morning sun shone down on the shady tree-lined streets and the huge grassy parade ground where once soldiers must have drilled and horses galloped. Now children were romping and rolling and tagging one another. Some of their parents strolled leisurely like tourists in a resort hotel.

"Come inside." A woman's voice called from a barrack window. It was Kitty Kaufman, who had found security in the fence. I entered her small partitioned apartment to find her stroking two cotton bedsheets. "In the caves of Italy I used to dream about bedsheets."

"And I used to dream about a mattress," her husband, Branko, a photographer, said softly. "How many years since we've seen a mattress?" He stretched out on the uncovered mattress. His face broadened into a smile that seemed to spread through his whole body.

The apartment had been furnished, GI style, with two metal cots, a small table, two chairs, and a metal locker. "Please sit down," Kitty insisted. "I'm sorry I have nothing to offer you to eat or drink."

The bedsheets were still in her arms when Margareta Spitzer called from the doorway of their apartment, "Come see how excited my mother is."

Her mother had opened the bedsheets and was fixing a cot ready for sleep.

"Bedsheets," her mother whispered in awe. Moses' Jews in the desert, I thought, must have whispered the same way as they watched manna falling from heaven.

She took off her shoes, lowered herself onto the precious bedsheet, and turned her head to the wall so that we would not see her cry. . . .

Note

1. The United Nations Organization was not created until 1945, but the term had already come into the language.

II

THEIR BROTHERS' KEEPERS

> To help the stranger and the sojourner, especially the refugee,
> victims of social, political, economic, cultural and racial movements
> which impinge upon people without their consent, is a divine
> imperative.
>
> M. FLETCHER DAVIS

MOTIVATIONS FOR aiding the dispossessed are varied. Many are
religious ("I do this because I am a Christian, a person committed
to 'bringing to life'"), many political ("I will not stand by and let
the fascist bullies attack these people"). Some are economic (as
when a person asks payment for assisting vulnerable individuals
or groups, or, in the extreme, traffics in human suffering by providing safe passage at outrageous cost). Many are personal. Noble
and mundane, selfish and selfless, the imperatives vary, but save
for those that are clearly exploitative, they seem to have in common a willingness on the part of committed people to extend
themselves to provide care and succor, assistance and advice, and
new homes for refugees so often "lonely and afraid." And many
do so at considerable risk. From ancient to modern times there
have been those who refused to turn away the stranger at the gate;
Good Samaritans who reached out to help others forced to flee
their homes and homelands; men and women of conscience and
concern who agreed with the sentiment of Emma Lazarus's immortal words, "Send these, the homeless, tempest-tost to me"—
and then did something to make sure they were welcomed and
cared for.

In the United States, from the time the statue that the poet
Lazarus called "The Mother of Exile" was erected, privately organized efforts to provide service to the uprooted have been a striking example of a very American process, the professionalization of
voluntarism. Like the field of social work which also began out of
a spirit of goodwill, noblesse oblige, and more instrumental motives (such as reducing concern about the dependency of the

downtrodden), refugee work had a parallel and overlapping raison d'être. Early social agencies were often called "settlement houses." One of their prime missions was to help Americanize the newcomers.

In this country, far more than in any other, there were also organizations specifically formed to greet, protect, and educate foreign migrants—be they people who were pushed out or those pulled in. Until 1950 there was no distinction in federal law between immigrants and refugees. Our first bona fide refugees were defined in the 1952 McCarran-Walters Act as "people fleeing communism," and only they were accorded that special designation and the privileges extended through the office of the attorney general. Only in 1980 were refugees recognized in the United States as they were under United Nations definitions, to wit: any person who, "owing to a well-founded fear of being persecuted for reasons of race, religion, nationality or political opinion, is outside the country of his nationality and is unable or, owing to such fear or for reasons other than personal convenience, is unwilling to avail himself of the protection of that country; or, who not having a nationality and being outside the country of his formal habitual residence, is unable or, owing to such fear or for reasons other than personal convenience, is unwilling to return to it."

The earliest of the voluntary associations established to aid newcomers was the Hebrew Immigrant Aid Society. An organization that still exists, it served as a model and catalyst for more than a dozen other religion- or nationality-based, privately funded agencies, including one that was nonsectarian from the start, now known as the International Rescue Committee. In addition to these agencies, some of which were—and remain—advocacy groups, especially for the protection and assistance of refugees, there have long been stalwart individuals who joined with like-minded acquaintances and mobilized campaigns to give voice to the needs of displaced persons, loudly oppose the forces that caused them to seek asylum far from home, and facilitate their resettlement, sometimes providing shelter themselves.

In the twentieth century, many of the most vocal spokespersons found sympathy and support in the big cities of the world— in Paris and London and, especially, New York, where all but two or three of the major nongovernmental refugees agencies had their headquarters. While regional offices were sometimes to be found in other large metropolitan areas such as Boston and Chicago, Los Angeles and San Francisco, there were some clusters of activity, both political and humanitarian, relating to the causes and consequences of targeted persecutions in out-of-the-way places too. One such center of activity, where political activists, clergymen, educators, philanthropists, and ordinary citizens rallied to the cause of saving the victims of Italian Fascism and German Nazism was in the Pioneer Valley of western Massachusetts. There a nexus of dedicated individuals, the most important of whom was William Allan Neilson, third president of Smith College in Northampton, gave special meaning to engaging the politics and morality of an enlightened refugee policy.

Neilson was a founding member of the forerunner of the International Rescue Committee, the Emergency Rescue Committee, a citizens' group that sent Varian Fry to Marseilles in 1940 to rescue over two thousand artists and intellectuals. Neilson's campus and its surrounding area became a haven for many of them. His colleagues, including men such as Michele Cantarella and Burns Chalmers, and his neighbors in the nearby towns of Cummington and Whately would prove that the quality of their mercy and good works was stretched by the extra efforts they gave to the cause.

This second section of our book represents a loosely connected but geographically grounded case study of active opponents of fascism and those who opened their institutions and their homes, believing that they were indeed "their brothers' keepers." Their interconnected stories are told in a series of essays that begins with an introduction to that key figure William Allan Neilson by the volume editor, Peter Rose; the Florida-based historian Charles Killinger, author of the biography of the Resistance fighter and Italian professor Gaetano Salvemini, focuses on the national antifascist movement that was centered in the Connecticut Valley; the religious scholar and minister, and former chaplain at Smith College, Richard Preston Unsworth weaves together the fascinating connections linking the French village of le Chambon in France, a Huguenot village made famous by its reluctance to let "the innocent blood" of numerous Jewish children given asylum there be shed, with the activities of another former chaplain of Smith, Burns Chalmers, and the hamlet of Cummington, Massachusetts, which became a haven for many refugees from Europe in the

1930s and 1940s. Two final essays—the first by a professor of German language, literature, and culture at Smith College, a person who is self-described as a "triple refugee," the Pomeranian-born, East Germany–raised, American-educated Gertraud Gutzmann, and the second by the writer and activist Deirdre Bonifaz—offer two perspectives on the lives and experiences of the refugees who came, respectively, to Cummington and to Whately, Massachusetts.

MAKING A DIFFERENCE

William Allan Neilson and the Rescue of Refugees

PETER I. ROSE

THE POET Robert Burns wrote, "O wad some Power the giftie ge us, / To see oursels as ithers see us." Smith College's Scottish-born third president, William Allan Neilson, had that gift. A perfect exemplar of an "outsider-within,"[1] in many ways President Neilson seemed to know and understand his adopted country, its noble ideals, and its foibles better than most of its native sons. And he often acted on that knowledge. Over his long life, in addition to his primary work as a teacher, scholar, writer, and college administrator, he played a number of civic and political roles in order to help his fellow Americans enjoy their full measure of "life, liberty, and the pursuit of happiness." He was also one of the leading forces fighting to provide care, succor, assistance, and shelter, mainly but not exclusively to refugee intellectuals.

A Worldly Philosopher

William Allan Neilson (known to his family as "Will") was born in Doune, Perthshire, Scotland, on May 28, 1869. He attended Montrose Academy and the University of Edinburgh, spending some of his time during his student years working at a settlement house in Edinburgh. He received his M.A. in 1891, the year he and his family immigrated to Canada. Shortly after their arrival he obtained an appointment as resident English master of Upper Canada College in Toronto. Four years later he moved to the United States to study for a Ph.D. at Harvard. He received the degree in 1898, became an American citizen in 1905, and, the following year, married Elisabeth Muser of Offenburg, Germany. The Neilsons had two daughters, Margaret and Caroline, and a son, Allan, who died of rheumatic fever at the age of seventeen.

A new career as professor of English literature took Neilson to Bryn Mawr and Columbia and then back to Harvard, where he taught from 1906 to 1917, the year he came to Smith.

NEILSON WAS an internationally recognized and highly respected scholar, the author of *The Origins and Sources of Courtly Love*, *The Essentials of Poetry*, *The Facts about Shakespeare*, and innumerable articles and essays. He was also co-editor, with Harvard president Charles W. Eliot, of *The Harvard Classics* and writer of most of the notes and introductions in that fifty-volume series. He was editor in chief of the second edition of *Webster's New International Dictionary*. And he served as president of the Modern Language Association, trustee of the Carnegie Foundation for the Advancement of Education, member of the Board of Overseers of Harvard, and president of Smith from 1917 to 1939.

By all accounts Neilson was a great teacher, an outstanding speaker, and a powerful presence. He was also a preacher of sorts—and a superb role player, too. One of his former students, whose words are quoted in the *Dictionary of American Biography*, described him as one who "could tease and cajole, scold, admonish and warn. Upon occasion he could be Moses, Jeremiah, or Isaiah, Lewis Carroll or W. S. Gilbert."[2] She was not alone in that assessment.

In his many years in the presidency of Smith, Neilson was a forceful advocate for the liberal arts and the broadening of traditional offerings. For him, such activity was necessary to achieve his academic goals, but it was hardly sufficient to satisfy his broader concerns. Neilson was a political man par excellence. And he did not hesitate to use his office as a bully pulpit to put forth his liberal agenda.

Although he was kind and generous—some say he was generous to a fault—he didn't suffer fools. He had as little patience for narrow-minded politicians as he did for ill-informed professors. He decried bigotry in its many guises and forcefully stood up against injustice. It was important, he told his friends and taught his students, to know facts and process them. But it was also important to act. His idea of a citizen was one who was both informed and engaged.

Not surprisingly, Neilson's advocacy made him quite controversial in some circles, especially when he would speak out on any number of issues far removed from his areas of acknowledged academic expertise. It didn't faze him. On the contrary, he was energized by those who opposed him.

William Allan Neilson was among the very few academic leaders who spoke out against the imposition of ethnic quotas in universities, who upheld the rights of defenders of Sacco and Vanzetti and others accused of "political crimes," who supported "suspect" groups such as the Women's International League for Peace and Freedom. During his tenure as president of Smith, he testified in the Massachusetts State House in Boston on many occasions, none more forcefully than in opposition to the Massachusetts Teachers' Oath Bill, which required all teachers to swear fealty to the federal and state constitutions in order "to protect youth from subversive doctrine."[3]

His civic activities frequently evoked the wrath of those who saw him as a subversive himself, even a "communist agitator." Indeed, he gained a kind of notoriety—his supporters would call it a distinction—by being included in Elizabeth Dillings's *Red Network*, where, according to his biographer Hubert Herring, Neilson was cited for having "trifled with Russia, blessed sundry organizations standing for civil liberties, and indulged in other 'communist' deeds."[4] (Neilson is reported to have responded to the attack by Dillings, doyenne of the DAR, by saying that he felt "proud to have been honored with a place [on her list]."[5]

Neilson was deeply concerned about racist and reactionary forces in this country and abroad. He rejected chauvinistic jingoism and nativist ideology, and he feared the consequences of "America First" isolationism. He was an outspoken antifascist who, early on, warned of the dangers being promulgated by Mussolini and Franco and Hitler, and who felt that Americans had to wake up to evils their policies portended. They had to be educated.

Neilson was a leading proponent of both the study and the practice of internationalism on his campus and far beyond it. During his first three years in Northampton, 1917 to 1920, he was proud to support the efforts of the Smith Relief Unit in France. The activities of the participants were reciprocated with the presentation of a replica of the gates of Grecourt, which mark the principal entrance to the college and were to become its long-familiar insignia.

In 1925 President Neilson established the second Junior Year Abroad program in the United States. (The first had been started by the University of Delaware two years earlier.) Thirty-two carefully chosen Smith College students, all with sufficient French skills to function in Paris, were provided the opportunity to study in France.[6] Theirs was definitely not to be the old-fashioned, casual Grand Tour, "when the traveler remained a stranger." Writing in the journal *Progressive Education* in 1930, President Neilson declared that *his* juniors were to be "steeped for a year in an alien civilization."[7]

Neilson also established a German house on the Smith campus in 1935. A French house was established several years later. To enrich the community and bring in different perspectives, Neilson also encouraged the enrollment of a number of foreign students and facilitated the visits of many lecturers and professors from abroad.

In recognition of Neilson's contribution to enhancing the exchange of students between France and the United States, in 1935 he was awarded the Croix de Chevalier de la Legion d'Honneur from the French government. He accepted the honor "as the representative of the French teachers of the College who have earned what has come to me."[8] The French decoration was to be but one of many honors bestowed on Neilson for his role in international understanding. A citation accompanying an honorary degree he received from Kenyon College in June 1940, for example, included these words: "A liberal in public affairs as well as education, you have sponsored many good causes and insisted upon an enlightened view of foreign affairs."[9]

For more than ten years, Neilson's compulsory Monday morning "chapel talks" were devoted to weekly reviews of current affairs, much of them based on what students were expected to read in the national newspapers. To ensure exposure, the president arranged to have copies of both the daily *New York Times* and *Herald Tribune* delivered to every house on campus and urged his students to read them.

William Allan Neilson was no summer soldier. His deeds were as important as his words. A man of principle and action, he was truly a man for all seasons. When he died in Northampton on February 13, 1946, at the age of seventy-seven, Neilson left a rich legacy. He was mourned by his family, former colleagues, fellow administrators, and other leading figures in higher education, by generations of students, and also by countless others far removed from ivied halls. His presence is still felt on the Smith College campus, in the President's House, which his wife, Elisabeth, helped to design; in the William Allan Neilson Library dedicated to his memory; and in a myriad of still-extant programs, many of which were pioneering ventures later to be copied on campuses all across America. He was especially mourned by a number of illustrious exiles who were the direct beneficiaries of his personal interventions and public activities. A number of such individuals had come to Smith through Neilson's efforts. He helped to place many others at a time when there was general reluctance to get involved or to extend special favors to the victims of fascism and Nazism in the American academy.

Neilson's benefaction extended far beyond the Grecourt gates of Smith. He had a profound effect on ensuring the civil rights of all Americans, including those long disenfranchised, and in establishing precedents for aiding the dispossessed. He played critical roles in many agencies concerned with these matters. Two of the many organizations in which he was a prime mover and active leader were the Legal Defense and Education Fund of the National Association for the Advancement of Colored People and the Emergency Rescue Committee.

In the first case, Neilson, who served on the board of directors of the NAACP from 1930 to 1946, was a key organizer and the first chair of the Committee of 100, a group of civil rights advocates who established, and found financial support for, the organization's Legal Defense and Education Fund in 1943, the year of the worst race riots since World War I. With Thurgood Marshall as its leading lawyer, the LDEF was to fight and win many battles in the courts, including the Supreme Court of the United States. Its most significant victory was the famous 1954 school segregation case *Brown v. Board of Education of Topeka,* in which the Supreme Court ruled unanimously that "separate could never be equal."

Fire Bells in the Night

Responding to another series of violations of human rights, in 1933 President Neilson became an active member of the EC, the Emergency Committee in Aid of Displaced German (later changed to Foreign) Scholars.[10] The members of this committee, departing somewhat from the approaches of those who founded the University in Exile at the New School for Social Research in New York and the Institute for Advanced Study at Princeton, were not so much concerned with establishing special academic sanctuaries for refugee scholars as they were interested in paving the way for scholars in exile to find positions in traditional institutions. Smith College was one place where, led by Neilson, the plan was put into action. In fact, when the W. A. Neilson Chair of Research was established in his honor, it expressly provided an "opportunity of inviting outstanding scholars to come into residence in the college without prescribing for them particular duties of any kind." Neilson used its flexible mandate to bring European scholars to the campus, a number of whom were political refugees. Among those given the special title of Neilson Professor was the psychologist Kurt Koffka, who had come to Smith in 1927. The literary scholar and author of *Goliath*, G. A. Borgese, was at Smith from 1932 to 1935. The music critic Alfred Einstein came in 1939, Carl Becker in 1941, and the art historian Edgar Wind served as Neilson Professor from 1944 to 1948. In addition, through Neilson's efforts—and those of his successor as president, Herbert Davis—many antifascists and exiles found a home at Smith and in the surrounding area. Some were from Italy; many more were from Nazi-dominated lands. Included in the first group were the likes of Michele Cantarella, who, with his wife, Helena, led a campaign from Northampton against the Fascist regime in Italy. Their circle included Gaetano Salvemini (who was teaching at Harvard), G. A. Borgese, Renato Poggioli, and, later, Massimo Salvadori. Poggioli, like Borgese, taught at Smith in the 1930s. In the late 1930s, Salvadori, a longtime (and once jailed) foe of Mussolini, who had spent some years in exile in Africa, was teaching at Saint Lawrence University in Canton, New York, leaving his post there to join the British forces in Montreal at the outbreak of the war in Europe. He came to Smith College after a brilliant career as an officer in the British commandos, having served for a time as senior liaison to the Italian partisans. Like Cantarella, Salvadori remained at Smith for the rest of his career.

Among the many other who also taught at Smith was the Czech scholar Hans Kohn (who first arrived in 1934 and stayed until 1950), and the German refugees Fritz Heider, Manfred Kridl, Anita Laurie Ascher, Martin Sommerfeld, Suzanne Engelmann, Annelies Argandler Rose, Walter Richter, and Walter Kotschnig. Those listed here represented a wide range of disciplines, including history, psychology, languages, and literature.

In the 1940s Kotschnig chaired the Neilson-inspired and Davis-supported Committee on Refugee Scholarships, which helped bring children of German, Austrian, English, and French exiles to Smith. Among those who benefited from one of the committee's scholarships was the Ukrainian-born Nelly Schargo, daughter of Simon Shargo, a prominent member of the American Jewish Joint Distribution Committee's campaign to aid refugees in Europe. Another was Marianna Simmel, daughter of German physicians and granddaughter of the sociologist Georg Simmel.

Oscar Seidlin was another German refugee who taught at Smith. Before taking a two-year leave of absence to serve in the U.S. Army, he was, with Elisabeth Muser Neilson, a most active member of the Committee of Loyal Citizens of German Birth, an organization made up mainly of anti-Nazi Germans living in the U.S.

The letters of many of the refugees Neilson brought to Smith (some of them available in the college's archives) acknowledge his special role and the extent to which his college served as a model for what could be done throughout the land. (I should note, too, that there were other havens for refugees in the Northampton area. These are discussed in subsequent essays; they include Jimmy and Blanche Cooney's Morning Star Farm and the Cummington community. And there were other members of the Smith College community, not least the chaplain Burns Chalmers, who were involved in their resettlement in western Massachusetts.)

On January 3, 1936, the *St. Louis Globe Democrat* reported on an address William Allan Neilson had given to a convention of scientists gathered in St. Louis, in which "he appealed to an innate sense of freedom and justice felt by all Americans and also to common sense [and] urged that our hard and fast immigration laws be relaxed to permit the unhampered entry of intellectuals who have been driven from foreign lands because they are not in sympathy with dictatorships in power there." He made special reference to Germany, Russia, and Italy. The article quoted Neilson: "The prescribing of subjects of research by political authorities, the imposing of conclusions to be arrived at, the choice of teachers and directors on grounds of political docility, the stifling of free discussion, all these and many more poisonous procedures are already having their bane-full effect on the science and scholarship of nations that formerly were leaders in their fields. They are committing national suicide." Interestingly in what was a news story, the reporter editorialized to the extent of stating: "Dr. Neilson is quite right in urging that 'it would be a profound mistake for our intellectual future if we permit a temporary economic emergency or hampering immigration regulations to prevent us from offering a generous hospitality to men whose consciences forbid them to forswear their intellectual birthright and who come to us stript and ruined but with hands laden with inestimable riches of the spirit.'"[11]

Such an endorsement was not so common in those days of economic depression, growing xenophobia, and widespread anti-Semitism in this country. Neilson knew it and did everything he could to alter the prevailing sentiments.

Worried about the growing power of antidemocratic forces and the scapegoating of Jews in Europe, especially in Germany, he was also quick to let his concerns be known. On learning about *Kristallnacht*, the rampage of anti-Semitic terror on the night of November 9–10, 1938, Neilson immediately expressed his outrage. Speaking at a mass meeting in Northampton, he stated unequivocally: "This is what we have to do. We have to say I will not stand by and be silent before these terrible things. I will not forget my common humanity, the common element in the whole race. I cannot be contemporary with these events and have it said by my children that I lived through that and did nothing about it—for no reason that I could honestly offer."[12] Neilson called for the immediate admission to the United States of at least 500,000 Jewish victims of Nazi persecution.

His impassioned pleas fell on deaf ears. No special accommodations were made until 1944, when, very reluctantly, U.S. authorities allowed a thousand refugees to be admitted on a temporary basis. All were brought to a former army post, Fort Ontario in Oswego, New York. Those refugees, escorted by another advocate and agitator for refugee admissions, the journalist and scholar Ruth Gruber, were confined to the base, to be kept there for the duration of the war then sent to back to Europe, though the repatriation order was later rescinded. (Excerpts from Ruth Gruber's firsthand account, *Haven*,[13] appear in Part I of this book.)

An article appeared in the *New York Times* on January 11, 1939, headed, "Northampton Ready to Care for 25 Refugee Children." A subhead stated, "Message from President Neilson, Mrs. Coolidge [wife of the late president, who had returned to their home in Northampton] and Others Urges State Department and Congressmen to Find Means to Admit Them to This Country." The text, datelined Northampton, January 10, explained that a meeting of the Northampton refugee committee presided over by President Neilson had approved a motion put forth by Professor Seth Wakeman of Smith to send the following wire to Congress: "Deeply moved by the plight of victims of religious and racial persecution in Germany, we have secured homes and funds in this community for a least 25 refugee children. Urge you to explore every possible means of admitting children to this country. Suggest possibility of admitting them at once on basis of quotas unfulfilled in past years, or by anticipating future quotas. We are confident you will share our concern."[14] It was further reported that Professor Otto Kraushaar of the Philosophy Department (later to become president of Goucher College in Baltimore) announced that Smith students had raised nearly $2,000 to assist students fleeing Germany to attend the college.

Neilson continued to voice his concerns and to encourage action. He fired up his students, rallied the community, and reached out to colleagues across the country. He did what he could to get his message of humanitarian intervention across to members of Congress—and the American people. He tried to do this in a variety of ways: writing letters to key figures and to the editors of major newspapers, speaking out at meetings of learned societies, and working with others—as he had earlier in his early involvement in the NAACP and various refugee support committees—to lobby for immediate aid to victims and for longer-term changes in policy and attitude on the part of influential Americans.

Long troubled and angered by what he saw as undemocratic tendencies in this country, such as the restrictive immigration "quota" laws passed in 1921 and 1924, he continued to be outraged by the fact that no provisions were made for the extenuating circumstances faced by those who were forced to flee their homes and homelands. He saw the obvious necessity of providing assistance and asylum to desperate people, and he saw the fringe benefits to the host societies as well. Addressing a broad spectrum of prominent figures and members of the public in a number of speeches, letters, and newspaper articles, he stated his beliefs in no uncertain terms.

In a typed note for a speech dated January 11, 1939, Neilson specifically addressed the advantages of welcoming refugee intellectuals into the ranks of American college faculties: "My theory is that the college executive should provide for his students the best teachers and scholars he can afford whether native or foreign." And later that same year, in a letter to the editor of the *New York Times* published under the title "Immigration as Trade Aid," Neilson ended with this powerful petition:

> The purpose of this letter is to appeal to American economists to examine the question [of the alleged harm to the economy that would be caused by the admission of refugees] in light of the conditions in this country and to let us

know whether it is true that increased population would diminish employment and prosperity here, or whether it is not probable that we can offer a refuge to the persecuted, not only without doing injustice to our own people but, on the contrary, helping our own recovery.[15]

In that same period, while the German juggernaut was rolling across Europe and one country after another was falling under Hitler's hegemony, Neilson and others sought to turn those words, "offer a refuge to the persecuted," into direct action. He was involved in the establishment of several organizations, most notably the Emergency Rescue Committee, which was to focus on the rescue of anti-Nazi activists, fellow intellectuals, and endangered writers and artists, and the National Refugee Service, whose board and staff were mainly concerned with saving and assisting Hitler's chief scapegoats, European Jewry.

The Emergency Rescue Committee

Long involved in supporting pro-democratic forces in Italy and Germany and those who lived in exile in the United States, in 1940 Neilson joined with Paul Hagen (also known as Karl Frank), an exiled leader of the anti-Nazi group Neu Beginnen, and Reinhold Niebuhr to help found the Emergency Rescue Committee (ERC). In addition to Hagen, Niebuhr, and Neilson, other sponsors were the distinguished foreign correspondent Dorothy Thompson, the popular radio commentator Elmer Davis (who would soon become head of the Office of War Information), and five other college and university presidents: Charles Seymour of Yale, Robert Maynard Hutchins of Chicago, George Schuster of Hunter College, Alvin Johnson of the New School for Social Research, and Frank Kingdon of Newark University. Among the ERC's most prominent early and longtime supporters were Max Ascoli, Thomas Mann, Jan Masaryk, Reinhold Niebuhr, Hendrik van Loon, and First Lady Eleanor Roosevelt; among its staff members was a young lawyer named Harold Oram, an expert fund-raiser and publicist who had already been involved in several political causes, including that of the Spanish Loyalists.

Oram had been a key figure in the American Committee to Aid Spanish Democracy, though he left it owing to factional disputes and debates about the role of the Soviet Union in the Loyalist campaign.[16] Oram's work with the committee had included soliciting money for the Spanish Refugee Relief Campaign to aid the Republicans in exile.[17] He was now prepared to play a similar role in rescuing Hitler's victims—and did. His roster of contributors was central to ensuring the underwriting of the activities of the Emergency Rescue

Committee.[18] Oram would soon become Neilson's son-in-law, marrying his daughter Caroline in 1941.

With the political support of the board and finances provided by Oram's efforts, the ERC's most successful endeavor was a clandestine operation carried out in Marseilles, the most critical point of embarkation for those trying to escape from Europe in 1940. The operation was led by a young writer and magazine editor named Varian Fry. Fry, a bookish, foppish Harvard graduate, seemed—despite his growing concern about the victims of the Nazis, doubtless influenced by what he had witnessed on the streets of Berlin in 1935—a most unlikely secret agent. But that is precisely what he became. And he was extremely successful, a true American pimpernel.[19]

The rescue mission, initially operating out of the Hotel Splendide under the cover of a YMCA-endorsed legitimate relief organization, was staffed by an international cast of characters. Socialists, Social Democrats, and a few socialites, they were as varied in background, personality, and temperament as the illustrious exiles they sought to spirit out of Vichy France.

Fry had left New York with a list of two hundred targeted for rescue. Yet his group managed to facilitate the escape of nearly two thousand foreigners and *apatrides* (stateless persons), including such luminaries as Marc Chagall, Marcel Duchamp, Lion Feuchtwanger, Jacques Lipchitz, Wanda Landowska, André Masson, Ylla (the animal photographer), Lotte Lenya, Hannah Arendt, André Breton, Heinrich Mann (brother of Thomas), Golo Mann (Thomas's son), Walter Mehring, Franz Werfel and his wife, Alma Mahler Gropius Werfel, Otto Meyerhoff, Hans Sahl, Max Ernst, and Giuseppe Modigliani.[20]

One important member of Fry's staff was Miriam Davenport. Contrary to her portrayal in the 2001 Showtime television movie *Varian's War*, Davenport did not go to Vassar.[21] She was a Smith College graduate, class of 1937, who, at the outbreak of the war in Europe, was studying at the Institute of Art and Archaeology at the University of Paris and taking painting classes with the cubist André Lhote. At the time of the German invasion of France, she managed to leave Paris for Toulouse at the last possible moment. There, through Charles Wolff, she met Walter Mehring and several others high on the German's "Most Wanted" list. Years later she would tell her friend Pierre Sauvage that Wolff had said their only hope was to get themselves to Marseilles to seek assistance from the American Varian Fry, who was setting up some sort of rescue operation there.[22] The exiles moved to the seaport city. Davenport did, too, volunteering to work with Fry. She also persuaded him to give a job to her friend Mary Jayne Gold, a wealthy, adventurous American expatriate. Davenport stayed with the ERC project in Marseilles until October 1941, when she moved to Ljubljana seeking a way to bring her fiancé to France. That proved impossible. After much work and many close calls, she and Sauvage managed to get to Lisbon and then to the United States on the Friday after the attack on Pearl Harbor.[23]

In 1941 Fry's ERC operation in Marseilles was forced to close down, and he returned to the United States. Several years later he wrote *Surrender on Demand*, a memoir of his thirteen months in Marseilles. He dedicated the book, first published in 1945, to five colleagues, Anna Caples, Paul Hagen, Frank Kingdon, Ingrid Warburg, and Harold Oram, "who made it possible."[24]

NOT LONG after the Marseilles operation ended, the International Relief Association, founded by Albert Einstein in 1933, merged with the Emergency Rescue Committee to form the International Rescue Committee to continue working to save those who, as their fund-raising flyers noted, were "Wanted by the Gestapo." Once again, William Allan Neilson played a key role in shaping the new organization, whose board included members of the old ERC council—Reinhold Niebuhr, Elmer Davis, Dorothy Thompson—as well as such other movers and shakers as John Dewey, Robert Maynard Hutchins, Alvin Johnson, David Dubinsky, and other well-known religious and academic figures, journalists, and labor leaders.[25]

From the start, the International Rescue Committee differed in certain critical ways from the majority of its sister refugee organizations. Unlike most of the others, which tended to be affiliated with Catholic, Protestant, or Jewish bodies, and were decidedly sectarian and, publicly at least, apolitical, IRC was intentionally neither. From its inception the organization, founded, endorsed, and supported by a broad cross-section of private citizens, had a rather singular raison d'être: to assist victims of totalitarianism, whether the oppressors be "black" or "red," in the old-fashioned sense of those words.

Well over a half century after its founding, the International Rescue Committee remains one of the principal nonsectarian refugee agencies in the United States. Whereas the ERC's focus was on refugee intellectuals, artists, and political activists, the IRC has long been involved in the rescue and resettlement of anyone forced to flee racial, religious, or political oppression. It has carried out its mission with considerable effectiveness in the aftermath of every conflict since World War II in places as different as Bangladesh, Budapest, and Bangkok (where the IRC ran the largest refugee resettlement service in Southeast Asia), as well as Rwanda, Bosnia, Afghanistan, and many other troubled spots. Sometimes, as in the case of the resettlement of Indochinese refugees, the IRC has worked under government contracts, but in the main, as in its earliest days, it remains heavily reliant on the support of private donors appealed to by latter-day Neilsons and other men and women of conscience.

The National Refugee Service

In the early days of the ERC's existence, Neilson also served on the board of the National Refugee Service (the NRS) along with a number of key figures in its campaign to save the Jews of Europe, find safe havens for them, provide resettlement assistance, and help refugees adjust to their new environs. Some of Neilson's colleagues on the board were Paul Baerwald, Joseph P. Chamberlain, David de Sola Pool, Charles Pickett, William Rosenwald, Lewis L. Strauss, Paul Warburg, Jonah B. Wise, and Abba Hillel Silver.

In 1940 the recently retired Smith College president helped to prepare the NRS handbook, *America Meets the Refugee*. It was a primer and guide for those, mainly volunteers, who were interested in becoming involved in aiding the "lucky few" who had managed to find asylum in America, in big cities like New York and Philadelphia and small ones like Northampton. Included in the text was a policy statement urging refugee workers to try to prevent "refugee ghettoes" from forming in New York or anywhere else. The New York–based NRS encouraged its representatives to "send [the refugees] to the smaller cities and towns throughout the United States on a planned basis . . . send them to places where they have a better opportunity to find work, where they have an even chance to make friends, where they will meet Americans."[26] (The fact is that many were reluctant to leave their "Guldene Medina," their city of asylum, where the Central Park West area became a veritable exile community, indeed affectionately called by some of its new residents "a refugee ghetto." As Neilson had feared, others called it the same thing, using a decidedly different tone.)

Concerned with long-range planning as well as immediate aid and assistance for those being settled either temporarily or permanently in this country, Neilson also served in the earliest days of World War II as the chair of the executive committee of the Committee on the Study of the Organization of Peace.

In 1940, in a small book, *The City of Man: A Declaration on World Democracy*, prepared at the end of a three-day conference of prominent figures in the arts and letters on the problems of war and peace which Neilson chaired, Herbert Agar, Lewis Mumford, G. A. Borgese, and others argued that their "City of Man," their good society, rested on two fundamental elements: freedom and justice, and an implicit world federalism. They wrote: "The City of Man must be much more than a League of Nations. . . . It must be the Nation of Man embodied in the Universal State, the State of States. . . . And the pluralistic system of the American Commonwealth, although prevented from reaching a complete expression . . . had shown its best age that the combination of local autonomy with unitary authority is . . . feasible on a continental scale, and therefore ultimately on a world-wide one."[27]

Two years later, in an introduction to *We Escaped*, a volume consisting of twelve personal stories of flight to America, a few written by the refugees themselves and the majority based on interviews by Neilson's daughter Caroline, Neilson wrote: "Not only has there been little relaxation of the restrictions of our immigration laws to meet the emergency, but scores of measures to increase these restrictions and to render the lot of the alien and the exile more difficult have been introduced into Congress. . . . And the great mass of our people seem to look on without indignation." He spoke out again in defense of the aliens who "are infusing new life into many industries, into our universities, into our art and music."[28]

Neilson did what he could both to change the laws and to assist those who had managed, somehow, to obtain scarce visas and make it to America. In addition to extending his personal welcome to refugee scholars and teachers (including some of those mentioned in *We Escaped*) to his campus, he appealed to his professional colleagues, legislators, Northampton neighbors, and students to do what *they* could to help the dispossessed.

In her biography *Neilson of Smith*, Margaret Farrand Thorp notes that

> while he worked toward the future, Neilson felt impelled also to promote justice and freedom by some action that would produce immediate and concrete results. For the plight of refugee intellectuals he felt particular concern. He had appointed as many as he could to the Smith College faculty and he tirelessly wrote letters and talked with his administrative friends in the endeavor to find posts for others. . . . With the ERC and the NRS Neilson worked both publicly and privately. Again and again he lent money from his personal funds or signed the affidavit guaranteeing financial support which made it possible for a German writer or teacher to gain entrance to the United States.[29]

Neilson was not only concerned with rescue and resettlement; he was also active in countering the still extant anti-alien sentiment. In the same year he worked on the NRS handbook and chaired the Committee on the Study of the Organization of Peace (1940), he took on yet another task, serving as co-chair, with Ernest Hemingway, of another committee, the sponsors of a forthcoming conference of the American Committee for the Protection of the Foreign Born, at which President Roosevelt was to be the keynote speaker. In a letter to the editor of *The Nation*, Hemingway invited the support of its readers for "work which I am certain will meet with their approval." He explained:

> You must be aware that the existence of the war in Europe has intensified the efforts of demogogic alien-baiters who seek to destroy our rights as Americans

behind the subterfuge of attacking the so-called alien. Because I am anxious to do my part in helping to defeat this attack upon American democracy, I have agreed to serve as co-chairman of the Committee of 100 Sponsors for the Fourth Annual Committee for the Protection of the Foreign Born. Dr. William A. Neilson, president emeritus of Smith College, is serving with me. An important undertaking of the conference is to prevent the passage of any of the seventy "anti-alien" bills in Congress. These undemocratic proposals for deportation of non-citizens, for concentration camps, for registration and finger-printing are a menace to the continued existence of American democracy.[30]

The conference was held on schedule and was widely reported and commented on. Here, for example, is how one small-town paper, the *Binghamton Sun* in upstate New York, handled the story under the headline "Nearly 100 Anti-Alien Bills Facing Congress." The article, written by Letty Lynn, begins with a lengthy quotation from President Roosevelt's speech:

> Every American takes pride in our tradition of hospitality to man of all races and of all creeds. One of the great achievements of the American commonwealth has been the fact that race groups which were divided abroad are united here as friends.... [T]hey have all made contributions to democracy and peace.
>
> Because of the very greatness of this achievement, we must be constantly vigilant against the attacks of intolerance and injustice. We must scrupulously guard the civil rights and civil liberties of all citizens, whatever their background. We must remember that any oppression, any injustice, any hatred, is a wedge designed to attack our civilization. If reason is to prevail against intolerance, we must always be on guard. We welcome therefore the work to maintain the rights of the foreign born.[31]

The rest of the article was about a different president, President Neilson. Lynn wrote:

> The American Committee for Protection of the Foreign Born, by the way, is not a radical organization. Unfortunately, many of the nation's worthy movements have won undeserved black eyes because other organizations masquerading as "patriotic" or "protective" are really subversive. However, men like Dr. William Allan Neilson, president emeritus of Smith College, have lent themselves to the committee. President Neilson is deadly earnest about the bills now before Congress. He warns that more than 20 proposals directed against the "alien" have been introduced since the opening of the Congress in January [1940] and that "It is essential that the American people voice their opposition to these anti-alien proposals immediately."[32]

A Special Legacy

There is much more to say about that "deadly earnest" man, but I must stop. But not without a final comment about President Neilson's special legacy.

Whether railing against anti-alien legislation or aiding the dispossessed, as in everything else he considered important, William Allan Neilson, often described as a "Gladstonian liberal," and sometimes as a "Jeremiah with a brogue," was informed, outspoken, and engaged. He thrived on diversity and controversy long before the former became a buzzword and the latter something to fear. He was the sort of person Bobbie Burns must have had in mind when he wrote, "The honest man, though ne'er sae puir, / Is king o'men for a' that."

Notes

This essay is, in several ways, a joint effort. My "partners" include the most helpful members of the Smith College Archives, which holds most of the Neilson papers, and three former students: first, Merril Winbanks, '94, whose spadework for "A Study of Refugee Intellectuals and Their Academic Environment as Specific to Smith College pre-1945," a fine paper prepared as a Special Studies Project under the joint supervision of professor of history emerita Nelly Hoyt and me in 1994, unearthed a number of important documents to read and a number of tantalizing leads to follow. The two others, both graduate students, Anja Klein, American Studies diploma '97, who came to Smith from the Netherlands, and Susanna Erlandsson, American Studies diploma '98, from Sweden, helped me follow those leads and many others. I thank them for their efforts.

1. Peter I. Rose, "Nobody Knows the Trouble I've Seen": Some Reflections on the Inside-Outsider Debate," 1977 Katharine Asher Engel Lecture, Smith College, Northampton, Mass., 1978.

2. *Dictionary of American Biography*, s.v. "William Allan Neilson."

3. Margaret Farrand Thorp, *Neilson of Smith* (New York: Oxford University Press, 1956), 189–90.

4. Hubert Herring, *Neilson of Smith* (Brattleboro, Vt.: Stephen Daye Press, 1939), 36.

5. Ibid.

6. Walter Hullihen, "Present Status of the Junior Year Abroad," *French Review* (January 1928): 25–37.

7. William Allan Neilson, *Progressive Education* (1930): 78.

8. Thorp, *Neilson*, 198.

9. Memo from G. B. Ford to Mr. Holding, January 23, 1946, Smith College Archives.

10. See Stephen Duggan and Betty Drury, *The Rescue of Science and Learning: The Story of the Emergency Committee in Aid of Displaced Foreign Scholars* (New York: Macmillan, 1948).

11. St. Louis *Globe Democrat,* January 3, 1936.

12. William Allan Neilson, December 1, 1938, Neilson papers, Smith College Archives.

13. See Ruth Gruber, *Haven: The Unknown Story of 1,000 World War II Refugees* (New York: Coward, McCann, 1983); and Sharon K. Lowenstein, *Token Refuge: The Story of the Jewish Refugee Shelter at Oswego, 1944–1946* (Bloomington: University of Indiana Press, 1986).

14. "Northampton Ready to Care for 25 Refugee Children," *New York Times,* January 11, 1939.

15. William Allan Neilson, letter to the editor, *New York Times,* April 2, 1939.

16. See Peter I. Rose, "Remembering Varian Fry," *Migration Today* 29, nos. 1–2 (2001): 35–42.

17. Mary Jayne Gold, *Crossroads Marseilles, 1940* (New York: Doubleday, 1980), xii.

18. Eric Thomas Chester, *Covert Network: Progressives, the International Rescue Committee, and the CIA* (New York: M. E. Sharpe, 1995), 14–15.

19. Gold, *Crossroads,* xvi–xvii. See also Andy Marino, *A Quiet American: The Secret War of Varian Fry* (New York: St. Martin's, 1999); and Sheila Isenberg, *A Hero of Our Own: The Story of Varian Fry* (New York: Random House, 2001). For a commentary on the Hollywood treatment of Varian Fry, see Peter I. Rose, "Debasing Good History with Bad Fiction: 'Varian's War,'" *Chronicle of Higher Education Review,* April 20, 2001, B18–19.

20. See Gold, *Crossroads,* epilogue; and Anthony Heilburt, *Exiled in Paradise: German Refugee Artists and Intellectuals in American from the 1930s to the Present* (New York: Viking, 1983), esp. 39–43.

21. See Rose, "Debasing Good History."

22. Draft of autobiography of Miriam Davenport Ebel, Varian Fry Project, 2–3, *www .chambon.org/ebel/bio.htm.*

23. Miriam Davenport Ebel, her friend Mary Jayne Gold, and many of those they helped to save would later write about their experiences during that critical and exciting period. See Gold, *Crossroads.* At this writing, Miriam Davenport Ebel's memoir, "An Unsentimental Journey," unfinished at the time of her death in 1999, is available on Pierre Sauvage's Web site.

24. Varian Fry, *Surrender on Demand* (New York: Random House, 1945), iii.

25. Aaron Levenstein, *Escape to Freedom: The Story of the International Rescue Committee* (Westport, Conn.: Greenwood Press, 1983), esp. 21–23.

26. *America Meets the Refugee* (New York: National Refugee Service, 1940), 6.

27. See Thorp, *Neilson,* 347.

28. William Allan Neilson, intro. to *We Escaped: Twelve Personal Narratives of the Flight to America* (New York: Macmillan, 1941), vi, vii.

29. Thorp, *Neilson,* 348–49.

30. Ernest Hemingway, letter to the editor, *The Nation,* January 27, 1940.

31. Letty Lynn, "Nearly 100 Anti-Alien Bills Facing Congress," *Binghamton Sun,* March 27, 1940.

32. Ibid.

FIGHTING FASCISM FROM THE VALLEY
Italian Intellectuals in the United States

CHARLES KILLINGER

THE FLIGHT of intellectuals and political activists out of Fascist Italy lasted for the duration of the regime, from the mid-1920s into World War II. The group was diverse, among them Nobel Prize–winning nuclear physicists Enrico Fermi and Emilio Segré, literary scholar Giuseppe Antonio Borgese, diplomat Carlo Sforza, journalist Alberto Tarchiani, conductor Arturo Toscanini, political scientist Mario Einaudi, historian of science Giorgio di Santillana, Nobel laureate virologist Salvador Luria, and historian Gaetano Salvemini. Their impact on American life, though limited in contrast to that of the German exiles, yielded significant results. An examination of the Italian exiles confirms some of the characteristics that scholars have attributed to the general exile community, while at the same time demonstrating that the Italian experience differed in substantial ways.

A useful starting point is to employ the most unadorned meaning of "intellectual" as a man or woman of ideas. Intellectuals were afforded status and deference in Europe, but not as widely in the United States. Italian intellectuals had regularly succeeded in politics, whereas American voters tended to regard intellectuals as lacking in adequate measures of pragmatism and real-world experience. Thus, the success of the legal and political scholar Woodrow Wilson in the presidential elections of 1912 and 1916 provides the exception to the American rule, whereas the rise of the economists F. S. Nitti (in 1919) and Romano Prodi (in 1996) to the office of presidency of the Italian Council of Ministers, though not the rule, is at least much less surprising. On the one hand, American anti-intellectualism, described by Richard Hofstadter as "disrespect for mind,"[1] sometimes subjected the exiles to culture shock and even contributed to a sense of alienation. On the other hand, H. Stuart Hughes, while acknowledging this phenomenon, noted the salutary effects of the American academic environment, including a certain openness. Hughes quoted the refugee philosopher Theodor W. Adorno, who appreciated the absence of "reverential silence in the presence of everything intellectual."[2]

It was Donald Fleming and Bernard Bailyn who in 1969 introduced the now standard term "intellectual migration" to describe the flight of scholars from Europe in the Fascist era.[3] The literature tends to focus on Jews from Nazi Germany—many, like Albert Einstein, Erich Fromm, Walter Gropius, Hannah

Arendt, and Herbert Marcuse, well-known figures. Considerable scholarly attention has been directed to this subject, some quantitative but most descriptive and interpretive, producing a useful, if shapeless, collective portrait.[4] Wilfred McClay argued in a 1994 article that the migration of scholars has not yet found a place in the mainstream of American intellectual history, and may never do so. Criticizing most of the existing work, McClay called for integrated cross-cultural interpretations emphasizing the refugee scholars' impact on American thought.[5] Among the scholars who have contributed to the study of the intellectual exiles is the sociologist Lewis Coser, who, in his 1984 book *Refugee Scholars in America*, differentiated between refugee intellectuals and immigrants.[6] Because of mass immigration, it is particularly important to understand this distinction when dealing with Italian Americans. For the most part, the Italian anti-Fascist intellectuals came to the United States in the 1930s and early 1940s, long after Congress had placed severe restrictions on immigration while at the same time exempting professors.[7] The Italian professors, like Coser's "refugee scholars," were forced to abandon positions in Europe that had afforded them relative comfort and status; they therefore had expectations of the New World that contrasted markedly with those of the immigrants who had arrived in steerage class a generation earlier. Consequently, the methodology applied to studies of mass immigration, often based on a scale of assimilation, are not applicable to the Italian professors and writers, who generally had little interest in becoming Americans.

Although the Italian intellectuals have been relatively neglected and much work remains to be done, enough evidence exists to argue that they played a role, particularly in a political context, that proved quite important in its own right. Fortunately, some participants, among them Salvemini, Sforza, Max Salvadori, and Luigi Sturzo, left first-person accounts.[8] Of special note in documenting the Italian experience are books and articles by Hughes, Salvadori, Vera Modigliani, Laura Fermi, Aldo Garosci, Philip V. Cannistraro, Charles Delzell, and John P. Diggins.[9] Invaluable are the collective memories of participants in the anti-Fascist experience such as Hélène and Michele Cantarella and their children Nelda and Francesco, now being recorded by Ann Blaisdell Tracy.

There are several reasons for the relative neglect of the Italians. First, their numbers were few, and thus their impact on American culture, though substantial, is less obvious. Second, Italy's military-industrial base, the "least of the great powers," limited the reality of Mussolini's threat. Even if Il Duce were as great a tyrant as the exiles claimed, how much real damage could he inflict? Similarly, perhaps as a by-product of cultural stereotyping, the full range of Americans—from the State Department, the FBI, the Roosevelt administra-

tion, and the press to the general public—regarded Italian Fascism and Mussolini as substantially more benign than Nazism and Hitler.[10] Finally, the
intellectuals suffered by being largely relegated to the shadows of obscurity
along with much of modern Italian history. Thus, there was a tendency to
ignore the Italians, particularly in light of the shocking awareness of the Nazi
death camps.

The horrors of Blackshirt violence against the enemies of Mussolini are
now well documented; that they were victimized is beyond question. It is
important, however, to avoid the trap of viewing the Italian exiles merely as
victims. Historians made this mistake in studying slavery in the American
South for years, to the great detriment of a more complete appreciation of the
social and cultural qualities that sustained the slaves in the face of adversity.[11]
To avoid that mistake, historians must attempt to understand the characteristics of the Italian exile experience that enabled the exiles to survive their own
extended forced flight.

THE ITALIAN political exiles called themselves *fuorusciti*, an epithet originally
applied to them contemptuously by the Fascists, but which they then adopted
as a badge of honor and a link to a proud tradition. The story of the political
exile in Italian history is an important one, running through lives and careers
from Dante and Machiavelli through Mazzini.

The historical record of the *fuorusciti* suggests several features that distinguish them from their German counterparts. The Italians began to arrive
earlier in the United States, some in the 1920s, and many brought a clearly
defined anti-Fascist agenda that they shared with cohorts in France, Switzerland, and elsewhere. It is this group of Italian political exiles, and not the
larger group of Italian refugee scholars, that provides the subject for this
inquiry. The distinction may appear superficial since the Italian scholars in
exile, even if not political activists, were generally in agreement in their opposition to the Fascist regime. Mussolini had co-opted much of the community
of Italian scholars through the 1931 Oath of University Professors, signed by
all but about twelve of a total of 1,200.[12] Thus, having pledged their loyalty to
the regime, even if disingenuously, these professors guaranteed their own jobs.
The renowned Neapolitan philosopher Benedetto Croce set the tone for the
"quietist resistance," publishing his influential journal *La Critica* throughout
the Fascist era. Because of the oath, Mussolini found no need to purge university professors, as Hitler did, on the basis of ideology. Not until 1938 did Il
Duce dismiss Jews from Italy's centralized university faculty. Consequently,
the high incidence of anti-Fascism among the Italian exiles is not surprising.

Anti-Fascism had actually begun even before the October 1922 march on

Rome by which Benito Mussolini became prime minister. In the summer of 1924 protest intensified, and when he could no longer tolerate the threat, Il Duce drove many of his critics into exile, where they formed new anti-Fascist groups. Most of the anti-Fascists who remained were relegated to a passive resistance.

Among the early icons of the Italian resistance were Giacomo Matteotti, Giovanni Amendola, Antonio Gramsci, Piero Gobetti, Carlo and Nello Ros-selli, F. S. Nitti, Sturzo, and Salvemini. Of the nine, only Nitti, Sturzo, and Salvemini survived in exile. Amendola and Gobetti died in France of injuries administered earlier by Italian Blackshirt thugs. The Rosselli brothers, proté-gés of Salvemini and politically active sons of a prominent family of Florentine Jews, were ambushed and killed in June 1937 by French Fascists at a resort in Normandy. Nitti settled in Paris, where his home became a meeting place for exiles until the fall of France. Sturzo lived in London until moving to the United States in 1940.[13]

Salvemini, driven from his office at the University of Florence by Black-shirts, was imprisoned, and his lawyer was beaten to death. Threats against his life appeared in the Fascist press, and rumors of his assassination circulated in Tuscany. His friend Ernesto Rossi noted the Fascists' strategic mistake: "This was one of Mussolini's gravest errors: He let slip through his hands his most decisive and intelligent adversary. If Salvemini had remained three months more in Florence, he would have been 'wiped out' in the bloody night of October 4."[14] Salvemini's name had been first on the proscription list the death squads carried in the Florence pogrom the night of October 4, 1925.[15]

AS THE FASCIST regime became a repressive dictatorship in 1926, it forced further changes in the anti-Fascist movement, accelerating the exodus of dis-senters. The best-known socialists, republicans, and communists fled for their safety and for the purpose of continuing their opposition. Filippo Turati, Giuseppe Modigliani, and Claudio Treves, all prominent socialists, departed for Paris, while the republicans Cipriano Facchinetti, Egidio Reale, and Ran-dolfo Pacciardi escaped to the Swiss Ticino. These *fuorusciti* joined the earlier exiles to form the backbone of the exiled anti-Fascist movement.[16]

The Wall Street collapse of 1929 transformed the ranks of exiled anti-Fascism just as it changed most everything. For the two previous years, *fuorus-citi* of the democratic parties had operated under a coalition known as the Concentrazione Antifascista. Turati and Pietro Nenni led the Concentration from its headquarters in Paris, while Claudio Treves edited its journal, *La Libertà*.

The major development in the exiles' movement in this period was the formation in 1929 of Giustizia e Libertà (GL), an organization that would challenge the Concentration and the Italian Communist Party (PCI) for the support of Italians abroad. After his bold escape from imprisonment on the island of Lipari, Carlo Rosselli would emerge as the moving spirit behind GL and would make it the most dynamic of the anti-Fascist organizations.

Rosselli favored a strategy of "revolutionary action," of bold gestures designed to galvanize world opinion. The "Giellisti," as they called themselves, operated both inside and outside Italy, embracing a broad spectrum of noncommunist opposition. As dramatic as were its heroic gestures, GL's real contribution to the anti-Fascist movement was to maintain a covert operation inside Italy that exploited each event. The Giellisti circulated pamphlets advocating "revolutionary agitation" to take advantage of the spreading depression. Police raided GL operations in Milan and Turin, driving the leadership to join Rosselli in Paris.

In 1930 Rosselli began to publish the *Quaderni di Giustizia e Libertà*, in which he spelled out GL's "revolutionary program": a revolution that would empower local committees, creating a decentralized socialist state within a disarmed, federated Europe. Rosselli's movement toward socialism alienated GL's more traditional liberals and at the same time threatened the Italian Socialist Party (PSI). And in offering a specific, grassroots program with a clandestine organization in place inside the country, Rosselli challenged the communists as well.[17]

The rise of Adolf Hitler to power in 1933 dispatched a sense of urgency through the ranks of Italian anti-Fascism. Rosselli warned that the spread of Fascism had brought Europe to the brink of war. He urged that anti-Fascists quickly join forces to win the support of all democratic elements in a revolution in both Italy and Germany. The PSI regarded Rosselli's new emphasis as unwarranted aggression, and demanded that the Concentration retaliate. GL pulled out of the Concentration, which dissolved shortly thereafter.

Meanwhile, Hitler's ascent forced communists and socialists toward a "Popular Front" strategy. The PCI and PSI eventually signed a series of agreements in 1934, made easier by the collapse of the Concentration. By mid-1934, Giustizia e Libertà was the only significant anti-Fascist organization to rival the new communist-socialist front in an era when Mussolini's foreign policy would suddenly attract worldwide attention. In response, Salvemini, with the help of Roberto Bolaffio and several others, organized a North American GL federation.[18]

A new phase of anti-Fascism developed in the fall of 1935, when Italian troops invaded Ethiopia. Patriotic support from Italians around the globe overwhelmed the feeble opposition. Nonetheless, anti-Fascists saw an opportunity to mobilize international forces against Il Duce's adventurism.

GL had been damaged by Rosselli's intellectual wanderings in its press, defections by Tarchiani and Emilio Lussu (a militant Sardinian republican and GL founder), and the arrests and sentencing of the GL leadership in Turin. Consequently GL was isolated when the social-communists called a congress in Brussels. In a show of solidarity, Italian émigrés of virtually every group condemned Mussolini as the aggressor and endorsed League of Nations sanctions. Rosselli opposed sanctions, trying unsuccessfully to persuade the PCI to join a propaganda campaign inside Italy.

In May 1936 Italian armies took Addis Ababa, and Il Duce triumphantly proclaimed King Victor Emmanuel III emperor of Ethiopia, leading to a surge in Mussolini's popularity. In July the League removed its sanctions. The anti-Fascist future appeared bleak.

Two months after the Ethiopian war, civil war erupted in Spain. Mussolini's decision to support General Franco's nationalist-fascist-clerical armies presented Italian anti-Fascist forces with their greatest challenge to date. By the fall of 1936, the Spanish Loyalist government had shifted to the left, bringing communists into the cabinet. At the same time, anarcho-syndicalists organized an autonomous Catalan government in Barcelona, as bitterly opposed to the communists as to Franco.[19]

The *fuorusciti* favored intervention against Franco's forces but disagreed as to which group to support. Carlo Rosselli threw GL's support to the anarchists of Barcelona, while Italian social-communists backed the Loyalists, thus isolating Rosselli from all other anti-Franco forces. The social-communists picked the Republican Pacciardi to command a Garibaldi Battalion. Both Rosselli's Italian column, primarily anarchists, and the communist brigades enjoyed some success. Rosselli, however, failed to match the social-communists, finding little support for his "Oggi in Spagna, domani in Italia!" (Today in Spain, tomorrow in Italy) campaign. Rosselli resigned his command after a defeat and, ill with phlebitis, returned to Paris to campaign in the press. Acting in Rosselli's stead, Aldo Garosci also failed to mobilize a successful effort.

In March, Mussolini's "volunteers" attacked the Garibaldi Battalion at Guadalajara in a monumental battle. Pacciardi heroically returned from leave to lead the victory. The Battle of Guadalajara, reported in newspapers around the globe, became the greatest triumph of the *fuorusciti* in the entire anti-Fascist campaign. But their celebration was shattered by internal discord. A bloody coup in Barcelona decimated anarchist opposition and killed two leaders, Camillo Berneri and Giovanni Barbieri.[20]

Political and military setbacks led Rosselli to pursue collaboration with the PCI. Meanwhile, his "Today in Spain, tomorrow in Italy!" broadcasts infuriated Il Duce. In June 1937, Carlo and his brother Nello were ambushed and stabbed to death by French Fascist Cagoulards at the resort of Bagnoles de l'Orne. Back in Spain, Pacciardi resigned his command in protest against the Stalinists and returned to Paris with Nenni to take up Rosselli's work. But in January 1939, Loyalist resistance collapsed and the communist leader Palmiro Togliatti barely escaped. In all, possibly 3,000 *fuorusciti* fought against Franco's forces. Of the total, 2,600 were casualties, a startling rate of 86 percent.[21]

The Spanish civil war had provided a defining moment for the anti-Fascists. They had taken their cause to the battlefield, only to be frustrated by ideological conflict and superior international force. It was both a bitter lesson and a dress rehearsal for the armed resistance in Italy. The PCI, in particular, had learned the benefits of Stalinist organization.

IT IS THIS intense commitment of the Italians to anti-Fascist activism—tested in battle, unable to shake the tradition of partisan infighting, faltering and reemerging—that sets them apart from the larger group of the "dispossessed." It seems apparent that some Italians such as Borgese and Salvemini traded scholarly productivity for politically driven attacks on the Fascist regime.[22] Irrespective of the degree of professional success in exile, however, the Italians remained highly politicized and focused on a European agenda—the restoration of freedom in Italy. This single-minded focus gave them a sense of purpose that proved invaluable in the face of enduring hardship.

The campaign of the anti-Fascist exiles in the United States was elevated in importance by the context in which they worked. They correctly anticipated a strong U.S. role in determining the future of Italy, and they feared that Washington would tolerate Mussolini or, failing that, an Italian kingdom governed by his Fascist collaborators. The overarching goal of the *fuorusciti* was to force their republican, secular Italian program on the Allies, who would surely dictate terms of peace and postwar settlements. Furthermore, the sheer size of the Italian American immigrant community, inundated by a steady flow of Fascist propaganda, magnified the importance of the anti-Fascist campaign.

Throughout their two decades of campaigning, the exiled anti-Fascists faced serious challenges. Repeatedly encountering material and spiritual anguish as they fled from Paris to Marseilles to New York, the exiles now confronted even greater political barriers. They faced the powerful machines of Fascist propaganda and organization.[23] And, at every rally, there were the ubiquitous Fascist spies.[24] If they had the good fortune to find a teaching job, they soon discovered Fascist sympathizers on campus. Philo-Fascists appeared in almost every academic institution, particularly in departments of Italian language and literature—at Harvard, at Columbia, and at Smith College. Furthermore, the exiles soon came face to face with the sobering reality of Mussolini's popularity in Italian America.[25] And, finally, they realized that both the Amer-

ican government and the American public would be loath to accept what the
exiles believed to be the awful truth about Fascist Italy. None of these problems, however, would stop the *fuorusciti*, who would campaign relentlessly even
beyond the fall of the Fascist state.

GAETANO SALVEMINI, like many of the exiles, had lived his life on the run.
Released from prison on a technicality, he fled across the Alps using a forged
passport, assisted by former students.[26] The Italian government seized his
property, including the rights to future royalties from his books. He truly was
"dispossessed." From 1925 until 1933, lecturing in London and Paris, he managed to support himself and his wife.[27] Eventually he was hired at Harvard,
settled in Cambridge, Massachusetts, and taught at Harvard through the 1930s
and 1940s while leading a vigorous anti-Fascist campaign. Hughes has compared Salvemini to the German exile social scientist Franz Neumann in the
"verve with which [both] attacked the fascist system."[28] It was around the
magnetic and relentless Salvemini and a few others that Italian anti-Fascists
would rally in the United States.

Hitler's invasion of Poland on September 1, 1939, infused the American
exiles with a sense of urgency. Three weeks later Salvemini joined Roberto
Bolaffio, Lionello Venturi, Renato Poggioli, and Michele and Hélène Cantarella at the Cantarellas' house on the Smith College campus in Northampton,
Massachusetts, to create a new anti-Fascist organization named after the Italian republican patriot Giuseppe Mazzini. The founders agreed to mount a
vigorous campaign to mobilize the American public and American policy
makers against totalitarianism, monarchism, and clericalism, with a particular
eye toward the postwar reconstruction of a democratic Italy. Three weeks later
at Venturi's apartment in New York City, the Mazzini Society formalized its
charter. Salvemini, Borgese, and Venturi were selected as an executive council,
with Poggioli as interim coordinator.[29] Centered in the Northeast, the Mazzini
Society would spread through a number of North American cities and to
Mexico and South America. With membership exceeding one thousand by
mid-1941, it would remain throughout the war the most important anti-Fascist
organization outside Italy.[30]

Although Salvemini provided the Mazzini Society with its most distinguished European intellectual, it was Hélène and Michele Cantarella who contributed steady organizational grit, editorial and linguistic expertise, and enormous personal support and comfort to the foot soldiers of the anti-Fascist
movement.

Smith College president William Allan Neilson hired Michele Cantarella in
1929, just seven years after he had arrived in Boston from Italy with his family,

unable to tolerate Fascism after serving as an officer with the Italian Alpine Corps in World War I. In the interim, Cantarella had swept floors at the Jordan Marsh department store, sold coal and life insurance to immigrants, designed scarves for a store on Boylston Street—all while studying English, tutoring in Italian, and completing a graduate degree at Boston University. In that same year, Michele and Hélène married, and Hélène returned from teaching at Hollins College in Virginia to take a position on the French faculty at Smith.[31]

Smith College, Harvard University, and the New School for Social Research readily employed Italian scholars, and in doing so provided what was often missing among the exiles—a critical mass of familiar culture and invigorating intellect.[32] The research clearly indicates that these were important factors in adjustment and productivity, and where they were missing, the exiles suffered devastating results.[33]

Although colleges and universities could hire the exiles, they could not fill the enormous vacuum in their lives. This is where the Cantarellas made one of their greatest contributions, by affording a safe haven between the more combative cities (anti-Fascists were facing hand-to-hand combat from the *fasci* in New York City in the 1920s).[34] Consequently, Northampton, ideally located on the rail lines from both Boston and New York, became the fulcrum of an anti-Fascist axis. New York featured a full range of Italian anti-Fascists from anarchists to communists, while in Boston the anarchist Aldino Felicani provided an anti-Fascist rallying point with his newspaper *Controcorrente*. From the 1930s through World War II, the Cantarella house in Northampton was an important center of anti-Fascist enterprise, overshadowed only by New York, Boston, and a few other urban centers.

It was in Northampton that the exiles composed and mailed to Italy anti-Fascist propaganda, sometimes concealed in innocuous packages, often eluding Italian censors; subscribed to official Fascist journals so as to criticize the regime based on its own statistics; and gathered on Belmont Avenue as Salvemini in his one wrinkled suit arrived by train from Boston for the weekend, occasionally accompanied by the Harvard church historian Giorgio La Piana.[35]

For a few of the most active years, anti-Fascists on the Smith faculty provided great energy: the literary critic Poggioli, before he moved on to Brown University and then Harvard; Borgese, who married Thomas Mann's daughter Elisabeth and sometimes returned even after his departure for the University of Chicago; and the underground leader Max Salvadori. Salvadori's Anglo-Italian heritage rendered him an ideal liaison between the Allies and the Italian underground. Having fled Italy with his father at age sixteen, he met the leaders of GL in Paris in 1929—Salvemini, Rosselli, Tarchiani, Lussu, and others—and on their behalf returned to Italy to assist in organizing the Roman underground for GL. After earning his Ph.D. at the University of Rome, Salvadori was arrested in 1932 and sent to prison and *confino* (internment). Upon his release, he traveled to East Africa, Spain, and, at the invitation of Salvemini, to the United States. After splitting with GL in 1937 over its leftward shift, Salvadori returned to the United States to take a faculty position at Saint Lawrence University in Canton, New York. In 1943 he entered the British Special Forces. In that capacity he accompanied the Allied invasion at Salerno and was injured in the Anzio invasion. In the fall of 1944 the Allies parachuted Salvadori behind German lines as a liaison officer with the northern Italian Resistance.[36] Salvadori joined the Smith faculty soon after the war and became a close, lifelong associate of Michele and Hélène Cantarella.

On regular visits to the Cantarellas throughout the 1930s, Salvemini wrote exposés of Mussolini's failed economic experiments and his brutal repression, facts largely unknown in the United States because Il Duce had duped American columnists and provided free use of the Atlantic cable to pro-Fascist Italian-language newspapers in the United States. Generously, Hélène Cantarella translated and polished Salvemini's articles for the *New Republic*, the *Nation*, and other journals—articles that reached prolific proportions of more than two per week throughout the entire decade of the 1930s.[37] And in the Cantarella home, all of the exiles could find among kindred spirits respite from a world that had stripped them of their careers, their livelihood, and their legal rights but had failed to wound their courage or their commitment to destroying Fascism.[38]

IN 1939 AND 1940 the influx of political exiles from Italy accelerated. Mussolini's anti-Semitic policies, implemented in the Manifesto of Fascist Racism in July 1938, produced a flood of Italian Jewish exiles, many of whom sought refuge in New York in 1939.[39] The fall of France brought another wave, including many veterans of the underground movement. By then the Mazzini Society had emerged as the dominant anti-Fascist exile organization of its day.[40]

The new wave of exiles invigorated the Mazzini Society with a wealth of talent and experience, thus enabling the group to accelerate its campaign and make a strong bid to influence American opinion and U.S. policy. Of note were Count Sforza, pre-Fascist minister of foreign affairs, who had negotiated the Treaty of Rapallo; Tarchiani and Alberto Cianca, both well-known journalists from the Milanese daily *Corriere della Sera*; Luigi Sturzo, former founder of the Partito Populare Italiano, the Catholic reform party; and the Spanish civil war hero Randolfo Pacciardi.[41] The harrowing stories told by Sforza and Tarchiani inspired a renewed effort. Salvemini joined the Italian Emergency Rescue Committee (IERC), which attempted to raise transportation money for the refugees and persuade the American government to admit them. The IERC succeeded in assisting hundreds of Italian anti-Fascists to escape France. Many moved to New York, transplanting the core of the external resistance movement across the Atlantic.[42]

In developing a diversified program to influence opinion on the "Italian question," however, the Mazzini encountered powerful forces that were destined to reshape the movement. Among the most influential members of the society was Max Ascoli, a former law professor who had been purged from his teaching job at the University of Cagliari and jailed. Ascoli found asylum in the United States through a Rockefeller Foundation fellowship in 1931 and joined the faculty at the New School for Social Research, the "University in Exile," in 1933. Husband of the heir to the Sears fortune, Marion Rosenwald, and benefactor of the New School, Ascoli maintained good relations with the Department of State and with the Roosevelt administration.[43] From the start, by advocating a pro-American strategy, Ascoli competed for intellectual dominance of the Mazzini Society with Salvemini, the acknowledged head of the exiles' faction.[44]

Having struggled in Paris, Marseilles, London, Geneva, and in the clandestine movement inside Italy, the anti-Fascist exiles had faced infiltrators, assassins, and *confino*. Weathered as they were, however, nothing had prepared them for one challenge they would face upon arrival in New York: how to win the hearts and minds of Little Italy. Not surprisingly, they found themselves poorly prepared for this task. By then the Mazzini Society had emerged as the dominant anti-Fascist exile organization of its day.

It was Hitler's aggression as much as anything else that altered the course of anti-Fascism and, with it, the direction of the Mazzini Society and the lives of the refugee intellectuals. In the spring of 1940, as speculation grew that Mussolini would enter the war, the society issued its first manifesto, sounding a familiar theme: the need to "distinguish between love of Italy and support of Fascism."[45]

Two weeks later, Mussolini's invasion of France forced further changes. When FDR bitterly labeled the invasion a "stab in the back," American attitudes—including the attitude of Italian Americans—and U.S. policy toward Fascism all changed dramatically.[46] This jolt prompted an emergency session in New York at which the Mazzini Society reorganized and revised its charter, explicitly pledging itself to the ideals of the U.S. Constitution. More significantly, Ascoli, later to become dean of the New School, took the reins of the organization.

With Ascoli's rise to power, the Mazzini Society now inherited his connections to American liberals and to the U.S. government. In turn, the society moved markedly toward an American emphasis. The implications were enormous. With the pressures of war now weighing on the group, Ascoli, with the endorsement of Sumner Welles and Adolph Berle, assured the group's absolute loyalty to the U.S. government, while at the same time committing to expansion by recruiting large numbers of Italian Americans.[47]

The group reached a watershed in the spring and summer of 1940. Once a small band of exiled European intellectuals, the Mazzini Society now reshaped itself to become an American mass movement—if a hyphenated one. The ultimate impact was that, in the process, the Mazzini Society would lose both its original zealous anti-Fascism and its most fervent anti-Fascists.

The logic here seems clear. It became virtually impossible to follow the Ascoli plan without accepting the influence and membership of some power brokers in the Italian American community who lacked fervor for the anti-Fascist cause. In building bridges to the Italian American power structure, Ascoli accepted a contingent of socialists and union leaders—especially Luigi Antonini, president of Local 89 of the ILGWU—who pursued their own agendas and clashed regularly with former exiled leaders such as Cianca, Tarchiani, and Venturi.[48] It was Ascoli who, by the sheer force of intellect and political efficacy, managed to reconcile the two factions, at least for a while. But by linking the Mazzini Society to official U.S. goals, Ascoli alienated the exiles, especially Salvemini, and further buried their original campaign in obscurity.[49] Salvemini's fear—and the basis for his objection to Ascoli's linkage to Washington—was his belief that FDR was going to give Churchill free rein in postwar Italy. Along with Churchill would come his conservative agenda, including support for the continuation of the monarchy and many of the elements that had championed Mussolini for twenty years.[50]

In addition to their efforts to connect with the *prominenti* (the successful businessmen and politicians who dominated the Italian American communities) and the community-based fraternal groups, the Mazzini faced a more pervasive challenge: to develop a propaganda campaign to reach the Italian American masses. The political importance of Little Italy had been recognized not only by the Roosevelt administration but also by Italian foreign minister Dino Grandi, who acknowledged Italian America's potential for "powerful influence" on U.S. policy.[51] Thus the Mazzini campaign would be contested at every turn.

At the same time, in developing a diversified program to influence opinion on the "Italian question," the Mazzini encountered other powerful forces that were destined to reshape the movement. The exiles who had founded the movement understood the extent to which Italians in the diaspora had developed in the United States a heightened sense of national pride, particularly in response to the discrimination they had faced as immigrants. Although some mistook national pride for Fascism, Sturzo noted that "their philo-Fascism was really nationalism with a Fascist label."[52] Similarly, Max Salvadori observed, "In Italy they had never been Italians, but in America they became Italian nationalists."[53] Salvemini believed that no more than 5 percent of Italian Americans were "out and out Fascists,"[54] a number that may, in fact, be exaggerated. Nevertheless, overwhelming numbers took pride in Mussolini, particularly after the Ethiopian war. Consequently, in denouncing Mussolini and his regime, exiles ran the risk of being labeled anti-Italian.

The primary obstacles to the anti-Fascist exiles' efforts were the *prominenti*, of whom the most imposing was Generoso Pope—favorite of Mussolini, millionaire construction magnate, publisher of the largest Italian-language newspaper in the United States (*Il Progresso Italo-Americano*, circulation in excess of eighty thousand), and chair of the Italian section of the Democratic National Committee. Despite an effort in 1941 to gain control of *Il Progresso*—an intrepid campaign that took them to the White House—Ascoli and Sforza failed to stop Pope.[55]

In the fall of 1941, Pope came out against the Axis powers, a move that began a trend among the "pre–Pearl Harbor Fascists." Soon, many former supporters of Il Duce had emerged as leading voices on the "Italian question." For the exiles, the failed campaign against Pope and the subsequent political scrambling among the *prominenti* served as a sobering reminder of the severe limits in which they worked, especially when it came to influencing the Roosevelt administration.

The Japanese attack on Pearl Harbor provided an even greater shock to the exiles than had Mussolini's invasion of France. Both through the press and inside the State Department, the Mazzini Society sounded a persistent theme: Washington must remove Italians in the United States from "enemy alien" status, which had proved especially threatening to the exiles, most of whom remained resident aliens in the United States.[56] Finally, on Columbus Day 1942, Attorney General Francis Biddle announced the lifting of "enemy" status.[57]

IRONICALLY, WHILE the entry of the United States into the war placed the Mazzini Society more squarely in line with U.S. policy, it made the task of the exiles both more important and more complex. Salvemini's long-held belief that the United States would weigh heavily in the future of Italy had now become a reality. Thus the stakes were much higher with respect to issues such as the future of the monarchy and the Catholic Church in Italy, not to mention the possibility of Fascism without Mussolini.

At the same time, the exiles now saw *prominenti* cannily changing their stripes. As the Roosevelt administration sought Italian Americans who could support the war effort, they turned to former philo-Fascists. In an editorial in *Nazioni Unite*, the Mazzini Society newspaper, Tarchiani sounded this very theme: "Little by little these people—Pope and the Sons of Italy at the head— have arrogated to themselves the right of . . . impersonating anti-fascist senti- ments. . . . And they have found among certain Washington officials . . . the most powerful support for their maneuver."[58] Thus, even though the Mazzini Society occupied the enviable position of being the only organized anti-Fascist group in the United States at this critical moment, the exiles saw their influ- ence waning.

Sensing the severity of the Mazzini Society's crisis, Tarchiani called for a national convention in June 1942. For two days, several hundred members met in New York and candidly debated the group's future in an atmosphere of growing tension. In his presidential speech, Ascoli attempted to rally the mem- bership behind his American plan, while Salvemini, in absentia, presented his own set of principles, in line with the exiles' purposes. The Ascoli plan was adopted almost in its entirety by the society's political committee.[59]

One issue arose to dominate the convention: the question of Communist Party membership. After a contentious floor debate, the convention adopted the Political Committee's anticommunist, pro-American proposal by almost three to one. Ascoli was reelected president, and labor leaders (Frank Bellanca president, Umberto Gualtieri treasurer) gained greater control of the Mazzini Society's executive committee and took over the funding. Several founders, including Salvemini and Lionello Venturi, had now left.[60]

The pivotal events of 1943 sealed the fate of the anti-Fascist exiles. In a letter to Adolph Berle, Ascoli explained, "I wanted to make [the Mazzini Society] an organ of unity among decent liberal Italian Americans, an organ whose advice would be useful to those who formulate U.S. policies for the Italians in Italy or in the Americas. Of course, I failed." He then noted with contempt that U.S. government agencies now were taking advice from the "'*Salon des Refusés*' of the Mazzini Society," the very forces the exiles had excluded.[61] Ironically, As- coli's own pro-American policy had handed the exiles' group to the *prominenti*.

Beginning with the Allied invasion of Sicily in July 1943, a number of exiles left the United States to resume a role in Italian political life. By that time, a food importer and socialist politician from Buffalo, James Battistoni, had taken the reins of the Mazzini Society, which now functioned primarily as an auxiliary of the New York Italian labor unions.[62] For the final years of the war, the group turned its attention to such matters as sponsoring a relief campaign for Italians and virtually abandoned the exiles' original campaign to convert Italian Americans to anti-Fascism.

By the fall of 1943, the Office of Strategic Services (OSS) identified the dominant American group organized to campaign for Italian interests as the "Pecora Committee," a virtual who's who of *prominenti*. Among them were Pope, Antonini, and the banker A. P. Giannini.[63] The OSS also noted that Antonini, who they said had "recently captured control of the Mazzini Society," was now cooperating with "former pro-Fascists."[64] This proved a devastating realization to the anti-Fascist exiles who had observed Antonini's meteoric rise to power in the Mazzini Society. The editors of *Nazione Unite*, while providing news from the war front, carried on several important editorial campaigns, especially the time-honored effort to distinguish between Italians and Fascism, and a new appeal to protect Italian territorial integrity at war's end. But the exiles' campaign in Little Italy was over.[65]

IN BOTH its successes and failures, the anti-Fascist campaign also served to sustain the exiles through an extended period of great difficulties. Much of the credit for maintaining that campaign goes to the Cantarellas and their Northampton haven. Their contribution was part of the broader role played by colleges and universities that sheltered the exiles and thereby met a number of important needs.

H. Stuart Hughes noted the distinctive tendency of Italians to "linger" on the European continent, developing an Italian culture-in-exile.[66] What they had known in Paris, London, and Geneva, the Italian exiles now restructured in the United States, sometimes assembling in New York or Boston, sometimes at Smith and other academic centers. The restructuring of Italian communities provided a safety net that protected against the worst hardships of refugee life. It was the support of this tightly knit group of anti-Fascist friends in the Northeast, who found Northampton a convenient hub, which sustained and nurtured them as well as their political campaign. This phenomenon was part of the general "reconstruction of social networks" among the European refugees, more typical of the later Jewish migration. In contrast, Italian scholars were often forced to make their adjustments "with very little sympathy from abroad."[67] But not in western Massachusetts, largely because the members of the Mazzini group were the beneficiaries of the great and good friendship of the Cantarellas and their colleagues among the small band of exiles.

Employment also proved critical, and on some occasions protected the exiles against being marginalized. A refugee with an international reputation, such as Albert Einstein, Thomas Mann, or Kurt Goedel, usually found a job at a well-known institution. Most scholars, however, could not find employment, and thus suffered debilitating losses of status and prestige. In his reflective memoir *From Berlin to Berkeley*, Reinhard Bendix invokes his father's poignant poem "The Lost Status:

> I live now, torn away from my life's work,
> a nameless shadow life I never knew,
> in which there is no struggle and no striving
> And no one cares to know what work I do.
> . . . .
> Accepting favors never was my aim—
> I feel I need to hang my head in shame.[68]

In the case of Salvemini, a Harvard position was the key to success. Referring particularly to the Widener Library, he wrote: "In the British Museum I thought I had found paradise. But the true paradise I discovered at Harvard."[69] Smith College provided a similar haven, not only for Hans Kohn and Felix Gilbert but for Renato Poggioli and Giuseppe Antonio Borgese as well.

Income was also a key. Because market conditions in higher education were dismal during the Great Depression, employment did not guarantee financial stability. Harvard paid Salvemini only $2,000 per year during the 1930s. By comparison, Columbia paid Béla Bartók $3,000 and Enrico Fermi $8,500 to $9,000.[70] Nevertheless, by living frugally, Salvemini, Borgese, Venturi, Poggioli, and the others escaped the humiliation and near starvation suffered by many exiles, a situation described graphically by Anthony Heilbut:

> In exile they assumed the haunted look of people who would barter any goods for a real passport to safety. Scurrying from place to place, "changing one's nationality almost as often as one changed one's shoes," they became adept at subterfuge and chicanery. Law-abiding citizens, now no longer citizens, became cunning outlaws, smuggling currency, property and people across the borders. Established members of the community became men on the run after that same community had banished them, denied them legal protection granted common criminals.[71]

The literature on the intellectual migration attributes the general lack of success among these scholars to frustration generated by institutional hostility and their inability to adjust. Many experienced "geographical and emotional displacement," which frequently "provided the shock that has set the mind off its familiar course."[72] Occasionally this proved stimulating, but more often it drained creativity. In contrast, the Italians at Smith defied this trend and, in a hospitable environment, thrived; moreover, by providing a refuge for exiles who, like Salvemini, were never fully accepted at their home institutions, the Cantarellas embraced the broader community and helped to overcome this serious obstacle.[73] Again, absence of community contributed to marginalization.[74]

IT IS CLEAR that the Northampton connection proved an ideal, sustaining force for a number of Italian exiles, and in the process produced the kind of subculture that Heilbut and others found to be nurturing. But, in the final analysis, the question remains: How important was their work?

There is no doubt that the exiles greatly improved the formal study of Italian history, culture, and language at American institutions of higher education, providing much-needed expertise.[75] In that respect, three of the exiles made particularly important contributions. Salvemini left an indelible mark on the study of Italian history in the United States. Before 1930, Italian studies at American universities (Harvard included) had focused on language, arts, and literature. The critical, systematic inquiry into modern Italy began only in the Fascist era, a phenomenon Hughes attributes largely to Salvemini.[76] Renato Poggioli's highly original interpretations, particularly in his *Theory of the Avant-Garde*, exercised a major impact on the fields of art history and literary criticism. Poggioli both influenced and transcended the study of Italian culture. In exploring the literature of his land of origin, the Florentine writer ranged widely through Dante, futurism, and Crocean idealism.[77] At the same time, Poggioli interpreted a vast range of world literature and art, focusing successively on Slavic (especially Russian) and Spanish writers and cubist painters, and provocatively integrated psychological and sociological perspectives into his literary analysis.[78] In addition to his influence on American thought, Poggioli was instrumental in creating a department of comparative literature at Harvard. At the same time, Giuseppe Borgese, like Salvemini, condemned the Fascist state, the cultural and historical dimensions of which he described in *Goliath* as a barbarian regime of "hollowness and nil."[79] And, like Poggioli, Borgese exerted an influence as novelist, poet, and scholar that reached well beyond Italian issues, influencing the way in which literary critics viewed their world in general.[80]

In politics, which was the exiles' passion, the answers are more elusive. Before the end of World War II the unions had taken over the Mazzini Society, and Italian American politicians had seized the initiative within the Roosevelt administration. Clearly, the exiles enjoyed little success influencing opinion in Little Italy or mobilizing Italian Americans behind their republican, secular agenda. In the end, it could be said, and not surprisingly so, that the Italian American community had proved durable and its culture and institutions resilient. In a certain sense, these European intellectuals had found it easier to influence national politics in liberal Italy, dominated as it had been by a narrow leadership class, than to induce change at the grassroots level in the Italian neighborhoods of the United States.

Nevertheless, there is little doubt about this point: the ability of the anti-Fascist exiles to sustain their campaign in a new and otherwise hostile environment allowed them to exercise substantial influence. They provoked serious debate about the future of Italy, both in the press and in the Roosevelt administration. And even though they failed to achieve their loftiest goals, they altered the parameters of American policy on postwar Italy. Certainly they made important headway in pushing the "Italian question" onto the U.S. agenda. As Salvemini had been insisting all along, in the critical months of Allied occupation, the United States demanded a democratic system in which the Italian people would determine their own political future.

Finally, in an existential sense, they fought a courageous battle against great odds on behalf of laudable human values. In her tribute to G. A. Borgese, Hélène Cantarella wrote of them all, "Unheralded, unknown in this country, no longer in the first flush of their youth, speaking little or no English, virtually without funds, confronted by what might have seemed insurmountable odds, they faced expatriation with singular courage, fortitude and gallantry."[81] It is most notably in this context that President Neilson, the Cantarellas, and Smith College each made an indispensable contribution.

Notes

1. Richard Hofstadter, *Anti-intellectualism in American Life* (New York: Knopf, 1966), 3.

2. H. Stuart Hughes, *The Sea Change* (New York: Harper and Row, 1975), 3–4.

3. Donald Fleming and Bernard Bailyn, eds., *The Intellectual Migration* (Cambridge: Harvard University Press, 1969).

4. Maurice Davie, *Refugees in America* (New York: Harper and Brothers, 1947); Stephen Duggan and Betty Drury, *The Rescue of Science and Learning* (New York: Macmillan, 1948); Rex W. Crawford, ed., *The European Scholar in America* (Philadelphia: University of Pennsylvania Press, 1953); Norman Bentwich, *The Rescue and Achievement of Refugee Scholars* (The Hague: Martinus Nijhoff, 1953); Donald P. Kent. *The Refugee Intellectual* (New York: Columbia University Press, 1953); Franz L. Neumann, ed., *The Cultural Migration* (Philadelphia: University of Pennsylvania Press, 1953); Robert Boyers, ed., *The Legacy of German Refugee Intellectuals* (New York: Schocken Books, 1972); Reinhard Bendix, *From Berlin to Berkeley* (New Brunswick, N.J.: Transaction, 1976); Jarrell C. Jackman and Carla M. Borden, eds., *The Muses Flee Hitler* (Washington, D.C.: Smithsonian Institution, 1983); Anthony Heilbut, *Exiled in Paradise* (New York: Viking, 1983); John R. Taylor, *Strangers in Paradise* (New York: Henry Holt, 1983); Michael R. Marrus, *The Unwanted* (New York: Oxford University Press, 1985); Felix Gilbert, *A European Past* (New York: W. W. Norton, 1988); Reinhard Bendix, "Intellectual Emigration from Hitler's Germany," *Society* 27 (March–April 1990): 51–58; Catherine Epstein, *A Past Renewed* (Cambridge: Cambridge University Press, 1993); Claus-Dieter Krohn, *Intellectuals in Exile*, trans. Rita Kimber and Robert Kimber (Amherst: University of Massachusetts Press, 1993); Mark M. Anderson, ed., *Hitler's Exiles* (New York: New Press, 1998).

5. Wilfred M. McClay, "Historical Research on the Refugee Intellectuals," *International Journal of Politics, Culture and Society* 7, no. 3 (Spring 1994): 513–24.

6. Lewis Coser, *Refugee Scholars in America* (New Haven: Yale University Press, 1984).

7. Johnson-Reed Act (Immigration Act of 1924), *United States Statutes at Large*, 68th Cong., sess. 1, vol. 43, pt. 1 (1923–25), 155.

8. Gaetano Salvemini, *Memorie di un fuoruscito* (Milan: Feltrinelli, 1960); Carlo Sforza, *L'Italia alle soglie dell'Europa* (Milan: Rizzoli, 1947); Max Salvadori, *The Labour and the Wounds* (London: Pall Mall, 1958); idem, *Resistenza ed azione* (Bari: Laterza, 1961); idem, "Antifascisti italiani negli Stati Uniti," in *Atti del congresso internazionale di storia americana* (Genoa: Tilgher, 1978); Luigi Sturzo, *La mia battaglia da New York* (Milan: Garzanti, 1949); Randolfo Pacciardi, "Gaetano Salvemini il grande esule," *Archivio Trimestrale* (July–December 1982): 614–19.

9. Hughes, *Sea Change*; Vera Modigliani, *Esilio* (Milan: Nuova editore, 1946); Salvadori, *Resistenza ed azione* and *The Labour and the Wounds*; Laura Fermi, *Illustrious Immigrants* (Chicago: University of Chicago Press, 1968); Charles Delzell, *Mussolini's Enemies* (Princeton: Princeton University Press, 1961); Aldo Garosci, *Storia dei fuorusciti* (Bari: Laterza, 1953); Philip V. Cannistraro, "Understanding America," and Spencer Di Scala, "Salvemini in the United States" in *Italian Socialism*, ed. Spencer Di Scala, (Amherst: University of Massachusetts Press, 1996), 177–82 and 167–76; John P. Diggins, *Mussolini and Fascism* (Princeton: Princeton University Press, 1972). See also James E. Miller, "Carlo Sforza e l'evoluzione della politica americana verso l'Italia, 1940–1943," *Storia contemporanea* 7, no. 4 (July 1976): 825–53; Antonio Varsori, *Gli alleati e l'emigrazione democratica anifascista (1940–1943)* (Florence: Laterza, 1982); idem, "La politica inglese e il conte Sforza (1940–1943)," *Rivista di studi politici internazionali* 43, no. 1 (January–March 1976): 31–57; Adriana Dadà, "Contributo metodologico per una storia dell'emigrazione e dell'antifascismo italiano negli Stati Uniti," *Annali dell'Istituto di Storia* (University of Florence) 1 (1979): 197–218; Charles Killinger, "Salvemini at Harvard: A Case Study in the Intellectual Migration," in *Italian Americans: The Search for a Usable Past*, ed. Richard N. Juliani and Philip V. Cannistraro (New York: American Italian Historical Association, 1989).

10. Diggins, *Mussolini and Fascism*.

11. See, for example, the comments of Gary Nash, *Red, White & Black* (Englewood Cliffs, N.J.: Prentice-Hall, 1992), 3.

12. Monte S. Finkelstein, "University Oath," in *Historical Dictionary of Fascist Italy*, ed. Philip V. Cannistraro (Westport, Conn.: Greenwood Press, 1982), 557; Renzo De Felice, *Mussolini il Duce* (Turin: Einaudi, 1974); Delzell, *Mussolini's Enemies*; Hughes, *Sea Change*, 4–5. Among the dissenters were two prominent anti-Fascists who participated in the Mazzini Society, Borgese and Venturi.

13. Garosci, *Storia dei fuorusciti*.

14. Ernesto Rossi, "Il non conformista," *Il Mondo* (Rome), September 17, 1957, 2; Gaetano Salvemini, "The Civilization of Italy," letter to the editor, *New Statesman*, November 7, 1925, 106.

15. Gaetano Salvemini, "Non mollare," in Gaetano Salvemini, Ernesto Rossi, and Piero Calamandrei, *Non mollare* (Florence: La Nuova Italia, 1955), 26–31.

16. Garosci, *Storia dei fuorusciti*; Salvemini, *Memorie di un fuoruscito*; Delzell, *Mussolini's Enemies*; Spencer Di Scala, *Italy from Revolution to Republic* (Boulder: Westview Press, 1998), 252–54; Alexander de Grand, *Italian Fascism* (Lincoln: University of Nebraska Press, 2000), 51–57.

17. Garosci, *Storia dei fuorusciti*.

18. "La Voce di Giustizia e Libertà Echeggia a New York," *Il Nuovo Mondo*, May 7, 1930; Gaetano Salvemini to Alberto Tarchiani, January 23, 1932, Tarchiani Papers, Archivio Giustizia e Libertà, Istituto Storico per la Resistenza in Toscana (Florence), hereafter ISRT; Salvadori, "Antifascisti italiani negli Stati Uniti," 274.

19. Delzell, *Mussolini's Enemies*, 149–64; Garosci, *Storia dei fuorusciti*, 172–90, 280–81; Aldo Garosci, *Vita di Carlo Rosselli* (Florence: Vallecchi, 1973), 2:200–204, 211–18, 259–68.

20. Garosci, *Vita di Carlo Rosselli* 2:389–411; Delzell, *Mussolini's Enemies*, 150–54.

21. Gaetano Salvemini, *Carlo and Nello Rosselli* (London: For Intellectual Liberty, 1937); "Il mandante" and "Le trovate del mandante," *Giustizia e Libertà*, July 30 and August 20, 1937; "The Rosselli Murders," *New Republic*, August 18, 1937; "Carlo Rosselli et la première lutte clandestine en Italie," *Giustizia e Libertà*, June 24, 1938; Garosci, *Vita di Carlo Rosselli*, 2:505–15.

22. Giuseppe Antonio Borgese, *Goliath: The March of Fascism* (New York: Viking, 1937); Gaetano Salvemini, *The Fascist Dictatorship in Italy* (1927; reprint, New York: Fertig, 1967); idem, *Mussolini Diplomatico* (Paris: Grasset, 1932); idem, *Under the Axe of Fascism* (New York: Citadel, 1936); idem, with George La Piana, *What to Do with Italy* (New York: Duell, Sloan and Pearce, 1943).

23. Gaetano Salvemini, *Italian Fascist Activities in the United States*, ed. Philip V. Cannistraro (Staten Island, N.Y.: Center for Migration Studies, 1977).

24. Charles Killinger, "Gaetano Salvemini e le autorità americane: documenti inediti del FBI," *Storia Contemporanea* (June 1981): 405–42.

25. Philip V. Cannistraro, *Blackshirts in Little Italy* (West Lafayette, Ind.: Bordighera, 1999); idem, "Fascism and Italian Americans," in *Perspectives in Italian Immigration and Ethnicity*, ed. S. M. Tomasi (Staten Island, N.Y.: Center for Migration Studies, 1977), 51–66; Salvemini, *Italian Fascist Activities in the U.S.*; Diggins, *Mussolini and Fascism*, 88–90; Alan Cassels, "Fascism for Export," *American Historical Review* 69 (April 1964): 707–12; Daria Bicocchi Frezza, "Propaganda fascista e comunità italiane in USA," *Studi Storici* 11 (October–December 1970): 661–97; Gian Giacomo Migone, *Problemi di storia nei rapporti fra Italia e Stati Uniti* (Turin: Einaudi, 1971), 25–41; Killinger, "Salvemini e le autorità americane," 403–39; Dadà, "Contributo metodologico"; Adriana Dadà, "I radicali italo-americani e la società italiana," *Italia Contemporanea* (June 1982): 131–40.

26. The major works on Salvemini include Gaspare De Caro, *Gaetano Salvemini* (Turin: UTET, 1970); Massimo L. Salvadori, *Gaetano Salvemini* (Turin: Einaudi, 1963); Enzo Tagliacozzo, *Gaetano Salvemini nel cinquantennio liberale* (Florence: La Nuova Italia, 1959); Ernesto Sestan et al., *Gaetano Salvemini* (Bari: Laterza, 1959); and Charles Killinger, *Gaetano Salvemini: A Biography* (Westport, Conn.: Praeger, 2002).

27. Ministero dell' Interno, Casellario Politico Centrale, "Salvemini, Gaetano," Archivio Centrale dell Strato (Rome).

28. Hughes, *Sea Change*, 105.

29. Report, "Propaganda antifascista," Italian Embassy, Washington, D.C., to Ministry of Foreign Affairs, May 17, 1939, Ministero dell' Interno, Casellario Politico Centrale, f. 4551, "Salvemini, Gaetano."

30. Michele Cantarella to Philip V. Cannistraro, November 22, 1975; Michele Cantarella interview by Charles Killinger, December 1979, hereafter Michele Cantarella interview; Renato Poggioli to Gaetano Salvemini, October 1, 1939, and memorandum, "The Mazzini Society," Fondo Mazzini Society, ISRT; Michele Cantarella, letter to *New York Times*, January 31, 1945; "Relazione della prima seduta della Mazzini Society," signed by Lionello Venturi and Renato Poggioli, n.d., "The Mazzini Society," Archivio Giustizia e Libertà, ISRT; Michele Cantarella to Cannistraro, November 22, 1975; Maddalena Tirabassi, "La Mazzini Society (1940–1946)," in G. Spini, G. Migone, and M. Teodori, *Italia e America dalla grande guerra a oggi* (Padua: Marsilio, 1976), 141–43. See also James E. Miller, *The United States and Italy* (Chapel Hill: University of North Carolina Press, 1986), 25; Max Ascoli and Arthur Feiler, *Fascism for Whom?* (New York: W. W. Norton, 1938); Italian Embassy to Ministry of Foreign Affairs, February 22, 1941, Ministero dell'Interno, DPGS (1920–1945), "Società Mazzini," Archivio Centrale dello Stato (Rome); Roberto Bolaffio to Salvemini, April 18, 1941, Archivio Gaetano Salvemini, ISRT; Max Ascoli, "Salvemini negli Stati Uniti," *La voce repubblicana*, December 20–21, 1967; Gaetano Vecchiotti (Italian Consul General in New York) to Ministry of Interior, February 28, 1939, Ministero dell'Interno, f. 34148 "Bolaffio, Roberto," Archivio Centrale dello Stato (Rome).

31. Michele Cantarella, draft of speech to the North Bennet Street Industrial School (n.d.); Cantarella application for agency, Metropolitan Life Insurance Company (n.d., 1923), Cantarella Papers, Smith College, Northampton, Mass.; Michele Cantarella interview; Hélène Cantarella interview by Charles Killinger, August 1991, hereafter Hélène Cantarella interview. On Neilson, see Margaret Farrand Thorp, *Neilson of Smith* (New York: Oxford University Press, 1956); Marjorie Hope Nicolson et al., *William Allan Neilson* (Northampton, Mass.: Hampshire Bookshop, 1947).

32. A cursory review of Catherine Epstein, *A Past Renewed: A Catalog of German-Speaking Refugee Historians in the U.S. after 1933* (Cambridge: Cambridge University, 1993) indicates that of the German scholars Epstein tracked, Smith College provided a total of nineteen "scholar years" of employment (to Hans Kohn, Frederick H. Cramer, Dietrich Gerhard, Felix Gilbert, and Frederick Sell), exceeding Princeton University, for example, but surpassed by the New School for Social Research, which accumulated more than thirty-five "scholar years." If one adds to the totals the Italian scholars, the Smith numbers increase markedly. The two Italians at the New School were Max Ascoli and Nino Levi. Dieter-Krohn, *Intellectuals*, 68.

33. Hughes, *Sea Change*, 2; Franz L. Neumann, "The Social Sciences," in Neumann, *The Cultural Migration*, 21–22; Herbert A. Strauss, "The Movement of People in a Time of Crisis," in Jackman and Borden, *The Muses Flee Hitler*, 57ff.

34. Cannistraro, *Blackshirts in Little Italy*.

35. Among the sources Salvemini employed were ministerial bulletins, banking reports, statistical abstracts, speeches, parliamentary debates and statutes, internal memoranda, memoirs, and diaries. Michele Cantarella interview.

36. See Salvadori, *The Labour and the Wounds*, passim; idem, *Resistenza ed azione*, pas-

sim.; and idem, "Antifascisti italiani negli Stati Uniti." See also Delzell, *Mussolini's Enemies*, passim. Max Salvadori interview by Charles Killinger, 1989. Before he died in 1996, the revisionist Italian historian Renzo De Felice alleged in an extended published interview that Salvadori had ordered the assassination of Mussolini on behalf of Churchill in April 1945. Friends and family have vigorously denied the charge. Renzo De Felice, *Rosso e Nero*, ed. Pasquale Chessa (Milan: Baldini & Castodi, 1995). See also "Mussolini ucciso dagli inglesi? Un coro di no alla tesi di De Felice," *Corriere della Sera*, September 3, 1995; "Il conte Max, agente doppio, forse triplo: la vera storia di Massimo Salvadori, fuoruscito col permesso del Duce," *Il Giornale* (Milan), September 15, 1995; Clement Salvadori to Renzo De Felice, September 22, 1995; Renzo De Felice to Clement Salvadori, September 30, 1995 (copies in possession of the author supplied by Hélène Cantarella.)

37. Michele Cantarella, ed., *Bibliografia salveminiana, 1892–1984* (Rome: Bonacci, 1986).

38. Michele Cantarella interview.

39. Renzo De Felice, *Storia degli ebrei italiani sotto il fascismo* (Turin: Einaudi, 1972); Susan Zuccotti, *The Italians and the Holocaust* (Lincoln: University of Nebraska Press, 1987), 28–51.

40. Tirabassi, "La Mazzini Society"; Varsori, *Gli alleati e l'emigrazione democratica antifascista* and "La politica inglese e il conte Sforza," 31–57.

41. Tirabassi, "La Mazzini Society"; Gaetano Salvemini to Alberto Tarchiani, October 7, 1936, and December 3, 1938, Tarchiani Papers; Salvadori, *The Labour and the Wounds*, 134–35.

42. Ministero dell' Interno to Casellario Politico Centrale, April 26, 1941, Casellario Politico Centrale, Archivio Centrale dello Stato (Rome); undated memo, "Italian Emergency Rescue Committee," Ministero dell' Interno, Casellario Politico Centrale, "Salvemini, Gaetano," Archivio Centrale dello Stato (Rome); Alberto Tarchiani to Giorgio La Piana, September 11, 1940, Giorgio La Piana Papers, Andover-Harvard Theological Library (Cambridge, Mass.); Garosci, *Storia dei fuorusciti*, 208; Salvadori, *Resistenza ed azione*, 189–91.

43. Philip V. Cannistraro, *Historical Dictionary of Fascist Italy*, s.v. "Max Ascoli"; Krohn, *Intellectuals in Exile*, 72; Antonio Varsori, "La 'Mazzini Society': Max Ascoli, oppositore del fascismo," *Nuova Antologia* (October–December 1980): 106–24.

44. Killinger, *Gaetano Salvemini*; idem, "Salvemini at Harvard"; Michele Cantarella interview; Ascoli, "Salvemini negli Stati Uniti," 16, 24.

45. Gaetano Salvemini, Giuseppe Antonio Borgese, and Lionello Venturi, "A Statement of the 'Mazzini Society,'" *Il Mondo* (New York), June 15, 1940.

46. Carlo Sforza, "Roosevelt's 'Stab in the Back': Was It an Insult or the Gospel Truth?" *Nazioni Unite*, March 19, 1942.

47. Varsori, "La 'Mazzini Society,'" 106–24.

48. Philip V. Cannistraro, "Luigi Antonini and the Italian Anti-Fascist Movement in the United States, 1940–1943," *Journal of American Ethnic History* (Fall 1985): 21–40.

49. "A.B.C.," Mazzini Society pamphlet (New York: Edizione delle "Mazzini News," n.d. [1940?]); Ascoli, "Salvemini negli Stati Uniti"; Lamberto Mercuri, ed., *Mazzini News* (Foggia: Bastogi, 1990).

50. Salvemini to Ascoli, February 12, 1942, Ascoli Papers, "Salvemini file," Immigration History Research Center, St. Paul, Minn.

51. Cannistraro, *Blackshirts in Little Italy*.

52. Luigi Sturzo, "L'Italo-Americano," *Nazioni Unite*, September 1, 1945.

53. Salvadori, *Resistenza ed azione*, 163.

54. Salvemini, *Italian Fascist Activities in the United States*, 18; Salvadori, *Resistenza ed azione*, 165; Diggins, *Mussolini and Fascism*, 79–80.

55. Philip V. Cannistraro, "Generoso Pope and the Rise of Italian American Politics, 1925–1936," in *New Perspectives in Italian Immigration and Ethnicity* (Staten Island, N.Y.: Center for Migration Studies, 1985); Ascoli, "Salvemini negli Stati Uniti."

56. Luigi Antonini, "The Burning Question of the 'Enemy Aliens'" (letter), *Nazioni Unite*, March 26, 1942.

57. "Italian Aliens," May 25, 1942, Records of the Office of Facts and Figures, Office of War Information, Record Group 208, National Archives, Washington, D.C.; "Confidential Duplicates of Board Meeting Notes," CWI meeting, May 18, 1942; board meetings, March 3, March 10, April 28, May 5, May 26, June 9, June 16, July 6, 1942, Papers of Archibald MacLeish, Miscellaneous Subject File, Manuscript Division, Library of Congress, Washington, D.C.; Gaetano Salvemini, "Good, but Not Good Enough," *Nation*, November 7, 1942, 477–78; James E. Miller, "A Question of Loyalty: American Liberals, Propaganda, and the Italian-American Community, 1939–1943," *Maryland Historian* 9 (Spring 1978): 60–64; Cannistraro, "Antonini."

58. Alberto Tarchiani, "The Thorny Question of the Exponents of Fascism in America," *Nazioni Unite*, January 7, 1943.

59. "Notes for the Congress," *Nazioni Unite*, June 11, 1942; Gaetano Salvemini to Roberto Bolaffio, May 27, 1942, "Mazzini Society," Bolaffio Papers, Archivio Giustizia e Libertà, ISRT (Florence).

60. *Nazioni Unite*, June 25, 1942.

61. Max Ascoli to Adolph Berle, February 17, 1943, President's Personal File, Franklin Delano Roosevelt Library, National Archives and Records Service, Hyde Park, N.Y.

62. "The End of Mussolini and the Italian Political Scene in the United States," confidential memorandum, Foreign Nationalities Branch, Office of Strategic Services to Director of Strategic Services, no. B-65, August 3, 1943; Tirabassi, "La Mazzini Society," 150–51; James Battistoni obituary, *Buffalo Evening News*, October 31, 1939.

63. Diggins, *Mussolini and Fascism*, 405–6.

64. "The End of Mussolini and the Italian Political Scene in the United States."

65. "Esponenti e complici non rappresentano il popolo Italiano" and "Misconceptions," May 7, 1942; "A Correct View," May 14, 1942; "L'Italia vera e antifascista, disprezza Mussolini aborre i Tedeschi" and "Il 24 Maggio," May 21, 1942; "Affermazioni ufficiali americane sulla neta differenziazione tra Italia e Mussolini sulla necessità di abbattere il fascismo" and "The American Official Recognition of the Antagonism Beetwen [sic] Italy and Fascism: A Frank Declamation of the Assistant Secretary Acheson," June 11, 1942, all from *Nazioni Unite*.

66. Hughes, *Sea Change*, 13.

67. Strauss, "The Movement of People in a Time of Crisis," 57–61.

68. Bendix, *From Berlin to Berkeley*, 276.

69. Gaetano Salvemini, "The Nelson Gay Risorgimento Collection in the Harvard College Library," *Harvard Alumni Bulletin*, February 22, 1935.

70. Fermi, *Illustrious Immigrants*, 5–8.

71. Heilbut, *Exiled in Paradise*, 37.

72. Hughes, *Sea Change*, 2.

73. Hughes, who knew Salvemini at Harvard, wrote: "I recall seeing him from a distance, walking as if in a trance. His heart must have been in Italy—certainly not in Cambridge." Salvemini's reception had been cool, as was the case with most émigré intellectuals hired at prestigious institutions. He made some close friends, but he remained outside the institution, a nontenured lecturer, never integrated into the department. H. Stuart Hughes to Charles Killinger, August 3, 1983.

74. Bendix, *From Berlin to Berkeley*, 2–8.

75. H. Stuart Hughes, "Gli studi di storia moderna Italiana in America," *Rassegna Storica del Risorgimento* 45 (1958): 273–74; idem, *Sea Change*, 4–13.

76. Hughes, "Gli studi di storia moderna italiana in America," 273–74.

77. Renato Poggioli, "Dante poco tempo silvano: or a Pastoral Oasis in the *Commedia*," *Annual Report of the Dante Society* (1962): 1–18; idem, "Tragedy or Romance? A Reading of the Paolo and Francesca Episode in Dante's *Inferno*" and "The Death of the Sense of Tragedy," in *The Spirit of the Letter: Essays in European Literature* (Cambridge: Harvard University Press, 1965), 50–102, 279–91.

78. Renato Poggioli, *The Theory of the Avant-Garde* (Cambridge: Harvard University Press, 1968); Dante Della Terza, *Da Vienna a Baltimora: la diaspora degli intellettuali europei negli Stati Uniti d'America* (Rome: Riuniti, 2001), 127–94.

79. Borgese, *Goliath: The March of Fascism*.

80. Dante Della Terza, "Reappraising G. A. Borgese," in *Giuseppe Antonio Borgese, 1883–1983: A Commemoration* (Northampton, Mass.: Smith College, 1983); idem, *Da Vienna a Baltimora*, 195–203.

81. Hélène Cantarella, untitled tribute to G. A. Borgese, in *Borgese: A Commemoration*.

A French Connection

Chambon, Chalmers, and Cummington

RICHARD PRESTON UNSWORTH

THIS ESSAY considers the anatomy of exile principally through the experience of people in two small rural corners of France and New England.[1] The citizens of each took the plight of the refugees as their personal responsibility. Several were pacifists, and many had histories of engagement with issues of international peace and justice. A consistent goal in the church communities of both towns was the prevention of war through the expansion of justice. But when war broke out, they responded to its victims with relief work, and later by efforts at rescue and refuge. While the war went on, they worked for the rehabilitation of individuals; and when the war was over, leading persons in these two communities connected with one another to heal the wounds.

Three Inseparable Components of Compassion

The refugee stories of every generation tend to focus on the most dramatic events of the experience: the hiding, the narrow escapes, the suffering, the death of family and friends, and all the other hardships refugees experience as they pursue escape or await rescue. The press features pictures of roads littered with broken-down vehicles, ragged and despairing people trying to get out of harm's way, and all the other poignant aspects of the dislocation of populations. These are often the experiences that mark and define the lives of refugees and their communities for decades—even generations—to come. We have seen that outcome repeatedly during the past century, through the eyes of Armenian Christians, Palestinian Arabs, Indian Muslims at the time of Partition, and Serbian Orthodox with memories of defeat and persecution that stretch back four hundred years.

Rescue, when and if it happens, is the climactic element of these stories; but relief and rehabilitation are equally important, albeit less dramatic, aspects of the tale. This essay centers our attention on a few people and a very few places, not because they have greater significance than others, but because they function as paradigms of the three moments that together constitute the refugee experience in the twentieth century, a period that saw more people driven out, dislocated, and only sometimes relocated than any other period in history. Most of these dislocations were the product of war; only a few were the consequence of natural disasters.

The Neilson Symposium, "The Anatomy of Exile," gave major attention to one of these dislocations: that of the Jews and others who were driven out or murdered in the Nazi period, with its organized contempt for fellow humanity. Theirs is only one such refugee story from the past century, but the one that was graven most deeply on the consciousness and conscience of Americans and Europeans. The purpose of the symposium was to search the fundamentals of such refugee experience in order to find more effective means for resisting its repetition. If one is to search the fundamentals, then relief, refuge, and rehabilitation must all be part of the story, for each lends a level of understanding to the whole refugee experience. All three components of compassion together compose the structure of resistance to the exile of populations.

Davids and Their Goliaths: Resisting Colossal Forces

The decade leading up to World War II was a time of mounting division among the populations of the future combatants, both politically and economically, in the United States and in Europe. Germans faced the rise of Hitler and his pretensions to a Third Reich. The French were torn between the inheritors of the Revolution of 1789, who had become the new political establishment, and the socially radical left-wing parties—the Communists, Christian Socialists, and others who had made economic injustice their cause and "internationalism" their watchword. England was not far removed from the days when Karl Marx labored daily in the British Museum to produce his manifesto and its formula for the secular fulfillment of religious hopes for a just society. Americans were entering a period marked by the most divisive cultural and political debates since the Civil War. Everywhere, it seemed, the remaining footprints of eighteenth-century enlightenment were being washed away by the inescapable realization that each of the western governments had been co-opted by the wealthy and would, on their behalf, aggravate the pain of the underclasses. One hardly needed prophetic powers to see that the outbreak of a second world-embracing war was rising to the level of inevitability.

But there were, in every nation, enclaves of resistance to the abuse of power and the glorification of war in the name of national pride and corporate self-interest. Some such enclaves were rooted in religious commitments, others in the quasi-religious faith of Marxism, still others in the pride of patriotism, a term most often interpreted as loyalty to the nation-state in its status quo. Two small communities, one in the western Massachusetts hills and the other in the French Massif Central, offer us a vivid sense of these enclaves.

As early as 1938, André Trocmé and his colleague Edouard Theis spoke from the pulpit in the temple[2] of le Chambon-sur-Lignon, a small town in a traditionally Hugenot area, about the coming trials under the Nazis in Germany, not imagining that France itself would become Nazified within three years. The two pastors told their congregation that they must be prepared for all this, and that they must become a city of refuge for the Jews and others who would inevitably be persecuted, routed from their homes, and driven out of Germany. What Trocmé and Theis preached in those years was not pacifist dogma, although both were absolute pacifists themselves, but something like nonviolent activism, a position of renouncing violence, whether as a product of war or a precondition of peace.

Across the Atlantic, another pastor in the Reformed tradition, Carl Sangree, soon considered the same necessity for his little town in the Berkshire foothills: Cummington, Massachusetts. He foresaw the Nazi terror leading to tragedy and dislocation for whole peoples, and he knew that the response that would be required of him would be not one of policy and strategy but one of solace and refuge. As the misery mounted in Europe, he, his wife, Elizabeth, and some members of his congregation established a hostel in the town designed to offer temporary shelter for European refugees. The hostel was quickly filled, and more space was found in homes in Cummington and other nearby communities. Sangree was to find, as Trocmé and Theis found in le Chambon, that the project struck some of his congregation as none of their business. In fact, a group of his parishioners were sufficiently disaffected from the whole enterprise that they circulated a petition designed to force his resignation from the Cummington church. Beyond the resistance and criticism, the Sangrees and their co-workers were faced with providing food, clothing, and job counseling for the refugees they took in.

Downhill from West Cummington, a community leader, William Allan Neilson, the legendary president of Smith College, also considered the notion of creating a city of refuge in the face of the advance of Nazism and all it represented. Neilson was an activist and an organizer, of the sort described by Peter Rose as "movers and shakers," who became one of the leading American figures in the effort to rescue Jews and others in flight from the Nazi terror.[3] His particular interest was in offering safe haven to intellectuals from the societies infected by the plague of fascism. His awareness of the threat to intellectuals—a common thread in totalitarian societies—was centered on its European manifestations. Only later did Americans deal actively with the exile of Russian and much more recently Chinese intellectuals.

Neilson was among the few educational leaders who recognized the threat early enough to help develop an escape route to the United States for key European intellectuals whose lot was made impossible at home. As early as the late 1920s he had already provided refuge for Italian scholars such as Michele Cantarella who had actively resisted the Fascist regime in their homeland. Cantarella was the first of many who would join the Smith faculty for longer or shorter periods. He and Massimo Salvadori, a longtime anti-Fascist who fought in the British army from 1939 to 1945, both remained at Smith until retirement. Others moved on to appointments elsewhere but remained part of the anti-Fascist Italian fellowship in the United States known as the Mazzini Society, a name they took to honor one of their own, Giuseppe Mazzini.[4]

These three men, Trocmé, Sangree, and Neilson, had many convictions in common, but each one came to them in his own time and from his own distinct perspective.

Neilson was the paradigm of the intellectual leader, a man who yoked his political and moral wisdom with his humane convictions. Although he was not a theologian, nor an active member of any established religious community, Neilson was a man who took very seriously the moral claims of the biblical tradition on the life of the intellectual.

Trocmé, by contrast, was distinctly a theologian and pastor. The Bible provided his framework for the interpretation of events, and truth was a value on which he felt compelled to build his decisions. Yet, thanks in part to his wife, Magda Grilli di Cortona, he was always and principally an activist in the way he saw the claims of his theology on the fabric of his daily life.

On the face of it, Carl Sangree was like neither of the other two. He was a complex, stubborn man with a plain and cheerful manner. He was born in a small industrial city in Pennsylvania and went to Haverford, a Quaker college in Philadelphia, the land of many Quakers and many Sangrees. One of them, Carl's uncle, had headed the delegation of Quaker peacemakers who, in the 1930s, met with and appealed to Hitler to abandon his war-bound course. At college, Carl Sangree took his stand as a conscientious objector during the First World War by refusing to heed the call of his draft board. He did not remain in the Quaker community, however, but was ordained a minister in the Congregational Church. Still, he had been marked for life by the Quaker tradition and often described himself as "a friend of Friends." (He might have said "a cousin," since that was literally the case for any member of the extensive Sangree clan of Philadelphia Quakers.) In any case, throughout his ministry he would always be much more interested in doing good than in being right.

He finished his training at Union Theological Seminary in New York, a seedbed for liberal theologians and political activists throughout the 1920s and 1930s and one of the places where both socialism and pacifism were most hotly debated. But Sangree considered himself neither a theologian nor a political scientist. He simply thought war a particularly inhumane sort of madness, a twisted design for imposing order which actually imposed chaos. He had little patience with theological or political abstractions about the matter.

The story is told of Sangree that, in 1940, he met with the secretary of the National Conference of Congregational Churches to discuss the churches' role in stopping the war that was already under way. He was told that the church could not tell people whether or not they should wage war; it could only help its victims. Sangree's response was to tell the secretary that it was insane to help the victims without also attending to the cause of their misery.[5] Nonetheless, Sangree marshaled the interest and the support of other churches in the area and established the hostel in Cummington that would serve as a refuge and rehabilitation center for about forty European refugees from Nazism.[6]

Trocmé was already a budding pacifist during his studies at the Protestant Theological Faculty in Paris. His friends Jacques Martin and Henri Roser had both decided to refuse the military service required of every young French male, and both served time in prison as a consequence. Trocmé's convictions were still those of a pacifist when he enlisted in the French army in 1921 for his two-year military obligation. With so many of his family members having served the French army with distinction during the First World War, he hoped to find a way to be both a loyal citizen and a pacifist Christian in the context of military service. Once enlisted, however, he found that there was really no way he could serve both masters. His military experience only convinced him that he must be even more resolute in his pacifism. Humans killing other humans was behavior altogether at odds with everything that was expected of a Christian; he felt that was an axiom for anyone who read the New Testament with an open eye. Interestingly, he did not try to resign his service, an option that would likely have brought him an even longer prison sentence than had been imposed on his friends. Instead, he simply refused to carry a rifle, leaving his officers to figure out what to do with such a soldier.

Fortunately he had the help of a friend, a Private Crespin, who worked in his army unit's office. Crespin had a more negotiable conscience, one burdened with fewer scruples than Trocmé's. So when their lieutenant returned to camp thoroughly drunk one night, Private Crespin slipped a transfer order into a pile of routine papers requiring the officer's signature, and the besotted lieutenant unwittingly transferred Trocmé to a geodetic brigade to serve as a map maker. The officer was furious when he sobered up the next morning and discovered what had happened; but it was too late, and in any case, he was frankly glad to be rid of a troublesome pacifist in his unit.

Even a noncombatant role, however, failed to assuage Trocmé's problems with military life. While on a tour of duty in Morocco, he simply ignored his commander's direct order to carry a rifle and ammunition on his geodetic sorties out into the Bled, the "outback" of southern Morocco. He solved his problem of conscience by wrapping both rifle and ammunition in the 1920s equivalent of duct tape, turning them in to the armory in Rabat, getting a receipt, and returning to his unit.

Neilson's approach was quite different. While no friend to the war makers and the warmongers, he was not a pacifist. He accepted war as a last-resort option for addressing power gone mad, as it had most certainly done in the Nazi instance. Neilson's response to the politics of the Nazis was to muster the influence and the resources needed to bring as many of Europe's leading intellectuals as possible out of harm's way. He took a lead role in the establishment of the International Rescue Committee,[7] an organization to which we will return later.

In due course, Neilson would provide the link that drew together the two towns of le Chambon and Cummington and their distinct but similar efforts to serve as cities of refuge. Nearly three decades later, Paul Ricoeur, by then a *grand philosophe* at the Sorbonne, would recall his early teaching experience in le Chambon and his later friendship with the Sangrees, observing that "there were really two centers to the universe: le Chambon and West Cummington"[8]

Burns Chalmers and the Growth of a Network

The link that Neilson provided was a Quaker scholar-activist, Burns Chalmers. Neilson appointed him to teach in the Department of Religion and Biblical Studies, and to occupy the newly established position of director of religious life at Smith. Like Sangree, Chalmers was a "birthright Quaker," but unlike Sangree, he had remained within the tradition. He was to prove both a timely and an effective religious leader for the college.

Smith had been chartered in 1871 in Northampton, a town known historically as the parish of the eighteenth-century American philosopher-theologian Jonathan Edwards. The community was culturally homogeneous, a place where being religious was generally understood as being Christian, Protestant, and Congregational. While not affiliated with any religious body, the college had been established by a churchly Congregational woman, Sophia Smith, with the spiritual direction of her Congregational pastor, the Reverend John M. Greene, and was presided over for its first thirty-seven years by another Congregational clergyman, the Reverend L. Clarke Seelye.[9] In the manner of the time, Seelye and subsequent presidents, whether clergymen or not, were expected to fill the role of religious leader and moral arbiter. Now, more than half a century later, Smith had become a more secular institution, and one with a national reputation, with students drawn from many regions and different religious traditions.

By appointing Chalmers to this newly designed post, Neilson had no intention of abandoning his own moral leadership. He simply recognized the changing realities of the college presidency and of a student body that was no longer made up nearly exclusively of New England Protestant women. He also continued his practice of addressing the college community regularly with Monday morning assembly talks that spoke as much to the implicit moral claims of public and political life as they did to the development of personal traits of character and spirit. Personal life and public obligation were intimately related, in the mind and speech of Smith's president.[10] But now it was time for some person other than the president to develop an approach to the college's religious heritage that would serve the multiple needs of an increasingly diverse student body.

Chalmers and his wife, Elizabeth Scattergood, herself the offspring of Philadelphia Quaker aristocracy, came to Smith in 1935, prepared to help its students better understand "that of God in every man."[11] and to live out the Quaker concern for building peace by ordinary deeds. Chalmers was not an ordained minister, since the Quaker tradition does not call for such singling out of leadership. So while his job was not focused principally on the conduct of Christian liturgy, he presided at the Sunday evening Vespers services in John M. Greene Hall and the smaller weekday gatherings in the Little Chapel in the college's library. Still, his major concern was with the development of discussion and action programs that expressed broad and fundamental religious convictions.

Chalmers's Quaker background made him a good interpreter of Neilson's intention to provide leadership that took ethical responsiveness as seriously as religious commitment. An appealing figure in both manner and appearance, Burns Chalmers was diplomatic by habit, and his religious and ethical commitments were as strong as they were soft-spoken. He was tall, lean, and athletic, accustomed to long climbs in New Hampshire's White Mountains near his summer home in Center Sandwich, a habit he maintained till near the end of his life. His bespectacled face conveyed kindness and attentiveness. In conversation, the raising of the eyebrows, the forward tilt of the head—often required by his height—and the directness of his gaze proclaimed that he was happy to listen and consider. When he disagreed, he did so in the best Quaker fashion, with a disarming manner calculated not to give offense but simply to open another possibility; and when he agreed, he did so with a manifest sincerity that let others know that they and he had connected at a depth that was more than intellectual. For Chalmers, censure was rare and laughter was common—the laughter of an extraordinarily perceptive person who accepted the ironies in himself and others, all the while remaining in firm possession of his principles.

Chalmers first based his work in an organization called the Smith Christian Association, a consciously interdenominational group of students who aspired to represent the several Protestant church traditions within the student body. It was still a time when Roman Catholic students were expected by their church to keep a safe distance from Protestant activities; and Jewish students, though growing in number, would have no chaplaincy on campus until some years later. Before long, Chalmers had led the SCA to change its name to the Smith College Association for Christian Work (SCACW), a designation that seemed to be accepted on all sides because it focused on social action projects without implying any specific doctrinal commitment.[12]

During their first years on campus, the Chalmerses lived in a white frame house on College Lane, where they looked out on the aptly named Paradise Pond. Hundreds of students passed by their kitchen door many times each day as they trekked back and forth from dormitories to classroom buildings and the library. Both Burns and Elizabeth Chalmers related easily to their new constituents. They were warm, straightforward, accepting, and intellectually impressive people who quickly gathered the respect and affection of a broad segment of the student body and the faculty. Their family life included all the threads of their Quaker heritage: the practice of silence, using "thee" and "thou" as the accepted form of address within the family, and a focus on justice tempered with love, and love as an instrument of justice.

Soon after his arrival at Smith, the skies began to darken everywhere as the seemingly inevitable war came nearer. By 1939 the SCACW's attention was focusing on the needs of the displaced and persecuted peoples of Europe. France's six-week debacle of May–June 1940 brought matters into focus when Americans, including the Smith community, learned about the hastily built "camps" in southern France, where thousands of refugees were crowded into facilities that supported only the most marginal amenities of ordinary life.[13]

The Focus on Relief: 1940–41

Chalmers took a very Quakerly decision when, on July 18 of that year, he wrote to President Herbert Davis, Neilson's immediate successor, asking for a year's leave to work with the American Friends Service Committee in the more than fifteen refugee camps in southern France for which the AFSC, together with other charitable American, English, and Swiss agencies, had taken a responsibility. On the same day, Davis wrote to inform the agency that Chalmers had been given leave to do relief work in France.

By August 5, Chalmers was flying across the Atlantic on the *Dixie Clipper* headed for Toulouse and, ultimately, AFSC headquarters on the Boulevard d'Athènes in Marseilles. The AFSC work there and elsewhere in Europe was headed by Howard E. Kershner, the "Directeur des Secours en Europe." The word *secours* can be translated into English by both "relief" and "rescue." When Chalmers arrived, the task was seen almost entirely in terms of relief. During his year with the AFSC, Chalmers was put in charge of counseling and work in the camps.

The first of these camps were established by the French government in 1938 and 1939 to deal with the flood of refugees from the Spanish civil war. At the end of that war, more than a half-million Spanish Republicans fled their homeland, many of them across the Pyrenees into France. In February 1939 the French, under the leadership of Premier Edouard Daladier, opened camps at Argelès and St. Cyprien, the first two of seven erected for Spaniards in the Catalan and Languedoc regions of France. These camps offered only minimal shelter, with windowless barracks, poor food, and a total lack of sanitary facilities and water supply. But they were better than living in the open, and the French regarded them, for the most part, as a humanitarian response to the plight of the refugees.

In 1939 the government set about building additional camps to accommodate some of the next half-million refugees, now internal refugees from the Anschluss in Alsace-Lorraine, together with a swelling stream of Jews, leftists, Gypsies, and others from central and eastern Europe. At first, the four additional camps built at Rieucros, Gurs, Les Milles, and le Vernet were euphemistically designated as assembly points for sorting out people who were French from those who were foreigners and citizens of nations at war with France. An important insight into the French situation in 1939 is the fact that among those foreign nationals were to be numbered all foreign Jews, Gypsies, communists, and expatriates.

There was no particular outcry among the French about the establishment of these camps. The need for relief work of the most basic kind had simply exploded in magnitude and urgency. The camps were seen primarily, perhaps only, as the government's attempt to deal with the crisis.

Then came the debacle of June 1940, which sent an estimated 5 million French fleeing from the Blitzkrieg tactics that put an end to French resistance in six weeks: "the greatest movement of humanity in all history," wrote Howard Kershner.[14] After the June 1940 armistice, the Vichy government added a new twist to the role of the camps by its open declaration that the purpose of these camps was to gather and oversee all "undesirable elements."[15] There was still no outcry of opposition to the establishment of these camps from the French citizenry, any more than there was a general outcry of Americans later, when Roosevelt approved the construction of internment camps for the confinement of Americans of Japanese descent.

Some sense of the early work of these groups can be gathered from Kershner's report on the activities of the AFSC for 1940–41. Chalmers's role in counseling and work projects was based on the hope that most of those interned would ultimately be able to rebuild their families and their lives, either within France or by emigration to Portugal, the United States, or other places of opportunity. So it made sense to find out what people required in the way of visas, temporary financial support, or vocational retraining. There was also the urgent necessity to provide the internees with meaningful work, in part to supply their own needs, in part to counter the debilitating boredom and hopelessness that usually dominate places of forced confinement.

A note of hope characterized Kershner's report for 1940–41. "The French Government," he wrote, "generously supplies railway transportation [of relief supplies] without cost."[16] And later in the same report he made this hyperbolic comment about the French nation, presumably including its government: "No nation in the history of the world has ever been so hospitable and generous in its dealings with foreigners who have been unwanted and have come without invitation. . . . [France] has generously allowed the persecuted of all lands to seek asylum within her borders."[17] Both comments now seem painfully innocent, and suggest a lingering refusal to look closely at the tragic course of events the Vichy regime had set in motion.

The government, understandably, expressed gratitude for the relief work offered by the Quakers and others. Marshal Pétain wrote to Kershner from Vichy on December 14, 1940: "The gift of vitamins to be distributed among the school children has been received with great thankfulness. I wish to assure you of my gratitude and that of my government. . . . I address to you on this subject all my congratulations for these activities which you have undertaken in favour of France."[18]

By this time, the Secours Suisse aux Enfants staff had also moved into the camps and, working with English and American Quakers and other groups, made an effort to improve conditions in these camps. An immediate need was proper shelter for pregnant women and nursing mothers, the latter established at a castle near Perpignan. But the relief agencies also endeavored daily to supplement camp rations with local produce bought with funds from Norway and other countries abroad, and with vitamin concentrates to keep the children from languishing under the pitiful diet.

Many of these relief agencies were already practiced in dealing with populations in flight and fear. As early as 1937, a combine of some twenty Swiss charitable organizations had come together, identified themselves as a Swiss chapter of the International Civil Service movement, and embarked on a major effort to provide help to civilians, particularly children and the elderly, who were dislodged by the Spanish war. That combine was the parent organization of the Secours Suisse aux Enfants, the relief agency that would later play a major part in establishing camps and homes of refuge for children in le Chambon.

Given the facts at this stage of events, it is not surprising that many of the relief workers who arrived in Marseilles in the early months following the German-French armistice of June 22, 1940, would focus their attention on relief rather than rescue. The unfolding sequence of developments also helps us understand the sometimes optimistic comments of people such as Burns Chalmers when reporting on their work. Thus it is that Chalmers described his own part in the "relief" effort this way in a letter home to President Davis:

> Since writing you last, I have been in and out on several missions. When in Marseille my responsibility has been to direct a department including refugee counseling and correspondence, and food and clothing for the internment camps. . . . I went to the camp of Gurs at the end of December and the first part of January. . . . Three of us as Quaker delegates made the trip. Our purpose in going was to take and distribute a thousand dollars worth of food for supplementary feeding, especially for the undernourished and old. We also took two thousand dollars worth of clothing.

And regarding the setting of the camp, he wrote:

> The camp is situated on a level stretch of country, though high. At present there are about 13,000 people there, mainly central Europeans. There are 13 *ilots* [blocks of buildings] now in use, each containing 20 barracks. The *ilots* are separated by barbed wire and each has a sentry, but permission to leave the *ilots* is frequently obtained. One is unavoidably impressed with the mud, which is deep, sticky and present everywhere except on the fine gravel road which stretches for two miles and divides the camp in half.

Chalmers also mentions that he was favorably impressed with the director of the camp and the prefect at Pau, who were both well aware of the severity of the camp situation. He also speaks about the progress made in coordinating camp committees, on which he served as Quaker representative. And he takes the Vichy government at its word, saying:

> Thorough-going governmental action toward better conditions is now launched. The situation of 4,000 children will be vastly improved. . . . On the whole, among

people in the camps the essential human dignity and integrity of mankind is strongly indicated. Our efforts will continue to be independent. We must be intelligent and resourceful in helping to meet the need and in working toward ultimate solutions.[19]

In November 1940 the number of internees in these camps was estimated by the external aid agencies at 53,610. The Vichy government promptly established three more: Rivesaltes, Noé, and Récébédou. But now the cast of the camps had become more sinister. A month earlier the new Vichy government had issued its first *statuts* concerning the place of Jews in French society, and Pétain had met with Hitler to work out the terms of collaboration between the two governmental entities. The degree of sinister purpose in these camps could not be fully discerned, however, until a second set of *statuts* was promulgated in June 1941 and the arrest and deportation of French Jews began.

From Relief to Refuge: 1941–42

One tends to forget at this historic distance that both the events and their meaning unfolded not instantly but over time, in France and in other countries, not least among them the United States. Only by such recollection, too, can one best understand how and when the work of the Quakers and their international counterparts widened the focus from relief to rescue, from one meaning of *secours* to the other.

Even as relief began to include rescue, and the relief organizations began creating false papers and doing what they could to get both children and adults out of the camps by whatever means possible, there remained on the part of many involved in relief work some degree of refusal to recognize the full import of the evil that was befalling the nation.

A young American named Tracy Strong Jr. accepted an appointment similar to Chalmers's about the time Chalmers's term was finished in the summer of 1941. Strong, the son of an American YMCA executive, went to Marseilles, as Chalmers did, to provide what help he could to those who were confined in the French camps. Strong kept a diary for much of his time in France, in which one finds a combination of realistic address toward the problems of internees and optimistic assessment of their lives and prospects. An example of this combination of optimism and realism is found in his entry for September 23, 1941:

I was in Toulouse and visited the two camps of Noé and Récébédou. The latter has about 1400 people in it, mostly old and sick people. It is well fixed up, and the director seems willing to help all he can. He has practically given us a free

hand. . . . At Noé I went straight to the Foyer where Mme Martin is carrying on a
fine piece of work. Things are really going there . . . [but] a visit to all the TB
barracks was pathetic. Here are young men who have little hope of getting better,
especially as the food isn't so good.[20]

The environment at Gurs was typical of that at several of these camps.
Auguste Bohny, the Swiss director of aid to refugees in unoccupied France,
estimated in his report that the Gurs camp held some twelve thousand internees. In his diary Strong describes the camp at Gurs on a cold, rainy November
day in 1941: "I met eight Dutch boys who had lost patience waiting at the
frontier and tried to go on. Result: Gurs. . . . The mud here is slippery clay so
that one feels [as if] he were running on an open field with tacklers on all
sides, and no cleats to help from dodging." The notes of optimism and pessi-
mism toggle back and forth throughout Strong's diary.[21]

André Trocmé later recalled the conditions he found when he went to Gurs
and other camps:

> The prisoners lived there in filthy conditions and completely destitute. Although
> we were in the so-called free south, the Gestapo was active everywhere at the end
> of 1940 [sic] and already organized the deportation of political suspects and Jews
> to Germany.[22] Families were separated without pity and the Protestant CIMADE
> [Commission Inter-Movement pour Assistance aux Deportés et Étrangers], un-
> der the leadership of Madeleine Barot, had succeeded in introducing several of
> its members into the camps as social workers.[23]

The situation that greeted Burns Chalmers on his arrival at the AFSC office
in Marseilles in July 1940 had steadily worsened on its downhill course to the
statuts of October and the disenfranchisement of Jews in French society. It
became increasingly apparent to the relief groups that their task would have
to include rescue. Jews were being deported to the forced labor camps in
Germany. Soon they would be transshipped to the death camps of eastern
Europe.

The several refugee aid groups in the area all recognized that the nourish-
ment, health, and safety of the children in these camps were the most urgent
of a series of urgent concerns. On the children depended the reconstruction
of the society once the hostilities were over. What Chalmers and his co-workers
did not, and probably could not, realize was how quickly these Vichy policies
toward Jews, both French and foreign, would become malignant. Few realized
until relatively recently that the regime in France, "alone among all occupied
Western European nations, wrote its own anti-Semitic policies, extending the
definition of Jew beyond contemporary Nazi practice. . . . This government created a climate in which anti-Semitism and informing on Jews was not only

acceptable but patriotic, and its legal system cooperated with Nazi goals to a greater extent than any other Occupied nation ... ultimately turning over 76,000 Jews ... 10,000 of whom were children—to be exterminated."[24]

Knowledge of the camps, their emerging purpose, and the conditions there had also gotten to many others in France, since communication between the prisoners and their friends and family was not forbidden. One of the ironies of the system of internment was that the help of relief and aid groups such as CIMADE was needed by the Vichy overseers, but those same volunteers became the source of the reports that spread throughout the region and sparked resistance.

Among those who learned the facts about the camps and their purpose were André Trocmé and his colleague Edouard Theis in le Chambon-sur-Lignon, about three hundred kilometers north of Marseilles (a two-day journey at that time). These two men were equally committed to an activist philosophy of nonviolence, and neither had any intention of standing to one side while others suffered the hardships of displacement. They decided that the circumstance of the camps demanded that one of them offer to help the aid groups at work there. The other would assume double duty as pastor to the parish and director of the Collège Cévenol, which Trocmé and Theis had established as part of their ministry to the youngsters of the Viverais-Lignon Plateau.[25]

Trocmé discussed their plan in his memoir:

I called the Church Council into a meeting and described our privileges, the easy servicing of our parish thanks to the presence of Edouard Theis, a part time minister, and other ministers such as Henri Braemer, a teacher at the Collège and Mr. Poivre who was retired. I asked the council to delegate me to the internment camps as ambassador to distribute food and other items which the parish would collect.

Edouard Theis was agreed and so was the council. They asked, however, that my project be investigated before I made the official first step. I went to Marseille to question American Quakers [American Friends Service Committee], and met Mr. Burns Chalmers who is today a Quaker official in Washington. He and I soon became very close friends. He advised me against living in the camps because the Quakers already had many inside contacts there. He said:

"You are telling me that you come from a village in the mountain where people are still living safely. Our problem is this: We have contacts with French doctors and officers who are in charge of the camps and through them we try to obtain medical certificates for as many adult people as possible so that they are declared unfit for forced labor. (Indeed, deportation in those days was still described as forced labor, *Zwangsarbeit* in German.) If and when we manage to have the father liberated, we include the mother and the children and, if and when the father and mother are deported, we recuperate the children. We then get permission, with great difficulty, to house unfit people outside the camp but the problem is that there are not many towns in France ready to take the risk of receiving adult, teenage or child[26] guests as compromising as our protégés. ARE YOU WILLING TO BE THAT VILLAGE?"

An unscheduled and unplanned task was lying there, right in front of me.

"But we will have to house, feed and send these children to school. How can we do this?" I asked.

"You find the houses and the people to take charge," Burns replied. "The Quakers and the Fellowship of Reconciliation will sustain you financially," he replied.

Burns' word was kept, even after the U.S.A. entered the war in 1941. American citizens had left France but the Quakers, the Fellowship of Reconciliation (Nevin Sayre), and the Congregational Churches provided funds through secret channels such as the International Ecumenical Council of Protestant Churches which had just been created in Geneva and also with Charles Guillon's [former mayor of le Chambon] assistance from Geneva as well. They didn't only provide funds for food and lodging but also created scholarships for young Collège students. Courageous emissaries secretly walked through the Franco-Swiss border with money in cash. Many were caught and one of them was executed by a German firing squad.

Back in le Chambon I won an easy victory with the church council. They were relieved to see that their minister had decided to stay.[27]

The challenge that Burns Chalmers put to André Trocmé sparked a response not only in the pastor but in his flock. There were already several *colonies de vacances* for children in le Chambon and other towns in the Plateau. They were the continuing product of an effort that began in 1891 with the formation of L'Oeuvre des Enfants à la Montagne, an organization founded to bring children from the industrial cities to the healthier environment of the mountains. These smoky industrial centers were indeed not a very healthy environment for children in the 1890s, nor during most of the century following.

Albert Camus bears witness to this in his notebooks. He spent several months in the winter of 1942–43 in Panelier, a village adjacent to le Chambon, working on his novel *The Plague* and dealing with his tuberculosis. Every week he took the little departmental train from le Chambon down to nearby St. Étienne for treatments. He describes that industrial city in his notebooks:

An old worker tells of his misery: his two rooms at an hour's distance from St. Étienne—two hours on the road, eight hours of work, nothing to eat at home, too poor to patronize the night market (*i.e.* black market). Meanwhile, the rain drowns the dirty landscape of an industrial valley—the acrid smell of its misery—

the frightful distress of its lives. . . . Saint-Étienne in the morning mist with si-
rens calling people to work in that jumble of towers and buildings with huge
chimneys bearing toward the shadowed sky their deposit of slag and cinders like
a monstrous sacrificial offering . . .[28]

The opportunity still offered to urban children by L'Ouevre des Enfants retained its original appeal to those who could afford to send their children off
to the mountains for a month or more of rehabilitation.

Le Chambon was one of the most popular centers of L'Oeuvre des Enfants
because it was already a town that attracted a considerable amount of family
tourism. Children who came alone were housed with farm families at first; but
by 1939 there were a dozen Maisons d'Enfants in the area from Fay-sur-Lignon
north to Tence, nine of them in Chambon.[29]

The habit of offering refuge to the persecuted was an old one in the area.
For nearly two centuries the pious but nonconforming peasants of the
Viverais-Lignon Plateau and companion regions to the south, known as "les
Camisards," were subjected to massacres and persecution because of their
insistence on freedom of conscience and of religious practice.[30] The Edict of
Nantes, promulgated in 1787, brought an end only to the worst of it. Le Chambon and other towns throughout the plateau had become and remained a
stronghold of Protestantism, and by extension a stronghold of resistance to
any authority that sought to compromise the people's freedom to worship
according to the dictates of conscience. The response of le Chambon, its religious leaders, and the Protestant communities in many surrounding towns to
Vichy persecution of Jews and others was part of a long continuum of witness
by civil disobedience.

If there was a difference between le Chambon and some of its neighboring
communities, it may only reflect the proportion of Protestants in the population of those towns. Where they were most numerous, the communal memory
of religious persecution was most vivid, and le Chambon had by far the
greatest concentration of Protestants in the plateau. The predominance of
Protestantism certainly affected both the political and the religious outlook
of the inhabitants. The census of 1936 for the seventeen communities of the
plateau counted 38 percent of the total population of 24,000 as Protestants of
one strain or another; but the population of le Chambon was 95 percent
Protestant.[31] An interesting related figure indicates the political orientation of
the plateau population in the same year: the towns of le Chambon and le
Mazet voted 92 percent and 95 percent, respectively, for the candidates of the
left.[32]

Although the habit of giving welcome to refugees had never been entirely
lost, the First World War had rekindled it among the people in the area, when

the Oeuvre des Enfants gave special attention to children who were displaced by the conflict to the north. Then, in the period between the two wars, these children's centers became even more popular. In 1918 the first of this new group of centers was established when Alice Matile opened Les Genêts. She soon found her facility entirely too small to handle the demand, and a number of others opened throughout the community. Their names give the flavor of their work: Les Heures Claires, Tante Soly, Chante Alouette, La Joyeuse Nichée. So when Trocmé was presented with Chalmers's challenge, his parish had an infrastructure ready to tap for supporting its positive response.

As the situation worsened in the concentration camps (which, by early 1941, they began to be called), efforts to counter their purpose were redoubled by the relief groups that had now become relief and rescue operations. One of them, CIMADE, undertook to rent a hotel in le Chambon, Le Côteau Fleuri, which it used as a staging center for children and adults who were being spirited out of France and into Switzerland on a kind of underground railroad (*filières de sauvetage*). More children's homes sprang up, five of them between 1941 and 1944: Les Genêts, L'Abric, La Guespy, Faïdoli, and Les Barandons.[33]

From Refuge to Rehabilitation

So far, the rescue and refuge efforts I have described were motivated primarily by religious commitments of one sort or another. But there were also many organizations and efforts whose motivation was secular and/or political. One of the best known is the Emergency Rescue Committee, of which President Neilson was a founder. The ERC's agent on site, Varian Fry, was assigned to see that key European artists and intellectual leaders were able to escape. Fry's tale has been well told by Neilson Symposium panelist Andy Marino in his book *The Quiet American: The Secret War of Varian Fry*. It is also recounted in Fry's own diary of events during the year he was active in Marseilles.[34]

Fry was in the business of getting his clients to places of refuge as quickly and effectively as he and his co-workers could manage. One of those clients was the German poet and playwright Walter Mehring, who had gained fame in the 1930s with his uncomplimentary portrayals of fascism. Mehring, once over the Spanish border, finally made his way to the United States and ultimately to Morning Star Farm in West Whately, Massachusetts. There he became part of a small community of refugees who were accommodated by James Cooney and his wife, Blanche, both intellectual radicals and pacifists with a web of connections in the literary community akin to Sangree's web of connections in the church community.[35]

Mehring was one of those who took refuge in America but had no interest in becoming American. Not long after the war, he returned to the life he had fled: that of the urbane European intellectual and writer. Farm life was not for him! Quite understandably, many others who spent part of their exile at Morning Star Farm or in the Cummington hostel did the same. For them, refuge was a temporary state of affairs; and for their helpers, the shelter and other necessities they provided were also temporary.

But there were those who were determined to start a new life in the United States, and these people required a different, more extended network of helpers to aid in their resettlement. One of them was Paul Amann, a German professor of French language, who for twenty-seven years had taught at the Goethe Realschule in Vienna.[36] In 1938 he was among those stripped of his teaching post. Because Amann decided to remain in this country, his story illustrates that different and extended networking.

Already fifty-seven years old when he arrived here in 1941, Amann, along with his wife, Dora, became two refugees among the flood. Their sojourn had taken them to Marseilles, where they were the beneficiaries of the relief efforts of the American Friends Service Committee. While there, they met Burns Chalmers, whose job with the AFSC was to counsel such people about their options for getting out of the Nazi encirclement.

The Amanns got to the United States thanks to an assignment given them by Julien Champenois, the AFSC's director of Group Emigration for Children. They were to shepherd fifty-six Jewish children, for whom places had been found in America. Typical of many others at the time, and owing to the American government's grudging constraint on accommodating refugees, their odyssey was a roundabout one. It took them from Marseilles to Lisbon, probably by one of the *filières de sauvetage* that Mehring and others had used as their escape route into Spain and beyond. From Lisbon they traveled to Casablanca, thence to Bermuda, and finally, on September 24, 1941, to New York. One can only imagine the daily challenges they faced in providing food, shelter, and safety for those children during the period of their transport.

Once in America, the Amanns had to start over, the common story of many refugee professionals. Paul Amman, now an itinerant professor with no permanent address, was recommended to the Cummington hostel by a friend and fellow refugee, the poet Jacob Picard. There Amann would spend the fall months improving his English and seeking a new start. Carl Sangree took him to visit fellow scholars at Smith and Amherst colleges in hopes of finding an appointment. Nothing worked out. Amann ultimately got his first break with an appointment as a visiting fellow at Yale University. There he resumed his scholarship and taught French. He spent the next academic year living in Northampton and doing manual labor in a paper plant in Holyoke, Massachusetts. Ever in search of intellectual companionship, he made connections, through Carl Sangree and Burns Chalmers, with members of the Smith College faculty. The network of his academic friends included Smith religion professor Ralph Harlow. In October of that year of manual labor, Harlow wrote on Amann's behalf to his friend David Porter, headmaster of Mount Hermon School:

> Dear Dave:
>
> A very cultured and fine German refugee and his wife are in our city and Marion and I are trying to do something for them. He speaks excellent English, though I am giving him some extra help in this.
>
> For years he was a teacher and longs to find work. His fields are French, German and History. I enclose his record. Both he and his wife are unusually cultured and fine people, making a good impression on all whom they meet.
>
> Do you happen to have any opening or know of any into which Dr. Amann might fit? I would be glad to bring him up for an interview if you have any hope to offer.

Nothing came of that inquiry right away. Instead, Amann landed another temporary appointment, this time as a visiting professor at Kenyon College in Ohio. But the following summer, the new headmaster of Mount Hermon, Howard Rubendall, discovered Harlow's letter of the previous fall. Eager to recruit language teachers to replace those who had gone off to military duty, he wrote Amann with an invitation to teach there beginning in the fall term. So began a more stable period of Amann's resettlement.

He taught with great success at Mount Hermon; but Rubendall recognized that he was at heart a scholar and a college professor. Halfway through his second year at the school, his headmaster shared with Amann his own dilemma: he faced the obligation to make room for returning faculty members who had been on leave to do their military service, including several from the foreign language department. He wrote a strong recommendation for Amann to the American College Council, a clearinghouse for professorial talent in that time of turbulent change in college faculties around the country. The result was another college appointment, this time to one of the cluster of upstate New York colleges which, according to Amann, had been established to provide for the education of returning servicemen. Now well settled in his new life, Amann maintained his connection with his Cummington and Mount Hermon friends. He wrote to Howard Rubendall in November 1950, asking for his sponsorship and help in becoming a citizen of his new country. Rubendall responded as one would expect. Once again the enclave of human concern had enclosed these two refugees, Paul and Dora Amann, with those who responded to their need.

At the end of the war, a new phase of work with refugees began, some of it aimed at establishing others like Amann in their new lives here, and some of it involving the reconstruction of the devastated European communities and economies in which returnees would rebuild their lives. Some of these efforts, here and in Europe, involved the same people who had been part of the enclaves of resistance, relief, and refuge during the war. One striking example is the new connection that emerged between le Chambon, Cummington, and Northampton. One could begin the tale anywhere around that circle of the concerned, but we pick up the thread here in the western Massachusetts hills.

Carl Sangree's wife, Elizabeth, had died of a brain tumor in 1944, during the period when they were deeply engaged in the hostel project. Now a widower, and connected through Amann, Rubendall, and others to the Northfield and Mount Hermon communities, he came in touch with Florence Lyons, a Smith graduate who had become the dean and assistant head of the Northfield School for Girls. She served a formidable headmistress, Myra Wilson, a religion professor who had left the Smith faculty for Northfield.

Florence Lyons came from a prosperous Long Island family. She also came from a deep tradition of human service. She was a person of quiet and somewhat restrained demeanor, but one who had a most engaging smile, a rich sense of humor, and a discerning sense of the practical. She exemplified—even though from Long Island—the best of the Boston Brahmin tradition of service above self. When, in the winter term of 1945, she announced to the Northfield girls in a morning chapel service that she was to marry Carl Sangree in just a few weeks, the excitement was palpable. Her faculty friends had never quite understood why she hadn't married, and her students, of course, presumed that she never would marry. It wasn't the last time that she would surprise both her friends and her students.

Florence and Carl Sangree set out to discover just the right project that would give them opportunity to participate in the task of rehabilitating both refugees and their societies. In the fall of 1945 they went to the national offices of Congregational Church in New York to see what people there might suggest. Carl and Florence were told by the legendary pacifist minister A. J. Muste of a French minister by the name of Trocmé who was in the city trying to raise funds for the school that he and a friend had organized in France just before the war. He was staying in the guest quarters, the so-called Prophet's Chamber, at Union Theological Seminary uptown. But he was scheduled to leave for France the next day. It was already evening, so without further ado the Sangrees hurried up to 120th Street and Broadway and knocked on the door of the Prophet's Chamber. Here is Trocmé's account of the encounter:

> Someone knocked on the door and I wearily said "come in."
>
> A man and a woman walked in. Their appearance was not impressing at all: He was short, somewhat chubby and didn't speak much. She was slender and more vivacious than he was. Her left eye was smaller than the right one and it spoiled the harmony of her face.
>
> "We have listened to one of your lectures the other day and we want to know what we can do for you."
>
> I had heard this "what can I do for you" formula at least fifty times and I knew it was a vague and polite form which, in most countries, ends up by giving a piece of advice such as: "You should go and see Mr. so and so, at the Ecumenical Council or at the French Protestant Federation. He is a nice man and will certainly be able to help you."
>
> These people, Carl and Florence Sangree, had a modest appearance and I thought that, like many other Americans, they came to apply for a job at Collège Cévenol because they liked traveling and also wanted to help suffering Europe. Indeed this was what they had in mind.
>
> "What are your qualifications?" I asked.
>
> "I am a Congregationalist minister, or rather I used to be, in West Cummington, Massachusetts," he said with great modesty. "I have resigned from the ministry because I divorced to marry my second wife Florence who is here with me.[37] I don't speak French, I have never taught school but I have worked as a football coach when I was younger . . ."
>
> "We don't play American football in Le Chambon," I interrupted, "and you Madam?"
>
> "I was the administrative director of the Northfield School for Girls but I resigned when I married Carl. I am a good accountant, however."
>
> "We already have a good accountant," I said, thinking of Mademoiselle Köing.
>
> "That's unfortunate," said Carl as they stood up to let me pack.
>
> As they opened the door, Florence said something which changed the course of events.
>
> "We forgot to tell you that, during the war, we opened a small house in West Cummington for Jewish refugees who had escaped from Nazism and we were particularly interested by your speech because of your interest for refugees. We have developed a few methods of collecting money to feed these Jews in which you may be interested. We organized small student committees in New England schools which we could perhaps revive to help Collège Cévenol."
>
> "This is quite different," I said. "It is very interesting. Please come and sit down."[38]

Thus began a friendship and an alliance that lasted throughout the lifetime of all three. Thus also began one of the innumerable postwar efforts at rehabilitation, both of individuals who had become refugees and of societies that had crumbled.

Of the many and varied efforts at rehabilitation that went on in France and elsewhere in Europe, the best known was certainly the Marshall Plan; but there were dozens of others that arose from individual and communal commitments outside of governments. One such effort was undertaken by William Danforth, whose huge farm feed company, Ralston Purina, produced an all-purpose food for human consumption designed to help the French and others survive their food crisis while they rebuilt their agricultural economy. Rural areas such as the Massif Central were among the neediest, and also among the first to be helped by the Ralston Purina company's shiploads of enriched food.

Another was the postwar building of Collège Cévenol, with the help of funders and the efforts of students recruited for the task from the ranks of the Collège, and abroad by Carl and Florence Sangree. Immediately after their meeting with André Trocmé in New York in November 1945, the Sangrees had traveled about the country exploiting all their contacts and acquaintances in the network of schools and colleges to arouse interest in the school that Trocmé and Theis had founded. Its original purpose had been to open opportunities for local children to further their education at the lycée and university levels. During the war years, the École Nouvelle Cévenol, as it was first known, expanded its mission as it became part of the network of refugee sites that had given flesh and blood to Trocmé's vision for le Chambon as a "city of refuge."[39] So it was a natural progression for the Collège, after the war, to gather an international group of students for the work camp that put up its first dormitories, four Swedish prefabricated buildings.

The Sangrees persuaded Trocmé to postpone his return to France long enough for them to introduce him to key church leaders and to bring him to a number of school and college campuses in the Northeast. Among their first stops were the Northfield and Mount Hermon schools and Smith College. Those were solid starting points, since Florence Sangree had been the assistant headmistress of Northfield and was an alumna of Smith. This is their account of the visit to Smith:

> We paid a visit to Burns Chalmers, chaplain of Smith, and were surprised to learn that André and he had worked together during the war, in aiding refugees under the aegis of the Quakers. Burns was enthusiastic about the Collège Cévenol and its future. He presented André to the president of Smith College [Herbert Davis] as well as several professors and a group of students. This was the beginning of a real interest in the Collège Cévenol on the part of students and professors at Smith College, interest which has survived during several generations of students and which is still very lively today.[40]

After Trocmé returned to France a short while before Christmas, the San-grees lost no time in putting together a group of American students who would join French students of the Collège Cévenol, plus English and Swedish students, in le Chambon to put up those first four dormitories and establish the first academic and administrative center. The students pitched their tents in the pasture of a farm known as Luquet, whose traditional stone house and barn complex they would renovate into a combination administrative center, classroom, library, gymnasium, student center, and refectory. A school with a mission but without a campus would now have a simple but proper home.

The Smith students in that first work camp were accompanied to le Cham-bon by Dorothy Ainsworth, the internationally known director of the physical education program at Smith College. Burns Chalmers was a strong ally of the Sangrees' effort, and when, in the fall of 1946, a group of work camp "alumnae" from Smith put together the notion of an American support group for the Collège, Chalmers became its first president. Over the next years, students from around Europe and the United States dug the trenches for pipelines, laid out a track and athletic field, painted the Swedish barracks that were to serve as dormitories, and laid the foundations of the first proper classroom build-ing. In the foyer of this "Bâtiment Scolaire" there hangs to this day a large plaque that describes the Collège as "An International Center for Peace."

The response that began as a relief project and progressed to one of rescue and refuge had now extended the work of rehabilitation into the postwar years. Burns Chalmers was at the center of the network that brought together André Trocmé, Edouard Theis, and Carl and Florence Sangree and two edu-cational institutions, Smith College and the Collège Cévenol. The parallel commitments of people in two small towns in rural areas of France and the United States, at first unknown to each other, had merged in an institution that, however modest in its aims, was an emblem of those enclaves of resis-tance to the forces that create refugees.

Notes

This essay was occasioned by the Neilson Symposium panel discussion "Anti-Fascists and Exiles in Western Massachusetts," whose members were Deirdre Bonifaz, Gertraud Gutzmann, Charles Killinger, and Richard Unsworth. In preparing the essay, I drew material from each of the four presentations (all represented in this volume) as well as from a number of other unpublished sources. The most prominent of these is "André Pascal Trocmé, His Life's Story, Written for His Children, Grandchildren, and Great-Grandchildren," translated by Jacques P. Trocmé, January 2001. All quotations from the memoirs of André and Magda Trocmé are published here with the permission of

Jacques Trocmé and Nelly Trocmé Hewett. References are to the English translation, except where otherwise indicated.

1. Le Chambon-sur-Lignon, in the mountainous Haute Loire region of the French Massif Central, and Cummington, in the Berkshire hills of western Massachusetts, were towns of roughly similar size, both with a mix of farmers and "summer people" (*estivants* is the French term), both predominantly Protestant, and both profoundly influenced by the pacifist ministers in their rural pulpits. A third pacifist leader, Burns Chalmers, the chaplain at Smith College, became a bridge between the two.

2. In the era of Roman Catholic establishment in France, Protestants were not allowed to refer to their places of worship as churches. They adopted, and still use, the term *temple*.

3. See "Making a Difference," Peter Rose's essay in this volume on Neilson's activities with the Emergency Rescue Committee and the National Refugee Service.

4. For a full account of this group, its Northampton center, and its widespread membership, see Charles Killinger's essay in this volume, "Fighting Fascism from the Valley."

5. Joan Livingston, newspaper article in *Hampshire Life,* July 22, 1944, 9.

6. The full story of the Cummington hostel is told by Gertraud Gutzmann in this volume.

7. See Peter Rose's essay on Neilson.

8. Ricoeur's remark was made to the author in a personal conversation while walking the hills of West Cummington after a visit with the Sangrees.

9. Smith College, chartered in 1871, appointed its first president in 1873 and received its first students in 1875.

10. A fine collection of these talks was assembled by Neilson in 1940 and published by the Hampshire Bookshop on Smith's seventy-fifth anniversary in 1956 under the title *Intellectual Honesty*.

11. The defining phrase used by its founder, George Fox, to describe the purpose of the Meeting of Friends.

12. What made the work "Christian" was unclear to many Jewish students and others, but Protestant terminology was still the established mode in the society.

13. Throughout these pages there are many references to the "camps," a word used with many differing connotations—refugee shelters, transit camps, detention camps for controlling "undesirable elements" of the French population, forced labor camps, and death camps. In fact, all these camps had one thing in common: they served as a means for "concentrating" populations whom the authorities decided should not or could not be absorbed, person by person, into the general population. A study of concentration camps has appeared in *Le Siècle des Camps* by Joel Kotek and Pierre Rigoulot (Paris: L. C. Lattès, 2000), in which we discover that the notion, in the West at least, of bottling up troublesome populations was first put forward in 1895 by the commander of the Spanish garrison in Cuba, who saw it as a way of depriving insurgents of their practical and logistical support by making a sweep of the villages where their sympathizers could both harbor and resupply them. Other nations picked up the

idea: first the British confining Boers in South Africa, then the Germans in present-day Namibia, the Russians with their gulags for dissidents, the Americans with their internment camps for Japanese and Nisei during World War II, the Chinese with their Cultural Revolution against traditionalists and intellectuals, and the Serbians with the Bosnians. Concentration camps seem to be a phenomenon whose rise coincided with those innumerable moves of displaced populations which became one of the hallmarks of the twentieth century.

14. Howard E. Kershner, *The American Friends Service Committee in France*, a report privately published by the AFSC of activities for the period of July 1940–May 1941, 21.

15. Vanessa Horesnyi, "Les Maisons d'Enfants du Secours Suisse au Chambon-sur-Lignon: 1939–1945" (master's thesis presented to the history faculty of Jean Moulin University, Lyon, 1997). This thesis was made available to me by Auguste Bohny, who directed the Swiss efforts in the Viverais-Lignon Plateau from 1941 to 1944. I am indebted to Vanessa Horesnyi and her careful scholarship for many of the particulars cited in this article concerning the work of the Secours Suisse aux Enfants.

16. Kershner, "American Friends Service Committee," 16.

17. Ibid., 27.

18. Ibid., 29.

19. Herbert J. Davis, "General Correspondence, 1940–45, 1947–48, 1950, n.d.," box 1, folder 1, Sophia Smith Collection, Smith College, Northampton, Mass. I am indebted to Gertraud Gutzmann for discovering this letter in the archives of Smith College.

20. Tracy Strong Jr., "Vichy Diary: May 29, 1941–October 20, 1942," manuscript provided by Pierre Sauvage, president of the Chambon Foundation. The extant pages begin with an entry on September 23, 1941, mentioning Strong's failed attempts to keep a diary during the first three months of his stay in France. The final entry is dated April 14, 1942.

21. Ibid.

22. Trocmé's recollection is off by a year. The arrests and deportations began in the summer of 1941, according to the chronological table in Pierre Bolle, *Le Plateau Viverais-Lignon: Acceuil et Resistance, 1939–1944* (Le Chambon sur Lignon: Société d'Histoire de la Montagne, 1992), 92.

23. Trocmé, "His Life's Story," pt. 1, 263.

24. Patrick Henry, "The French Catholic Church's Apology," *French Review* 72, no. 6 (May 1999): 1101.

25. The Collège Cévenol was a school established in 1938 by Trocmé and Theis to provide rural students a better preparation for baccalaureate studies at the urban *lycées* in nearby St. Étienne and Le Puy. The Nouvelle École Cévenole, as it was first called, also became, during the war years, an educational haven for many children from the displaced populations of France and other European countries.

26. Although the translator uses the word "infants" here, the original French text (243) uses "enfants" to refer to "children."

27. Trocmé, "His Life's Story," pt. 1, 252.

28. Albert Camus, *Carnets, 1942–1951* (Paris: Éditions Gallimard, 1964), 2:38–39.

29. Serge Bernard, "La construction de la mémoire légendaire au Chambon-sur-Lignon" (thesis presented to the social sciences faculty of the University of Paris, Jussieu, September 2000), 43.

30. *Les Camisards* (Cevennes: Musée du Désert, 1986).

31. Bolle, *Le Plateau Viverais-Lignon*, 132.

32. Ibid., 26.

33. Horesnyi, "Les Maisons d'Enfants," 23.

34. Varian Fry, *Surrender on Demand* (1945; reprint, Washington, D.C.: Johnson Books/U.S. Holocaust Memorial Museum, 1997). Fry's dates in Marseilles—August 1940 to September 1941—are virtually the same as Chalmers's time there.

35. The account of Mehring's sojourn in refuge is given in this volume by Deirdre Bonifaz in "A Haven in Whately: The Refugees Who Came to Our Farm."

36. The material on Amann is taken from research done by Gertraud Gutzmann and depends chiefly on the archived files of the Northfield–Mount Hermon School.

37. Trocmé's recollection is in error. Carl Sangree had indeed divorced his first wife when both were very young. He had been a widower, however, since Elizabeth's death the year before.

38. Not surprisingly, Trocmé's account includes some errors, this section having been written some twenty-three years after the fact. It was Elizabeth, not Florence, Sangree who had been involved in the organization of the Cummington hostel. Thus the remark about the Cummington hostel must have been made by Carl Sangree.

39. The change of name from École Nouvelle Cévenole to Collège Cévenol came about at the end of the war years when the administration decided to focus its attention on secondary education and discontinue its primary grades.

40. Edouard Theis, ed., *Collège Cévenol: 30 Ans d'Histoire* (privately published), 30b. The translation is my own.

ACCULTURATION, TRANSFER, AND INTEGRATION
Exiled Scholars and Writers in Western Massachusetts

GERTRAUD E. G. GUTZMANN

THE UNITED STATES was the chief country of exile for scholars, writers, and artists from Nazi-occupied Europe.[1] In the 1930s a number of distinguished refugees gained entry to the United States and found teaching or research positions at prestigious American colleges and universities. Erich Auerbach, for instance, professor of Romance languages and literatures, came to Yale University, where he gained worldwide renown in the field of comparative literature. In an essay on Auerbach's stellar career at Yale, Henri Peyre, professor emeritus of the Department of French at that institution, goes so far as to call the United States a "paradise for exiles."[2] Admission to the American academic "paradise" was not granted readily, however, and not to all refugee intellectuals, even though in 1940 the U.S. State Department established a procedure for issuing "emergency visitor visas" for endangered refugee scholars, artists, and politicians whose achievements were of interest to this country.[3] To gain access to prestigious American institutions of higher learning, the refugees had to be experts in their fields, and give proof of at least three years' teaching experience, requirements established by major agencies or foundations that controlled the placement of émigrés at colleges, universities, museums, and private schools.[4] Even then, the refugee scholar had to be a quick study in determining the value of his expertise or prestige on the academic market of his host country.[5]

The prospects of acquiring financial security and prestige in the American cultural arena, however, had changed considerably by 1940–41. Colleges and universities were overcrowded by that time with exile academics, and the hostility toward émigré scholars was intensifying.[6] Yet these were the years when European intellectuals, politicians, and artists were arriving in the United States in vast numbers, having escaped from southern France and the Nazi threat by a hair's breadth. Initially, many of the newly arrived had not sought to leave Europe for overseas countries, but rather hoped to wait out the collapse of the Nazi regime in their exile in France. To many exiles—Heinrich Mann, Walter Benjamin, Anna Seghers, and Paul Amann, for instance—France had been an intellectual homeland all along, even though French laws had imposed considerable restrictions and hardships on them. By the summer of 1940, after the defeat of France by Hitler's army, the situation of German and Austrian refugees in France had become untenable. Once Marshal Pétain had signed the armistice with the Germans, most exiles were in extreme danger. Vichy France, according to Article 19 of the armistice, agreed to deliver on demand to the Gestapo any of the thousands of resisters to Nazism residing, hiding, or held in camps in the region. Many a well-known critic, writer, or political activist—Walter Mehring, Anna Seghers, Lion Feuchtwanger, Heinrich Mann, Walter Benjamin, and Kurt Breidscheid, to name just a few— ranked high on the Gestapo's "Most Wanted" list. Yet hundreds of lesser-known exiles were trapped in southern France as well—political activists, working-class people, staff members of publishing houses or newspapers, teachers, translators, and critics who had all been part of their countries' cultural tapestry on which the famous had been accorded a central place.

The stories of such famous exiles as Thomas Mann, Heinrich Mann, Lion Feuchtwanger, Walter Mehring, and Franz Werfel have been richly documented over the years, particularly in Andy Marino's *Quiet American: The Secret War of Varian Fry*. In this essay I explore the experiences of "ordinary exiles," as the lesser-known European writers, scholars, and artists have been called. In recent years their lives and paths in American culture have become the focus of exile studies. Hanna Papanek goes so far as to consider the letters of less well-known refugees, their unpublished or incomplete manuscripts and diaries hidden away in archives all over the world, as the "true literature of exile," for they document, in her view, the harsh realities of life in flight and exile with greater detail and more perceptible urgency than do the autobiographical fictions of famous men.[7]

Paul Amann, an Austrian-Jewish educator, writer, and translator whose story I am about to retell, is one such less famous exile. In June 1942 he became a guest of the Refugee Hostel in Cummington, in western Massachusetts.[8] He was to work on improving his English and to translate chapters of his book *Tradition und Weltkrise* (Tradition and World Crisis, 1934) for publication in the United States so as to enhance his prospects of finding a teaching post at the college or university level in French, German, or cultural history. I reconstruct from letters, official documents, and other unpublished materials Amann's situation in southern France and his last-minute rescue through the efforts of such famous friends as Hermann Broch and Thomas Mann in the United States, as well as assistance from Quaker organizations and the Emergency Rescue Committee in Marseilles.[9] His experiences in the United States, however, in particular the process of his assimilation to daily life and to the academic culture of western Massachusetts and greater New England, are the main concern of my essay. In particular, I explore the tensions arising from Amann's eagerness to become part of the educational world of his host country, and his lapses into European concepts and values in regard to culture and education. His vacillation between the wish to adapt to new conditions and the need to insist on his Viennese social status and cultural self-understanding find instructive expression in his letters to family members and to close personal or famous friends. While Amann, in his more intimate correspondence, frequently expresses pride and enjoyment in his new teaching appointments, however temporary they may have been, he tends to detract from these experiences, measuring them by European standards when writing to his more prominent friends.

Amann had difficulties acquiring in western Massachusetts the kind of financial security and prestige he had enjoyed in Vienna. He nevertheless did assimilate to daily life and academic work—though not, as he would have preferred, at prestigious institutions such as Amherst or Smith, but rather at Mohawk and Champlain colleges in remote upper New York State, where he was hardly shielded from the realities of American life and culture. Despite his advanced age, he managed to succeed as a teacher of German, so much so that he held his position until the age of sixty-eight. As a scholar, however, Amann did not establish a reputation among his American peers in the field of German or French languages and literatures. He continued to struggle to find his own voice when writing in English—an understandable struggle, indeed. In addition, his area of expertise, as well as his reluctance to adapt to American academic conventions—he regarded the annual conventions of the Modern Language Association, for instance, as a "cattle market for academics"—did not exactly enhance his chances of making an impression on his peers.[10]

Yet Amann was not the only specialist in the field of Romance or German studies not to accept and adapt to American conventions in the area of research and publication. Leo Spitzer and Erich Auberbach were exceptions among exile scholars of Romance languages and literatures who succeeded at prestigious American universities. The experiences of Leonardo Olschki, an authority in Romance language studies, formerly of the University of Heidelberg, are far from resembling Auerbach's or Spitzer's successes. Looking back on his attempts to continue in the United States his distinguished European career, Olschki concluded near the end of his life: "I have gotten nowhere in this country, because there is no use for old-time humanists such as I am; and since scholarship without a use value is considered nonsensical by definition in this pragmatic society, I cut, at best, a comical figure."[11] Amann, in his letters dating from his American years, in particular those addressed to Thomas Mann, arrived at a similar assessment.

At the time when he was preparing for emigration to the United States, Amann was neither an Auerbach nor an Olschki. Nevertheless, between 1910 and 1939 he had gained considerable fame in Austrian, German, and French literary circles, especially as a distinguished translator of literary works from French into German. Hermann Broch, Thomas Mann, and Hermann Hesse were among his famous friends, as were French writers such as Georges Duhamel, Jean Richard Bloch, Romain Rolland, and Maurice Minot, whose works he had translated into German with enviable success for the Zsolnay publishing house in Vienna and Kurt Wolff in Munich. Born in Prague in 1884 to a middle-class Jewish family, he grew up amidst different ethnic and racial groups, an experience that informed his lifelong interest in cultural studies, which had culminated in his book *Tradition und Weltkrise*, published by Schocken of Berlin in 1934. It was a study of cultural differences within Europe, especially those between France and Germany. Since the Nazis pulped the book shortly after its publication because of the author's critical stance on racial "theories," Amann did not receive the critical reception he had hoped for.[12] The fate of *Tradition und Weltkrise* became an obsession for Amann in his American years. He had plans for its publication in English, updated and adapted for American audiences, in the hopes of establishing his reputation as a scholar of distinction. He tried for ten years, mostly under adverse circumstances, to complete this project, an effort that was thwarted throughout.

Amann had studied German and French literature as well as philosophy in Vienna and Prague, where, in 1905, he earned his doctorate in German literature with a dissertation on the nineteenth-century Jewish writer Leopold Kompert.[13] The same year he passed with distinction the examinations for secondary school teachers in French and German. In 1910 he traveled to France, a trip that marks the beginning of his lasting interest in French literature and culture. In addition to his translations of writers such as Romain Rolland and Jean Richard Bloch, Amann published a number of essays on sociocultural topics, "Western Jewish Dynamic" of 1919 among them.[14]

Amann's status in German and Austrian literary circles was, in part, linked to his correspondence, beginning in 1915, with Thomas Mann. His reflections on culture and literature, including Mann's own writings, were received with generous attention and appreciation. In fact, Mann was initially so taken by Amann's writing that, he said, he wished their exchange of ideas would never end.[15] Their correspondence was abruptly broken off, however, after Amann, in an essay published in a Munich cultural journal, accused Mann of plagiarism.[16] They resumed communication eighteen years after that rupture and met, for the first time in fact, at a dinner in 1937 held in Vienna in Mann's honor. Meanwhile, Mann had already been sent a copy of Amann's *Tradition und Weltkrise*.[17] He apparently regarded the study highly enough to take it along, with a limited number of other books, into exile.[18] Amann came to rely heavily on Mann's generous letter of appreciation of the book and its author in his efforts to gain a faculty appointment at various distinguished institutions of higher learning in the United States.

Hermann Broch, another of the famous exiles, became acquainted with Amann through a translation project. In 1935 Broch's novel *Die Schlafwander* (The Sleepwalkers) came out, and Amann was so taken by the book that he offered to translate a chapter into French and have it published in the prestigious journal *L'Europe*. It was the beginning of a lifelong and life-saving friendship, for Broch was instrumental, together with Thomas Mann, in getting Amann on the list of endangered intellectuals, a prerequisite for gaining an emergency visa to the United States.[19]

Amann and his family had left Vienna in February 1939, a year after the annexation of Austria by Nazi Germany. Because he was Jewish, Amann, at the age of fifty-four, was dismissed from his teaching position at the Goethe-Realschule. His *Tradition und Weltkrise*, as well as the French novels he had translated, were on the Nazis' list of banned books. Having witnessed for a year the rampant anti-Semitism in the streets of Vienna, the Amanns decided that it was time to head for France. After a year in Paris and environs, where they had friends and felt quite at home, they had to leave again, along with thousands of others, once the Germans marched into Paris in June 1940. Thanks to Amann's writer friend Georges Duhamel, an ardent anti-Nazi, they were able to travel by train to the unoccupied zone of southern France, for Duhamel had secured for them from the German authorities the *sauf-conduit*, a document required of persons of foreign origin wishing to travel to that part of the country. Amann and his wife, Dora, found a place to stay in Montpellier, their residence until their departure for the United States in September 1941.[20]

In Montpellier, Amann befriended Edmond Vermeil, a professor of German literature and as staunch an anti-Nazi as Duhamel, both of whom ranked high on the Gestapo's list of French enemies of the Third Reich.[21] Vermeil, cognizant of Amann's expertise as a translator, invited the Austrian to help him develop examination materials for French students of German language and literature at the University of Montpellier. Vermeil and Duhamel, as well as Hermann Hesse, would write letters of reference for Amann, attesting to the high quality of his work as a teacher, translator, and writer. Letters of this nature were essential for a refugee intellectual to convince the Emergency Rescue Committee (ERC) and Varian Fry, as well as other aid organizations in Marseilles, of his scholarly worth. They were but one of the many kinds of documents a refugee hoping to get out of southern France had to procure for

the relevant authorities and agencies. Amann's letters to friends and to officials in Marseilles, as well as an unpublished satirical prose sketch, give insight
into his despair and depression as a refugee trapped in southern France in
1940-41. They confirm the "reality" of *Transit* (1944), Anna Seghers's exemplary
novel of exile, which encapsulates the predicament of refugees from Nazi-
occupied Europe in the Marseilles of those times. It was a city overrun by
people in flight, caught in an obscure, menacing world of bureaucracy—of
consulates and French administrative offices—and subjected to the abuse of
hotel managers, the police, and small business owners determined to make a
profit from their plight. As Seghers's narrator observes: "At that time, everybody had just one wish—to sail; and just one fear—to be left behind. Anywhere—as long as it took you away from this shattered country, this shattered
life, this star! People listened to you avidly as long as you told them about
ships that had been captured or had never arrived, and visas that had been
bought or forged, and countries that were issuing transit permits."[23]

Meanwhile, Amann's friends in the United States did their utmost to secure
affidavits, visas, and ship passage for Amann and his family. The American
Guild for German Cultural Freedom, in particular Wolfgang Sauerländer, a
former associate of the Kurt Wolff publishing house, in collaboration with
Broch and his secretary, Viktor Polzer (an acquaintance of Amman's because
of their association with Zsolnay publishers in Vienna), after a year of desperate efforts managed to get Amann and his family out in September 1941. It all
began with a letter of August 15, 1940, from Broch to Sauerländer at the Guild's
office at 20 Vesey Street, New York City. Broch tried to make a case for Amann,
"an experienced Viennese secondary school professor, extremely well qualified
to teach French, German and history here in the United States." In closing he
asked: "What can be done for the man? His dream is to teach at the high
school or college level, possibly this fall?"[24] Two months later Viktor Polzer
urged the Guild to step up its efforts on a colleague's behalf. Polzer describes
the Amanns' situation as desperate, with the potential for family suicide.
"Thomas Mann is very interested in Amann," Polzer continues to plead; "he
knows him personally and thinks highly of him and is ready to put his esteem
in writing."[25] A letter to Mildred Adams of the Emergency Rescue Committee
(ERC) in New York seems to have got the wheels turning, for on November 28,
1941, Broch reported to his friend in southern France:

> This is the situation with regard to your visas: you rank high on the list of the
> endangered European intellectuals with the Rescue Committee, due in large
> measure to efforts and extraordinary support of our friend Thomas. We are
> working currently on an affidavit for you. Our hopes to secure you a professor's

visa did not materialize. Colleges and universities are already overcrowded with exiled academics, and the hostility to émigré scholars in American academic institutions is intensifying.[26]

At the same time, he assured Amann that a suitable position would be found, and that he should not lose his admirable courage.

Shortly thereafter, Viktor Polzer was able to send Amann the happy news that affidavits and visas for the entire family had been secured. What remained to be done was to raise the money for the ship passage to bring them to the United States, the most difficult part of the Guild's efforts on the Amanns' behalf. Sauerländer and Polzer apparently went so far as to beg strangers for money and to contribute from their personal funds to the Amanns' travel costs, set at $1,200. Yet the Guild had been able to raise only $600, leaving it to Amann to come up with the rest. Thanks to the intervention of Julien Champenois, a French Quaker in Marseilles, Amann, on July 10, 1941, got to present his predicament to Varian Fry. Although the ERC was willing to assist him with daily expenses, the committee was not ready to cough up the $600 Amann needed.[27] By the summer of 1941, the Gestapo was closing in on southern France. Ships rarely left Marseilles harbor for ports overseas, and the Amanns had every reason to fear for their lives. Had it not been for the American Friends Service Committee, Julien Champenois in particular, their fate would have been sealed. Champenois, once he had learned of Amann's predicament, secured the Amanns' passage in return for accompanying a transport of fifty-six Jewish children from Marseilles via Spain and Portugal to New York. They left the European continent on the *Serpa Pinto* on September 9, 1941, and arrived seventeen days later in New York, where Polzer welcomed them all and led them to their temporary residences.[28]

For their first months in the United States, the Amanns remained in the care of the Quakers. From October 1941 to the end of February 1942, they were guests at a refugee hostel in Haverford, Pennsylvania, where they attended the Cooperative College Workshops for uprooted German and Austrian intellectuals interested in teaching. The goal was to help such refugees adjust to American life and acquire a speaking knowledge of American English. Christopher Isherwood, one of the mentors at the workshop, noted Amann's determination to find a teaching position by the time the workshop ended. In his perception, Amann stood out among the rest, whom Isherwood describes as "badly rattled middle-aged whose life-line to the homeland had been brutally cut and whose will to make a new start in a new country was very weak."[29] In a letter to Lilian Cohen, his Quaker caseworker, Amann proudly reports that his English had greatly improved and that he had benefited, with regard to

American ways of teaching, from observing classes in French and history at Haverford College. "I would be too happy to find myself some work to do as a teacher before my time at the workshop is over," he writes in closing.[30]

His hopes, however, did not materialize. He received a three-month fellowship instead (March–May 1942) at Yale University, as a guest of the Department of French. The time at Yale would further acquaint him with American academic institutions and their scholarly standards and teaching practices. In Henri Peyre of the French department, Amann found a loyal friend and generous mentor who, in a letter of recommendation, wrote about his refugee charge:

> I knew Mr. Amann well in 1942, while he was a visiting fellow in French at Yale. He gave several scholarly talks at our Romance Club and at our group saw a good deal of students, was well liked by every one, students and colleagues. He is a man of fine intellectual caliber. He has also a very pleasing and modest personality. We have found him remarkably adaptable and more likely to succeed with American boys and in an American institution than many other refugees.[31]

While Paul Amann was at Yale, his wife and children had to remain in Philadelphia in Quaker care, with Dora Amann providing for the family as a seamstress and cook. The family was to be separated in subsequent months as well, when Amann came to the Refugee Hostel in Cummington (June–October 1942) after his fellowship at Yale ended. He was fortunate to be invited to Cummington, thanks to the initiative of Jacob Picard, a German-Jewish writer, poet, and lawyer whom Amann had befriended at the Haverford hostel.[32]

The months Amann spent in Cummington, a village in the hills of western Massachusetts, were perhaps the toughest and most instructive challenge in his adjustment to American life. At the age of fifty-eight, a time when many academics look forward to retirement, Amann, spurred on by his sponsors and mentors, chief among them pastor Carl Sangree of Cummington, began looking for a teaching position in French or in German at prestigious area colleges such as Smith, Amherst, Mount Holyoke, and Williams.

It may come as a surprise that refugee poets, painters, sculptors, journalists, scholars, and politicians from such cultured metropolitan centers as Vienna, Prague, Berlin, and Frankfurt should have wanted to come to Cummington. The village was, however, not just a remote hill town; it was also a summer center for the arts. The Cummington School of the Arts attracted poets, writers, and painters.[33] Moreover, it was the home of the prestigious Cummington Press, which produced books of lasting value.[34] Greenwood Camp, for young musicians up to the age of eighteen, with famous artists among its teachers, added to Cummington's reputation as an artistic center.

The key figure in bringing exiles to the town, however, was the Reverend

Carl Sangree, the village pastor, a lover of the arts and an activist Congregational minister. Nelly Baar Wieghardt, an accomplished sculptor, wife of the painter Paul Wieghardt, both temporary residents of the refugee hostel, writes in her memoirs:

> Carl Sangree may have been only the minister of a small country church, but his vision and interests went far beyond. Probably not more than ten years older than Paul he had traveled widely, was interested in all the arts, and was more of a teacher than a preacher. He worked with great skill to promote the artists at the hostel, and succeeded in arranging the first exhibition for Paul and me in this country. That was to be early in December at the Berkshire Museum in Pittsfield, Massachusetts.[35]

Sangree had turned a house he owned on Main Street in Cummington into a hostel in which, between 1940 and 1944, up to twelve refugees could be safely lodged, if rather cramped for space at any given time. There they found respite from their recent experiences of flight and displacement. They were also given the chance to acquire practical work skills while improving their English and their understanding of American habits and customs. It was largely meant for Jewish refugees, especially those whom other refugee committees did not support. Yet these newcomers were not received with undivided enthusiasm in Cummington's Yankee community. They were, after all, the first sizable group of foreigners in their midst. Yet the town accepted them after a while and found them to be decent people.

After Pearl Harbor, all of that changed. The widespread obsession with Nazi spies, presumably ready to land on the shores of Long Island Sound, ready to infiltrate the American Northeast, had taken hold of the Cummington community as well. Local residents wanted the foreigner to leave. Some threatened to shoot any refugee who would dare to show up on the village streets.[36] But Sangree "soothed" the refugees, as Gloria Gowdy recalls; he "translated for them, interpreted for them, took the criticism for them, chaired the meetings, scoured the countryside looking for donations and craft materials . . . and tried to maintain his ministry in Cummington, which was frequently a prickly situation."[37] If spies were to make their way as far as Cummington, he told his parishioners, they would hardly resemble any of the refugees, who spoke English with an accent, whose clothes were worn out and their pockets empty. Real German spies, Sangree argued, would have perfect command of American English, impeccable citizenship papers, and lots of dollars. Sangree was determined to turn the experiences of his exiles into success stories, even though his charges often misread or resisted his efforts on their behalf, as a number of Amann's letters to his wife, Dora, suggest.[38]

Amman had come to Cummington for the purpose of improving his English, in order to translate a chapter of his book *Tradition und Weltkrise* for submission to an American publisher, and to find a teaching position at one of the schools and colleges in western Massachusetts. In a letter of June 27, 1942, written to Major Eugene Freedman, M.D., his affidavit sponsor, Amann describes his new situation as follows: "Now for two months I am invited at this little home in western Massachusetts in a lovely country and here I am writing the outline of my book for my former editor Kurt Wolff. He is starting again a publishing job and said to me: Ihr Buch interessiert mich brennend [your book is of great interest to me]. Smith College is very near to this place and there I have friends among the professors who can help me to correct my English."[39] Kurt Wolff, the famous German publisher, himself an exile in New York by 1942, who had been associated with Amann in the 1920s, had indeed expressed interest in Amann's study, but eventually decided against its publication.[40] In fact, that was to be the fate of the English-language manuscript of *Tradition und Weltkrise* for the next ten years: one rejection after another by university presses such as Harvard, Princeton, and Chicago.[41]

Amann was but one of the many exiled writers and scholars who found it difficult to understand and accept the differences between the European and American styles of academic writing and publication. For American critics and publishers, "European" or "central European" was synonymous with "too erudite," "too long," "too thorough," "too esoteric," "too philosophical," or "too subjective, not scholarly enough."[42] Amann was loath to adapt to American scholarly conventions in his field. It was only at the urging of his friend Henri Peyre of Yale University that he joined the Modern Language Association and presented a paper at the group's annual meeting, a professional gathering he called "a meat market for teachers."[43] Having been socialized in Prague's and Vienna's early-twentieth-century café culture, where he had taken part in the sustained exchange of ideas and debates between artists and intellectuals, Amann found the MLA's mass dispatch of intellectual goods discouraging. And yet he also felt professionally isolated, frequently overcome by self-doubt and resignation. In times such as these he had an ever-ready escape hatch: the letter of recommendation from Thomas Mann, describing Amman as a "scholar and author of great rank" whose *Tradition und Weltkrise* had made "a tremendous impression" on him.[44]

It would appear, then, that Amann's stay in Cummington did not serve its initial purpose, which had been to come up with an outline and a translation of one chapter of his book, and to find a publisher and a teaching position in a nearby college. Yet he benefited in other ways from the four months he spent at the refugee hostel. To begin with, he enjoyed the companionship of his writer friend Jacob Picard and that of Gustav Wolf, a distinguished artist and former professor at the Arts Academy at Karlsruhe, Germany. Wolf was to become artist in residence at the nearby Northfield School. Of these friends Amann wrote to Dora: "You know Picard who is very dear to me, despite his many quirky ways and the many little unpleasant things he does and says. ... Gustav Wolf, the painter and graphic artist in our midst, is as superb a human being as he is an artist."[45] While the gifted poet Picard, as the hostel's gardener, had to do mainly physical work, Wolf and Amann were free to concentrate on their artwork and translation project, much to their friend's envy and resentment. European notions of class, work, and status were being played out here, as one of Amman's letters to Dora suggests. In describing to her the other hostel residents, he draws a satirical picture of a "bourgeois" Viennese couple, the "Gutmanns." Amann was astonished to meet up with "such people" in a hostel supposedly meant primarily for "artists and intellectuals."[46]

Amann, Picard, and Wolf seem to have shared many walks through the Cummington countryside, a habitual recreational activity for Europeans of their background. Walking was as natural to them as it was perplexing to their host community.[47] The western Massachusetts landscape reminded Wolf, Amann, and Picard of their homelands. It was here that Gustav Wolf became acquainted with America. Having left the unsettling rhythms of New York City, he regained in Cummington, and later on in Northfield, that inner peace he urgently needed for his creative spirit. Picard, in letters, essays, and several poems, pays tribute to the beauty of the area and to the small hamlet of Cummington.[48] Along with Greenwood Music Camp, the Tod Morden Estate, as it is referred to these days, was one of the three friends' favorite destinations. In the summer of 1942 it apparently was a guesthouse run by a Miss Abendrot.[49] Here they would enjoy a meal, play croquet, or engage in conversation with other guests, experiences of which Amman told Dora, "The subject matter, or the nuances of what is being said, continue to elude me; still feel like a mentally deaf person."[50]

Amann, Picard, and Wolf were in "transit," hoping for steady employment and a place to settle down. Carl Sangree untiringly fended for them. As Amann comments in one of his letters, Sangree was for "doing things, looking at things."[51] For example, he set up interviews for Amann with the departments of French and German at Amherst and Smith; he even drove his refugee charges to these institutions.

One of the many telling examples of Sangree's efforts to familiarize his refugees with American ways of life is an evening at a local church where Amann was to give a talk. In a letter of September 9, 1942, his describes that experience:

Last night, C.S. took me to West Cummington. We first drove to his farm in the hills. . . . Then we drove to the town for church supper. I sat next to local farmers and we soon got talking and became comfortable with each other. I was the main attraction with my talk about our refugee experiences. . . . People complimented me on my good English, which was good to hear; for when picking apples, I often don't speak a word to anyone for most of the day."[52]

Sangree knew quite well what he was doing: he had his refugees interact on a personal level with ordinary Americans, who generally knew little about the exiles' background. Amann seems to have caught on to Sangree's objectives, for he would later write to his minister friend, "Looking back on my stay at the guest-house, I fully realize what a blessing have been these months of quiet preparation for an American life." He goes on to reminisce about his "exchanges of ideas and experiences" with Sangree, as well as his interactions with local people. "In the slow-motion picture of the rural life," he writes in closing, "it was easy for us to notice general trends of that New Life which would be our and our children's life in the near future."[53]

By the end of October 1942, despite sustained efforts Amann had still not found a teaching position anywhere. A small window of opportunity seemed to open up when Herbert Davis, president of Smith College, on September 12, 1942, asked Amann to come and see him at his office. Apparently Davis agreed to ask Paul Graham of the German department to design a few courses that Amann could teach at Smith. The salary would come from the Oberlaender Trust, which, in collaboration with the Emergency Committee in Aid of Displaced German Scholars, was known to support such appointments, provided there was a prospect for longer-term employment at the institution.[54] To Amann's great disappointment, however, Graham seemed unwilling to "create" courses for him. In addition, support from the Oberlaender Trust did not materialize, nor did the opportunity to teach French at Amherst College. His friend and mentor Henri Peyre at Yale had tried to dissuade him all along from applying for a position in French because colleges gave preference to native speakers or Americans specialists in the field.[55] Carl Sangree seems to have been as disappointed as Amann was, for he went so far as to contact a friend who was a trustee of Smith College in the hope that a position of sorts might be set up for "his refugee."[56]

Despite all of these setbacks, Amann decided to move to Northampton. Reunited with his wife and children, from whom he had been separated for about eight months, he found an apartment at 66 West Street, within walking distance of Smith College and Forbes Library. In addition, the Ammans had some friends in the Smith community, President Herbert Davis, Professor Hans Kohn, and Ralph Harlow chief among them. Amann ended up taking a job in a Holyoke paper mill, while his wife worked in Northampton as a seamstress. In a letter to his eldest son, Ernest, in Mexico, Amann writes: "Both of us are thoroughly fed up with our make-shift arrangements of war-jobs, but we must stick to them for the time being. I am living now, without any real contact but am, nevertheless, observing a great deal, for what purpose, I don't know."[57] And observe he did: aspects of raw American reality, experiences from which he probably would have been shielded teaching at an Ivy League institution. In an unpublished prose sketch titled "In der Papiermühle" (At the Paper Mill), he describes the informality of interactions between bosses and workers. Instead of the employees calling their superiors "Herr Direktor," which he, as a European, would have expected, he hears them call out, "Hello, Bob." He also notes with appreciation that the workers are not constantly supervised, for as a laborer he was clumsy and inept at most tasks. His fellow workers' teasing was mitigated by their respect for his ability to speak five or more languages, which he gave away when speaking with a French Canadian, a German, a Czech, and a Pole, respectively, in their own languages.[58]

By October 1943 Amann was teaching at Kenyon College in Gambier, Ohio, albeit not as a member of its regular faculty. Kenyon at the time was home to the Army Special Training Program, to which Amann had been appointed for about eight months as a teacher of German and French for GIs bound for Europe. It was his first teaching appointment in the United States. "Working with these eager and intelligent soldiers has been one of my best teaching experiences," he wrote to Thomas Mann in January 1944, expressing at the same time his regret at having to leave the program by the end of April of that year.[59] It comes as no surprise that Amann should have been successful in teaching nontraditional students, for he had mentored adult learners, many of them working-class people, in an evening school in Vienna from the mid-1920s until 1938.[60] Amann's ability to adjust his style of teaching to his learners' abilities and skill levels finds further expression in a letter to President Davis:

> For the time being it is very satisfactory work. In this ASTP we have soldiers who are supposed to learn German or French, especially how to talk one of those languages within nine months. And therefore we had to devise and apply rather new methods of intensive training. The results are not unsatisfactory as yet, I think, and anyway we are extremely satisfied with the kind of students we got: nice and decent young fellows and many very gifted and clever boys among them.[61]

At the end of the program he felt he had learned to teach "American style."[62]

Nevertheless, at the age of sixty, Amann was still without steady employment. He aimed high once again, applying for a position at Stanford Univer-

sity, hoping that a letter from Thomas Mann would be sufficient "pull" to
land him a job at that famous California institution of higher learning. As was
to be expected, the Stanford position did not materialize, for by 1944 the
teaching market, in the humanities in particular, was overcrowded. Instead,
Amann was hired by Mount Hermon Preparatory School in Northfield, Massachusetts, where he was to teach French eighteen hours a week, replacing
teachers drafted by the U.S. Army. At Mount Hermon, Amann was able to
expand his understanding of American teaching practices. Looking back at his
time at that institution, he wrote to David Rubendall, the school's headmaster:

> To notice your guidance in this school was a great experience for me, American
> education at its best. To you I owe the opportunity to have lived and taught at
> Mt. Hermon and to have the inside story of such a model institution. I am proud
> to have had my share in the collective work and, perhaps, to have left my mark
> on some young minds, the grain which did take root in deep good soil, by a
> happy chance.[63]

At the same time, while at Mount Hermon, Amann felt isolated, as a letter
to his friend Hugo Bergmann suggests. "All social accessoires of a refugee are
really dead: homeland, companionship of friends except a few such as you
are," he writes mournfully, missing "our furniture, books, social standing and
record, professional know-how, strategies for living and the little pleasantries,
the Vienna Cafés, or a walk through the parks at Schönbrunn castle, all of
that is gone. There is only a faint shadow left of the former self that is trying
to build a new life at the age of 60."[64] In the same letter he also expresses his
frustration with teaching elementary and intermediate language courses, longing for a situation where his vast knowledge would be appreciated. "Americans
are good at coping with life, but not very inclined towards things intellectual,"
he finds. "Life here in the States is not easier, but less demanding intellectually,"[65] a leitmotif of all of his comments on America. Like a great number of
exiles of his generation, he missed in America an appreciation for intellectual
work without a use value. And yet he also mentions having met in Northfield
and environs bright and admirable people, the Reverend Burns Chalmers of
Smith College chief among them. Amann had met Chalmers in Quaker relief
quarters in Marseilles in 1941, and Chalmers became the Amanns' sponsor at
the time they converted their visitors' visas to immigration papers.[66]

In 1946, at the age of sixty-two, Amann was back on the job market, still
hoping for a more permanent teaching position. "The papers are full of statements that New England and other parts of the country begin to feel a short-
age of teachers. Should that not improve my prospects?" Amann asked Else
Staudinger, his advocate at the Emergency Committee for Refugee Scholars,

Writers, and Artists.[67] Despite Amann's close proximity to the traditional American retirement age of sixty-five, Staudinger managed to place Amann in the public college and university system of upstate New York, where he taught German from 1946 to 1952, his longest appointment at any American institution of higher learning. He started out at Mohawk College in Utica, and then moved on to Champlain College in Plattsburgh.

How much farther removed from Vienna or Paris and their cultural ambience could a man of Amann's background find himself? To be sure, he continued to struggle with such European notions as social prestige and professional stature. At the same time, he appears to have thrived in upstate New York, removed from the German and Austrian exile centers. He enjoyed teaching at both Mohawk and Champlain, finding the experience "agreeable, interesting and successful."[68] At the same time, he expressed frustration over the poor background knowledge of his students. "Teaching in this country," he complains to Thomas Mann in a letter of June 15, 1951, "you have to be shockproof, when in a class of twenty-year-olds not one has heard of 'muses,' or a Berlin born ex-GI who fought in the Battle of the Bulge asks me what an 'oracle' might be."[69]

At the same time, at Champlain College, Amann for the first time in a long while was close to a city with a good library, concerts, and street life. He was eager to become part of a community, not just an academic setting. In one of his letters he describes for Thomas Mann a Plattsburgh town meeting. His surprise at meeting so many intelligent, refined, independent-minded individuals caused him to change his opinions about Americans. "What astounded me most," he wrote Mann, "are the women, ladies who, by their looks, seemed to have stepped out of the dreams of our youth! Except for their energized, articulate presence!" On the local level, he concludes, one is apt to encounter the worst that America has to offer, but also "all that is indestructible, strength and basic goodness."[70]

AMANN'S MAY not have been an Erich Auerbach success story in North American academia. His inability to write and publish in English is a recurring theme in almost all of his letters of these years, especially those addressed to Hermann Broch, Thomas Mann, and his friend Hugo Bergmann. "There is a strange inhibition preventing me from putting into literary shape the manifold research I have done during the last twelve years," he confesses to Bergmann.[71] In a letter to Thomas Mann he goes so far as to admit his dislike for the kind of research that requires file cards and footnotes. One gains the impression that Amann "published" his work in his many long letters to such friends as Thomas Mann, Hugo Bergmann, and Romain Rolland. Looking back on his life, he concluded that the intellectual exchange in the form of letters may well have been his genuine scholarly accomplishment, not all the research projects he started but never completed.[72]

Yet Amann had no intention of returning to Europe. Instead, he moved in his retirement to Fairfield, Connecticut, where he lived until his death at the age of seventy in February 1958. In a melancholy note to Thomas Mann he concludes, "On y plante ses choux (et roses) àla Candide, ist Hauswirt einer Robin-Familie und hört das Nebelhorn drüben vom Sund" (You plant your cabbages and roses here, like Candide, play the role of landlord to a family of robins, and listen to the foghorn from across the bay).[73] For Amann and others of his generation, America remained "die Fremde," the foreign country, despite the fact that he succeeded in securing teaching positions into his sixties and enjoyed the esteem of his students and fellow teachers. As Dora Amann concluded, in looking back on her husband's life in the United States, "In seiner geistigen Welt hatte Paul viel Heimweh nach Europa" (Intellectually and emotionally, Paul was quite homesick for Europe).[74] At the same time, he had recognized all along that, for his children, the United States was indeed a land of great opportunity. Amann's son Peter became a professor of history, his daughter Eva an accomplished artist. Despite all its wrongs and flaws, Amann felt a deep gratitude toward his country of rescue, an "active gratitude," as he stated in a 1955 letter to Hans Kohn. "We have to make our contribution, for it is a country that is eager to learn, to become educated and cultured."[75]

Notes

Amann's papers, housed in the Leo-Baeck-Institute of New York, among them unpublished short stories, plays, poems, essays, and notes, contain a wealth of insight into the promises and problems of cultural mediation.

1. See Claus-Dieter Krohn, *Intellectuals in Exile: Refugee Scholars and the New School for Social Research* (Amherst: University of Massachusetts Press, 1993), 21–29.

2. Hans Helmut Christmann, "Deutsche Romanisten als Verfolgte des Nationalsozialismus," in *Exilforschung: Ein Internationales Jahrbuch*, Bd. 6, *Vertreibung der Wissenschaften und andere Themen*, ed. Thomas Koebner, Wulf Köpke, Claus-Dieter Krohn, Sigrid Schneider, and Lieselotte Maas (Munich: text + kritik, 1988), 75.

3. For an instructive, richly detailed discussion of anti-immigrant sentiment in America between 1931 and 1941, see Stephanie Barron, "European Artists in Exile: A Reading between the Lines," in *exiles + émigrés: The Flight of European Artists from Hitler*, ed. Karen Jacobson (Los Angeles: Museum Associates, Los Angeles County Museum of Art, 1997), 11–29.

4. See Karen Michels, "Transfer and Transformation: The German Period in Amer-

ican Art History," in Jacobson, *exiles + émigrés*, 304–16. Michels refers to the Emergency Committee for Displaced Foreign Scholars as well as to the Rockefeller and Carnegie Foundations. We should not overlook, however, the outstanding efforts of the American Committee for Refugee Scholars, Writers, and Artists of New York City, and its effectiveness in placing displaced intellectuals at American preparatory schools, colleges, and universities. Paul Amann, whose story is at the center of my essay, relied heavily on the assistance of this committee.

5. Sven Papcke, "Fragen an die Exilforschung heute," in Koebner et al., *Exilforschung*, 6:23.

6. This is how Hermann Broch describes the situation at American institutions of higher learning in a letter to Paul Amann, dated November 28, 1940, folder "Amann, Paul," American Guild–EB 70/117, Exilarchiv, Deutsche Bibliothek, Frankfurt. All further references will be to Guild–EB 70/117, folder "Amann."

7. Hanna Papanek, "Reflexionen über Exil und Identität, Staat und Menschenrechte," in *Exilforschung*, Bd. 17, *Sprache–Identität–Kultur: Frauen im Exil*, ed. Claus-Dieter Krohn, Erwin Rotermund, Lutz Winckler, Wulf Koepke, and Sonja Hilzinger (Munich: text + kritik, 1999), 29, 17–23.

8. See Richard Unsworth's essay in this book, "A French Connection: Chambon, Chalmers, and Cummington."

9. I thank the archivists at the Leo-Baeck-Institute, the Exilarchiv at the Deutsche Bibliothek Frankfurt (DB), the Stadtbibliothek Lübeck, and the librarians at the Northfield–Mount Hermon School for their generous assistance of my research. All translations of archival materials from German to English are mine unless otherwise indicated. The greatest debt of gratitude I owe, however, to the Cummington Historical Society, Barbara and Allan Goldsmith in particular. Without their assistance in introducing me to the files on the Refugee Hostel that the society maintains, my search for such exiles as Amann, Jacob Picard, and Gustav Wolf would never have been realized. Gloria Gowdy, a writer and Allan Goldsmith's sister, granted me an interview, shedding further light on the history and context of the hostel. This essay is dedicated to them.

10. Letter of September 2, 1942, to Dora Amann, in Paul Amann Collection (hereafter PAC), Leo-Baeck-Institute, New York, 5C, 2.

11. Christmann, "Deutsche Romanisten als Verfolgte des Nationalsozialismus," 78.

12. For extensive information on Amann's life, see Robert Gangl, "Paul Amann: Leben und Werk" (M.A. thesis, University of Vienna, 1995). Gangl cites many of the sources I have also consulted in the archival holdings on Paul Amann at the Leo-Baeck-Institute in New York.

13. I am indebted here to Gangl, "Paul Amann," in particular the biographical notes, 12–20.

14. Paul Amann, "Westjüdische Dynamik," *Der Jude* 4 (July 1919): 145–51. Martin Buber was the editor of this journal.

15. Letter of June 13, 1915. See Thomas Mann, *Briefe an Paul Amann, 1915–1952*, ed. Herbert Wegener (Lübeck: Max Schmidt-Römhild, 1959), 28.

16. *Münchner Blätter für Dichtung und Graphik* 1 (February–March 1919): 25–32 and 42–48.

17. Paul Amann, *Leopold Komperts literarische Anfänge* (Prague: Carl Bellmann, 1907).

18. Mann writes on May 15, 1942, in Pacific Palisades, California, the following diary entry: "After lunch, reading in Amann's *Tradition und Weltkrise.*" Thomas Mann, *Tagebücher, 1940–1943*, ed. Peter von Mendelssohn (Frankfurt am Main: Fischer, 1982), 429.

19. Dora Amann, "Erinnerungen," 2:4–5, Nachlass Dora Amann (hereafter NDA), Leo-Baeck-Institute, New York. See also Thomas Mann, *Tagebücher, 1937–1939*, ed. Peter de Mendelssohn (Frankfurt am Main: Fischer, 1980), 10.

20. NDA, 39.

21. Rita Thalmann, *Gleichschaltung in Frankreich, 1940–1944* (Hamburg: Europäische Verlagsgemeinschaft, 1999), 111, 155–57.

22. For Amann's correspondence during his exile in France, 1939–41, see PAC, 5D.

23. Anna Seghers, *Transit*, trans. James Galston (Boston: Little, Brown, 1944), 155.

24. "Amann Paul" folder, American Guild—EB 70/117, exile archive of the Deutsche National-Bibliothek, Frankfurt.

25. See Amann's letter ("Liebe gute Freunde") to Polzer, written on June 10, 1941, in Marseilles, in which he mentions his fear of a breakdown in "this European hell." PAC, 5D.

26. See NDA, folder 1.

27. See Amann's letter to his friend Hugo Bergmann of November 4, 1944, PAC, 5F.

28. See Amman's letter to his son Ernest of March 3, 1955, PAC, 5C.

29. Christopher Isherwood, *Diaries*, Vol. 1, *1939–1960* (New York: HarperCollins, 1997), 188.

30. Letter of November 3, 1941, PAC, 5F.

31. Letter in Amann folder in the archival holdings of the Northfield–Mount Hermon School, Northfield, Mass.

32. See Jacob Picard's letter to Amann, April 19, 1942 (PAC, 5F), in which Picard writes: "In case you don't know where to turn at the end of your Yale fellowship, there is a chance that you could stay here. I would do everything I can on your behalf."

33. Gloria Gowdy, "Refugee Hostel," on Cummington and its refugees. I am grateful to Gloria, who, as a teenager, befriended some of these foreigners, for allowing me to quote from her unpublished manuscript.

34. See "The Cummington Press in Third Year," *Publishers' Weekly*, July 3, 1943, 39; and S. Lane Faison Jr., "Cummington Press Keeps Alive an Ancient Art," *Berkshire Eagle*, March 12, 1955, sec. 2A, 1.

35. Nelly Baar Wieghardt, "Our First Year in the United States" 1 (unpublished manuscript). I thank Gloria Gowdy for a copy of these memoirs and Nelly Baar Wieghardt for permission to quote from her materials in this essay.

36. Among the many sources documenting these conflicts, Robert Groetsch, "In den Hills," *Neue Volkszeitung*, November 11, 1943, is particularly revealing. Groetsch and his wife spent a few weeks at the hostel in the fall of 1943, two years after the conflicts had first occurred.

37. Gowdy, "Refugee Hostel," 3.

38. See Paul Amann, correspondence with family members, 1934–47, PAC, 5C.

39. PAC, 5F.

40. Kurt Wolff, *Briefwechsel eines Verlegers, 1911–1963*, ed. Bernhard Zeller and Ellen Otten (Frankfurt am Main: Scheffler, 1966), 45. Hermann Broch may have dissuaded him from publishing the Amann book, which he criticized as "amateurish" and confused.

41. For an excellent in-depth discussion of Amann's literary difficulties in the United States, see Gangl, "Paul Amann," 445–46.

42. Wulf Koepke, "Exilautoren und ihre deutschen und amerikanischen Verleger in New York," in *Deutschsprachige Exilliteratur seit 1933*, Bd 2. *New York*, Teil 2, ed. John M. Spalek and Joseph Strelka (Bern: Francke, 1989), 1410.

43. See letter of September 5, 1942, to Dora, in which Amann reports that he has sent the five-dollar membership fee to Henri Peyre as well as a manuscript of a paper on Molière he was to present at the December 1942 MLA meeting. PAC, 5C, 2.

44. Thomas Mann, "To Whom It May Concern," carbon copy in archives at the Northfield–Mount Hermon School, folder "Paul Amann."

45. Letter of June 20, 1942, PAC, 5C.

46. Letter of July 9, 1942, PAC, 5C.

47. Gowdy, "Refugee Hostel."

48. In Wolf papers at Northfield–Mount Hermon School, see copy of a flyer issued by the print department, Boston Public Library, May 17, 1950; also Jacob Picard, "Spring in Cummington," a poem in *Lest We Forget: A Newsletter from Your Congregational Christian Committee for Wartime Victims and Services* 4 (September 1942): 3.

49. Letter of July 20, 1942.

50. Ibid.

51. Letter to Dora, undated, but must have been written shortly before the letter of September 5, 1942.

52. September 9, 1942, PAC, 5C, 2.

53. Letter of February 10, 1942, PAC, 5F.

54. Claus-Dieter Krohn, *Intellectuals in Exile: Refugee Scholars and the New School for Social Research*, trans. Rita Kimber and Robert Kimber (Amherst: University of Massachusetts Press, 1993), 27–29.

55. Letter to Dora, September 10, 1942, PAC, 5C.

56. Letter of October 2, 1942, PAC, 5C.

57. PAC, 5C.

58. Paul Amann, "In der Papiermühle," PAC, 1V.

59. Paul Amann to Thomas Mann, 1939–1955, letter no. 3, Familienarchiv Mann, Archiv der Hansestadt, Lübeck.

60. Hans Altenhuber, "Vorbemerkungen zu den österreichischen Beiträgen," in *Erwachsenenbildung und Emigration. Biographien und Wirkungen von Emigrantinnen und Emigranten*, ed. Volker Otto und Erhard Schlutz (Bonn: Deutscher Hochschul-Verband, 1999), 95–103.

61. Letter to Herbert Davis, October 18, 1943, PAC, 5F.

62. Letter to Hermann Broch, March 12, 1944, PAC, 5F.

63. Copy of letter in the Amann folder, Northfield–Mount Hermon archives.

64. Letter to Hugo Bergmann, November 4, 1944, PAC, 5A.

65. Ibid.

66. Ibid.

67. Letter of March 20, 1943, PAC, addenda box.

68. Letter to Hugo Bergmann, October 29, 1946, PAC, 5A.

69. Paul Amann to Thomas Mann, 1939–1955, letter no. 8.

70. Ibid., letter no. 5.

71. Letter of May 27, 1950, PAC, 5A.

72. Letter to Dr. Karstadt of the Stadtbibliothek Lübeck, December 27, 1957, PAC, addenda box.

73. Paul Amman to Thomas Mann, 1939–1955, letter no. 9.

74. Letter of July 25, 1958, PAC, addenda box.

75. Letter of August 14, 1955, PAC, 5F.

A Haven in Whately

The Refugees Who Came to Our Farm

DEIRDRE BONIFAZ

My family settled in Massachusetts in the hill town of West Whately in 1943, after the United States had entered World War II. Our two-hundred-acre farm was a few miles from Whately Center, a pristine New England village located between Northampton, home of Smith College, and Greenfield, a mill town. Whately Center consisted of a tiny general store with a large glass case full of penny candy and a post office inside the store; also a gas pump, the town hall, and the fire station. Inside the town hall was a small room with books and magazines, the town's library. Across the way stood the Whately Inn. American flags blew in the wind up and down the wide main street lined with colonial houses, stretching from the graveyard and the two-room red brick schoolhouse at one end to the homes at the other end beyond the big white Congregational church whose tall steeple you could see from Route 5. The inn stood at the corner of the winding road that led back to our hilltop, where the views of the valley below, across the Connecticut River to Amherst and the rolling hills beyond, were even more breathtaking than down in Whately Center.

At that time Whately was a very tight-knit Yankee community of small dairy farms passed on from one generation to the next. The townspeople referred to as "the Polish farmers," some of whose families had immigrated to the community in the early 1900s, lived on the other side of Route 5, in East Whately. They were the minority, the "newcomers"—that is, until we arrived.

We must have been an odd presence—a young family arriving at a time when America was at war to buy old Vic Bardwell's rundown tobacco and dairy farm in West Whately, moving from Bug Hill Road in Ashfield over sixteen miles away. We arrived in our old blue Marmon with my father's type-writer, violin, and all our books and records piled high in the back and still more books in the trunk with the Victrola. My mother sat in front beside my father, my three-year-old brother Michael on her lap. I knelt at the rear window watching our home disappear, clutching my doll Lilly. For a while I kept my eyes on sweet Lady Una, our beautiful Morgan horse trotting behind us, pulling the hay wagon that contained the rest of our worldly possessions secured with rope. On top I could see rolled up the deep red rug that had been in my mother's bedroom when she was growing up in New York City; the carved wooden headboard my mother painted a sunflower-yellow one summer day; the stiff, uncomfortable sofa with horsehair coming out in the corner where the red velvet upholstery was torn. Uncle Paul, my mother's brother, held Lady Una's reins, and sitting up front beside him was Shirley, my new aunt from Chicago. They'd met on the Hechalutz farm in New Jersey, a kibbutz where my uncle was studying cooperative farms when Pearl Harbor was bombed. He told the draft board that he was "an internationalist," that nationalism was archaic and he considered himself a citizen of the world. He didn't believe in fighting for one piece of the world versus another, my uncle told them, but if they could get all the bad guys and line them up against the wall, he'd shoot. On those grounds, the draft board turned him down for a deferment, and he had to leave the Hechalutz farm, where he had been tolerated until there was a possibility of his being arrested.

Soon we left them behind, too, as the Marmon slowly followed the bumpy dirt road to the smooth blacktop in Ashfield, passing by Elmer's General Store on the corner, where I first discovered ice cream in a cone, then through the village of Conway to another dirt road leading to our new home.

Our neighbors who lived on dairy farms along the road leading to the hilltop first saw us in our old car as we passed slowly up the steep hill, followed a couple of hours later by the horse and wagon, and my Uncle Paul and Aunt Shirley. No one knew anything about us except that we were from somewhere else; we were definitely not New Englanders. The information gathered about my family began with the story of our arrival, followed by the observations of the curious mailman who delivered letters and shared whatever he learned about us with others on the rural free delivery route. But the stories spread in earnest when I first entered the two-room schoolhouse down in Whately Center. Just before my sixth birthday I left my protected life for first grade, and faced all the bewildering questions about who we were.

MY FAMILY came from New York. My mother, born Blanche Rosenthal, was a first-generation American. My grandmother, Bertha, was the sixth and last child to be born to Blume and Shamul Goldenberg, a Jewish family living in the ancient Danube port city of Galati. Bertha would never forget the terrifying pogrom—led by Christians—which she witnessed before leaving Romania with her widowed mother and sisters in the summer of 1900, when she was nine years old. My grandfather, Joe Rosenthal, was a Russian Jew who arrived with his family around the same time. They were both part of the great exodus of Jews from eastern Europe who crossed the Atlantic Ocean in steerage and grew up on the Lower East Side of New York in wretched tenements overcrowded with other eastern European refugees escaping oppression and poverty. My grandmother worked by day in sweatshops and eventually became an accomplished milliner; by night she attended classes at the settlement school. She developed a deep reverence for education and culture, learning quickly from her dedicated teachers, while Joe, the man she married when she was in her twenties, had no patience for learning from books; he preferred to get his education on the street.

My father, James—whom I always called Jimmy—was the eldest child of Emily and Thomas Cooney. My paternal grandfather came from County Armagh in Ireland. He left his family's farm in the late 1800s when extreme poverty forced the wrenching parting of the eldest children, who crossed the sea in search of work. Before his marriage, my grandfather was working to save money so he could return to Ireland. My paternal grandmother, Emily Magdalene Delahanty, was born in New York with Daughters of the American Revolution lineage on her mother's side. Her father was an immigrant from Alsace-Lorraine. After my Irish grandfather's unexpected marriage to an educated American, he was elevated to the status of a fireman on Long Island. When he first met Emily on a streetcar, he was the driver and she was a schoolteacher in Flushing, a career she kept until retirement. My grandfather's rigid Catholicism, and the tragic death of Thomas, my father's younger brother, contributed to driving my father from the church and from his parents' home when he was eighteen.

My mother was seventeen, my father twenty-six, when they first met in Greenwich Village in the 1930s. She was an art student eager to be free of her middle-class Jewish family, searching for adventure, scorning what she perceived as her mother's bourgeois life and the middle-class financial comfort her father provided before the shaky marriage disintegrated in the first divorce in the family. My father was twenty-seven, a struggling writer living in a cold-water flat in the Village. He had finished teachers' college, but after a couple of years in the classroom, he quit. Deeply affected by the Great Depression, he had briefly joined the Communist Party before being thrown out for disobeying orders. His first novel, a thinly disguised autobiography, had just been accepted for publication when he met my mother.

I was the first child of this Jewish-Christian union that left my maternal grandmother sitting shivah—briefly—for my mother. My paternal grandmother, a devout Catholic (raised as an Episcopalian), was by then a widow and unaware of her son's marriage until after my birth. She grieved when she learned I was not to be baptized, believing that my soul was in mortal danger. I was born in New York City, at the same hospital where my mother came into the world, delivered by the same doctor, almost twenty years later. My maternal grandmother was brokenhearted all over again when she watched my mother leave the city with me to rejoin my father—a "Christian," with all the dread memories that word stirred in her, a stranger in the family, a poor man who was educated but had no interest in money. She imagined her eldest child slipping back into the poverty she had known in Romania and as an immigrant on the Lower East Side. She imagined her first grandchild growing up in primitive, rural places many miles from the New York Public Library, the Metropolitan Museum of Art, far from the curtains going up on Broadway and the sounds of music filling Carnegie Hall.

My parents were pacifists, radicals. We lived in Woodstock, New York, in a writers' and artists' colony called The Maverick, where I'm told I was the only baby. We stayed in a long, narrow, one-room stone house, known as The Salamander. It was at The Maverick that my father first published the *Phoenix*, a literary quarterly that was antifascist and antiwar. Henry Miller was the European editor, Anaïs Nin a contributor. My mother designed the cover, a fiery hand–silk screened image of the mythical bird, the phoenix, rising from the ashes. It was March 1938 when the first issue appeared.

In Europe, this was the moment when Hitler marched into Austria, and Walter Mehring, Hertha Pauli, and Carli Frucht were fleeing Vienna by train for the temporary safety of Paris. Less than a decade later they would be with us in West Whately at Morning Star Farm.

ON THAT first day of school my father had accompanied me into the classroom where the first-and second-graders were waiting for the school bell to ring. He was there to tell my teacher, in the sudden quiet of the room, that I was NOT to pledge allegiance to the flag. I stood by his side as he explained to Mrs. McKay that he wanted his child to have allegiance to humanity, not to a government or a country.

I had no idea of the significance of his words, or of the consequences. It was the autumn of 1943, two years after Pearl Harbor was bombed. The hill towns around us had "lookout towers" where there was a view for miles, and local citizens took turns searching the horizon through binoculars for enemy planes. Once a warning siren went off when it was thought that a flock of geese were Japanese warplanes. This was before the refugees, who spoke with accents, some of them German, began to arrive on our farm.

It would be a long time before I understood why my classmates shunned me. My mother, attending her first and only meeting with other mothers of children at the Whately School, was ignored after revealing that we didn't belong to any church. Our neighbors watched us through their lace curtains as we drove up the hill to our house. It was scary the way people stopped talking as I followed my father and Michael into the Whately general store to choose, in the uneasy silence, our box of Cracker Jack with the present waiting at the bottom. It was scary the way the men looked at my father. People kept their distance. Acceptance was not in the air.

These incidents, among many others, contributed to the stories spinning through the hills in the years following our arrival: My family must be spies for the enemy. We chose the hilltop so signals could be sent out (where?). Our lights could be seen burning late at night, another ominous sign. Foreigners, people with accents, stayed at our farm, and there was a "Negro woman married to a white man" who lived with us for months with their child. Cars with New York license plates drove up to our end-of-the-road farm. My parents heard about all the rumors from Charlie, "the hired hand" who helped my father and lived with us. Every Saturday night Charlie found his way to the Whately Inn, where he'd sit at the bar defending us and drinking up all his weekly pay until he was thrown out.

A young man from neighboring Conway was paid by the FBI for many years to inform on my father, during and after the war. One of his assignments was to record the license plate number of every vehicle heading up to our farm. Our telephone was a party line shared with five other families. Whenever it rang for us—one long and two short rings—clicking could be heard on the line as neighbors, and perhaps the FBI informer, listened in. "Is everyone there?" my father sometimes asked, before speaking to the caller.

So THIS was still the local climate in 1945, before the war ended, when Walter Mehring and his French wife, Marie Paul, stepped off the New York train arriving in Northampton. They were closely followed by Hertha Pauli, E. B. Ashton, and their three small dogs—Dolly, Bambi, and Bonzi—along with three typewriters and luggage for an indefinite stay on our farm.

They came first, as "paying guests," because another refugee, Lucy Sabsay, told them about us. Lucy was their friend, as well as Roger Coster's. She knew them through her friend Carli Frucht, and they all lived near one another around West Seventy-sixth and Seventy-seventh streets, by the Museum of Natural History and Central Park, in cheap residential hotels. At night, after work, she would join them at the hotel café across from the museum, where refugees gathered throughout the day to share information about the war, news about those missing and those arriving, about possible publishers and galleries interested in their work.

Earlier that spring before president Roosevelt died, and before the reports of Hitler's suicide, Roger Coster had settled in the front guest room of our farmhouse with his Haitian wife, Laura, and their baby boy, "petit Roger." It was the preferred room, where guests could awaken to the sweeping views of the green valley below and distant violet-blue hills to the east. Through the windows facing north, beyond the blacksmith's shop, the icehouse, and the hay field, you could see the little red cottage built in the late 1700s. This was where the new arrivals chose to stay, a short walk up the road on the edge of the pine forest.

By 1940, when Roger was forced to escape from France, the country of his birth, he was already a well-known photographer in Paris. He first met Lucy in Lisbon, where she was helping the flood of Jewish refugees, like herself and Roger, find a boat out, a visa to any country willing to accept them. Roger went first to Brazil. From South America he found his way to New York after *Life* magazine published his photographs of Brazilian miners. He met Laura while she was working with the Quakers, helping to settle refugees arriving in the city.

Laura was Haitian, from a middle-class family in Port-au-Prince. After her marriage to Roger, it was hard to ignore landlords' many excuses for not renting an apartment to them. They were living in Harlem when their son was born, and Roger decided it was time to find a place in the country for his family. The League for Mutual Aid in New York told him about a family that was taking paying guests on a farm in New England. Refugees were welcome.

Roger came up from the city every weekend to be with Laura and his son. He watched us though the lens of his camera, often photographing my father working on the farm. Two of Roger's black and white photographs appeared in *Coronet* magazine. One shows my family gathered under the old maple tree in front of our house—a neglected seventeen-room colonial farmhouse with a large porch stretching across the front. We're sitting on grass overgrown with clover and dandelions which my father never had time to mow, pretending to have a picnic because Roger needed to show his editor in New York a "typical American family" celebrating the Fourth of July. My mother sits beside Michael, who is offering her something to eat on a white paper napkin. She's wearing a simple striped cotton dress with long sleeves and a high neckline for the photograph. Her dark, curly hair looks the way she always wore it at that time, braided then pinned around the top of her head. There's sadness in my mother's lovely face, her features a mixture of her Romanian and Russian roots, with the distinctive high cheekbones I always wished I had. She looks quietly down at Michael, her hand resting gracefully in her lap, her slender body momentarily in repose as she waits for the French photographer to say he is finished. Sitting uncomfortably at the center is my father. My mother had great difficulty persuading him to change into a clean shirt in the middle of the afternoon and trim his red hair and mustache for Roger's important photograph. He is looking down, as if listening to Michael, his expression one of melancholy mixed with some impatience because he didn't like posing for the camera. "He looks so Irish," people often said when they first met him and noted the intense blue of his eyes. I am seated with my back to my father, mother, and brother, facing my Aunt Shirley, who was cut out of the photograph when it was published. I am the only one smiling. I'm wearing my most despised hand-me-down, a red and white gingham sundress from Great Aunt Selma, who, on her one and only visit to our farm, thought my hair needed brushing and took it upon herself to improve my appearance by making two braids out of my thick hair. Then she pulled my braids so tight on top of my head it felt as if all my hair was being yanked out by the roots, and then pushed her hairpin straight down into my scalp until I cried out in pain.

The second photograph, featured in the same issue of *Coronet* depicting how America was living through the war, showed a close-up of my father's hands, scarred from working in the fields, gently holding a newly hatched chick, and Michael's amazed expression as he looked on.

One weekend Roger brought his friend Lucy Sabsay to stay with us. She was in her late twenties when we met, the same age as my mother. Her long, dark hair was pulled back from her pretty face, and she was soft and curvy. She seemed very short for a grown-up. "You're almost as tall as I am!" Lucy gasped, her face coming close to mine as she gave me a big hug. "Disgusting!" she teased. "You're seven going on eight. And I'm twenty-eight!" She was joyful. Of all the refugees who ever stayed with us, she seemed the happiest to begin a new life in America.

Lucy spoke quickly when she told my mother about her childhood. Her mother died when she was born, in Odessa, and she never knew her name or saw her face. There were no photographs. Lucy lived in Estonia with her father, Emmanuel Sabsay, who owned a textile factory with his brothers in Tallinn. When she was five, he married a young pianist from Russia, and Lucy became Russian Orthodox, like her father's new wife. Soon afterward the family moved to Berlin, where Lucy began school. At the same time, her father decided she should become a Protestant.

When she was eight she was sent away to school in Switzerland. From then on she was always at boarding school, returning home only for holidays. At the age of ten, her childhood was forever changed: her father suddenly died. After that loss, she spent her vacations at school, with the nuns.

Lucy's father left a huge fortune for her with the young stepmother. She continued to attend the best boarding schools, and while at an especially fancy one in Nice, she decided to become a Catholic so she would be permitted to enter the chapel with the other girls. "First, I was exorcised!" Lucy laughed at my mother's expression. "Yes! They said the devil was in me. I was led to a small room with high windows, a chair, a priest, and the nuns. The door was shut. I had an idea! I climbed up on the chair and pushed open the window, and the nuns and priest became absolutely furious with me. I explained I was only helping the devil get out of me! Then, when I was sixteen, I discovered a wonderful secret! I was really Jewish, and she," her stepmother, "wasn't my mother!!! Can you imagine my relief?"

Lucy never learned from her father's brothers why she had not been told about her own mother, nor why her Jewish identity had been kept a secret. The mystery surrounding her birth remained unsolved, even after trips back to Estonia to question her uncles.

The night before Lucy left our farm to go home to New York, I was allowed to sit on the little chair by the kitchen hearth while the grown-ups ate supper and told their stories.

"When did you leave France?" my father asked Lucy.

"In 1939. I had been living in London, attending the School of Economics to please my Uncle Boris, who was also my guardian. But I was not at all interested in economics!" Lucy reached for a cigarette as everyone laughed. My father struck a wooden match on the sole of his shoe and reached over to give her a light, then lit his own. He leaned back in his chair, and I watched him blow smoke circles into the candlelight.

"I returned to Cannes that summer after learning my stepmother's villa would be empty. She was in Spain with her lover, Raoul, and I could have the place to myself. At the end of the summer, I met some people my age on the beach, and we became friends. They were Jewish refugees who had just escaped from Germany and were trying to decide where to go next. Where could they be safe? I invited them to the villa for meals, and then to spend the night. They had been sleeping out on the beach."

She paused, watching my father put another log of fragrant apple wood on the fire as a shower of sparks went up the chimney. Her stepmother's servants were suspicious of the foreigners, who spoke always in German with Lucy. One of them informed the police that "undesirables" were at the villa. The authorities arrested Lucy's friends and took them away. She never saw them again. Then the police arrested her, using the excuse of her Estonian passport to expel her from France. Lucy was given twenty-four hours to leave. She went to Lisbon. (She found a visa to Portugal with her passport; her stepmother's lover, Raoul, must have known she would need it one day.) She packed everything she could in her trunk for what she believed would be a temporary stay, and departed alone by train the next morning. It was September 1939. Lucy was twenty-three.

"And what about the fortune? What happened to that?" my mother asked, remembering Lucy's story earlier that day.

"Oh, I never saw the fortune my father left for me. But you know," all at once her voice changed, "I was one of the lucky ones to escape with my life." She took a last sip of her wine and looked back into the fire. "I am just so lucky to be here!"

In the long silence that followed, while everyone watched the flames dance around the disappearing apple wood, Lucy noticed my concern. She laughed away the solemn moment. "But don't look so serious, *ma petite*. I may not have a family, but you see," she left the table and bent down to hug me, "I have very good friends, and they are my family. This way I can choose. Will you be one of my new friends?"

Lucy had a job in New York working in a film cutting room, a skill she had learned in a youth training camp in Florida when she first arrived in America. Because there weren't enough men around with this skill during the war, jobs traditionally reserved for them suddenly opened to women. Lucy was one of the first to be hired, a pioneer. That marked the beginning of her long, exciting career in film, an interest awakened during her time of exile in Lisbon.

Before leaving for the train back to New York with Roger, Lucy told my parents she had never dreamed that people living on a farm would have a house filled with books, or that a farmer would play classical music when he came in from his chores. She was amazed to see prints of Goya and Picasso and Van Gogh paintings covering cracks in the plaster walls. She lowered her voice, knowing that Roger was upstairs saying good-bye to his family. "He isn't an intellectual, maybe that's why he didn't tell me what to expect before I came here." Lucy smiled. "Maybe that's part of the reason I didn't want to marry him!"

"Marry him?" My mother and father were startled.

"It was five years ago, when we were both in Lisbon. He was leaving for Brazil—you know, everyone was so desperate to get out of Europe—and I no longer had a country, nor papers. Estonia was gone! It was dangerous. So partly to protect me, he wanted us to get married. That way I could depart with him. But you can see we're still good friends." She looked over at me, and put her finger to her lips. I knew she wanted me to keep what I had just heard a secret.

She would not return until she could bring Carli, she said. "We have to wait for this terrible war to end."

Carli Frucht, the man she loved, was back in Europe as a soldier in the U.S. Army. Having escaped several times over from the Third Reich and come to America as a refugee in 1941, Carli told Lucy he had to join the army after Pearl Harbor was bombed. He didn't believe in killing, but this was "his war." He had to return to danger.

"In the meantime," Lucy promised, "I will send you our friends, Hertha

Pauli and E. B. Ashton, Walter Mehring and Marie Paul." They all needed a quiet place to work, and since none of them really had a job, they couldn't afford to stay any longer in the city.

And so that's why, several weeks later, Lucy and Carli's friends arrived at the Northampton train station.

MARIE PAUL was the only one who wasn't a Jewish refugee; she was an art student from France who had come to attend school in New York. She was renting a small furnished room on the West Side in the neighborhood where so many of the refugees were staying. One day as she was walking down the street near Central Park, a piece of paper floated from the sky, landing at her feet. She bent down to pick it up and was startled. It was written in German. She could not read the words, but she recognized the language. She looked up at the building she was passing when the mysterious paper appeared, but there was no sign of anyone. How could it have fallen from the sky?

At that instant Hertha Pauli, who was walking her adopted dog, Bambi, also saw the paper float to Marie Paul's feet. She was curious. She did not hesitate to peer over the stranger's shoulder, and immediately recognized the writing. "But I know this handwriting! I know the man who wrote these words!" she shouted for everyone passing by to hear. "He's the famous poet Walter Mehring!"

This was how Hertha realized that Walter had finally arrived in New York after landing first in South America. That was how Marie Paul first met Hertha, who then introduced her to the famous new arrival. Walter Mehring was in town!

The first thing you noticed about Marie Paul was how emaciated she was; from a distance, walking beside the others, she looked like a boy. As soon as the New England weather warmed up, she wore, every day, leather sandals on her bare feet, and a man's blue-striped shirt that was so huge it completely covered her bikini. Her oval face often had a worried, frightened expression, and when she sat at the kitchen table listening to the discussions, her dark, gentle eyes followed my mother as she moved around the room preparing meals. Perhaps she had trouble understanding English. She seemed most comfortable when she was with Hertha, who was about fifteen years older.

Marie Paul offered to give me French lessons if I would help her find the words she didn't know in English. We met at the cottage, the building I loved most of all on our farm. It was much older than our big house, a four-room antique Cape with low ceilings, small windowpanes, and a cooking fireplace that was so big you could walk into it. The central room was the one with the cooking hearth. From there the windows looked out to the east, to the rolling mountains beyond the huge ancient maple tree near the stone wall; to the south you could see the farm buildings below, the dairy barn, the milk house, the stable, the chicken house, the workshop, and the icehouse. The kitchen was small and narrow with some shelves on the wall for dishes. There was an icebox to keep the milk cold (Marie Paul and Hertha came every morning to refill their milk can) and a wood stove for cooking and warmth. A ladder led straight up from the kitchen to the sleeping loft with its low, slanted ceiling and a small window looking out to the slate rooftop of the dairy barn. Marie Paul and Walter climbed the ladder to sleep up in the loft because they were smaller than Hertha and Ashton, who chose the bedroom downstairs on the other side of the central chimney. Their view faced north to the woods that reminded Hertha of the Black Forest. The wide pine floorboards were very worn and uneven. In the small entry there was a secret door in the wall. Someone told my father it had once led to an underground tunnel where people could hide "in case of an Indian attack." Another person told him it was for escaped slaves, part of the Underground Railroad. The privy was at the edge of the hay field, twenty-five steps through the deep grass. Marie Paul counted each step in English. On one side of the weathered gray boards was the cutout shape of a crescent moon, on the other side a star. Queen Anne's lace bloomed along the path to the privy door.

By day, Hertha and Walter worked in different corners of the cooking hearth room, and Ashton worked at a table in the bedroom he shared with Hertha. Bambi, Bonzi, and Dolly slept together on the couch—which was really a single bed with soft pillows pushed against the wall.

All around the cottage the grass was very deep, and I was extremely watchful as I made my way up to the old batten door. My Jewish grandmother from New York City once made me promise her that I would always watch my step whenever I walked through high grass. "You never know what might be hiding there," she warned me. In the warm weather a huge garden snake often sunned itself on the huge stone step that was covered with moss around the edges. Marie Paul was as scared of snakes as I was, but everyone else thought we were ridiculous and laughed when we screamed, "Watch out for the snake!"

My lessons began at four, when the writers finally left their typewriters and went for a walk down the hill, or to watch my father and Charlie at work in the tobacco fields up past the pond. When the hot summer days came, we changed the hour to after lunch, up at the pond, where Hertha and Marie Paul went swimming every day and then stretched out in the sun to get tan. Hertha had been the Austrian breaststroke champion, and she wanted to teach me, but our lessons were interrupted by the appearance of a gigantic snapping turtle in the pond.

Marie Paul let me watch her make pen and ink drawings on the sketch pad she carried everywhere. One day she gave me a drawing of the view from the cottage. It now hangs in my study, the paper beginning to yellow around the edges, a treasured memory of a view long gone. Before Marie Paul left us, she wanted to make a crèche. She was raised a Catholic, but she didn't go to church anymore, she told me; still, the crèche was something good for me to know about, she thought, and we could keep it for Noël. It was the walnut shells that my mother was going to toss into the fireplace that gave her the idea. Selecting one perfect walnut shell, she lined it with a bit of hay to be a bed for the tiny naked baby doll she found in the 5 & 10 in Northampton. "Voilà!" She was pleased that the pink plastic form fit so perfectly into the walnut shell. "We pretend it is the *bébé* Jesus." Marie Paul placed the shell on the sweet-smelling hay that covered the bottom of a shoebox turned on its side. "Now we have the most important part of the crèche, we can finish."

I watched her make the baby's mother and father out of paper, then helped her paint them with watercolors, and we put more hay on top of the box, and Marie Paul suspended a yellow star hanging from a thread above it all. Walter stood with his arms crossed, frowning as he considered her creation. Then, after several moments of silence, he took a long puff on his cigarette and told her she forgot the cow! "Tu as oublié la vache, ma chérie." Ashton glanced politely at it and gave a nervous little laugh, while Hertha clapped her hands and shouted with delight, "Bravo, Marie Paul!" She knew all about the crèche because in Vienna, her mother, who had killed herself when Hertha was young, had been a Catholic. "She was a pacifist and feminist, like I am," she told my parents. Hertha's father was Jewish.

WALTER MEHRING, because of his fame as an antifascist poet and playwright in the 1920s and 1930s in Berlin, was one of the first to be expelled from Hitler's Germany. His antifascist plays were known throughout Europe. He fled to Vienna, where he soon linked up with Hertha Pauli, then a young actress at the beginning of her career who also ran a literary agency with her friend Carli Frucht. In her book *Break in Time*, Hertha relates the story of Mehring's escape from Berlin.

A fellow passenger on the train to Vienna had recognized him and warned him of the Austrian ban on his new book. Then the stranger produced a copy of the book from his suitcase and respectfully asked for Mehring's autograph.

"But who are you?" Mehring had wanted to know.

"Well, I'm the censor . . ."

"Mehring never tired of telling the story, usually to prove his point that our situation was 'hopeless but not serious,'" Hertha wrote.

Walter was in his late forties, a gaunt, slightly bent-over man who always had a cigarette drooping from his mouth. Sometimes he forgot it was there, and I'd watch as the ashes became so long they finally spilled down the front of his shirt. The first time he sat down at the kitchen table, I noticed how pale his skin was and how his bloodshot eyes nervously searched the room, watching everyone, even while he was arguing with my father. He enjoyed those arguments, especially at night, after dinner, after drinking wine, after everyone else was too tired to utter another word about writers or the existence of a God in a world gone mad.

Walter Mehring seemed out of place in the country. He was a city man. The quiet, remote hilltop made him restless; he missed the crowds of people, the sounds and pace of city life, his coffeehouses and newspapers. He missed being recognized. When he was staying with us, he had to wait for a ride into the nearest town—it was too far to walk—for the *New York Times,* and for more cigarettes. He always ran out of cigarettes. My father shared his tobacco with him when he ran out, rolling the cigarette himself and handing it to Walter. He was appreciative, but he needed a pack in his possession. It made him even more anxious to be without cigarettes.

The ride into Northampton usually occurred only once a week because of gas rationing. My father would turn off the ignition and coast down all the hills between our home and Route 5 in order to save gas. The trip always had to be combined with other errands, including a stop at the Public Market on Main Street, where the owner, Sam, my mother's new friend, would come out from behind the meat counter, wiping his hands on his white apron, to give her a hug. They'd talk about the visiting guests and the war while she walked through the narrow aisles of the small, overcrowded store. I'd help find the essentials on her list: peanut butter for Michael; Maltex, the hot cereal we had to eat every morning; cornmeal, coffee, tuna fish, and Hellmann's mayonnaise. She picked up bags of flour for baking bread, and yeast, raisins, and her ration of sugar from the coupons she kept in her pocketbook. She bought matzos for Passover (and ate them with our freshly churned butter) and tangerines at Christmas. Eggs, milk, cream, and butter came from our farm, as did vegetables harvested from the garden through the summer, and then canned for the long winter by my mother and Aunt Shirley, who helped my mother with the guests. She lived in the ell with my baby cousin Ilanna while my Uncle Paul spent the rest of the war far from his family, in federal prison, as a conscientious objector.

I could tell right away that Walter Mehring was not at all interested in children; I knew not to bother him with my questions. The famous poet preferred the cows. Every morning he took a walk before beginning his work at the typewriter. I watched him pause at the pasture by the dairy barn. I stood near the door of the chicken house, holding a basket, while my father collected all the smooth brown eggs, cautiously placing one beside the other, careful not to let any shells crack. I saw Walter lift his black beret from his head and then make a deep, sweeping bow before the curious cows, who gathered on the other side of the stone wall to observe their visitor. It was like the drawing of Christopher Robin bowing at the gates of Buckingham Palace.

"Bonjour!" he said with solemn respect. "Bonjour, mes amies." Then replacing his beret, he continued on his walk.

Mehring started writing *The Lost Library* while he was staying in the cottage. There was a chapter on my parents, and I remember how furious my mother was at his inaccurate portrayal of them. Rereading his words years later, I can still understand her dismay at his distortions, the made-up details about my father that he weaves in for effect, and to make a point. Yet it is interesting to read, a glimpse of how he viewed his time on the farm, and in particular his view of "the farmer." True or not, it is his perception. Or misperception. In the chapter "Epilogue on a New England Farm," Mehring writes:

> Throughout my exile I had carried around with me the idea of writing the autobiography of a literature, or to put it more precisely, the story of a library to which I was intimately related. In my youth such a library was as much part of the household of a progressive European as the crystal chandeliers, the landscapes on the walls, the Pre-Raphaelite allegorical nudes, the Japanese prints, the pianino and the Persian rugs, the gaslight, the feather mattress on the marital bed, and the champagne in the "special cupboard."
>
> The idea was old, but the decision to write the book came to me on a New England farm whose remoteness made me remember step by step what I had read, forget what I had lost; whose roughhewn integrity recalled me to myself. All my aimless agitation, the after effects of Europe, vanished into the blue mist above the waves of hills that rose up to either side of the Housatonic. [Here Mehring is avoiding naming the Connecticut River—which is what he means—so that the reader will not easily identify my family.]
>
> ... The name of the tyrant which had echoed from every radio and every headline and had pursued me from country to country, from dream to dream, all the way across the ocean to the Antilles and the American continent, now occupied my imagination less than the melodious evening call of the whippoorwill which incessantly repeated its own name.
>
> In this rural environment I would also have recovered from the loss of my library, had I not again been led into temptation. But the farmer at whose place I was boarding had intimidated me by his gruffness at out first meeting, when he called for me in his car at the village railroad station—and then later, in his clapboarded colonial house, had completely baffled me by his reproductions of

Picassos and Braques, his collection of records extending from Vivaldi to Stravinsky, and above all by a library containing Hindu and Chinese philosophy, the Greeks, English literature from Chaucer to D. H. Lawrence, and those dangerous, insidious Americans (Poe, Melville, Ambrose Bierce, O'Neill, Thomas Wolfe, Faulkner).

. . . He advertised in the newspaper for summer boarders ("writers preferred") and hired men ("race, religion, previous experience unimportant; Thoreauists, pacifists and lovers of Beethoven welcome"). He himself, in fact, might well have been the protagonist of a Tolstoyan parable: a peasant's son who had gone back to the bosom of nature, whose adolescent thirst had remained unsatisfied in the city, and who was now doing penance for earlier sins by monogamy, pacifism, vegetarianism and tilling the soil. . . .

He was as self-righteous and obstinate as an Ahab, as intolerant as Ibsen's country pastor in his creed of God's goodness. And as soon as we reached the point during our midnight disputes—for by day he plowed his tobacco fields and I tilled my typewriter—he would interrupt me in the middle of a sentence, tramp over to his bookcase and proceed to crush me and everyone else present by reading aloud for hours.

His chief and only thesis was: "God is love!"

And he spoke the phrase so ferociously, so challengingly, that the devoutest believer would have been provoked into contradicting him.

No argument could touch him. It was no use demonstrating that the Incarnation of eternity and infinity should not be assigned human attributes, which involved temporal and spatial limitations; nor to refer to recent European history for examples of the opposite, nor to suggest that it was beyond human strength for men enduring incendiary bombs, gas chambers and death in freight cars to summon up the faith, love or hope which our friend demanded of them.[1]

Mehring finished *The Lost Library* after the war was over. He dedicated it "To my wife whom I love as I once loved France and Europe." It received little attention in the United States. Soon after the book was published, the ceiling of his cheap hotel room fell in on Walter, covering him with plaster. He couldn't afford another place to live in the city, and decided America was not for him, George Grosz felt sorry for him, as did all his surviving friends who had known him at the height of his fame. The celebrated artist gave Mehring money to return to Germany with Marie Paul, who still didn't speak German or feel she could learn. She finally left him to go back to France, and the marriage that began with a piece of paper falling from the sky was over.

HERTHA PAULI was intense, a woman in a state of outrage against all the injustices of her time. Her hair was short and the color of copper, full of light like her green eyes. She called herself a feminist and a pacifist, and she spoke to me in the same voice she used for the grown-ups. She was the first to teach me about Eleanor Roosevelt, who had added Hertha's name to the select list Varian Fry took with him when he went to rescue people trapped in Marseilles, saving them from the fate of the less famous.

I admired Hertha's spirit, her rage. And her glamour! She wore high-heeled sandals with her shorts and halter top during the day, showing off her golden tan and long legs. At night, when the guests in the cottage joined the other grown-ups for supper in our house, Hertha changed into a dark silky skirt, with a fringed shawl covering her bare shoulders. Waiting for the mailman to arrive was an important event on our hilltop. Everyone gathered around for the moment, except my father, who was usually working in the fields. Hertha would arrange herself on the front lawn in a way that made her look like the actress she once was, posing for the camera. The mailman was impressed. I noticed he often glanced at her as he called out the names on the letters he distributed, one by one.

She was proud of her famous brother, Wolfgang Pauli, the only remaining family she had, who won a Nobel Prize while she was with us. I think she loved animals more than people. Hertha's three dogs, rescued after she found them abandoned on the streets of New York, were always with her, competing for her attention. She became quite upset if my father shouted unkindly at the workhorses, who took the place of a tractor on our farm.

"Look, Jim, of course they will refuse to work for you if you speak to them in that angry voice," she said, her green eyes filling with tears as she comforted the big animals, murmuring to them in German. "You must treat them with respect!" Unlike Walter, she was not at all intimidated by my father. In fact she was fond of him, agreeing with many of his beliefs. Once during a violent thunderstorm Hertha managed to pull a frightened horse through the cottage door. When my father went to search for his lost animal in the upper pasture, he was astonished at the sight of the horse's face looking out at him from inside the cottage.

Every evening my father would turn on our crackling radio, kicking it in the belief that this improved the reception, as the grown-ups gathered nervously in the living room, trying to listen to the latest news of the war through the maddening static. From my secret listening place at the top of the stairs (I was not allowed to stay in the room when the news was on), I wanted to understand what was happening that made the grown-ups groan and Hertha cry out in German.

Ashton was from Munich. He had been a very rich man before the war. He was once a lawyer, educated at Oxford, and became a respected translator.

That is how he met Hertha, at Scribner's, when he was her translator. She was writing children's books at the time, a story about the Statue of Liberty, followed by the history of the song "Silent Night." She always gave me a copy of her current new book, and I pretended to read each one and be interested, but they were the most boring stories on my bookshelf, until I read her autobiography, *Break of Time*. (By then I was already a mother with young children, living near Philadelphia, years away from my childhood with the refugees.) I loved reading Hertha's story, understanding finally those years of flight from Vienna to Paris to Marseilles to the final escape over the Pyrenees, led by her friend Carli.

Ashton rarely took his eyes off Hertha when they were in a room together. He sat close to her at the kitchen table, shoulders touching, always hunched over, dressed in the same old gray suit he wore no matter what the temperature, always with a colorful paisley silk scarf around his neck as if to soothe his incessant cough. Like Hertha and Walter, he smoked one cigarette after another, lighting the new one before extinguishing the old. He remained calm in contrast to Hertha's high emotions, reaching out to protect her whenever she became too distraught or hysterical about some new injustice. He adored her.

We never saw Walter and Marie Paul again after they left, but Hertha and Ashton came back the next summer. They still had very little money; it was before Ashton received his reparations from Germany, and before they bought their house in an apple orchard in Huntington, Long Island, near their friend George Grosz. They arrived again on the New York–to–Northampton train with Bambi, Bonzi, and Dolly, and were dependent on my father for rides into town. My mother did not learn to drive until I was in high school.

One day they asked to borrow the car. Friends were arriving at the Northampton train station and my father couldn't get away. He was in the middle of haying, trying to beat the forecast of rain.

Our cars were always much older than most cars on the road—in fact, valuable antiques, if only we had kept them all instead of trading in one gem for another! My father and brother, Michael, often lamented, for years afterwards, how rich we could have been if only we had kept a particular car. The blue Marmon that first took us up the steep hill to the farm in West Whately was now abandoned at a cemetery of cars in Hatfield. I wept when we passed it, left with all the other cars that no one wanted anymore. The car we had after the Marmon was hideous. It was a 1927 Lincoln, pea soup green with black trim and a high running board. I always begged my father to let me off at the corner so I could walk the rest of the way to the Smith College Day School, pretending I lived in Northampton. At first Michael would walk with me. Then he decided I was silly, and he was driven around the circle and dropped right at the school door. Just what I was trying to avoid! My classmates couldn't miss that car. "Your father should get an award for driving the ugliest car in Massachusetts!" someone said.

My father explained to Ashton, on the day he borrowed the car, how the old Lincoln had more power in reverse. "You have to remember to drive backwards to get up our steep hill. You'll need enough speed to make it all the way up," he reminded him.

Ashton laughed politely. "Thanks, Jim." He thought my father was a little crazy.

The next thing I remember about that day is the dreaded sound of the fire engine echoing through the hills, roaring to the scene from Whately Center, the siren growing louder. My father was still haying in the top meadow. I ran with Michael and my mother past the sandpit and down the hill to our nearest neighbor, Olive Damon, who had called minutes before saying our car was on fire. Ashton and Hertha, their European friends just off the New York train, and the three dogs were all standing by the Damons' mailbox, the rescued luggage that had been strapped onto the Lincoln's roof scattered all around them. The terrifying Doberman and German shepherd I had to pass on my way to the school bus at the bottom of the hill were barking ferociously at all the strangers, including Bambi, Bonzi, and Dolly. Even Hertha could not make friends with them.

The fire engine arrived too late. The silvery heap smoked for hours afterward. Michael said he never saw anyone jump as high as my mother did that day; she was overjoyed to learn our pea green car was beyond saving. Ashton was full of apologies. He had tried several times to go in reverse, to build enough speed at the bottom of the hill to make it up the steepest part, as my father advised. Maybe the motor overheated. Maybe a neighbor's dog crossed the road at the wrong moment and Ashton lost momentum as Hertha screamed out: "Attention! Le pauvre chien!" Or maybe he just had trouble driving backwards as fast as he could without going off the road, or hitting a tree, or worse.

CARLI FRUCHT'S first love was Hertha Pauli. Until Hitler marched into Austria, they ran a literary agency in Vienna, Austrian Correspondence, described by Carli as representing "all shades of opinion except the Nazi shade." Walter Mehring connected with them after fleeing Berlin, and the three remained friends for the rest of their lives. In *Break of Time*, Hertha describes their narrow escape in 1938 as the streets of Vienna were filled with Austrians welcoming the Third Reich. They sat in a dark corner of an obscure café, where Mehring ordered one cognac after another, Hertha and Carli drank black coffee, and Carli took charge of their desperate exit:

> On the way to the station Carli said each of us should travel alone, in the order of peril: "Mehring, you first, then Hertha, then I." There were no objections.
>
> [They walked Mehring to the train station. He became terrified when he saw the black uniforms around the main gate, and wanted to turn back.]
>
> Through an unguarded side entrance we finally slipped into the terminal, and Carli went to the ticket window while I stood chatting with Mehring. . . . On Track I the train was waiting. "Vienna-Zurich-Paris Express—all aboard," the conductor called just as Carli brought the ticket and the little suitcase. Mehring set out for the train. Then as the S.S. man came over, Mehring's filigree figure all but faded in the shadow of the black uniform.
>
> "Who's that?" The enemy pointed at the shrinking poet. Carli stepped in. "Our French teacher," he said quickly and drew out his student card as if to offer it in evidence.
>
> The S.S. man's attention shifted to us. While the student card underwent his malevolent scrutiny, I heard a sound and glanced sideways: Mehring seemed to have vanished. The train whistle blew. A slight figure climbed onto the platform of the last car.
>
> "Stop!" someone shouted.
>
> We froze. Then we saw S.S. men converge on a group of four or five people still heading for the train. Carli was right: Groups were riskier. The four or five were surrounded and taken away as the train pulled out slowly and the rumbling wheels blended into the roar of the bombers circling above.[2]

LUCY KEPT her promise: one day after the war ended, she returned to Morning Star Farm with Carli. He had survived without visible wounds as an American soldier in the worst battles in Europe, on the beaches of Normandy and the Battle of the Bulge. Because of his fluency in German, he had served as a translator, interrogating prisoners of war; more than once he found himself face to face with a classmate from Vienna.

Moments after Carli sat down at our kitchen table, I remember my father asking, "Who do you like to read?"

He filled wineglasses with Chianti, and poured Manischewitz (the sweet wine we were allowed to drink on special occasions) in a shot glass, one for Michael and one for me; my mother unwrapped the large chunk of cheddar cheese Lucy had brought from New York, placed it on a breadboard, and I brought it to the table while she filled a basket with crackers. There was a clinking of glasses all around, a welcoming toast. "Shalom!" Carli said softly when our glasses touched. I kept my eyes on Lucy, who looked radiant, and on the handsome man beside her, who seemed shy, smiling back at us.

First Carli appeared not to understand my father's question or to notice that his intense blue eyes were still focused on him, waiting for an answer. It was one of the questions my father often asked, a kind of test, I realized when I grew older, for what it revealed about the person.

"Who do you like to read?" my father asked again, lighting a cigarette and leaning back in his chair. "Which writers?"

Carli then met his gaze, restlessly shifting in his chair as if trying to find a more comfortable position. He was no longer smiling. He attempted to change the subject, but when my father persisted, he suddenly stood up and exploded in anger: "Look, I don't have to answer your questions! It's NONE OF YOUR GODDAMN BUSINESS WHO I READ!" He pushed his chair back. "I don't have to answer anyone's questions any more!"

And with that he stomped out of the kitchen, down the long hallway, and out the front door. From the living room window I watched to see which direction he would choose, down the road or up. He turned up the road, toward the cottage and pine forest. I thought about running out to keep him company. Often when I knew guests were upset by something my father said, I would try to explain that he didn't mean to hurt their feelings, that he was like that with other people, but this time I returned to the kitchen.

My father rose to put another log on the fire. Lucy was looking down, her delicate fingers tracing circles around scars on the old pine table's surface. The loud ticking of the steeple clock over the fireplace filled the silence. My mother kept sipping her wine and soon began talking to Lucy as if nothing had happened, calmly asking her about the film she was working on. I was so afraid they would want to leave the next day and we would never see them again.

The next morning, after my father finished milking the cows, he came in to have more coffee and put on his new record of Erik Satie's piano music. There must have been words of peace between Carli and my father that I missed, because I remember being totally surprised and overjoyed when I heard their voices, followed by laughter. They were talking about writers Carli knew, people my father admired, like Ernst Toller, who took his life after coming to America. Amazingly, the two difficult men remained good friends for a long time after that first meeting.

As for my own first introduction to Carli, "This is my young friend Deirdre (Lucy pronounced it "Dare-dra," as did all the refugees); she's eight."

"I'm almost nine now," I corrected her.

"Almost nine? I'm almost ten!" Carli responded, pretending to be very serious. I soon discovered that he stood firmly with us and was ready to take on the voice of authority (my parents), despite Lucy's gentle scolding: "Don't cause trouble!" He enjoyed doing just that, especially if it made us—the children—laugh until we cried.

When my mother said, "O.K., children outside, time for the grown-ups to have some privacy!" Carli obediently got up from the table and followed us out the front door to the porch steps, where the three of us collapsed in hysterical delight. Carli did not want to be identified as one of the "grown-ups," a quality that endeared him to young people, whom he usually preferred to people his own age because they had not yet "sold out" or "settled down."

I liked to listen to the stories of how people who loved each other first met. Lucy told their story, which began in Lisbon. She was living with Suzanne Chantal, a famous journalist and editor of *Cinémonde,* the woman who was Lucy's mentor. "Lisbon was my university education!" Lucy stayed in Suzanne's apartment, a meeting place for many famous refugees passing through Lisbon. Despite the darkness and terror of that time, it was mixed with excitement for her. "My life began in Lisbon!"

While an exile, Lucy worked with a Portuguese Jew, a Dr. Desaguy, who had approached her in a café the day after she arrived in Lisbon. She was sitting alone, lighting a cigarette, trying for a certain worldly bravado. He had paused at her table, introduced himself, and inquired whether she was Jewish.

"What's it to you?" she asked the stranger.

He wanted to know if she would like a job. She learned he was a doctor, connected with the Refugee Committee, who had turned his clinic into an emergency rescue center for the flood of European Jews appearing every day in the city. Lucy, who could speak five languages, plunged into the first job of her life the next morning. All day she listened to refugees' terrible stories, recorded each history, then assisted with visa applications, often becoming an interpreter, accompanying people to those consulates willing to take in refugees. One day, after Lucy had been working many weeks without a break except to sleep at night, Dr. Desaguy saw she was unable to cope with one more record of human brutality. He found her sitting on a back staircase unknown to the refugees, ravenously eating chocolates. "Take time off," he told her. "Go to the beach, stretch out in the sunlight, you need rest."

That was when Lucy first met Carli, who would pass through Lisbon every six weeks, pausing to restore his strength after the arduous climb over the Pyrenees, leading one group of refugees after another to the safety of the Portuguese capital. Lucy had found lodging for all the people he helped rescue, but they had never met before. Unwinding by the sea, they talked with each other for hours, two young people taking time out from the drama of the rescue effort.

"One day," Lucy said, "I decided I so completely trusted this man that I read him pages from my journal! I had never done that before, not with anyone. There I was sharing my most intimate thoughts with him, my feelings of disbelief about what was happening to all of us, mixed with the exciting nightly discussions at Suzanne Chantal's apartment. He was stretched out beside me on the sand, exhausted from his journey. His eyes were closed, but I knew he was listening, so I continued. Then when he didn't respond for a very long time I realized he was sound asleep!" Lucy laughed. "And you know, that's when I knew this was the man for me!"

"Why?" I asked.

"Because I knew he would not let me feel sorry for myself!"

They lost each other during the frantic final exodus, leaving on separate boats at different times, Carli sponsored by Varian Fry, Lucy by a U.S. consular officer in Lisbon, who knew her well because of her work with the other refugees, and knew it was time for her to get out of Europe. "Do you want to go to America?" he asked, and she said of course. She knew everyone wanted to go there, but to her "America was like the moon!" They arrived in different ports, Carli in Baltimore, Lucy in New York; both encountered trouble with immigration authorities when they tried to enter the United States. Lucy was sent to Ellis Island. She gave the filmmaker George Friedland's name as the person she'd be staying with in New York, a temporary arrangement she'd made with Friedland, a new friend from Estonia, before he left Lisbon.

"He's your fiancé?"

"No, he's my friend."

"Are you going to marry him?"

"Of course not! He's just my boyfriend!"

After seeing the words "Moral Turpitude" stamped in bold black letters across her papers, she was horrified. "What kind of disease is that?" she asked on the way to Ellis Island.

Carli was not allowed off his ship in Baltimore because, when the authorities searched his address book, they found the names of well-known communists and socialists. That's when the American journalist Eric Sevareid came to the rescue. Sevareid immediately wired money to Carli after learning that he was in grave danger of being sent back to Europe. Having money gave Carli immediate respectability in the eyes of the authorities (he referred to himself as a "new capitalist"), and they finally permitted him to disembark.

Months later Lucy and Carli found each other in a hardware store on Broadway. It was hours before the old year—1941—ended. Each heard the other asking for lead, explaining to bewildered salesclerks in their broken English that it was "for melting over fire, an old New Year's Eve tradition."

IT WAS NOT from Carli, nor from the other refugees, nor even from Lucy that I learned he was one of the heroes; he was too self-effacing. He would mention something to me in passing about "taking people over the Pyrenees," vague references to a time in his life I sensed was extremely important to him. But it wasn't until shortly after Carli died, in 1990, that I fully appreciated his part in the rescue effort that saved so many lives. That was the day I stepped into the space in the Holocaust Museum in Washington, D.C., where there was a special exhibit and tribute to the forgotten Varian Fry, to the people who had helped him, and to the people they saved. There were all the familiar faces looking back at me—Hertha Pauli, Mehring—and suddenly there it was. Sketched in ink in Carli's familiar handwriting, a map captioned: "Early Autumn tour in the Pyrenees recommended to illegal tourists. For crossing frontier on foot, choose siesta time, French guards will be asleep." There is his watercolor sketch of the vital route, more instructions, and the final words: "Descend and surrender to Spanish frontier guards."

In the winter of 1940 Carli was sent to Meslay du Maine, a French "internment camp" where "enemy aliens" were held to be sent to death camps. One frigid day the journalist Eric Sevareid—then working for the *Paris Herald*—suddenly appeared to interview those who had been imprisoned by the French authorities. He was deeply shocked by the conditions he witnessed, and could barely recognize Carli—whom he had met months earlier on the Left Bank, where Sevareid was living with his wife—when Carli called out his name. After a long, painful interview with Carli, who told him everything he knew about what was happening to "enemy aliens," Sevareid took off the new camel's hair coat he was wearing, feeling embarrassed beside the gaunt, shivering prisoners who had nothing but a threadbare blanket to wrap around them in the raw winter.

"You take this. You need it more than I do." He handed the luxurious coat to Carli before following his military escort out the gate ringed high with barbed wire. The coat almost reached Carli's ankles, but he was immensely grateful for the warmth. Sevareid wrote down his Washington, D.C., address, telling Carli to call when he reached the United States. His intention was to leave with some hope, but Carli saw he was weeping as he turned to go. This was the only story I heard Carli tell about the camp.

Months later Carli escaped from Meslay to the French countryside, finally reaching Marseilles, teeming with desperate refugees, in early August 1940. There he rejoined Hertha and Walter Mehring, and at last met Varian Fry.

Carli wrote of that period in a 1983 letter to Cynthia McCabe, curator at the Hirschhorn Museum in Washington, as she prepared for the belated tribute to Fry.

I kept busy preparing faked receipts of fictitious shipping lines for supposedly paid passages to the United States. With these receipts some of us obtained visa to China and transit visa through Spain and Portugal in doctored-up Czechoslovakian passports provided with the compliments of the outgoing Czech consul in Marseilles. This activity of mine was independent of that of Varian Fry and worked only in rare instances. . . . Varian Fry seemed to be the man to get us out of France by hook or crook. He asked me to assist him by reconnoitering the border between France and Spain and especially in the Banyuls area find suitable crossings over the Pyrenees. I eventually found myself accompanying groups of refugees from Banyuls to the border on a route I found best suited for medium mountain climbers until the day I had to accompany Hertha all the way South to Lisbon because she had fallen ill.

Carli left Lisbon in February 1941, sailing on the *Maria Christina*, a freighter loaded with cork. In the middle of the Atlantic the steering broke down, and they had to drift for a week until setting course again for America. Carli wrote:

> While aboard I wanted to practice my English on an ancient typewriter, but I had no paper to write on. I stole the toilet paper to start a treatise on "Nostalgia." Every once in a while one of the 5 passengers on this 2500 ton freighter would come and pull out the roll, interrupting my chain of thought. The essay remained unfinished. I feel nostalgic ever since. Arriving in Norfolk, Virginia, the immigration authorities there did not let me off the ship. In my address book they had discovered the names of well-known European communists and anarchists: they overlooked the names of monarchists and Christian-Democrats. When however Eric Sevareid sent me $50, a large sum in 1941, c/o the shipping line, I could go ashore a capitalist.

NOSTALGIA STAYED with him throughout his years in America. During the summers and my nonresident terms at college in the late 1950s, I lived with relatives in New York City, downtown near Washington Square and the Village. Marley and Dinny were related to me through my Jewish grandmother, who died in 1945, after the war was over and the refugees living at the farm had returned to New York.

Lucy and Carli lived uptown on West Eighty-first Street, off Amsterdam Avenue. By then they had given up on having a child of their own. In the early 1950s they had been on the verge of adopting a French orphan, but after working through all the bureaucracy, they were told that France was refusing to allow the child, a boy, to leave. All males born in France were needed to serve in the army; therefore, he was not free to leave.

I saw them often when I lived in the city. By then they had bought an old car, which started only after Carli muttered his magic Chinese prayer. With their combined salaries, they purchased a little summer cottage on Bayberry Lane in Huntington, Long Island, a short walk from the harbor and a brief car ride to where Hertha and Ashton lived. I was always invited to their wonderful parties, in Huntington and Manhattan. Their circle of friends—writers, artists, translators, and filmmakers—remained mostly "European transplants," as Carli called them, and himself. No one spoke of the war anymore.

"We have tickets to *The Threepenny Opera*. It's important for you to see it," Lucy told me. I attended previews of movies she worked on, and once a month I'd have dinner with Carli down in the Village at a small family-owned restaurant called Monte's. It was Lucy's suggestion that I keep him company while she was at her union meetings. She said I cheered him up. Her job was always filled with excitement—the film celebrities she met, the interesting people she worked with and brought home. Carli's job was boring. Working as a technical writer for some big company left him feeling frustrated and utterly useless at the end of the day.

Sometimes we had serious discussions during our monthly dinners together. Other times he was in a silly mood and we giggled like adolescents about nothing in particular, or he was subdued, using his paper placemat to make an amazing drawing of all the people sitting around us. I knew he was restless, that he felt like a failure, but I didn't know then what I know now: like Varian Fry, whom he kept in touch with until his death, Carli could not adjust to the mundane daily rituals or the comforts of middle-class life after the defining drama of his time. He spoke of finding work that had more meaning, but his low opinion of himself seemed to paralyze his efforts. He was not a great writer, artist, musician, poet. Therefore, in his own eyes, he was nobody. It's not that he felt sorry for himself; he never did. I just felt his disappointment.

After our meal at Monte's, we'd wander over to Eighth Street, stopping at the secondhand bookstores that used to fill the area. Carli would find a book he wanted me to read, often written by someone he knew whose story he wanted to share with me. One day he found a copy of *The Age of the Fish* by Odon von Horvath.

"He was a charming guy. Hertha was deeply in love with Odon."

"What happened to him?"

"A freak accident! He was killed while walking on the streets of Paris. There was a sudden storm, high winds, a tree fell, and he was gone . . ."

Once we went to the Russian Tea Room while Lucy was working on a documentary in the Bowery. It was a frigid January day, and we had walked against the wind after seeing a Paul Klee exhibit. I was totally self-absorbed, nursing my first true heartbreak. Carli ordered Irish coffee for us both and smiled sympathetically at me.

"Ah, dear Deirdre." He took my hand in his after the waiter left our warming drinks. "It's so good you can feel sadness!"

He knew that would make me laugh, that it would blow away my tragic expression. "Why do you say that?"

"Because it means you're ALIVE! How I envy you. To suffer is to be alive!" He scooped the whipped cream from his glass to mine. "Look around you—everyone's dead! I'm dead. We don't weep anymore."

"I ALWAYS knew you would marry a foreigner!" Hertha told me when she first met Cristobal and heard his accent.

At the airport that is now called JFK, in the spring of 1963 Lucy and Carli, Hertha and Ashton were the last familiar faces we would see on this side of the Atlantic. They'd come to say farewell before we flew off to Paris, en route to the Sudan. They all approved of Cristobal. He was born in Quito, Ecuador. His father, ambassador to France in the 1960s, grew up in Nice but was forced to leave France before entering the university because Cristobal's grandfather, Neptali, had decided to run for president in Ecuador. So the family returned to the Andes after World War I.

After earning his doctorate, Cristobal had accepted a UNESCO post, helping to set up a teacher's training school in Khartoum. When we left the United States that day in 1963, John F. Kennedy was the new president, Martin Luther King Jr. was in Birmingham, change was in the air, and our expectations were high. Like the first tide of Peace Corps volunteers, people our age going to Africa, we believed we were going to "make a difference."

"I'm jealous!" Carli whispered as we hugged good-bye. "I should have worked for the UN."

"You still can!" I whispered back. And he did. Soon after our departure, he finally uprooted—well, the roots were never very deep—from America and went to work for the World Health Organization in Delhi for years. Then later, when his age required him to retire from the UN, he headed an animal rights group based in Zurich.

Lucy was with him through these years, having given up her film career when they first left New York City for India. She knew it was his turn to have exciting work. But she would not go to his final destination: back to Vienna, to his mountains, in the hope of finding something he'd lost. She came back to New York, where Carli returned periodically to be with her.

Carli wrote his own story of growing up in Vienna, of the war, published in Austria shortly after he died. Written in German, a language I can't read, it is titled *Verlust Anzeige*.

He was disturbed by the revived anti-Semitism, which never had really ceased in Austria. He spent his last years visiting the schools, speaking to the students about the Third Reich and his experiences, determined to make the war vivid to them. Because of his rapport with young people, they listened. Finally, he spent many hours each day in the national library, making certain that Hertha's archives, and the archives of all the other writers he knew, were complete and accurately catalogued.

Once when I was in college, Carli sent me a poster from an exhibit in Paris, "De Giotto a Bellini." This was the year I was about to sail off to France for the first time, to study at the Sorbonne. On the back of the poster Carli wrote a letter to me in watercolors. While I was working with Harold Isaacs at the Center for International Studies at MIT, he offered to make a frame for the poster. Since then it has been on the wall of every home I've lived in. Coming to the end of this reminiscence of Carli, I yearned to see his letter, hidden since Harold framed it over four decades ago. On the eve of winter solstice 2001, I picked up the poster from the framer. Harold's pine frame was still in place, but now there was glass on the back revealing the letter, written in 1957, though it could have been yesterday:

> Dear Deirdre
> Here goes the last leaf of autumn—
> [drawing of a tree losing the last leaf]
> How many silly leaves spoiled with type did
> You turn since I saw you last? How many
> Did you spoil yourself? But never mind—
> There'll be new green leaves come spring—
>   A spring with strontium
> In a world radiating at 2725 dis-
> Integrations per minute.
> Did you look at the Moon lately? The
> Israelis have landed there . . .
> But us, Lucy and meself, you'll find
> In New York now, dead or alive
> Come and let's be gloomy!
> Exit crying. . . .
> . . . . Curtain!
>   Carli

Lucy, eighty-seven as of this writing, is the only one of the refugees who came to Morning Star Farm in the 1940s who is still alive. She lives alone, fiercely independent, a defiant smoker, surrounded by the library she and Carli collected over the years, many of the books written by friends, in French, German, Russian, English. She keeps rediscovering them. The George Grosz paintings were of no interest to the thieves who robbed Lucy and Carli's apartment on West Eighty-first Street in the 1950s and early 1960s. They still hang on her walls, crowded with mementos of her years in India. The steamer trunk Lucy took with her when she was given twenty-four hours to leave France is still with her, filled with fading photographs treasured over a life-time, and all the journals—Carli's and her own—including the journal she read from when they were on the beach in Lisbon.

In 1945, while World War II still raged and twenty-nine-year-old Lucy was first visiting our farm, she said to me: "I have very good friends, and they are my family. This way I can choose. Will you be my new friend?"

To Lucy's question I whispered, "Yes!" happy I was chosen, an eight-year-old child just learning about the refugees and the war that never seemed far away.

Over five decades later, I am still Lucy's friend and she is still mine.

Notes

1. Walter Mehring, *The Lost Library*, trans. Richard Winston and Clara Winston (London: Secker and Warburg, 1951), 265–67.

2. Hertha Pauli, *Break of Time* (New York: Hawthorn Books, 1972), 13–14.

III

ÉMIGRÉS AND THEIR IMPACTS

The nature of the intellectual skills that the refugees brought to this
country was one of the major determinants of their relative success or
failure in finding a niche in America.

LEWIS A. COSER

MOST SOCIETIES are wary of strangers, especially those who,
forced to flee, threaten to be dependent on others for their care
and succor. Even those nations that pride themselves on their diversity frequently erect barriers to prevent the influx of those fleeing persecution. Today the mass media are filled with stories of
such resistance, especially in the countries of Europe where "asylum policy" in regard to would-be petitioners from eastern and
central Europe and North Africa are topics of considerable concern and the source of new nativist campaigns.

Many Americans are offended by the seeming hard-heartedness
of those in Europe, forgetting that this country has not been immune to such sentiments and practices, and to what Gilburt
Loescher and John Scanlan have called our own policy of "calculated kindness." Few better examples of such a protectionist attitude are to be found than in the reluctance of U.S. authorities to
welcome the victims of the Third Reich to these shores in the late
1930s and early 1940s. The fact is that those who were selected to
be allowed to enter the United States were a relative few out of
hundreds of thousands of petitioners. Among those in that cohort were several thousand refugee intellectuals—writers, editors,
artists, architects, musicians, filmmakers, scientists, psychiatrists,
and physicians—people Laura Fermi once called our "illustrious
immigrants."

Despite the generally negative policies of the Roosevelt administration toward the admission of refugees and the widespread
animosity toward them expressed in many quarters in the country, those who did manage to come had profound effects on our
society and culture. (To a lesser extent, the presence of their coun-

terparts had a similar impact in many other countries where
small groups of intellectuals and professional were admitted.
Among those societies that benefited most were the United Kingdom, Canada, Australia, South Africa, and, for very special reasons, Turkey.)

In this section we examine the careers, contacts, and contributions of a select group of such émigrés, most of them writers, and
all within the subset of professionals who are usually placed under the rubric "Arts and Letters." It was they who, as the historian
H. Stuart Hughes clearly noted, helped to "deprovincialize" American society and culture. He called this a "sea change." Hughes
was one of a number of scholars who studied the cultural migration of European intellectuals in the 1930s and 1940s. One after
another of these writer-researchers noted a perverse irony: how
much the United States benefited from Hitler's desire to make his
nation *Judenfrei*—and also free of all others who would not accept
the Nazi definition of proper art, music, science, thought, or
opinion.

The United States became the second home of the Frankfort
group of social scientists and the Bauhaus school of artists and
architects. It became the base of operations for the likes of Albert
Einstein, Enrico Fermi, Niels Bohr, Edward Teller, and many
other scientists; for psychologists and psychiatrists such as Eric
Erikson, T. W. Adorno, Else-Frankel Brunswick, and Bruno Bettel-
heim; for historians Hans Kohn, Haja Holborn, and Peter Gay;
and social theorists and sociologists such as Leo Strauss, Paul
Lazarsfeld, Leo Lowenthal, and Kurt Lewin. And it became the
creative haven for Kurt Weill, Erich Leinsdorf, George Szell,
Bertolt Brecht, Kurt and Helen Wolff, Billy Wilder, Peter Lorre,
Marlene Dietrich, and many other composers and musicians,
writers, publishers, actors, and filmmakers. Few had an easy time,
though some fared far better than others did. This was not only
because of the nature of the intellectual skills they brought with
them but also because of their own cultural baggage and the re-
ceptiveness of the host society. Some, especially in certain fields of
science and social science, found welcoming colleagues and comfortable environments in universities and institutes and adapted
fairly quickly. Many others never adjusted. Among those who had
the hardest time were the writers, individuals who may have been
literary virtuosos in their native language of German or French or

Italian but found writing in English for American readers a most difficult and frustrating exercise.

In the essays that follow, our writers discuss the contributions of both well-known and lesser-known refugee intellectuals of the 1930s and 1940s and their impact not only on this country but on others as well. The authors are as varied in background, interests, and disciplines as those about whom they write. Turkish-born and educated Lâle Burk teaches chemistry at Smith College; Karen Koehler, a specialist on the Bauhaus, is on the faculty of Hampshire College, where she teaches art history; Saverio Giovacchini, an Italian historian of American culture and politics, is the founding chair of program in Media Studies at the University of Maryland; and Krishna Winston, a noted translator, is a professor of German language and literature at Wesleyan University in Middletown, Connecticut.

An Open Door

German Refugee Scholars in Turkey

LÂLE AKA BURK

A LARGE number of German intellectuals who left their homeland because of Nazi persecution found refuge in the Republic of Turkey in the 1930s and 1940s. Many were academics, artists, and politicians with established international reputations, and experts in their fields. Invited by the Turkish government under the leadership of Kemal Atatürk, they arrived in Turkey with their families and often their assistants to teach at the Turkish universities and participate in the reforms of the young republic. Many were instrumental in securing additional academic posts in Turkey for fellow refugee scholars. How was the Turkish republic able to employ in its government and universities so many refugees at a time when other countries were experiencing difficulty finding positions for such individuals? Were the events that led to the intellectual migration, which affected Turkey so profoundly, planned, or were they coincidental, resulting from unpredicted turns of history? To answer these questions, one must consider the developments in Turkey preceding the Nazi takeover in 1933, the atmosphere in Germany during the early days of the Nazi regime, and the response of the international community.

Turkey before 1933: Educational and Other Reforms

Until the nineteenth century, higher education in the Ottoman Empire followed the Islamic tradition. Secular schools were established during the Westernization movements of the 1800s; these were mostly professional institutions such as Mekteb-i Tibbiye-i Şahane (the Imperial Medical School) and Mekteb-i Mülkiye (the School for Civil Servants). The only state university was Dar-ül-Fünun-u Şahane (the Imperial House of Science [or Knowledge]) in Istanbul, which was restructured as a secular institution in 1900.

In 1915 the Ottoman government invited, as part of an educational reform initiative, a German assistance mission to help upgrade the Dar-ül-Fünun. Twenty German academics from a variety of fields were given teaching posts at the institution. One of the most significant achievements of the German professors was the establishment of the first academic department of chemistry, Yerebatan Kimya Enstitüsü (the Chemistry Institute at Yerebatan), founded under the leadership of Fritz Arndt from Breslau University. For the first time in Turkey, chemistry became an independent discipline, separate from medicine and biology. The institute was housed in a new building planned by Arndt and equipped with supplies and chemicals from Germany. The curriculum was based on the German model, and the facilities were modern for the times. The institute trained students who eventually received chemistry degrees. Fritz Arndt was a talented pedagogue and linguist. He learned the language in one year in order to be able to teach in Turkish. He also provided two much-needed Turkish textbooks, which were published in Arabic, then the official alphabet of the Ottoman Empire. The university reforms of 1915 were interrupted with the onset of World War I. The activities of the German professors were terminated at the end of the war, when the Ottoman Empire, then aligned with Germany, was defeated. German nationals were forced to leave Istanbul. Arndt returned to Breslau in early 1919 to resume a successful teaching and research career.

The collapse of the Ottoman Empire and occupation of Ottoman territory by English, French, and Greek forces were followed by the War of Liberation, from which Turkey, led by Mustafa Kemal, emerged victorious. The Turkish nation proclaimed its independence, and a secular republic replaced the fallen Islamic state: the sultanate was abolished on November 1, 1922, and Mehmed VI, the last Ottoman sultan, fled the country on November 17. The Republic of Turkey, with Mustafa Kemal as president, was established on October 29, 1923. The new republic, looking to European nations as models, and operating under the six principles of Kemalism (republicanism, secularism, nationalism, populism, statism, and reformism), pushed ahead to create a revitalized, modern Turkish state. In the quest for national identity, other Turkish roots were sought to replace the Islamic past of the Ottomans.

The reforms that were undertaken in the early years of the republic included the abolition in 1924 of the caliphate (the Ottoman sultan had been the caliph, or leader of Islam, since the sixteenth century), the adoption in 1926 of a new civil code granting women equal social rights, and the adoption in 1928 of the Latin alphabet.[1] Reforms in teaching at all levels were given priority. German-Turkish relationships in higher education resumed during the early years of the republic. The High Agriculture Institute in the new capital, Ankara, the Ankara Yüksek Ziraat Enstitüsü, was founded in 1928 with the help of German experts who established programs and taught there. These individuals, like the German professors who taught in 1915 in Istanbul, were not refugees; their appointments involved the cooperation of both governments.

In 1931 Turkish educational reforms were directed toward raising the standards of the university in Istanbul, the Dar-ül Fünun, which had been neglected and in decline since the end of World War I.[2] Alfred Malche, professor of pedagogy at Geneva University and a well-recognized educational expert on teaching methodologies in higher education, was asked to evaluate the university. He visited Turkey for the first time in 1932 and submitted his report within five months. Malche found major weaknesses in the existing university, including inadequate library resources, low faculty salaries, isolationist governance policies, lack of communication with the government and the public, and obsolete methods of instruction. He noted in particular the overreliance on memorization, lack of foreign language instruction, lack of coherence in the curriculum, and the unnecessary duplication of courses in the various institutes. For instance, Malche found the site of the medical school problematic. The Dar-ül-Fünun, housed in the buildings of the former Ottoman War Ministry in Beyazit, on the European side of Istanbul, was isolated from its medical school, located in Haydarpaşa, across the Bosporus in Asia. In sum, Malche believed that the Dar-ül-Fünun in its present state was poorly equipped to train the nation's next generation of teachers.

The Turkish government, determined to remedy these problems, decided to take action and initiate major reforms. The goal of these reforms was the establishment of an institution that would be comparable to contemporary European universities. Following Malche's suggestions, a plan for the new university was drawn up which included on its faculty an internationally diverse group of professors. Malche, however, had also emphasized that simply establishing and filling chairs with foreign professors was not sufficient; a new philosophy, or spirit, was essential to revitalize the institution. Although the government agreed with Malche's suggestions, implementation was not simple. It was unclear, for instance, who would constitute the proposed foreign faculty. Where would these individuals come from? The year 1932 ended with no action taken and no new appointments made. The next year, however, turned out to be crucial for the realization of the university reforms.

Germany, 1933: Persecution and International Response

On April 23, 1933, Herman Kantorowitz, professor of philosophy and history of law at the University of Kiel, received a questionnaire addressed to university professors, who were then considered civil servants in Germany. Kantorowitz answered regarding the racial background of his grandparents:

> Since there is no time to inquire as to which sense of the term "race" is being utilized, I shall limit myself to the following declaration: as all four of my grandparents died a long time ago and all the necessary measurements, etc., were never made, I am unable to ascertain scientifically (anthropologically) what racial group they belonged to. Understood in its common significance, their race was

German, as they all spoke German as their mother tongue, which means that it
was Indo-European or Aryan. Their race in the sense of the first supplementary
decree to the Law of April 7, 1933, section 2, paragraph 1, sentence 3 was the Jewish
religion.[3]

Kantorowitz's sarcasm became irrelevant, for he had already been dismissed
under the Law for the Restoration of the Professional Civil Service, along with
a number of other professors. Sixteen prominent names from this group were
published in the *Deutsche Allgemeine Zeitung* on April 14.[4]

Shortly after the Nazis came to power at the end of January 1933, many
academic professionals in Germany started losing their positions because of
the Aryan policies of the National Socialists, often because of their race or
religion. Being Jewish, or having family connections such as a Jewish husband,
wife, parent, or grandparent, meant termination of employment. Some individuals were persecuted for their political affiliations or beliefs. Artists whose
works were considered "degenerate" lost commissions and opportunities for
work. Fearing for the welfare of their families and themselves, many intellectuals left Germany in the months that followed. Others, though not personally threatened, found the political situation stifling and left because of their
personal convictions. Of the estimated 1,200 Jewish professors in Germany
who lost their positions in 1933, the largest numbers were in departments of
medicine (412), social sciences (173), law (132), physics (106), philology (95),
chemistry (86), and technology (85).[5]

The international community soon condemned the actions of the Nazis. In
the United States, the Emergency Committee in Aid of Displaced German
Scholars, later renamed the Emergency Committee in Aid of Displaced Foreign Scholars, started organizing at the end of May 1933. In a letter sent to
colleges and universities on May 27, 1933, Stephen Duggan, head of the Institute of International Education, stressed the need to rescue the displaced
academics. In response to that and a second letter, twenty-three prominent
educators, all college and university presidents, including President William
Allan Neilson of Smith College, consented to serve on the Emergency Committee.[6] The committee confined its aid to academics and gave no help to
lawyers, doctors, civil servants, or other professionals displaced by the Nazis.
A second organization in the United States, the Emergency Committee for
Displaced German Physicians, was established through the initiatives of Dr.
Alfred Cohn of the Rockefeller Institute for Medical Research, before the end
of the year.

In England, the Academic Assistance Council, a similar rescue organization,
was conceived and founded in early May 1933 under the leadership of Lord
William Henry Beveridge, director of the London School of Economics and

Political Science. Beveridge later described the formation of this rescue committee in *A Defence of Free Learning*:

> Twenty-five years ago, on an evening at the end of March 1933, I was enjoying myself with friends at a café in Vienna; the friends included the Austrian economist Ludwig von Mises and Lionel Robbins of the London School of Economics and his wife.[7] As we talked of things in general, an evening paper was brought in giving the names of a dozen leading professors in German universities who were being dismissed by the new Nazi régime on racial or political grounds. As Mises read out the names to our growing indignation, Robbins and I decided that we would take action in the London School of Economics to help scholars in our subjects who should come under Hitler's ban.[8]

The response to Hitler's policies was similar in other British universities. The formation of a rescue organization rapidly gained support. The founding of the organization, which was named the Academic Assistance Council, was announced in a document dated May 22, 1933, and signed by forty-one leading scholars and influential scientists, including Nobel laureates and heads of universities and learned societies. The prominent chemist Lord Rutherford, who headed the Cavendish Laboratories in Cambridge, was among the founding members of the Academic Assistance Council and assumed a leadership role in the organization.[9] The purpose of the Academic Assistance Council was similar to that of the U.S. Emergency Committee in that it was to help only university teachers and investigators. The news of the formation of an English rescue committee appeared in the press on May 24, and checks started arriving the next day.[10]

The rescue efforts of the U.S. Emergency Committee and the Academic Assistance Council were often coordinated. Relocating the displaced scholars, however, was not easy. Both the U.S. and English committees experienced financial difficulties in securing employment for these individuals. The years after World War I were a time of economic hardship for many countries, and the United States, in particular, suffered from the effects of the Great Depression, which weakened its educational institutions financially and increased competition for academic openings and other jobs. In the spring of 1935, a representative of the U.S. Emergency Committee asked the Academic Assistance Council to stop sending displaced scholars to the United States, because "the country was already as full of such people as it could hold."[11]

Another rescue committee for assisting displaced academics, Notgemeinschaft Deutscher Wissenschaftler im Ausland (the Emergency Society of German Scholars Abroad) had formed in Switzerland somewhat earlier than the U.S. and English committees. The membership of the Swiss committee was unique in that its members were all displaced scholars themselves. The Notgemeinschaft was headed by Phillip Schwartz, an early victim of Nazi racial persecution who was eventually removed from his position as chair of general pathology and pathological anatomy at Frankfurt am Main. As Schwartz described in his memoirs, on the afternoon of March 23, 1933, he met his friend A. W. Fischer, the administrator of the Association of Docents, in the gardens of the city hospital. Fischer asked, with great concern, why Schwartz had not already left the country, and warned that if he did not disappear immediately, he would be arrested. Schwartz's house had been searched a few days before by the police under the pretext of looking for hidden machine guns. Within an hour of his conversation with Fischer, the head of the Professors' Association telephoned Schwartz and advised him to leave as soon as possible. Schwartz and his son left by train that evening for Zurich, where his wife had relatives. His wife and young daughter followed him a few days later.[12]

A small academic refugee colony was already established in Zurich by the time Schwartz arrived. He immediately organized the Notgemeinschaft, and by the end of March, the rescue committee was in place and functioning. In April the formation of the committee was announced in the *Neue Zuricher Zeitung*, and also in an unofficial memorandum that circulated in Germany. Immediately the committee received numerous inquiries from academics who had lost or were about to lose their positions, along with applications for help in relocating. In May a postcard arrived from Turkey with an announcement of the availability of academic openings at Istanbul University.[13] This historic communication was to change the fate of many displaced German scholars.

"Not 3 but 30"

May 1933 was a turning point in the realization of the Turkish university reforms. Once contact between Turkish officials and the Notgemeinschaft was established, events developed rapidly. On May 31 the Turkish government passed a law regarding higher education (legislation no. 2252), which stated that the Dar-ül-Fünum would cease to exist on July 31, 1933, and that the Ministry of Education would be given the charge to establish a new institution under the name Istanbul University. This was to be a new establishment in no way connected to the old university. The faculty of the new university would consist of three groups: those rehired from the Dar-ül-Fünun, new Turkish faculty who had been educated abroad, and foreign professors. The last category was to be the largest.

In June 1933 representatives of the Academic Assistance Council met with

Phillip Schwartz in Zurich to discuss the possibility of coordinating the rescue efforts of the English and Swiss committees. Schwartz, however, preferred to work independently.[14] In the first of two trips, which followed shortly afterward, he arrived by train in Istanbul on July 5 and continued on to Ankara, the capital. There he met with Reşit Galip, the minister of education, other government officials, representatives from the university, and Alfred Malche, the author of the critical 1932 evaluation of the Dar-ül-Fünun. In a congenial meeting that lasted for seven hours, Schwartz was asked to help fill professorships in a variety of fields at the new Istanbul University. Schwartz, hoping to find posts for three, had brought with him the Notgemeinschaft's list of displaced professors.[15] But the question, "Can you recommend anyone in the area of..." was repeated thirty times, and Schwartz continued suggesting names from his list. Conditions for the hiring of thirty German professors were then drawn up. The salaries offered to the German professors were typically higher than those of the Turkish faculty and compared favorably with the former salaries of these individuals in Germany. The language of instruction initially was to be German, with the use of translators, but after three years, teaching was to be in Turkish. Contracts would be renewable after five years. The government would pay for travel and moving expenses, and the professors could bring family members and assistants. An agreement written in French, and signed by Reşit Galip and Phillip Schwartz, gave Schwartz the charge of implementing the appointments.

Schwartz was happy with the unexpected positive outcome of the meeting. From Ankara he sent a telegram that evening to the Notgemeinschaft which read, "Not 3 but 30."[16] The next day, Schwartz met again with Reşit Galip. The agreement had been forwarded to the president, Mustafa Kemal. Galip asked for replies from the German professors within two weeks, since the planned opening of the university was set for August 1. Galip also gave assurance that individuals who were invited and employed by the Turkish Republic would be protected to the fullest extent by the government.[17] On the same day, Schwartz met with Refik Saydam, the minister of health, to discuss the staffing of two new medical institutions that were being established in Ankara. Later that day Schwartz left for Zurich, where he made the necessary contacts with his displaced colleagues.

The early success of the Notgemeinschaft, within months of its formation, was remarkable compared to similar rescue activities in England and the United States. In their books on the English Academic Assistance Council (renamed in 1935 the Society for the Protection of Science and Learning), both Norman Bentwitch and Lord Beveridge describe the activities of the Notgemeinschaft and the role of Phillip Schwartz in helping place hundreds of displaced German scholars in Turkey. It is curious that in *The Rescue of Science and Learning*, which describes the story of the U.S. Emergency Committee, the authors Stephen Duggan and Betty Drury do not mention this significant event, nor the forty-two German professors who secured posts in 1933 at Istanbul University. This may well be the largest number of refugee professors emigrating to a single host institution, and many more were to arrive in the next few years. In comparison, according to Duggan and Drury, "30 arrived in 1933 [in the United States]."[18]

At the end of July 1933, Schwartz returned to Istanbul with the well-known surgeon Rudolph Nissen (who eventually came to teach at Istanbul University) from Berlin, who gave advice on the new medical programs and facilities. Nissen's teacher, the famous surgeon Ferdinand Sauerbruch, also came to Istanbul and served in an advisory capacity. At Schwartz's suggestion, three scientists, all formerly from Göttingen, and all well-known experts, were invited by the government and served as consultants. These were the physicists James Franck and Max Born, and the mathematician Richard Courant.[19]

In mid-August, Reşit Galip, who had argued strongly for hiring the refugee professors, and who had played a central role in arranging for their positions, was involved in a serious automobile accident and nearly died. After a two-week period of uncertainty, the minister of health, Refik Saydam, took over Galip's vacated office and reassured Schwartz that the original plans would be carried out. Much relieved, Schwartz returned to Zurich and pushed ahead to finalize the appointments of the refugee professors. Official papers were prepared by the Turkish ambassador, Cemal Hüsnü, in Geneva and by Alfred Malche. The opening of the university was moved to the beginning of November; this allowed time for some of the professors to visit Turkey before accepting their offers.

Arrival in Istanbul

Istanbul University started its 1933–34 academic year with forty-two refugee professors occupying high academic positions.[20] Schwartz, at the urging of Malche and Turkish officials, came to Turkey as director of the Pathology Institute, which he headed for twenty years.[21]

Schwartz described his friends arriving in large numbers (he estimated 150) all through October, accompanied by their wives and children, sisters, mothers, mothers-in-law, and assistants. Some brought their household help. Many came directly from Germany, where they had been forced to abandon their homes. Others came from England or from Paris. These individuals were encountered everywhere in the city, including the museums, mosques, boats, and beaches. In the evenings the refugees would enjoy the view of the Bosporus and the Sea of Marmara from the terrace of the Park Hotel and talk about their daily activities. They were living now "among hospitable people in comfort and peace of mind, as loved and respected guests."[22]

On October 29, 1933, the German professors attended, as guests of honor, the official celebrations of the tenth anniversary of the founding of the Turkish Republic at Dolmabahçe Palace. Ernst Hirsch, who taught law at Istanbul and Ankara universities between 1933 and 1952, wrote about this event in his autobiography:

> And here I was, belittled in my country for being Jewish and expelled from my position because I belonged to an "inferior" race; forced to leave my home and country to escape to foreign lands: a refugee. Here I was, in a country far far away, in Turkey, in a throne room of the past, surrounded by crystal, marble, priceless objects, carved furniture, rugs and paintings. Here I was, considered among the thousand most honored people in the country. Here I was, a respected German professor.[23]

In his book on the intellectual migration to Turkey, the economist Fritz Neumark, who taught at Istanbul University between 1933 and 1952, also wrote about this event:

> The Turkish Republic, whose soil we set foot on in October 1933, had just turned ten years of age. Hence, at the end of October, within a couple weeks of our arrival at the most, we had the opportunity of joining various celebrations held in Ankara and in Istanbul. On one such occasion, all of the foreign professors were invited by Dr. Tevfik Rüştü Aras, the foreign minister at the time, to a reception at Dolmabahçe Palace, held in honor of the Russian delegation, which was headed by the Commissioner of War, Marshall Kliment Woroschilow. From the outside, Dolmabahçe Palace resembles a decorated cake, not unlike, in my opinion, the famous cathedral in Milan. With its impressive interior decor and its magnificent location on the Bosporus, Dolmabahçe is a prototype of an Eastern dream palace. On this occasion, the latter impression was reinforced by the gold plates and service, and the rich assortment of Turkish foods.
>
> For those of us who did not own formal attire, it became necessary to pay a visit to a tailor. Fortunately, a Greek expert in the profession provided the necessary suit in three days. Dressed for the occasion and feeling somewhat shy, I entered the great ballroom, which was decorated extravagantly with flowers and flags. Having just left Nazi Germany, you can imagine how we felt at the sight of the Turkish crescent flying next to the Russian crescent and star, at the sound of the Turkish national anthem followed by the the Russian "Internationale" so hated by the Nazis, and witnessing Marshall Woroschilow opening the dance

with Madame Aras and the Foreign Minister following suit with Madam Woroschilow.[24]

Istanbul University started its fall session in November 1933. The opening address was delivered by the new minister of education, the historian Hikmet Bayur. At the end of his speech Bayur introduced the faculty to the student body. As each introduction was made, the students greeted their professors, Turkish and foreign alike, with applause. The continuing faculty from the Dar-ül-Fünun were received with particular enthusiasm.[25] Istanbul University had become the institution with the largest number of outstanding German refugees on its staff in the whole world. In the words of the refugee professors themselves, it had become the best German university.[26]

In the following years, refugee professors were given posts at other institutions in Istanbul, including the Fine Arts Academy (Güzel Sanatlar Akademisi) and the architecture division of Istanbul Technical University (Istanbul Teknik Üniversitesi Mimari Bölümü). In Ankara, the founding of Ankara Üniversitesi in 1935 and the State Conservatory (Ankara Devlet Konservatuvarı) in 1936, in addition to the establishment of new medical institutes, provided more academic openings. Refugee academics fleeing persecution continued to arrive from Germany and Austria, and, to a lesser extent, from other European countries. Most were employed in the capital, Ankara, some moving there from Istanbul. A few were given positions at the Ankara High Agricultural Institute, which was largely staffed by German professors who were not refugees. The Faculty of Social Sciences (Ankara Siyasal Bilimler Fakültesi) had no foreign staff except for Ernst Reuter, who came to Turkey in 1935.

Istanbul University expanded throughout the next decade. The size of the faculty increased from 180 in 1933–34 to 249 in 1942–43, with the number of assistants nearly doubling, from 142 to 300. The 65 foreign faculty members in 1942–43 constituted 26 percent of the total.[27] In all, around 300 displaced academics found homes in Turkey, along with three times that number of family members and assistants.[28]

Phillip Schwartz continued to work with Turkish officials in recruiting government specialists and academics. In an interview some years later, he estimated that he personally had been able to engage 250 "first-rate scientists" for the Turkish government, and that many of the young assistants who came to Turkey in 1933 eventually became renowned scholars elsewhere. The refugee intellectuals, Schwartz stated, helped change the face of the Turkish republic through their activities in higher education and their contributions to every governmental and organizational field.[29] Fritz Neumark, referring to this intellectual migration, used the phrase "the German-Turkish miracle."[30]

The Refugee Professors

While it is not possible to list all of the refugees who so profoundly influenced Turkey, in this section I discuss a number of those who were prominent in the social sciences and law, humanities, and arts, and in the sciences and medicine.

THE TURKISH government engaged refugee experts in political science, sociology, economics, and law to serve as advisers, and to design programs and teach at its universities in these fields. Many of the reforms undertaken by the Turkish republic in the early years of its formation were intended to help establish a new social order, and the refugee professors worked closely with the government toward this end.

Ernst Reuter was one of Turkey's most beloved refugees. In 1935 Reuter escaped to Ankara, where he was initially given an agricultural advisory post. He traveled extensively in Turkey and spoke the language well. He eventually taught political science and helped found university programs in urban studies. He also served as the director of the Ankara office of the Internal Rescue Committee. After World War II, Reuter returned in November 1946 to Berlin, where he became mayor. He lived in Berlin until his death.[31]

Among the well-known economists who made significant contributions were Fritz Neumark, Alfred Isaac, Alexander Rustow, Wilhelm Ropke, and Umberto Rici (who fled Fascist Italy and joined the faculty at Istanbul University in 1942). Neumark and Isaac left Germany because of racial persecution, Rustow and Ropke for political reasons. Neumark helped reform Turkey's income tax system. He spoke excellent Turkish and taught at Istanbul University for almost two decades, starting in 1933. He returned in 1952 to Frankfurt, where he became rector of the university while continuing to teach, and sat on the advisory boards of various federal ministries. Neumark received an honorary degree from Istanbul University. His book on the intellectual migration to Turkey is an insightful and significant document of the times; it includes detailed accounts of Istanbul University, his German and Turkish colleagues, the Turkish students, relationships with the Turkish government, and the refugee experience in general.[32]

Alfred Isaac, who taught in Turkey from 1937 to 1951, was an expert on business administration. Well liked and respected for his unassuming personality, he wrote extensively on the economics of business administration and helped the government establish its social security system. Isaac became very active in the Society for the Protection of Animals in Istanbul, and has been described as becoming "the soul" of this organization.[33]

For Alexander Rustow and Wilhelm Ropke, the period in Istanbul was one of contemplation in addition to teaching and consulting. Participating in the social and economic rebuilding of the young Turkish republic helped the two men formulate theories on how a new nation should be built. Rustow began teaching at Istanbul University in 1933. On several occasions his friends and former colleagues who had gone to American institutions such as the Rockefeller Foundation and the New School for Social Research in New York urged him to join them. Turning down these invitations, as well as offers from Harvard and Yale, Rustow remained in Turkey and wrote a number of works, including *Freedom and Denomination*, in which he stated:

> To write this German book I had to emigrate in 1933 from a Germany whose stifling atmosphere after Hitler's conquest left me no air to breathe. The most important and pressing task imposed by the catastrophic world situation upon historian and sociologist alike, it seemed to me, was to determine just what had really happened and just what position we really occupy on the historical continuum. Since then I have been engaged in this attempt to fix our bearings in relation to the present, to identify the historic coordinates of our time.[34]

While in Turkey, Rustow cooperated in the activities of the Office of Strategic Services and the International Rescue and Relief Committee, both United States-based organizations. Rustow taught at Istanbul University until 1949, when he returned to Germany to teach at Heidelberg University until his retirement.

Rustow's close friend and colleague Wilhelm Ropke spent a shorter period (1933–37) in Turkey. He left Istanbul University for the Institut Universitaire des Hautes Études Internationales in Geneva, where he taught until his death in 1966. Both men eventually became influential in the post–World War II recovery of Germany.

The sociologist Gerhard Kessler, an immediate target of the Nazis because of his activities opposing National Socialism, came to Istanbul University in 1933. He trained many Turkish students in labor economics and founded, with his students, the first labor union in Turkey. Extremely popular, like Ernst Reuter, he spoke the language well and traveled extensively throughout Turkey. In his classes he referred to Turkey as "our country."[35] Kessler returned to Germany in 1951 and taught at Göttingen.

In the field of law, both Andreas Schwartz and Ernst Hirsh trained numerous legal scholars and made significant contributions in the adoption of new laws in Turkey. Schwartz had a long teaching career at Istanbul University, from 1934 until his death in 1953. Hirsch, an expert in international trade law and legal philosophy, taught between 1933 and 1952 at both Istanbul and Ankara universities. His autobiography, like Neumark's book, is a rich source of information about this period.[36] Hirsch returned to Germany and served for two terms as rector of the Free University (Freie Universität) in Berlin.

AMONG THE initiatives undertaken in a search for a national identity were studies relevant to the origins of the Turkic peoples. The Turkish History Commission and the Turkish Language Commission (Türk Tarih Kurumu and Türk Dil Kurumu), founded in 1931 and 1932, respectively, as official branches of the government, helped formulate policies for developing programs in these areas. A new Turkish language (*yeni Türkce*) which substituted words with Turkish roots for Arabic and Persian terms evolved under the oversight of the Language Commission. A number of refugee professors, including Fritz Arndt in chemistry, Wolfgang Gleissberg in astronomy, Ernst Hirsh in law, and Fritz Neumark in economics, participated in the language reforms and advised the Language Commission on the adaptation of terms specific to their fields.

Refugee scholars of the humanities employed in areas relevant to Turkic studies were the Assyrologist Benno Landsberger, the Hittitologist Hans Guterbock, the Sinologist Wolfram Eberhard, the Indologist Walter Ruben, and the Orientalist Helmut Ritter (the brother of the historian Gerhard Ritter). Clemens Bosch, in ancient studies and archaeology, took a Turkish name, Emin, when he became a citizen in 1939.

Programs in the area of Romance languages and literature were initiated by Leo Spitzer, who arrived at Istanbul University in 1933 and taught until 1936, when his responsibilities were taken over by Erich Auerbach, who left Istanbul University for the United States in 1947. Auerbach wrote his best-known work, *Mimesis*, while in Turkey. Spitzer and Auerbach helped bring many refugees in their fields to Turkey and trained numerous students.[37]

In classical languages, Georg Rohde taught between 1935 and 1949 at Ankara University, where he founded the Institute of Classical Philology and established its library. Rohde also founded a program for the translation of major works of European literature into Turkish. In philosophy, Ernst von Aster taught at Istanbul University between 1933 and his death in 1948. Hans Reichenbach came to Istanbul University in 1933. In addition to teaching philosophy, Reichenbach trained the first skiing team in Turkey. He left for UCLA in 1938.

MANY OF the refugee scholars were prominent in architecture and the arts. Architects including Martin Wagner, Bruno Taut, Gustav Oelsner, and Clemens Holzmeister trained students and designed buildings in the new republic. The Austrian Holzmeister directed the architecture division of Istanbul Technical University between 1938 and 1954, and designed the parliament building in Ankara. Oelsner left Germany in 1933 for the United States, and from there, in 1940, came to Istanbul Technical University, where he taught architecture and city planning. He participated in the republic's urban planning programs and eventually received an honorary degree from Istanbul Technical University. Oelsner returned to Hamburg in 1950.

Bruno Taut, a founder of the Bauhaus with Walter Gropius and others, came to Turkey in 1936 with the help of Martin Wagner, who was teaching at the Fine Arts Academy in Istanbul.[38] His buildings (mostly schools) designed for the Turkish republic during 1934–38 were simple, modern, and functional. Taut's designs, fitting the philosophy of the new republic, did not incorporate elements of traditional Turkish architecture or Islamic features. Nor did they reflect Taut's Bauhaus style. Taut founded the first school of architecture in Turkey, the Architecture Division at Istanbul Technical University (Istanbul Teknik Üniversitesi Mimari Bölümü). He was exceptionally prolific during his four years in Turkey; his numerous designs included plans for a modern Chemistry Institute at Istanbul University. Taut designed Atatürk's catafalque in Ankara only months before his own death, which occurred suddenly and unexpectedly at the end of 1938.

Among the well-known refugee artists who trained Turkish students at the Fine Arts Academy in Istanbul were the German sculptor Rudolf Belling, who also taught at Istanbul Technical University, and the French painter Léopold Lévi.

Cultural reforms in music addressed all areas, including education, performance, and scholarship. Refugee musicians trained hundreds of young Turkish musicians and performed for Turkish audiences. Turkey enjoys a rich musical heritage, perhaps one of the richest in the non-Western world. Turkish music is remarkably diverse, and its influences on neighboring cultures are well recognized. In the early years of the republic, Atatürk addressed the weaknesses in the area of music, which he took very seriously. The issues were not necessarily those of Eastern versus Western music, or monophonic versus polyphonic; rather, the problem was the absence of modern methodologies in the musical practices of the nation. For instance, there was no documentation in the area of folk music; its survival relied solely on aural memory.

On the suggestion of Wilhelm Furtwängler, Paul Hindemith was invited to help found the new State Conservatory in Ankara. Bringing many refugee musicians to Turkey, Hindemith played a major role in the creation of this institution during 1935–37. Carl Ebert, the former director of the Berlin City Opera who came to Turkey in 1939, was responsible for the development of Turkish opera. He taught at Ankara State Conservatory until 1947 and helped bring additional refugee musicians to Turkey. For Ebert, Turkey became a "second mother country."[39] He eventually left for Glyndebourne in England, and from there to San Francisco. Other famous refugee musicians in Turkey included Lico Amar (who performed widely with Hindemith and others in Europe in the Amar String Quarter); Ernst Praetorius, and Eduard Zuckmeyer (the brother of the writer Carl Zuckmeyer). With his Turkish colleague Adnan Saygun, Béla Bartók traveled in Turkey, documenting folk melodies and researching the similarities between Turkish and Balkan music.

During these years, the young Turkish pianist İdil Biret, later an internationally famous performer, was recognized for her exceptional talent and sent to France to pursue her musical education at government expense. As Fritz Neumark, who had heard young İdil play, later commented, in supporting the young pianist, the government demonstrated its serious commitment to reforms in music.[40]

MANY WELL-KNOWN refugee physicians directed medical institutes, taught, and treated patients at teaching hospitals and government clinics. In spite of the difficulties they faced, the physicians made significant contributions in all areas of medicine and public health. They helped eradicate diseases, established medical programs, and trained future Turkish doctors. In addition to Phillip Schwartz in pathology and Rudolph Nissen in surgery, who both had participated in establishing the various medical programs in Turkey during the summer of 1933, the physicians included Hugo Braun in microbiology, Friedrich Dessauer in radiology, Albert and Erna Eckstein in pediatrics, Joseph Igersheimer in opthalmology, Alfred Kantorowitz in dental surgery (he also organized the skiing center at Uludağ, near Bursa), Wilhelm Liepmann in gynecology and women's health, Werner Liepshitz in pharmacology, Eduard Melchior in surgery, and many others. In his memoirs, Rudolph Nissen (for whom many Turkish babies were named "Nissen") described his experiences and the challenges facing the refugee physicians.[41] Nissen left Turkey in 1939 for the United States, and from there he eventually went to Switzerland.

Among refugees prominent in the sciences were Fritz Arndt in chemistry, Erwin Freudlich and Wolfgang Gleisberg in astronomy, Alfred Heilbronn in botany, Curt Kosswig in zoology, Richard von Mises (the brother of the economist Ludwig von Mises) in mathematics, Wilhelm Salomon-Calvi in geology, and many others. Of these, Arndt, Kosswig, and von Mises eventually received honorary degrees from Istanbul University.

For the author, a chemist whose native country is Turkey, Fritz Arndt holds a special place. He is remembered with great affection as the "leader of modern chemistry in Turkey."[42] Arndt knew Turkey well, for he had founded, during the Ottoman regime in 1915, the country's first chemistry department at the Dar-ül-Fünun. In 1919, at the end of World War I, Arndt, as a German national, was forced to leave Turkey. He returned to Breslau, where he pursued a successful career in teaching and research, contributing significantly to the field of synthetic methodology and to the development of the emerging discipline of physical organic chemistry. Arndt played a major role in the evolution of resonance theory, and was among the first, if not the first, to propose the concept of a "resonance hybrid," so fundamental to our current understanding of the phenomenon of resonance, or electron delocalization.

Arndt's academic career in Breslau was interrupted in 1933, when the Nazis removed him from his position. On the invitation of Sir Robert Robinson, he went to England.[43] Arndt was also invited by the Turkish government to come back to Istanbul University to head the department he had founded some two decades earlier. He returned to Turkey in 1934. Fritz Arndt's second sojourn in Turkey was as productive as the first. For the next twenty years, he helped train a new generation of Turkish chemists. His Turkish students were among the first in the world to learn about resonance from the expert himself. Arndt was a gifted linguist, and taught and wrote in Turkish, striving constantly for clarity of expression. His Turkish textbooks, written between 1934 and 1954, reflect his expertise, his gifts as a teacher, and his wit and warm personality.[44] In one of these texts (which is co-authored by his colleague and former student Lütfi Ergener) Arndt includes the following biographical footnote on Ernest Rutherford:

> Lord Rutherford (1871–1937, English). He was born in Nelson, New Zealand, and became professor at Montreal, Canada, in 1898. He came to Manchester in 1907, and shortly afterward moved to Cambridge University. His great contributions are evident in the contents of our text. His laboratory in Cambridge was a shrine to modern nuclear physics, where the best-known atomic physicists of our time were trained. Lord Rutherford founded, during the reign of the darkest dictatorship in Europe, a worldwide committee to protect the freedom of science and of ideas.[45]

The last sentence is quite atypical for a chemistry text. The statement regarding Rutherford's leadership in the Society for the Protection of Science and Learning, which was instrumental in Arndt's going to England in 1933, reflects Arndt's appreciation of Ernest Rutherford as a humanitarian as well as a great chemist.

The forewords to Arndt's textbooks are valuable resources for gaining insights into the history of the times. In them Arndt frequently referred to the reforms being made in the Turkish language. Over the centuries, the court language of the Ottomans had incorporated many Arabic and Persian terms, and this official language was not easily accessible to the majority of Turks, especially to those who were not educated. The language reforms addressed these issues. In an effort to improve communication nationwide and with the outside world, words with Turkish roots took the place of Arabic and Persian equivalents. Nonetheless, aspects of these reforms, particularly the constant changes of usage, generated problems for the refugee professors, including Arndt, who were teaching and writing in Turkish, and for their students as well. Arndt believed that the constant changes, which introduced difficulties in communicating with the students, were especially challenging for chemistry students, who had to acquire, in addition, a scientific vocabulary unique to their field. Arndt played an active role in the language reforms in Turkey, and advised the government on the incorporation of scientific terminology. He was one of the few nonnative speakers who served on the government's language commission (Terim Komisyonu), and in this context dealt personally with Atatürk.

When Arndt retired from Istanbul University in 1955, he returned to Hamburg, where he remained professionally active, traveling and lecturing worldwide, until his death in 1969. He received many honors, including an honorary degree from Istanbul University shortly before his death. Arndt's Chemistry Institute has been hailed as a successful example of the university reforms.[46] Many of Arndt's Turkish students and assistants followed his model, became successful teachers themselves, and trained many of the new generation of Turkish chemists.[47]

THE LENGTH of stay of the refugee intellectuals varied. Until 1950, those who left went mostly to the United States. Those leaving between 1950 and 1956 tended to return to Germany or Austria. By 1981, only three refugee professors remained in Turkey.

"The folly of tyrants"[48] had given the Turkish government the opportunity to engage hundreds of outstanding scholars whose contributions influenced the nation profoundly. Their main mission had been to train the younger generation of teachers and scholars, and this goal, for the most part, was accomplished. Some years later, Phillip Schwartz stated:

> The hopes that were bound up with the foundation of the new Universities have not been fulfilled in every aspect. Nevertheless, all of us foreign and Turkish professors, who collaborated in so many new cultural Institutes of the Republic, must be content. We have been able to remain loyal to the spirit which is the foundation of modern civilization and humane feeling, and to impart that spirit, even in these dark days of history, to thousands of gifted young persons.

Happy are we who could carry on our work uncompromisingly, and happy
are the people whose leaders opened the doors to productive men compelled to
leave their former place of work for grotesque reasons.[49]

The vacancies left by their departures were eventually filled by Turkish
faculty, often their former assistants or students. In addition, the legacy of the
refugee professors encompasses the professional journals they established, libraries they helped build, and a large body of collaborative work with Turkish
colleagues and assistants, including work resulting from projects specific to
Turkey in a variety of fields.

In spite of difficulties, the refugees worked hard in Turkey and, to paraphrase Atatürk, accomplished much in a short time. They won the respect and
affection of the Turks, forming long-lasting professional associations and special friendships. During their exile, these professors taught in a country where
teachers are revered, and perhaps this was the key to their success.

Notes

I am indebted to Peter Rose for organizing the "Anatomy of Exile" project, and for his
friendship, encouragement, and efforts in putting this volume together. I am grateful
to the Smith College Kahn Institute and Marjorie Senechal for giving me the opportunity to pursue this research, which has been most enriching. My special thanks go to
fellow members of "The Anatomy of Exile," and in particular to Gertraud Gutzmann,
Ingrid Sommerkorn, Karen Koehler, Krishna Winston, and Denitza Jilkova. I thank
Rene Heavlow for her unending support, and the Smith College Library staff for all
their help. My sister Esin Atıl provided me with valuable contacts, and I thank her, and
all my friends and colleagues in Turkey and in the United States who helped with
various aspects of the research. I am particularly grateful to the late Heinz Arndt, and I
thank Mary Flesher, Cemal Kafadar, Filiz Ali, Tuvana Alton, Oya Bain, and my former
student Eva Doll. My deepest thanks go to my husband, John, for his insightful suggestions, and for being there always with his ceaseless patience.

1. The refugee intellectuals who arrived in Turkey in 1933 were to witness additional
changes and reforms in the young republic the next year, including the adoption of
Sunday, instead of Friday, as the official weekly holiday, the granting of equal political
rights to women, and the adoption of surnames. Prior to 1934, Turks did not have
surnames; Mustafa Kemal chose the surname Atatürk.

2. For an excellent and detailed account of Atatürk's university reforms, see Horst
Widmann, *Atatürk Üniversite Reformu: Almanca konuşan ülkelerden 1933 yılından sonra Tür-
kiyeye gelen öğretim üyeleri—Hayat Hikayeleri—Çalışmaları—Etkileri*, trans. Aykut Kazanci-
gil and Serpil Bozkurt (Istanbul: Istanbul Üniversitesi Cerreahpaşa Tıp Fakültesi Atatürk'un Yüzüncü Doğum Yılını Kutlama Yayınları, 1981); Turkish translation of Horst
Widmann, *Exil und Bildungshilfe: Die deutschsprachige akademische Emigration in die Turkei
nach 1933* (Bern: Herbert Lang, 1973). Hereafter cited as Widmann.

3. Quoted in Saul Friedlander, *Nazi Germany and the Jews,* vol. 1, *The Years of Persecution, 1933–1939* (New York: HarperCollins, 1997), 49.

4. Ibid., 345.

5. Norman Bentwich, *The Rescue and Achievement of Refugee Scholars: The Story of Displaced Scholars and Scientists, 1933–1952* (The Hague: Martinus Nijhoff, 1953), 4.

6. Stephen Duggan and Betty Drury, *The Rescue of Science and Learning: The Story of the Emergency Committee in Aid of Displaced Foreign Scholars* (New York: Macmillan, 1948), 173–77. Duggan and Drury served on the U.S. Emergency Committee from the time of the formation of this rescue organization in 1933. In 1944, Drury joined the Committee for the Study of Recent Immigration from Europe, and her responsibilities at the Emergency Committee were taken over by Francis Frenton Park, who was dean at Smith College between 1924 and 1928 (ibid., 179).

7. Ludwig von Mises's brother, the mathematician Richard von Mises, was released from his post in Berlin in 1933. He went to Turkey to head the Mathematics Institute at Istanbul University between 1933 and 1939; from there he went to Harvard University.

8. William Henry Beveridge, *A Defence of Free Learning* (London: Oxford University Press, 1959), 1.

9. Ernest Rutherford (1871–1937) was awarded the Nobel Prize in chemistry in 1908 for his pioneering contributions to atomic physics and radioactivity. His work in nuclear chemistry was very influential and founded the basis of our current understanding of atomic structure.

10. Beveridge, *Defence of Free Learning,* 1–5.

11. Ibid., 127.

12. Quoted in Widmann, 160.

13. For a facsimile of the postcard, see ibid., 224.

14. These groups remained separate until the Notgemeinschaft moved to England in 1939.

15. The Notgemeinschaft's list of displaced scholars became very useful for other rescue organizations.

16. Widmann, 44.

17. The German refugee professors did in fact enjoy the full support and protection of the Turkish government during their stay in Turkey. This was not the case, for instance, in England, where some were interned and deported as enemy aliens. See Beveridge, *Defence of Free Learning,* 69.

18. Duggan and Drury, *Rescue of Science and Learning,* 25.

19. All three were very influential in their fields. James Franck received the Nobel Prize in physics in 1925. He came to the United States after the Nazis assumed power, and held professorships at Johns Hopkins and the University of Chicago. The laboratory that he headed in Chicago during World War II became central to the Manhattan Project. A great humanitarian, while in Germany, Franck spoke openly against the racial policies of the Nazi regime, and later, in the United States, voiced his objection to the use of the atomic bomb. Max Born collaborated with Franck and others who became well known the area of quantum physics, including Werner Heisenberg, Enrico Fermi, and J. Robert Oppenheimer. When he was forced to emigrate in 1933, Born went

to Cambridge, where he taught for three years. He worked with Sir C. V. Raman in India during 1935–36, and from there went to Edinburgh, where he remained until his retirement. He was awarded the Nobel Prize in physics in 1954. Richard Courant was offered a position at Istanbul University in 1933, but went instead to New York University. There he founded and headed the Institute of Mathematical Sciences, based on the Göttingen model. In honor of its founder, the institute in 1964 was renamed the Courant Institute of Mathematics.

20. According to Widmann (39, 54), the restructuring of the university resulted in the following numbers: at the Dar-ül-Fünun, which was closed on July 31, 1933, the number of faculty and assistants combined was 240 (88 ordinarius professors and professors, 44 docents, 108 assistants). Of these 240 individuals, 157 were let go; this number included 71 ordinarius professors and professors. In contrast, in its first year (1933–34) the total number of faculty and assistants at Istanbul Universty was 323 (65 ordinarius professors, of whom 38 were foreign and 27 Turkish; 22 professors, of whom 4 were foreign and 18 Turkish; 93 docents, who were all Turkish; and 142 assistants, of whom 43 were foreign and 99 Turkish). In sum, in 1933–34, of the 180 faculty, 42 were foreign (23 percent), and of the 142 assistants, 43 were foreign (30 percent).

21. Schwartz's position at the Notgemeinschaft was taken over by Gehaimrat Demuth, formerly director of the Political Academy in Berlin.

22. Quoted in Beveridge, *Defence of Free Learning,* 129.

23. Ernst E. Hirsch, *Hatıralarım: Kayzer Dönemi—Weimar Cumhuriyeti—Atatürk Ülkesi,* trans. Fatma Suphi et al. (Ankara: Banka ve Ticaret Hukuku Araştırma Enstitüsü Yayını, 1985), 240; Turkish translation of Ernst E. Hirsch, *Aus des Keisers Zeiten durch Weimar Republik in das land Ataturks: Eine unzeitgemasse Autobiographie* (Munich: Schweitzer Verlag, 1982). Translation from the Turkish by the author. Hereafter cited as Hirsch.

24. Fritz Neumark, *Boğaziçine Sığınanlar: Türkiye'ye İltica Eden Alman İlim Siyaset ve Sanat Adamları, 1933–1953,* trans. Şefik Alp Bahadır (Istanbul: Istanbul Üniversitesi İktisat Fakültesi Maliye Enstitüsü Yayını 1982), 42–43, Turkish translation of Fritz Neumark, *Zuflucht am Bosporus: Deutsche Gelehrte, Politiker und Kunstler in der Emigration, 1933–53* (Frankfurt am Main: Knecht, 1980). Translation from the Turkish by the author. Hereafter cited as Neumark. One of Atatürk's ideals for the Turkish republic was to maintain a peaceful existence. Toward this goal, he worked to end ancient wars and animosities with Russia and also with Greece. His phrase "yurtta sulh, cihanda sulh" (peace in the nation and peace in the world) became symbolic of his antiwar sentiments and was quoted often.

25. Hirsch, 241.

26. Helge Peukert, "Ein Lehrstuhl am Bosporus: Vor 60 Jahren: Deutsche Wissenschaftler emigrieren ins Land Ataturks," *DAD Letter* 1 (1994): 10–14. A parallel has been suggested between the University of Paris in the Middle Ages, where, reportedly, none of the famous faculty was French. See Bentwitch, *Rescue,* 54.

27. There was a similar increase in enrollment: in 1933–34, the number of students was 3,417; 18 percent of the student body was female. By 1942–43 the number of students had nearly tripled; of the 10,178 students, 50 percent were female. The university contin-

ued to grow at a similar pace in the following years; the number of foreign faculty, however, started declining in the 1950s.

28. Stanford J. Shaw, *The Jews of the Ottoman Empire and Turkish Republic* (New York: New York University Press, 1991), 252.

29. Beveridge, *Defence of Free Learning,* 129.

30. Neumark, 11.

31. Ernst Reuter's son Edzard, who later became president of Mercedes-Benz in Stuttgart, was seven years old when his family came to Turkey. A dedicated proponent of maintaining strong German-Turkish relationships, he stated in an interview in 1991 that the warmheartedness of the Turkish families, and their willingness to take in refugees, had had a lasting influence and shaped both his parents and himself. Peukert, "Ein Lehrstuhl," 14.

32. See Neumark.

33. Widmann, 206.

34. Alexander Rustow, foreword to *Freedom and Domination: A Historical Critique of Civilization,* trans. Salvator Attanasio (Princeton: Princeton University Press, 1980); abbreviated English translation of Alexander Rustow, *Ortsbestimmung der Gegenwart,* 3 vols., ed. Dankwart Rustow (Erlenbach-Zurich: Eugen Rentsch Verlag, 1950, 1952, 1957).

35. Quoted in Widmann, 206.

36. See Hirsch.

37. The Turkish Shakeaspeare scholar Mina Urgan, who attended Istanbul University between 1935 and 1939, was a student of both Spitzer and Auerbach. Urgan later held a chair in Romance languages at Istanbul University, where she taught until her retirement. In her memoirs, *Bir Dinozorun Anıları* (Istanbul: Yapı Kredi Kültür Sanat Yayıncılık Ticaret ve Sanayi A.Ş., 1998), 174–81, she describes the influence of the refugee professors on her career and refers to her student years at Istanbul University as "a glorious period."

38. Taut had previously visited Turkey in 1914 to participate in a competition for the design of a Turkish-German House of Friendship. The German architectural tradition had existed in Turkey since the latter part of the nineteenth century. For example, the two railroad stations in Istanbul, which are on opposite sides of the Bosporus, were designed by German architects. On the European side, Sirkeci Station, the last stop in Europe of the Orient Express, combined Islamic elements and contemporary design, symbolizing to the passengers arriving in European Turkey that they were entering an Islamic culture. In contrast, Haydarpaşa Station, on the Asian side, was designed in the neoclassical German style. Passengers continuing their voyage east departed from this station, built in a strictly Western tradition. The designs of the German architects thus bridged East and West both geographically and culturally.

39. Widmann, 210. Many other refugees spoke of Turkey as their "second country," including Fritz Arndt, Ernst Hirsch, Gerhard Kessler, Curt Kosswig, Fritz Neumark, and Ernst Reuter.

40. Neumark, 133–34.

41. Rudolf Nissen, *Helle Blätter, dunkle Blätter: Erinnerungen eines Chirurgen* (Stuttgart: Deutsche Verlags Anstalt, 1969).

42. Yunus Akçamur, "Modern Kimya, Fritz Arndt ve İlk Araştırma," in *Türk Dünyasında Kimya Bilimi ve Eğitim Tarihi*, ed. Ahmet Hulusi Koker (Kayseri: Erciyes Üniversitesi Gevher Nesibe Tıp Tarihi Enstitüsü Yayını, 1988), 53.

43. Sir Robert Robinson was one of the founding members of the Academic Assistance Council in England. He received the Nobel Prize in chemistry in 1947.

44. Lâle Aka Burk, "Fritz Arndt and His Chemistry Books in the Turkish Language," *Bulletin for the History of Chemistry* 28 (2003): 42–53.

45. Fritz Arndt and Lütfi Ergener, *Denel Anorganik Kimya*, 2d ed. (Istanbul: Kutulmuş Basımevi, 1953), 356; translated from Turkish by the author.

46. Widmann, 177.

47. Muvaffak Seyhan was a student of Arndt's at Istanbul University, and later became his colleague. He took over Arndt's chair in 1955 when Arndt retired, and wrote a number of newspaper articles about his mentor and colleague and about the university during the years of the intellectual migration. In one article, "Fen Fakültesinin Altın Çağı," *Cumhuriyet*, March 5, 1972, 2, he referred to this period as "the golden age" of the Science Faculty of Istanbul University.

48. Beveridge, *Defence of Free Learning*, 122.

49. Bentwitch, *Rescue*, 55.

Angels of History Carrying Bricks
Gropius in Exile

KAREN KOEHLER

> Whether it is a person, a stretch of shoreline, or the sound of a lan-
> guage, when something basic to one's identity has been torn away,
> nothing in the world is ever the same again. . . . Exile is less like the
> death of one's beloved than like a betrayal from which it is impossible
> ever to become fully healed because the prospect of a pathway home,
> of a return that is also a mutual pardoning, continues to exist. For the
> exile, hope is itself part of his torment.
>
> MICHAEL ANDRÉ BERNSTEIN, "Exile, Cunning, and Loquaciousness"

THE CRITICAL reaction to the German architect Walter Gropius
has long been polarized: Gropius is either revered for his spatially dynamic
structures or blamed for every bad tract house built since World War II; admired for the individual freedoms inherent in Bauhaus pedagogical programs
or criticized for his dogmatic design formulas; ultimately praised for the
breadth of his twentieth-century visions or mocked for his utopian ideologies.
What are the sources of this dichotomous portrait? It is my contention that
the emigration of Gropius to the United States in 1937, the difficulties of
assimilation, and the political exigencies of his exile have significantly contributed to the dualities of his legacy. Specifically, I believe that evidence of what
sociologist Rubén D. Rumbaut referred to as "exile shock"[1] can be detected in
two projects from 1938: the Bauhaus exhibition at the Museum of Modern Art
in New York and Gropius House in Lincoln, Massachusetts. These projects
demonstrate—both visually and conceptually—the material effects of his exile.
When we consider the work of an exiled writer, we readily accept the difficulties surrounding the problems and frustrations of translation. But what of the
work of an exiled artist or architect? Surely there is also demonstrable evidence
of the effects of visual and spatial translation—visual manifestations of the
effects of exile. The first design projects completed by Gropius in the United
States are indications of how he himself struggled with exactly these issues of
translation. The exhibition was a temporary display at the Museum of Modern
Art (MoMA), which traveled throughout the country, and Gropius House was
built as his own permanent residence; therefore, these two projects can be seen
as metaphors for the dualities of the exile experience. The juxtaposed sensa-

tions of transience and permanence are essential characteristics of any exile's disposition; for Gropius they are the tensions that defined his art in 1937–38.

Gropius is perhaps best known as the director of the Bauhaus, the experimental art school he founded in Weimar Germany in 1919, in the revolutionary aftermath of World War I, a school whose history has by now been well rehearsed: the Bauhaus immediately came under attack from conservative elements in Weimar, and in 1925 the school reopened in Dessau, in buildings designed by Gropius and outfitted by the Bauhaus workshops. After a decade of opposition from nationalist and racist groups, Gropius resigned as director and returned to private practice in 1928. Closed in 1932 by the Nazis, the Bauhaus briefly reopened in an abandoned telephone factory in Berlin, until it was searched and shut down by the Gestapo in 1933.

It had been increasingly difficult for Gropius to find work in Germany in the early 1930s.[2] Modernist architecture was disfavored by Nazi commissioners and eventually outlawed, a condition that caused Gropius to confront the president of the Reich Council for Art in 1934. "How do you think," Gropius wrote, "a German like myself must feel. . . . My homeland . . . shuts me up and people like me while [others] mislead the public opinion. . . . Is it now really true that this strong, new architectural movement of German origin shall be lost for Germany? I cannot accept always being labeled from a merely formalist point of view as originators of cubes with flat roofs; this point of view ignores the comprehensive work in design and sociology which we have been doing for German society as a whole." Gropius then admits, in 1934, to a member of the Reich, that he had a social agenda—and one that he linked with design. He goes on: "You demand the German man. I feel very German—and who can make himself a judge over what is German and what is not . . . I feel . . . that I am outlawed in Germany along with all that I have built in my life."[3]

On September 5, 1934, Hitler spoke out against modern art in his now infamous Nuremburg speech.[4] In October, Gropius and his wife, Ise, left for a conference in Rome, after which they exchanged their return tickets to Berlin for one-way passages to England.[5] Gropius remained in England from 1934 until 1937. He and Ise lived at Lawn Road Flats in Hampstead, a housing project designed by Wells Coates and developed by Jack Pritchard, who had invited Gropius to London. This experimental community was a haven for many painters, architects, and designers then in exile from Nazi Germany. Lawn Road Flats was also part of the larger avant-garde milieu in Hampstead, which included Julian Huxley, George Orwell, Ben Nicholson, Barbara Hepworth, and Henry Moore. Among the émigré artists were John Heartfield, Piet Mondrian, Naum Gabo, Marcel Breuer, and Lázló Moholy-Nagy. During Gropius's stay in England, he worked with the architect Maxwell Fry on a handful of projects, most notably the Cambridge Village College at Impington. He also joined Pritchard's design firm, Isokon, gave numerous lectures to art and academic organizations, and consulted on the design school being developed at Dartington Hall.

During his time in England, Gropius made only a few brief return trips to Germany, each time under increasing threat. In 1936, in a complicated series of events, he was repeatedly intercepted, detained, questioned, and searched. He continued to be cautious about his relationship with German authorities— fearing both for members of his family, his former colleagues, and former Bauhaus students still in Germany, as well as for his funds, which were held at that time by the Nazi authorities. When asked by a London newspaper to write about the arts in Germany, he refused; to do so, he said, would be "risking very unpleasant consequences."[6]

Despite the support of Pritchard, Fry, and others, Gropius's attempts at finding architectural work in England were only partially successful, and when he was invited to join the faculty at Harvard in 1937, he of course accepted.[7] As he was leaving England for the United States, Gropius gave a farewell address. When he first came to England, he said, he had been "in a state of bewilder-ment"; now, again, he was being "plunged into an entirely new world." Yet he hoped that his upcoming appointment at Harvard would be "further proof of the American ability to reconcile . . . the most diverse type of people to create a new form of life of typical American stamp. My stamp is definitely German and to Germany I owe the whole of my education and the possibilities of building up a world of my own. The greater part of my life has been spent there and very often I feel rather homesick. But in the different stages of my life I have always found it impossible to tackle new problems with my head turned back."[8] Gropius departed for the United States in March 1937 (fig. 1). I believe that despite his claims to the contrary, he continued to look backward and forward, and that the disjuncture of his perceptions is revealed in the work he produced in the years immediately after he came to the United States in 1937.

Gropius House and the Ornament of Exile

When Gropius first came to Massachusetts, he moved into a hotel in Cam-bridge. He did not immediately start teaching, but rather spent time arranging for his office materials to be sent from Berlin, as well as the contents of his homes in Germany and in England. He did this cautiously and continued to avoid any kind of a confrontation with the authorities.[9] His academic duties began officially in the fall of 1937.[10]

In the summer of 1937, Gropius went on a driving tour of the New England countryside looking for a place to live; he particularly like the "old white painted colonial homes, unpretentious and genuine in plan and appearance."[11] Soon after renting an old colonial house in Lincoln, he was given some land by Mrs. James Storrow, a local philanthropist, in order to build a house for himself. Thus, his first architectural commission in the United States was the design and construction of his own residence, positioned on the crest of a hill in a former apple orchard in Lincoln—a somewhat rural community just west of Cambridge and Boston, and a short walk to Walden

Fig. 1. Photograph (detail) of Gropius leaving England, March 1937. From Reginald Isaacs, *Walter Gropius* (Boston: Bullfinch, 1991).

Pond (fig. 2). Winfred Nerdinger tells us that Gropius and his partner Marcel Breuer took great care in planning the house, with the expectation that it would be "the calling card of the new Harvard professor's view of architecture."[12] Nerdinger sees Gropius's residence as probably his best and most important building in America. I agree with these findings, yet I also see Gropius House as a very curious structure, full of unusual forms and materials and peculiar juxtapositions, and because of this a work that indicates the extent to which we need to reconsider Gropius's modernism—particularly the formalistic, allegedly international modernism so often associated with his name and with the Bauhaus.[13] Rather than following a dogmatic, abstract equation, Gropius used colonial references and industrial materials as a form of ornamentation in his house in Lincoln—an attempt to integrate his former work into its new territory.

It may seem incongruous to use the term ornamentation in relation to Gropius and modernist architecture. Yet the definition of ornament is a difficult one, and at different moments in history it has designated much more than mere surface decoration. Ornament is by all accounts a slippery term, tied to the differences between applied arts and high arts, existing in the shifting spaces between simple functionality and aesthetic pleasure, migrating between the frivolous expressions of decadent superficiality and the manifestations of society's moral condition. Put simply, if there a discrete meaning for ornament, it is in all cases a historically specific definition.

Certainly what ornament meant to Gropius in 1937–38 and what it means to us today is not likely to be the same thing, and so I want to consider the writings of two of his contemporaries, Ernst Bloch and Siegfried Kracauer, who described in their writings many of the contradictions present in the concept of modernist ornament. Like Gropius, both Bloch and Kracauer were German intellectuals who wrote during the Weimar Republic and later lived in exile in the United States.[14] If, as these writers contend, ornament is a kind of morphological *Kunstwollen*, a historically determined Ur-expression, then this is indeed the only way to proceed.

The German utopian philosopher Ernst Bloch wrote "The Creation of Ornament" in 1918—a characteristically enigmatic and extremely difficult essay.[15] According to Bloch, the machine has forced us to live in an era of "technological coldness," a time in which the producer and his machine have "murdered the imagination," producing stuff that is lifeless and inhuman. To Bloch, that was not surprising. "Where should the vital, beautifully formed utensil come from," he asked, "when nobody knows how to live permanently anymore?" He lamented the alienation of life and labor caused by the machine, yet he also realized that we cannot go back to the days of the handcrafted object. After

Fig. 2. Gropius House, Lincoln, Mass., 1937–38. Photo courtesy Society for the Preservation of New England Antiquities, Boston.

the "rupture of a vital productive tradition," after the "burst of power with which the machine commenced action," he doubted whether we would ever need individually designed, luxurious objects again. And, although he referred to the work of painters such as Wassily Kandinsky and Paul Klee as manifestations of the current spirit, expressionist paintings could not save the modern structure or object, according to Bloch, because they were not able to function as ornament—they could only be surface coloration—and there was simply too much distance between the passion of the painting styles and the essential sobriety of the machine-made form. The machine, he explained, can take over the drudgery of life, and so he imagined the emergence of a new kind of ornament: overexuberant, expressive, and distinct, yet also a kind of enigmatic explosion or discharge. Both form and formless, this ornamentation would be a kind of spontaneous expression, parallel to but separate from technology.

Bloch explained this modernist ornament by considering the history of the human need for ornament to express the *Kunstwollen*, or will-to-form: the artistic spirit of different epochs. For Bloch, Wilhelmine ornament was a swindle, a kind of kitsch that ran morally counter to the honesty represented by modernist design. Yet the abstract bareness of the architectural cube created a sense of alienation. One needed ornamentation in order to express the imaginative properties of the human spirit; the question was how to do it. Somehow ornament had to grow again out of the inner workings of humankind, which is itself also more searching, "more homeless," he wrote, "assuming more of a form like a current."

For the critical theorist Siegfried Kracauer, ornament was also something that arose from the current of humanity. Yet for Kracauer, ornament was not the deepest expression of the emotionally driven inner workings of the individual spirit; on the contrary. In his 1927 essay "Mass Ornament," Kracauer tells us that historical processes can be determined most strikingly from an analysis of inconspicuous surface-level expressions, which, he believed, "provide unpremeditated access to the fundamental substance of the state of things."[16] In fact, for Kracauer, ornament was something far grander than mere decoration. Using his famous example of the "Tiller Girls," he explained that ornament was a geometric-conceptual model of human actions and gestures within the socioeconomic systems of capitalist production. The way we move collectively—the choreography of our actions as a society—determines the ornament of our epoch. Kracauer questioned the international popularity of the Tiller Girls, who performed their dancing, gymnastic spectacles, in which they moved together in simultaneous fashion, before packed arenas. "They condense into figures in the revues," he wrote, creating performances of "geometric precision." For Kracauer, the Tiller Girls were "no longer individual girls, but indissoluble girl clusters." Similarly, the movement of traffic on the urban street or the repetitive patterns of the hands of factory workers were an expression, for Kracauer, of a type of "mass ornament"—that is, an ornamental expression of the substance of the modern era.

Yet this is not necessarily a bad thing. Kracauer stressed that "the ornament is an end in itself"—like capitalism. Because of mass production, we no longer move independently, and this he tied, like Bloch, in Marxist terms to the alienation of labor: like the mass ornament, "the capitalist production process is an end in itself." The mass ornament of the Tiller Girls, then, was the aesthetic reflex of the severe rationality of the current economic system. Yet Kracauer made it clear that the "aesthetic pleasure gained from ornamental mass movements is legitimate." We may like the Tiller Girls because we are all cogs in the factory wheel—but that doesn't mean we like them any less, or that our connection to them is insignificant.

These different theoretical models delineate a modern view of ornamentation that is more complex and more structurally connected to the conditions of modernity than either the apologists for modern architecture or its postmodern critics admit. Ornamentation was seen as both an emotional and a psychological (that is, individualistic) expression. It was also seen as the product of a modernist Zeitgeist that was intuitively connected to contemporary social, political, and economic conditions. What is important, then, for the study of Gropius House is the extent to which ornamentation was believed to be tied to the psyche, spiritually as well as socially; these elements are precisely why I see Gropius House as an illustration of the exile experience.

There is a strange eclecticism in Gropius House that is contrary to the harmonious abstraction of Gropius's domestic commissions in Germany. Built the year after he arrived as an exile from Nazi Germany, in an effort to incorporate the architect's new residence into its geographic and historical context, the house included many direct references to local New England vernacular architecture, as in the use of white painted wood, a fieldstone foundation, brick chimney, retaining walls, and trellises. Yet in so many cases the expectations for the use of these colonial details are completely subverted. For instance, the horizontal clapboards—an important feature of colonial New England buildings—are turned vertically and, furthermore, moved to the interior of the house (fig. 3). The central staircase, which you see as you walk into the entryway, is turned away from the entrance, clearly demarcating the public space of the downstairs rooms from the private space of the second floor; yet these elements run counter to the spirit of the entryway common to traditional New England homes. And, most important, these disjointed colonial details are combined in a collage-like fashion with a European modernist vocabulary—asymmetrical plan, flat roof, ribbon windows, plate glass—and with a sense of abstract spatial relationships inside and out. Whenever possible, Gropius used industrial materials and fixtures—bought in standardized sizes from catalogues and supply houses—a practice at that time reserved for factory and commercial construction. He used glass brick both to separate his office from and join it to the living room, thereby invoking the American factory complexes which he had admired from the earliest days of his architectural career, and which had greatly influenced his work in Germany.[17]

This peculiar yoking together of historical, modernist, and industrial forms, and the strange oblique angles often used to combine them, created an unusual sensation of disjunction. In contrast to Gropius's modernist interpretation of the fully designed *Gesamtkunstwerk*, where each element of a dwelling was similar in materials and form,[18] at Gropius House the effect is one of confusion and dislocation: the "mass ornament" of exile. The language of distraction and alienation is revealed in the montaged network of ornamental

Fig. 3. Gropius House, entryway. Photo courtesy Society for the Preservation of New England Antiquities, Boston.

details that he employed—fragmented, bizarre references to both the historical and factory architecture of his newly adopted home—here applied to a structural type that he had, only three years earlier, identified as "wholly German" in his confrontations with Nazi authorities. Indeed, I believe that the peculiar grafting together of elements in Gropius House indicates the extent to which, for Gropius in 1938, he was still the German—or at least partially so—grappling with the psychological difficulties of emigration. In 1936 Gropius wrote to a colleague about the profound sadness he had experienced while closing his Berlin office and "sorting out my life from the files and drawings."[19] He also wrote to Herbert Bayer, still in Germany, that "we are like children here" and must make an encampment "to avoid getting homesick."[20] Certainly coming to Harvard represented financial security and a sense of safety that many intellectuals still in Germany, in hiding, in concentration camps, or in exile throughout the world did not have. But we must also keep in mind the real tensions that Gropius experienced in the late 1930s and 1940s in the United States. For a German in the United States, one's position was uncomfortable and difficult. There is some extant evidence that Gropius's desire for a sense of safety and privacy in his house played a role in its design—concerns seemingly justified by FBI files during World War II detailing unsubstantiated accusations that Gropius was a German spy who stored weapons in the basement of his "supermodern" house.[21]

What did it mean that he chose to build a permanent home when so many exiles insisted on maintaining a sense of impermanence? According to the exiled writer Henry Pachter, many émigrés insisted on living only in temporary housing—outfitted with nothing but lawn furniture—lest they give they impression that they might not be returning to their homelands.[22] By contrast, Gropius ultimately settled into Lincoln; yet he also continued to look backward and forward.

In 1936 Gropius's first treatise in English, *The New Architecture and the Bauhaus,* was published in England and in the United States. Using his buildings in Germany from 1911 to 1932 as examples, he wrote, "The morphology of dead styles has been destroyed, and we are returning to honesty of thought and feeling." What he called the New Architecture was "the inevitable logical product of the intellectual, social and technical conditions of our age." Only true modern architecture, not mere formalist imitation, can meet our material and psychological requirements and become the "concrete expression of the life of our epoch in clear and crisply simplified forms." Echoing, then, both Bloch and Kracauer, Gropius stated that machine production and rationalization had acted as a purifying agent liberating architecture from a welter of historical ornamentation. Yet that was only the material side. Equally important, he stressed, was the "aesthetic satisfaction of the human soul."[23] Until there is an art form that grows instinctively from the machine, according to Bloch and to Gropius, there will never be a true psychosocial expression of ornament. If, however one considers ornament as an expression of the inner psyche of the individual *and* as an expression of a collective social consciousness, it can be argued that this is precisely what Gropius House reveals: the desire of an exiled architect to unite references to both his homeland and his new home, combined in a way that reflected the fragmentation and disassociation of his uprooted existence at a time of great social and political upheaval.

For example, if we return to the shift in orientation of Gropius's New England clapboards, it is clear that the decision to turn them vertically was a complicated one. Here Gropius took an element that was one of the most recognizable signatures of New England vernacular architecture and entirely disorients our expectations in favor of a dynamic design component.[24] The psychological effect of this design choice was not unconscious or accidental. Gropius would, in fact, go on to research the perceptual effects of these kinds of design decisions throughout the 1940s and 1950s, as indicated by the comments and illustrations in an essay on the language of communication published in 1947 in which he discussed the different effects of horizontal and vertical stripes in architecture and in fashion. According to Gropius, the woman illustrated in the bathing suit with horizontal stripes looks thinner.[25]

In terms of Gropius House, the most important essay by Gropius after his emigration—and about his emigration—was published in January 1938. "Ornament and Modern Architecture" was likely written while the house was being designed. Rather than describe his past projects in Germany, in this case Gropius ventured to discuss the future. He began with the question, "Why do modern architects use so little ornamentation?" History, he wrote, has proven that "genuine ornamentation originates only during harmonious periods of the human race, when man, following his natural impulse to play and to adorn his environments seeks to shape the inward intentions of an established society rather than mere personal feelings. It shows that true ornament is the result of the unconscious work of a whole period of civilization, not of individuals." The nomad had reason for using oriental rugs which we cannot understand. Today's human beings have become lost in the increasing chaos of mechanization, and the resulting mess of historical ornamentation was an attempt at sedating the troubled soul. Modern architecture, however, will rid of us these "hopeless narcotics" and find a "true expression which may mirror our very life of the machine age." We desperately need quiet and repose from our "distracted nerves" and the "continuously changing scene of life." Yet the new ornament that will help us adjust to our changing lives does not exist because we have not yet reached the new social structure, the new conception of existence. He stressed the new industrial textures available to the architect, listing many of the materials used in Gropius House—"ribbed, corrugated . . . mottled, derived from manufacturing process"—and mentions the innumerable wealth of combinations to which they lend themselves. One day, he predicted, these new materials may surpass the ornamental glamour of old styles. "Our confused minds," he wrote "will become proud and confident at last in the knowledge that we have at our disposal such brilliant new means for shaping the image of our modern life." Writing as if he were describing the nomadic conditions of his exile, searching for a way to adjust to "the continuously changing scene of life," Gropius was surely describing his own state of mind: looking forward with his head turned back. As he himself concluded in this 1938 article: "Forward to tradition! The ornament is dead! Long live the ornament!"[26]

Equally disjunctive are Gropius's comments at the Museum of Modern Art in January 1939 in a lecture accompanying the Bauhaus exhibition there. He opened with a series of poetic metaphors about the human capacity to perceive time and space. He then defined the Bauhaus educational program as "an objective method of approach appropriate for any country." Then, in contradiction, he discussed the effects of different historical and geographic contexts on artistic production. In the end, Gropius paraphrased a conversation he "once had with Stravinsky, the famous composer, about people using modern forms and inventions without properly understanding their progressive spirit. He said they were like people sitting in an automobile and lashing with a whip." Gropius wanted his audience to "reverse this parable," to consider the infidelity of those today who "disguise our new achievements behind masks of bygone eras." The irony is that Gropius concluded his lecture with a slide show of his own house, emphasizing the combination of modernist and colonial materials, "in order to give a personal example of transplanting to American soil some of the ideas which I have explained."[27]

Objects in Exile: The Museum of Modern Art, 1938

When Gropius came to the United States, he acquired financial security, prestige, and influence. Still, his position as a German exile in the late 1930s was not without its complications and difficulties—personally, professionally, and politically. One must consider the historical conditions not only in Germany but also in the United States to begin to reconstruct Gropius's transplanted position.

In 1938 the House Un-American Activities Committee (HUAC) began to monitor the movements of communists, socialists, and foreigners in the United States, while right-wing extremists like Father Coughlin and groups such as the German-American Bund preached a message of anti-Semitic hatred. In 1938 an extension of the New Deal brought an end to a decade of labor unrest in the United States (supported in part by American communists), while wealthy industrialists continued to brand Roosevelt's initiatives as "Bolshevist." Also in 1938, Germany invaded the Rhineland and annexed Austria. In *Kristallnacht*, Nazi storm troopers destroyed synagogues, robbed Jewish homes, and began the deportation of thousands to concentration camps. In that same year, the Museum of Modern Art in New York (MoMA) mounted "The Bauhaus, 1919-1928," an exhibition of the work of modern German artists from the Bauhaus, many of whom had been declared degenerate and condemned as Marxist, communist, Jewish, and Bolshevist by Hitler in the "Entartete Kunst" (Degenerate Art) exhibition in Munich the previous year. Gropius's design for his house in Massachusetts must be seen in the context of his response to these political events. His other major project of 1937-38 was designing and curating the Bauhaus exhibition, and this project is equally an illustration of the effects of the exile experience on Gropius's professional work. The MoMA exhibition must be interpreted in the context of international political events—as both the organizers and the critics knew at the time.

The Bauhaus exhibition was designed and organized at the museum's suggestion by Walter Gropius under the directorship of Alfred Barr, with contributions by many other Bauhaus teachers, notably Herbert Bayer, with assistance from Josef Albers and Alexander Dorner. The exhibition ran from December 7, 1938, until January 30, 1939 (fig. 4). The show, including some seven hundred objects, had originally been scheduled to open the previous spring but was postponed because of the considerable difficulties involved in locating the Bauhaus materials in Germany and the clear political risks for the former Bauhaus members still in Germany, where the Nazi purging of museums, which had started in 1937, was legalized ex post facto in 1938.[28] There were problems not only with getting objects out of Germany but also with getting them through customs once they reached the United States. The scale model of Gropius's Dessau Bauhaus, for example, was held up in customs because of the tariffs on removing artworks from Germany at this time. Furthermore, and even more critically, of course, there was the problem of getting people out of Germany. Alexander Dorner and Herbert Bayer and his wife used an invitation from MoMA to work on the exhibition as a means to get a visa to leave Germany.

The exhibition was, as a result, limited to those objects that were available, and was composed mainly of reproductions, including many large photo-

Fig. 4. "The Bauhaus, 1919–1928"; installation shot. Photo courtesy the Museum of Modern Art, New York, © 2001.

graphs, which were wrapped around posts, hung from the walls at strange angles, and were used to represent original works of art. Furthermore, both the exhibition and the catalogue skewed chronology, favoring work produced after 1923. Many of those who worked on the exhibition intentionally neutralized the social and political history of the Bauhaus and its radical, albeit contradictory, ideological ambitions. Although much contemporary work by Bauhaus artists in the United States was included, there was no mention of the communist emphasis of Hannes Meyer, director of the Bauhaus from 1928 to 1930, to give an example of just one of many such distortions. For very good reasons, Walter Gropius and Alfred Barr refused to allow the real history of the Bauhaus to be discussed. (Barr notes in the catalogue preface that a number of the works exhibited at MoMA were shown without the consent of the artists still in Germany, and that it was "considered advisable" to delete their names.) Nowhere, however, are the utopian passions of the school's early years, or the vehemence of the reactionaries' hatred, or the intrigues involved in closing the school fully discussed or, more important, judged. The Bauhaus was in effect being seen through the eyes of its National Socialist detractors, in retreat from its origins.

Furthermore, anti-German propaganda had been part of American visual culture since the First World War and was still prominent in 1938 (fig. 5).[29] The Bauhaus artists were Germans, and people in the United States were anxious about Hitler and, by extension, everything German. Most were also afraid of the Soviets, and the Bauhaus artists had of course repeatedly been labeled Bolshevist, most recently in Hitler's "Degenerate Art" exhibition. It is also important to remember that as the exhibition was being planned, HUAC was investigating foreigners with ties to communism and socialism, with the intention of deporting those found to be subversive. The regulations requiring that all refugees from Germany have employment in this country had been eased in the spring of 1938; yet there was continuing controversy surrounding the number of German and Jewish émigrés, especially in New York City.[30] Whatever side they came down on, the Bauhaus artists were potentially a threat. Americans were nervous and frightened of war and invasions—military invasions as well as the immigration of so many ethnic and political refugees then fleeing fascism in Europe and allegedly competing for depression-era employment.

When the exhibition first opened in December, Barr wrote to Gropius that he expected hostile criticism. He particularly feared that the exhibition would be considered "Jewish." Gropius wrote to Herbert Bayer: "Barr wrote me a long letter making suggestions. . . . He wanted also to make a statement about the number of Jews on our faculty."[31] Gropius refused to allow such a statement, writing back, "We should try to make it [the exhibit] somewhat less aggressive against the Nazis so that it will look like a very objective statement."[32] While Barr dreaded the response of the American critics, Gropius was unsure of himself, and feared for the lives of Bauhaus students and staff still in Germany. Yet nearly all the reviews of the exhibition make mention of the international political tensions and the position of the Bauhaus within that setting. In other words, despite the effort to avoid political issues, the fact that these were German artists exhibiting in the United States works of art that had been banned abroad was clearly not going to go unnoticed. Headlines and photo captions from newspapers, magazines, and art journals throughout the United States included references to the Nazi persecution of the Bauhaus—references to both the charges of degeneracy by Hitler and the position of many former Bauhaus members as exiles.[33] These responses to the exhibition make it clear that avoiding political controversy was simply not going to work—at least not in the immediate sense. It was impossible to erase history and politics from the Bauhaus, and the attempt to do so was—and is—itself political. Yet it is by their conspicuous absence that these issues are manifested in the exhibition and in the catalogue.

When the Bauhaus members exhibited their work in Germany, it was always

Fig. 5. "Wings over Europe," cartoon by Daniel Fitzpatrick, *St. Louis Dispatch*, May 15, 1940.

as part of an ensemble, an architectural surround, a *Gesamtkunstwerk*; Bauhaus work had been displayed to demonstrate how it would be used in a domestic setting. By contrast, at the Museum of Modern Art, the works were abstracted and presented as objects of high art, dislocated from their functional surroundings. The audience at MoMA essentially turned into passive observers who would not use or experience the things in a utilitarian—that is, social— way. The Bauhaus objects on display in New York existed not in the everyday world but in isolation, in the realm of untouchable aesthetics; they became formalist experiments. For example, among the objects on display were rugs made in the tapestry studios in Germany. Here they were strangely suspended in space, a presentation separating the object from the world of usefulness; one could not walk on them. The exhibition design created a totality; it was a design, however, that existed only in the sacred space of the museum. The exhibition format isolated objects that were intended by the Bauhaus to be, in all cases, part of an architectural, pedagogical, or practical context. The museum display turned what were intended to be socially embedded products of artistic labor into art world commodities denied the syntactic substance of their initial historical and economic situation. The museum setting made these objects seem somehow no longer utilitarian, but also no longer German, and perhaps no longer Marxist, Jewish, Bolshevist, or "degenerate."

Enhancing the decontextualizing elements of the exhibition was the fact that many objects were represented by photographs rather than the real thing, thus further accentuating the sense of alienation. The effects of photography on works of art was a topic that concerned the German theorist Walter Benjamin, who was himself in exile from Nazi Germany when he wrote his now canonical essay "The Work of Art in the Age of Mechanical Reproduction" in France in 1937. According to Benjamin, the act of recording a work of art in a photograph removed the quality of rarefication of the art object by allowing it to exist in multiple places and formats; because of its replication, the "aura" of the original work of art was diminished in preciousness.[34] In the Bauhaus exhibition in 1938, what the audience witnessed was a strange deviation from Benjamin's argument: the Bauhaus objects—themselves often reproductions or prototypes which were intended to be mechanically duplicated—were forcibly given auras by the style of display in the museum setting. Consequently, the Bauhaus works were removed from the historical context that informed the moment of their initial creation. As I have argued elsewhere, the objects on display in the museum were, like the artists, in some sense in exile.[35]

Exile and Critical Theory

There are many connections between Gropius's writings, Gropius House, the 1938 Bauhaus exhibition, and the work of other German intellectuals then in exile. As demonstrated by the diversity of the essays in this volume, many activists, scholars, writers, and participants have tried to describe or configure the experience of exile—what it means not only for the individual's life but also in terms of cultural history as a whole. According to the exiled German writer Henry Pachter, being in exile was not just "a matter of needing a passport"; it was a state of mind, "a universal mode of existence."[36] For many Germans in the United States during the 1930s and 1940s, exile came to be a way of life in which they could never avoid the feeling of being in limbo, of being suspended in a space of nonexistence, of "constantly lingering between arrival and departure," as Pachter states. Exile meant "the loss of the environment that nourished talent morally, socially and physically."[37] As Gropius remarked, it was only in Germany that he'd had the "possibility of building up a world of my own."[38] I am reminded here of the words of Bertolt Brecht after his exile—

> Dem gleichen ich,
> der den Backstein in mit sich trug
> Der Welt zu zeigen
> wie sein Haus aus sah—

"I'm like the man who carried a brick with him to show the world what his house looked like."[39] Gropius was given a position of tremendous prestige at Harvard; he had a sense of comfort and safety that many others did not share. The sad fate of Walter Benjamin, who committed suicide after a failed attempt to escape from Marseilles, and of the Bauhaus artist Otti Berger, who died at Auschwitz, are poignant reminders of this.[40] Yet it does not necessarily follow that Gropius did not suffer from exile shock, or that his experience of exile did not manifest itself in his work.

For Pachter, exiled individuals must come to admit that their visions, and consequently their history, was a mistake; in particular, they must come to see their past contributions to ideological production as ineffective and misplaced. In order to survive, to find a new way of being, the exile must recognize the failure of his or her own point of view. For Gropius and the other Bauhaus artists, this would have meant admitting the failure of their modernist, utopian program, which in turn would have meant admitting that they did in fact have a social agenda. This would have given credence to Nazi claims that the Bauhaus was essentially a political organization. And this in turn would ultimately have meant admitting that Hitler's charges against them had some basis in truth—that modernism worked against the Nazi scheme not only in formalist terms but also "sociologically," to use Gropius's phrase in his correspondence with Eugen Honig of the Reich Council for Art.

After he came to the United States and found himself transplanted into an ambiguously hospitable environment, was it easier for Gropius to hide behind the abstraction of a Bauhaus idea and to turn history into a tabula rasa? Rather than look backward and recognize the falsehood of his claims of being apolitical, or confront the failure of his architectural dreams, was it safer simply to detach his work from its Weimar ideology and reposition it in a new space—the abstracted museum setting—a place without history? Was it expedient to fuse together the German modernism of his architectural designs with New England vernacular details, thereby avoiding the psychosocial difficulties of truly "transplanting to American soil" a Bauhaus style? I believe that if one considers the historical and biographical dimensions of exile shock, these are worthwhile speculations.

There are many other provocative connections between the work of the Bauhaus artists and the writings of German cultural theorists and intellectuals many of whom were also in exile. In 1938 the critical theorists Georg Lukás and Ernst Bloch argued extensively in print and in private over the role of modernism and its connection to social radicalism.[41] It is perhaps no coincidence that these writers associated with the Frankfurt school were debating the nature of modern art and its social contextualization at precisely this time, many from the New School for Social Research in New York and at Columbia University. Yet perhaps the most interesting connection between Gropius and the exiled German theorists (albeit a poetic one) is to Benjamin's "Thesis on the Philosophy of History," also written in exile in France. In his state of despair, Benjamin turned to a print that he owned by the Bauhaus artist Paul Klee, the *Angelus Novelis* (fig. 6). He refers to Klee's figure as "an angel looking as though he is about to move away from something he is fixedly contemplating." According to Benjamin:

> This is how one pictures the angel of history. His face is turned toward the past. Where we perceive a chain of events, he sees a single catastrophe which keeps piling wreckage and hurls it in front of his feet. The angel would like to stay, awaken the dead, and make whole what has been smashed. But a storm is blowing from Paradise; it has got caught in his wings with such violence that the angel can no longer close them. This storm irresistibly propels him into the future to which his back is turned, while the pile of debris before him grows skyward. This storm is what we call progress.[42]

Benjamin's "Angel of History" is of course the reverse image of our Janus-faced Gropius, wanting not to turn back, straining to keep his eyes looking forward; yet the shared vision of history as catastrophic and the witnesses, whatever their position, as powerless is appropriate here.

Gropius tried to turn his back on the past by collapsing the various historical circumstances of the Bauhaus's controversial history into a single Bauhaus "idea" in the 1938 exhibition at the Museum of Modern Art. In his house in Massachusetts, Gropius tried to diffuse the modernist radicality and the twentieth-century German origins of his design by yoking it together with regional references. It can be argued that through these strangely ahistoricist maneuvers, Gropius intended to spare himself from complicity with his detractors, or from political accountability—either for the current actions of the Bauhaus members or for their programs in the past. In 1938 he looked back, and he looked around him; in 1938 he was justifiably in fear of his position as a German exile.

Fig. 6. Paul Klee, *Angelus Novelis*, 1920. © 2004 Artists Rights Society (ARS), New York/VG Bild-Kunst, Bonn.

Notes

Portions of this paper were presented at the Neilsen Seminar, Kahn Institute Collo-quium, "The Anatomy of Exile," Smith College, April 2001; and at the College Art Association Conference in New York, February 2000. My thanks to Peter Rose, Ger-traud Gutzmann, Barbara Kellum, and Mimi Hellman for their comments on earlier drafts. Portions of this paper have been previously published as "Walter Gropius und Marcel Breuer von Dessau nach Harvard," in *Bauhaus: Dessau–Chicago–New York*, ed. George W. Kültzsch and Margarita Tupitsyn (Essen: Folkwang Museum, 2000), 70–81, and "Gropius in Exile and the Museum of Modern Art, New York, 1938," in *Art, Media, and Culture under the Nazis*, ed. Richard Etlin (Chicago: University of Chicago Press, 2003); thanks also to the editors of those volumes for their useful comments.

1. See the final essay in this volume by Rubén D. and Rubén G. Rumbaut.

2. In many ways throughout the Weimar period, Gropius and other Bauhäuslers were, in essence, internal exiles.

3. Walter Gropius to Eugen Hönig, Berlin, March 27, 1934, in Reginald Isaacs, *Gro-pius* (Boston: Bullfinch Press, 1991), 180.

4. See Jonathan Petropoulos, *Art as Politics in the Third Reich* (Chapel Hill: University of North Carolina Press, 1996), 23.

5. Gropius was asked to speak on theater design to the Fondazione Allesandro Volta Symposium; see Isaacs, *Gropius*, 182–83. According to Isaacs, "Mindful of possible repri-sals against his and Ise's families and Bauhäuslers and confiscation of their possessions were he to leave Germany without permission, Gropius wrote [on September 19, 1934] to Eugen Hönig requesting authorization to attend the Rome conference . . . and for a permit to work temporarily in England."

6. Gropius, letter to the BBC, London, May 12, 1936, ibid., 204.

7. Gropius remained in the United States for the rest of his life, and he continued to build internationally until his death in 1969. Yet even as late as 1947, when he was put forward as a nominee for the board of design for the United Nations building in New York, his participation was rejected on the grounds that Germany was not then a member of the UN. Gropius was still considered to be a German, although by then he was an American citizen who had been teaching at Harvard for a decade. See Eric Mumford, *The CIAM Discourse on Urbanism, 1928–1960* (Cambridge: MIT Press, 2000), 160.

8. Walter Gropius, "Farewell Address," March 9, 1937, Walter Gropius Archive, Houghton Manuscript Library, Harvard University, Cambridge, Mass., b MSGer 508.

9. See Isaacs, *Gropius*, 230–31. As Isaacs explains, Gropius was also at this time trying to adopt his recently orphaned niece, Ati, who was at this point in England, and he did not want to affect adversely the outcome of his adoption petition. As he wrote to George Nelson, a British journalist, "I am anxious that no political hints whatsoever should be given as to the general German attitude against the art I am an exponent of."

10. See Peter Hahn, "Wege der Bauhäusler in Reich und Exil," in *Bauhaus-Moderne im Nationalsozialismus*, ed. Winfried Nerdinger (Munich: Prestel, 1993), 202–13, and idem,

"Bauhaus and Exile: Bauhaus Architects and Designers between the Old World and the New," in *Exiles and Émigrés: The Flight of European Artists from Hilter*, ed. Stephanie Barron (Los Angeles: Los Angeles County Museum/Abrams, 1997), 211–23; cf. Kathleen James, "Changeable Agenda: From Bauhaus Modernism to U.S. Internationalism," in Barron, *Exiles*, 235–52. For a discussion of Gropius's years at Harvard, see Jill Pearlman, "Joseph Hudnut's Other Modernism at the 'Harvard Bauhaus,'" *Journal of the Society of Architectural Historians* 56, no. 4 (December 1997): 453–77. Although I find Pearlman's discussion of Gropius's first years at Harvard quite useful, I nonetheless take issue with her minimalization of the effects of political events in Germany and in the United States in the late 1930s, as well as her descriptions of Bauhaus pedagogy.

11. Isaacs, *Gropius*, 232.

12. Winfried Nerdinger, *The Walter Gropius Archive: An Illustrated Catalogue of the Drawings, Prints, and Photographs in the Walter Gropius Archive at the Busch-Reisinger Museum, Harvard University* (Cambridge: Harvard University, 1990), 3:33; and idem, *Walter Gropius* (Berlin: Bauhaus-Archiv; Cambridge: Busch-Reisinger Museum, Harvard University, 1985), 194. Among the initial obstacles was the mortgage: the Federal Housing Administration would not insure a mortgage on a flat-roofed house in a colonial neighborhood; see Isaacs, *Gropius*, 232. For other interpretations of Gropius House, see Sabine Kraft, *Gropius baut privat* (Marburg: Jonas, 1997), and Joachim Driller, *Breuer Houses* (London: Phaidon, 2000); see also Koehler, "Walter Gropius und Marcel Breuer."

13. For a discussion of the political implications of the International Style, see Terence Riley, *The International Style: Exhibition 15 and the Museum of Modern Art* (New York: Rizzoli, 1992), a detailed analysis of the exhibition and book by Henry Russell Hitchcock and Phillip Johnson, *The International Style: Architecture since 1922* (New York: Norton, 1937).

14. Kracauer spent eight years in exile in France before finally arriving in the United States in 1941. Ernst Bloch went first to Switzerland after learning that he was on a list of those about to be arrested by the Nazis; he was expelled in 1934 for resistance activities, and from there went to Paris and Prague, finally emigrating in 1937 to the United States, where he settled in New York and then eventually, like Gropius, at Harvard.

15. All citations are from Ernst Bloch, "Erzeugung des Ornaments" (1918), in *Geist der Utopie* (Frankfurt am Main: Suhrkamp, 1973), 15, 18, and passim; English translation in *The Utopian Function of Art and Literature*, trans. Jack Zipes and Frank Mecklenburg (Cambridge: MIT Press, 1988), 78–103.

16. All citations are from Siegfried Kracauer, *Das Ornament der Masse* (Frankfurt am Main: Suhrkamp, 1963), 50, 53, and passim; in English, *The Mass Ornament: Weimar Essays*, trans. and ed. Thomas Y. Levin (Cambridge: Harvard University Press, 1995), 75–87.

17. See Karen Koehler, "Gropius the Cowboy," *Architecture and Ideas* 2, no. 1 (Spring 2000): 9–23.

18. A comparison between Gropius House and the Masters' Houses that Gropius designed in Dessau in 1925 makes this point explicitly.

19. Gropius to Martin Wagner, December 27, 1936, in Isaacs, *Gropius*, 215.

20. "Wir sind hier wie die kinder und glauben uns belagern zu müssen damit wir nicht 'homesick' werden." Gropius to Bayer, June 4, 1937, Gropius Archive, Houghton Manuscript Library, Harvard University, b MSGer 508.

21. See Margaret Kentgens-Craig, *The Bauhaus in America* (Cambridge: MIT Press, 1993), 238–40.

22. Henry Pachter, "On Being an Exile," *Salmagundi* 10–11 (Fall 1969–Winter 1970): 12–51; reprinted in *The Legacy of the German Refugee Intellectuals,* ed. Robert Boyers (New York: Schocken Books, 1972), 16–19.

23. Walter Gropius, *The New Architecture and the Bauhaus* (New York: Museum of Modern Art, 1937), 17–18.

24. The vertical clapboards also altered the effect of the many modern prints and paintings that Gropius displayed, and rotated on a regular basis in the house.

25. Walter Gropius, "Design Topics," *Magazine of Art* 40 (December 1947): 298–304; cf. Mark Wigley, *White Walls Designer Dresses* (Cambridge: MIT Press, 1995), esp. 93–109.

26. Walter Gropius, "Towards a Living Architecture: Ornament and Modern Architecture," *American Architect and Architecture* (January 1938): 21.

27. Walter Gropius, lecture at the Museum of Modern Art, January 10, 1939, Walter Gropius Archive, Houghton Manuscript Library, Harvard University, b MSGer 508.

28. For a further discussion of the political context of this exhibition, see my essay "Gropius in Exile and the Museum of Modern Art, New York, 1938," in *Art, Media, and Culture under the Nazis,* ed. Richard Etlin (Chicago: University of Chicago Press, 2003), 287–315.

29. For further examples, see Anthony Rhodes, *Propaganda, the Art of Persuasion: World War II,* ed. Victor Margolin (New York: Chelsea House, 1976), and Peter Paret, Beth Irwin Lewis, and Paul Paris, *Posters of War and Revolution from the Hoover Institution Archives* (Princeton: Princeton University Press, 1992).

30. See David S. Wyman, *Paper Walls: America and the Refugee Crisis, 1938–41* (Amherst: University of Massachusetts Press, 1968), and Richard Breitman and Alan M. Kraut, *American Refugee Policy and European Jewry* (Bloomington: Indiana University Press, 1987).

31. In Isaacs, *Gropius,* 239.

32. Walter Gropius to Alfred Barr, December 17, 1938, Walter Gropius Archive, Houghton Manuscript Library, Harvard University, b MSGer 508.

33. Koehler, "Gropius in Exile."

34. Walter Benjamin, "The Work of Art in the Age of Mechanical Reproduction," in *Illuminations,* ed. Hannah Arendt (New York: Schocken Books, 1986), 217–51.

35. Koehler, "Gropius in Exile."

36. Pachter, "On Being an Exile," 16.

37. Ibid., 17.

38. Gropius, "Farewell Address."

39. Quoted in Boyers, *Legacy,* n. 37.

40. Gropius insisted on acting privately to help Bauhäuslers still in Germany. His

urgent letters to foreign consulates on behalf of the textile artist Berger are an especially poignant example. Unfortunately in her case, he was not successful. By contrast, Gropius refused to work publicly with the American Guild for German Cultural Freedom, even to help identify artists who might need financial assistance to emigrate. See Gropius's correspondence, 1937–39, Walter Gropius Archive, Houghton Manuscript Library, Harvard University. See also Hahn, *Exiles and Émigrés*, 216–19. For the despair of Benjamin's last days, see Lisa Fittko, "The Story of Old Benjamin," in Walter Benjamin, *The Arcades Project* (Cambridge: Belknap Press of Harvard University Press, 1999), 946–54.

41. See *Aesthetics and Politics: By Ernst Bloch, Georg Lukás, Bertolt Brecht, Walter Benjamin, Theodor Adorno*, ed. and trans. Ronald Taylor (London: Verso, 1980).

42. Walter Benjamin, "Theses on the Philosophy of History" (1940), in *Illuminations*, 257–58. For further discussion of the print and its relationship to Benjamin's writings, see the two essays by O. K. Werckmeister, "Walter Benjamin, Paul Klee, and the Angel of History," *Oppositions* 25 (Fall 1982): 102–25, and "Walter Benjamin and the Angel of History, or the Transfiguration of the Revolutionary into the Historian," *Critical Inquiry* (Winter 1996): 239–67.

THE JOYS OF PARADISE
Reconsidering Hollywood's Exiles

SAVERIO GIOVACCHINI

IN MOST OF the scholarly as well as nonscholarly literature dedicated to the anti-Nazi Hollywood refugees, the anti-Nazi filmmakers who came to Hollywood in the 1930s are characterized either as intellectual sellouts, completely integrated into the Hollywood system, or as perennial exiles, eternally unable to enjoy the fruits of the paradise surrounding them.[1] In 1980 Wolfgang Gersch argued that the precondition for Hollywood success was compromising one's talents to the demands of the Hollywood system. For those modernist artists who were unwilling to compromise—such as the Russian director Sergei Eisenstein—adjustment and success were impossible.[2] The titles of some of the best-known English-language studies of the Hollywood anti-Nazi refugees represent the other side of the coin, the stereotype of the Hollywood German as perennial exile: John Russell Taylor's *Strangers in Paradise*; John Baxter's *Hollywood Exiles*, with its pivotal chapter on "the taste of transitoriness"; and, finally, Anthony Heilbut's more important yet deeply traditional *Exiled in Paradise*. Heilbut, himself the son of German émigrés, has written what is possibly the most comprehensive account of the American fate of the German-speaking anti-Nazi intellectual refugees in the English language, but his chapter on Hollywood repeats the traditional account: these émigrés are characterized as "a club of discontented Europeans."[3]

Both interpretations are based on the assumption of a radical discontinuity between the modernist European past of these filmmakers and their Hollywood experience. Such emphasis on discontinuity and on the opposites of marginality and assimilation hardly fits the experience of these filmmakers in Hollywood. Rather, it reflects the classic twentieth-century suspicion of mixing "real art" and mass-marketed cultural artifacts and the tendency to lump together the Hollywood Germans with the rest of the German anti-Nazi exiles, thereby downplaying the specific place of film culture in European and American modernism of the 1920s and 1930s. In this essay I describe the experience of Hollywood Germans as framed neither by complete assimilation nor by total marginality, instead recasting their experience within the translational history of modernism. Neither sellouts nor marginal bystanders, these filmmakers actively participated in resurrecting the intellectual life of the Hollywood community. With varying degrees of success, they often tried to bend

Hollywood narrative styles and techniques toward shaping a message of a democratic modernity that could appeal to the masses and engage them in the anti-Nazi struggle.

THE EMPHASIS on loneliness and marginality in the Hollywood destinies of these refugees, while making their experience homologous to the experience of other anti-Nazi émigré intellectuals, is indeed a little surprising. Hollywood Germans were not the first foreigners to arrive at the Southern California studios. The film citadel had always been home to a contingent of foreign performers. In addition, a large proportion of Hollywood's founding generation was born abroad—those whom the American press soon began to call "moguls" as a mark of their foreignness.[4] As is also well known, after the First World War the American film industry lured several foreign stars away from Europe in order to undermine "continental" competitors. Among this first generation of Hollywood Europeans, to name only a few, are Ernst Lubitsch, Emil Jannings, Pola Negri, Friederich Wilhelm Murnau, Paul Fejos, Ewald André Dupont, Paul Leni, George Wilhelm Pabst, Berthold Viertel, and his wife, screenwriter Salka Viertel.[5] More Europeans came after 1928 to direct or act in foreign-language versions of Hollywood films for export to the European markets (among others, William Dieterle and Fred Zinnemann).[6] Frédéric Louis Sausser (better known as Blaise Cendrars), who visited Hollywood in the 1930s, thought that MGM was dominated by a "powerful German-American trust" and characterized by a "German order," revealed by "the solid accent of the majority of the studio's employees."[7]

Of course, German-speaking filmmakers were not the only new arrivals. As a matter of fact, the Italian journalist Arnaldo Fraccaroli remarked that the charm of Hollywood lay in its being "a formidable, chaotic assemblage of humanity, a mix of races and of languages."[8] At least in part, foreigners stood out because they were separated from the rest of the community. Already, however, this separation and isolation were also the result of a careful marketing job done by the studios and by the foreigners themselves. The non-domestic, the "exotic"—especially if associated with the high end of European culture—served to define an actor or a director as a "genius" and his or her films as highbrow masterpieces. According to Greta Garbo—herself a captive of the roles Hollywood imposed on Scandinavian performers—"in Hollywood a Rumanian is not a nationality, it is a profession."[9] The British journalist Cedric Belfrage noted, "It is undoubtedly true that many foreigners are getting contracts at the studios on reputations abroad which are entirely mythical. . . . Hollywood casting directors still make remarkably little effort to check the claims of actors from foreign countries."[10]

Those who could not claim a foreign origin often made one up. Thus Theda
Bara, born in Chilicothe, Ohio, into a lower-middle-class family of Romanian
Jewish descent (her father was a tailor), was reported in the fan magazines to
be Egyptian-born, the daughter of a Frenchman and an Arab woman.[11] Perhaps her Jewish origin was not "exotic" enough, and was too close to that of
the many immigrants who crowded the working-class neighborhoods of
American cities and worried so many American legislators.[12] For the same
reason, Erich Oswald Stroheim, the eldest son of a Jewish Viennese hatmaker,
forged an aristocratic pedigree, adding a "von" here, a monocle there, and
wrapped it all in the attitude of a spoiled aristocrat—transforming himself
into Erich Oswald Hans Carl Maria von Stroheim.[13]

The mark of the exotic often defined the work of Hollywood Germans in
the 1920s and early 1930s. With a few exceptions, such as Ernst Lubitsch's film
on World War I veterans, *The Man I Killed* (also known as *Broken Lullaby*, 1932),
between 1920 and 1935, Hollywood Mitteleuropa was engaged in the construction of a celluloid Europe whose "otherness" to the reality outside the movie
theaters was emphasized by what the film scholar Guido Fink terms *papier
mâché*, referring to the blatantly unrealistic fairy-tale quality of the studio
settings of these films.[14] These *papier mâché* constructions were superimposed
by the cinema of the Hollywood Germans onto real or imaginary places (such
as the Marshovia of Lubitsch's *The Merry Widow*, 1934), all in the end made
very much alike by the recurring operetta approach to the Old World.[15]

Quite interestingly for our purposes, these 1920s migrants were not disappointed by what they found in Hollywood. Reading what they wrote at the
time about their Hollywood experiences, one has the impression that these
accounts should be situated within the more general context of the German
intellectuals' quest for modernity after the end of the First World War. Indeed,
the intellectual pilgrimages made to Hollywood by European filmmakers in
the 1920s mirrored the travels, studied by Molly Nolan, which other German,
Italian, and Soviet "Fordists" were making to the "fabulous" factories of Henry
Ford at Highland Park and River Rouge.[16] In many cases, German travelers to
Hollywood sent home admiring accounts of the American genius and por-
trayed a society less dominated by the narrow ethnic and cultural boundaries
of the *Kulturnation*. The actor Owen Gorin, for example, returning from a brief
sojourn in Los Angeles, reported a liberatingly modern Los Angeles, far from
what had been until then the stereotypical, Karl May-ish "dream-like image"
of the American Southwest, with its "night of tropical forests, the gigantic
storms, and the waterfalls." The "sensational California" ("das sensationelle
Kalifornien") was, instead, the image of modernity—a modernity that Gorin
identified as racially and culturally open to hybridization. Upon arriving in

Los Angeles, the actor found himself plunged into "screams in all languages. Objects flying into the waiting automobiles. Japanese, Chinese, blacks, Mexicans, and whites drive their cars over the giant bridges of the Los Angeles River, in which there is no water. Passing between high apartment buildings and one-story bungalows, one arrives in Hollywood."[17] In 1927 Ernst Lubitsch echoed this impression, stressing that "it is overall the art of American organization to tame the God of chaos, so that everything goes forward according to the plan, as it has been previously laid out in theory."[18]

Reading these émigrés' expressions of admiration for the United States, one wonders whether these utterances hint at a larger context, one in which embracing the Fordist efficiency of the Hollywood studios signified a very political rejection of the petrified Wilhelmine culture. "How Germany bores me," Bertolt Brecht wrote in 1920. "It is a nice average land, beautiful for its pale colors and its surface, but how about its inhabitants! A decaying peasantry, whose ignorance yields no fabulous nuisance, only a quiet brutality; a fat middle class and feeble intellectuals! Remains America."[19] As Martin Jay and Anton Kaes have suggested, for the German intelligentsia, and perhaps even more so for the urban and Jewish intellectuals, Hollywood and the United States were the antithesis of German authoritarianism and militarism, and especially of the powerful concept of *Kulturnation*, or "cultural nation," against which they increasingly posited American mass culture, "as a vehicle for the radical modernization and democratization of both German culture and life."[20]

For some of those modernists who felt threatened by the idea of *Kulturnation* because of their racial, political, or sexual identity, modernity—and Hollywood—may not have seemed such a bad idea compared with the rigid German traditions. Therefore, it is not surprising that Wilhelm Murnau's first American film, *Sunrise*, reflects no signs of artistic discontinuity with his past films, but instead gestures toward continuity with modernism while "celebrat[ing] [American] modernity itself."[21] American modernity certainly did not prevent the creation of superior films. Murnau, the gay, highbrow creator of *Faust* and *Der Letzte Mann*, asserted in 1928 that "to me America has offered new ways to pursue my artistic plans."[22] As a Jew, Billy Wilder might have felt likewise. In fact, he once recalled a song popular among Univerum-Film AG (UFA) filmmakers of the late 1920s: "Dolly is doing well / she sits in Hollywood / at a table with Lillian Gish / and where am I? / where am I?"[23] "I would have come to Hollywood Hitler or no Hitler," the director told Max Wilk in 1973. "We were picture people. We were in exile where we wanted to be."[24]

Ultimately, these filmmakers' admiration for Hollywood technologies has been papered over as a result of the narrow boundaries we have imposed on modernism, and because of what Andreas Huyssen has called the "anxiety of contamination," which makes us suspicious of any marriage between high and low, modernism and mass culture.[25] If one is part of the former, one cannot really admire the latter. Yet Hollywood cinema was, as Miriam Hansen has suggested, an integral part of twentieth-century modernism, albeit a "vernacular modernism" able to offer its audiences "a sensory-reflexive horizon for the experience of modernization and modernity."[26] For the members of this generation of European filmmakers, Hollywood represented the place where the technology of their trade had advanced the farthest. Largely untouched by the contempt for American modernity that characterized much of contemporary literary modernism, the "picture people" were where they wanted to be.

WHEN THE exiles began to arrive in Hollywood in the early 1930s, they were surrounded by an already established community of Hollywood Mitteleuropeans. In 1929, when Frederick Kohner of the *Berliner Tageblatt* arrived in Hollywood, the screenwriter Hans Kräli immediately invited him to dinner at his place, where Kohner met a German-speaking crowd including the actor Albert Conti, director Ernst Lubitsch, the Hungarian producer Alexander Korda, screenwriter Ernest Vajda, director Paul Ludwig Stein, and Lubitsch's assistant Henry Blanke.[27] These 1930s exiles may have shared some of the 1920s interest in Hollywood and its version of modernity, which may in turn have helped ease their adjustment to their new surroundings. Yet according to most of those who have analyzed the Hollywood exiles, once in place, the 1930s wave of Hollywood Germans became a club of permanently "discontented Europeans," irremediably separated from the community around them and filled with contempt for the very culture that they were producing.[28]

But how discontented were the Hollywood exiles? Unlike filmmakers, literary exiles often made the choice to come to the United States as a last resort. In his autobiography Carl Zuckmayer recalls that when Franz Horch offered him the opportunity to emigrate to the United States, "we said no, like stubborn children. We are European and we remain in Europe. What can we do in a country where one pours ketchup over ribs? And where our highest linguistic aspiration would consist of the phrase: 'I am not able to express myself.'"[29] In the 1950s, the Columbia University sociologist Donald Kent published the first comprehensive study on the diaspora of German intellectuals during the 1930s. Based on a large sample of interviews, his work did not encompass refugee filmmakers, whom he did not consider intellectuals. Tellingly, his interviewees related "a conviction of personal and cultural superiority" with regard to the United States and in many cases had waited until the last moment before deciding to emigrate overseas.[30]

In stark contrast, German-speaking filmmakers went to Hollywood in the early 1930s even at the cost of abandoning a promising career in Europe. As the director of the well-known Josefstadt theater in Vienna, Otto Preminger was on his way to a distinguished career in the theater when he accepted Twentieth-Century Fox producer Joseph M. Schenck's offer and moved to the United States in the fall of 1935. He decided to go, he remembers, because going to Hollywood "was an old dream of mine and had nothing to do with Hitler."[31] What he found there did not disappoint him. "Two things are first rate here," the director wrote his friend Ferdinand Bruckner, "the unique beauty of the land and the unimaginable organization of film production."[32] The correspondence between Kurt Weill and Lotte Lenya hints that the couple's decision to emigrate to the United States—and to Hollywood—was not entirely motivated by Nazism. Like many other German intellectuals, at first Weill did not take Hitler's rise to power seriously. In a letter to his publishing house, Universal Edition, Weill expressed the opinion that "what is going on [in Germany] is so sick that it can't last longer than a few months." What contributed to Weill's motivation to move to the United States was his interest in American popular culture. When he received a letter from Marlene Dietrich about the possibility—never realized—of a job at Paramount collaborating on a project with the actress and the director Josef Sternberg, the composer wrote his lover, the singer Lotte Lenya, "One can only say yes to this, no?" Lenya concurred and was enthusiastic as well: "Wouldn't that be some triumph! . . . Imagine the faces of [Eric] Charell, [Bertolt] Brecht . . . , and all those people in Berlin. A musical film with Sternberg and Marlene! It's unbelievable how great that would be."[33]

German-speaking filmmakers often seemed willing to go out on a limb in order to get to Southern California. Billy Wilder's move in 1934 set back his career from working director in France to semi-employed screenwriter in Hollywood. In Europe, Wilder had already made the leap from writing films to directing them. After his escape in 1933, in the middle of a brilliant screenwriting career, he moved to Paris, where he had contacts and could work in a language in which he was fluent. Acquainted with many of the German-speaking producers who had opened shop there, Wilder soon graduated to direction his first feature, *Mauvaise Graine*, an interesting film about Parisian car thieves.[34] Perhaps concerned by the possibility of Hitler's expansionism, but certainly intrigued by the opportunities in Hollywood, the director gave up his fledgling French career and left for California in 1934.[35] Although his fame allowed him to arrive in Hollywood with a contract, Fritz Lang made a similar choice when he left France for California in 1934 after debuting in the French film world with *Liliom*.[36] The same could also be said of director Henry Koster's choice to leave an established career in Paris in 1936.[37]

Obviously my point here is not to downplay differences between the 1920s and 1930s waves of Hollywood Germans. Nor is it to deny the Hollywood Germans the moral stature of antifascist exiles. In the first place, their antifascist commitment played a very relevant role in their lives and directly transformed the intellectual and political life of the Hollywood community in the second half of the 1930s. Second, the turn from uncoerced migrant to refugee in the new context of the Nazi takeover was also an obvious change, though one that American immigration authorities failed to appreciate when they continued to keep in place the robust "paper walls," to use David Wyman's expression.[38] Third, many of the members of the 1920s migration had been contacted by Hollywood producers prior to their departure. By contrast, quite a few of the filmmakers who went to Hollywood in the 1930s had had no contract with any studio before their arrival.

A further contrast is that, as the 1930s wore on, the atmosphere in the United States became increasingly hostile toward refugees in the film industry. There had been concerns before: from 1934 to 1937, the chairman of the House Committee on Immigration, Samuel Dickstein, had called for an investigation of foreigners in the film industry. In February 1936 *Variety* announced that Dickstein had proposed a bill to limit the "influx of alien film and stage talents and musicians in effort to prevent unfair competition with native performers and prevent foreign gigolos from grabbing American brides as well as fat paying U.S. jobs."[39] Unlike later enemies of the Hollywood Germans, however, Dickstein was neither an isolationist nor an ultraconservative politician. A Jewish, liberal Democrat from New York, the congressman was a staunch supporter of the New Deal, and he suspected that American producers were importing talent from Europe in order to keep American wages low. His bill proposed to link the number of visas for foreign performers with the number of Americans who were performing abroad. In stark contrast with what was to happen in later years, Dickstein's proposal failed to resonate with the American public, nor did it frighten the industry brass. According to *Variety*, producers applauded Congressman Emanuel Celler of New York, who had "insisted that American producers must have freedom to import English butlers to play parts of English butlers and French maids to 'oui, oui madame' convincingly." The trade paper concluded that the bill had a very poor chance of passing, noting that "motion picture interests, confident of the ability to kill the legislation in the Senate in the event it ever passed the House, boycotted the Committee."[40]

The following year Dickstein tried again, though with no better success. Testifying before the committee, studio representatives Gabe Hess and Joe Seidelman stressed that if passed, the bill would hurt the economic standing of the American entertainment industry by weakening its ability to undermine its competitors. According to Hess, if Hollywood were deprived of foreign talent, "the superiority of American motion pictures which makes possible their distribution to all parts of the world would fall away," because "the preeminence of American motion pictures in the entertainment of the people of this country and of the world may be credited largely to the accessibility of producers to the creative, acting, artistic and literary talents of the world." Were the bill to be approved, "the talents of such foreign artists would be used to build up motion picture industries abroad instead of being utilized to maintain the leadership which America now holds."[41] *Variety* mocked the congressman, arguing that he wanted to levy a tax on Toscanini as if he were "maccheroni."[42] Even one of the directors of the recently founded Screen Actors Guild, the Danish-born actor Jean Herscholt, declared that "a good majority of the board [of SAG] were against the bill as it stands today."[43] In March, *Variety* reported the "probability is that the legislation will be laid away without ever leaving the Committee."[44]

The very poor performance of the Dickstein investigation affords some insight into the kind of reception foreigners were likely to encounter in Hollywood prior to 1937. A liberal congressman close to the FDR administration and to labor concerns, Dickstein represented less a hostility toward the refugees than American labor's traditional suspicion toward unlimited importation of foreign labor.[45] The newly founded Hollywood Anti-Nazi League termed his hearings a "Nazi investigation." But Dickstein's efforts were quite different from later attempts to regulate Hollywood's refugees.[46] David Wyman has shown that the congressman held progressive views about refugee issues. Dickstein drew a distinction between "the foreigner in Hollywood as contract laborer" and the "foreigner as a refugee." Although he wanted to limit the access of the former to the American job market, he nonetheless wanted to support the needs of the latter.[47] Furthermore, the failure of his campaign shows how important the foreigners were to the film industry and how eager the producers were to retain their services. The lighthearted tone with which the issue was treated in *Variety* and the *New York Times* was also far from the heated debates of later years. Hollywood producers were allowed to defend their right to import talent from Europe without raising any of the implications that the connection between "moguls" and European talent would carry in later years. The outcome of the hearings was also totally in favor of the producers' rights. Even though, at the end of 1937, William Randolph Hearst voiced the possibility of his support for a measure "to curb the influx of foreign talent," the Labor Department stated that no "changes in Immigration policies affecting entertainers or actors" were in sight.[48]

The situation worsened radically after the Nazis annexed Austria and the economic downturn seriously hit the Hollywood film industry.[49] In the second half of the 1930s, attacks against Hollywood's foreign community became increasingly frantic and were often tainted by anti-refugee and anti-Semitic sentiment. Perhaps because of this, liberals like Dickstein abandoned their efforts to limit the influx of foreigners in Hollywood. Their place was taken by shriller and more ominous voices. In June 1939 the refugee magazine *Aufbau* informed its readers of "antijudische Attacke in Hollywood." This campaign had targeted the "judische Vorherschaft" (the Jewish leadership) of the studios, accusing them of favoring refugees over American workers.[50] That same month, *Hollywood Now*, the organ of the Hollywood Anti-Nazi League, reported the text of a flier authored by the so-called Committee on Unemployment which had been handed out at the studio gates. It contained an appeal to "unionized labor" to join "a campaign of anti-Semitism" against the Jewish producers allegedly hiring refugees in place of natives.[51] California Nazis often received help from Washington personalities. The chair of the House Committee on Un-American Activities, the Texas Democrat Martin Dies, notoriously coupled vehement anticommunism with shrill xenophobia. In 1940 Dies attacked Hollywood as a place where "un-Americanism has made more progress . . . than in any other parts of the country" because the Jewish producers' panicky reaction to Nazism had made them easy targets of communist propaganda.[52] Dies was aided by the isolationists of the America First Committee, who accused Hollywood of being in the hands of a warmongering clique dominated by Jews and refugees.[53] In 1939 the conservative columnist Hedda Hopper charged, "It's been a street corner joke in Hollywood that if you wanted a job here, you'd better say that you were a foreigner, preferably a refugee."[54]

In September 1940, G. Allison Phelps, a nationally syndicated radio broadcaster, also accused Hollywood of hiring refugees in preference to American artists.[55] In response, the Motion Pictures Producers and Distributors Association (MPPDA) published the results of a survey it had conducted, which showed that the Hollywood film industry employed only 18 refugees out of a total of 19,511 employees.[56] Even the *New York Times* regarded these figures as ridiculous. According to the paper, refugees were far more numerous and had been able to find jobs in Hollywood through the intervention of the European Film Fund.[57] Refugees counterattacked. The New York–based refugee magazine *Aufbau* accused Hopper and others of being "dupes" of the Nazis and announced that the FBI was now looking into the origins of these slanderous and false accusations.[58] Compared with the first half of the 1930s, the situation was now becoming increasingly problematic for the refugees. In 1941 *Aufbau* published a report by Franz Bunfel concerning the job opportunities available for refugees in the Los Angeles area: "In just the last two years, when the influx of emigrants to the West Coast has seen a great boost, increasing difficulties have presented themselves to the newcomer trying to make a living.... The possibility of making a living in the film industry in the Hollywood studios is clearly available only for exceptional individual cases with outstanding accomplishments."[59]

TO FIND a job with a studio, relatively unknown refugees often relied on a network of solidarity that connected them with the more established Hollywood Germans in the film community. Favors and assistance were asked of the German stars, and because of their position in the studio hierarchy and in the Hollywood mode of production, producers and directors were often the first to be called upon. The producer Joseph Pasternak obtained a contract for his friend, the director Henry Koster, who wanted to move to Hollywood in 1936. Carl Laemmle did not seem impressed by Koster's credentials. Pasternak did not relent. He demanded a contract for Koster as a condition of his own coming to Universal, and finally convinced Laemmle, who responded, "Bring Koster if he works for $250 a week." The producer supposedly said, "He can make one picture, but then he has to get the hell out of here."[60] In 1937 Ernst Lubitsch wrote Hal Wallis, a top executive at Warner Brothers, to ask for a contribution for the widow of Paul Grätz, a German actor who had recently died.[61] And Paul Weigel, another refugee, begged Henry Blanke for any kind of employment on the set of *The Life of Emile Zola* (1937).[62] In 1936, when Otto Klemperer, the director of the Los Angeles Philharmonic, recommended Frederick Kolm, a German actor, to Fritz Lang, Lang recommended Kolm to Ernst Lubitsch and to the Hollywood refugee producers Henry Blanke, Joseph Pasternak, and Gregor Rabinovitch.[63]

Refugee technicians needed particular help because they were often excluded from the ranks of the union which controlled most of the technical jobs in the studios. Douglas Sirk employed cameraman Eugene Schuftan in his first three American films (*Hitler's Madman*, 1942; *Summer Storm*, 1944; *A Scandal in Paris*, 1945), though Schuftan was not a member of the union. Edgar G. Ulmer did the same, allowing Schuftan to work in his most technically challenging works, including *Bluebeard* (1944), *Strange Illusion* (1945), and *The Wife of Monte Cristo* (1946). The "credits," however, never went to the Germans but to different front men: Jack Greenhalgh, Archie Stout, and Guy Roe for the films by Sirk and Jockey Feindel for Ulmer's films.[64]

The only qualification necessary to join the refugee network was unquestionable antifascism. "Everybody considers [Reinhold] Schünzel a Nazi," the agent Paul Kohner wrote in 1937. Kohner, a stalwart anti-Nazi himself, believed that the director was innocent, but his crime—to have lingered in Germany until 1937—made him unpalatable to many refugees.[65] In 1937 Lang told his friend Charles Katz about Oskar Fischinger, who had worked in Nazi Germany and was now in Los Angeles: "I personally don't like that kind of opportunism . . . [It] was enough reason for me not to help him and not to pull any ropes for him. Because I think that we have enough other people who are really in distressed situations and really need a job."[66]

As the European crisis deepened, the number of refugees arriving increased, and the attitude of American pundits became more hostile. The informal network was not sufficient any longer, so in 1938 the refugees institutionalized their solidarity drive. Organized in November 1938 by Paul Kohner, Charlotte Dieterle, and Elizabeth Frank, the European Film Fund (EFF) soon became the center of the refugee rescue efforts. Unlike the Hollywood Anti-Nazi League (HANL), which since its founding in 1936 had gathered together the resources of both native and foreign antifascist filmmakers in the anti-Nazi struggle, the EFF was funded by the employed refugees via semi-regular contributions and was almost entirely composed of refugees, its activities being confined to the aid of refugee artists.[67] Once they found gainful employment, the fund's beneficiaries were supposed to return the money they had received and begin, in turn, to contribute some of their own income to aid other needy refugees.

A thorough study of the EFF is long overdue, but it would exceed the scope of this essay.[68] Here, suffice it to say that the fund's activities involved hundreds of refugees. The EFF did provide help to many even though it seems to have operated in a somewhat hierarchical way, privileging de facto the famous over the ordinary exiles.[69] Donations could be made either "blind" or *ad personam*, that is, earmarked for the benefit of an individual "exillant." In a EFF list of "Loans to Specific Beneficiaries" referring to the period from May 1, 1941, to April 30, 1942, Bertolt and Helen Brecht are named as the recipients of "$50, and $50, $25." For the fiscal year after that (May 1, 1942, to April 30, 1943), the EFF list of "Gifts for Special Beneficiaries" includes $525 for the Brechts.[70] Well into January 1945, when Brecht had begun to make some serious money in Hollywood, Fritz Lang and others were still paying the debts incurred by the playwright. So, for example, in January 1945 the treasurer of the EFF, Fred Keller, wrote to the accounting firm of Button, Herzog, and Butts that "we will have to accept as repayment an amount of $125 which was repaid by Mr. Lang and Mr. Feuchtwanger."[71] Not all refugees, however, were equal. The actor Steve Gerai had not returned a loan of $90. In this case no leniency was to be granted: "You are instructed to start suit if the money is in [sic] paid within three days," Keller wrote to the accounting firm."[72]

EVEN WHEN we take into account the increasing problems facing refugees in Hollywood, we cannot see the Hollywood Germans solely as desperate or uprooted. On the contrary, in the second half of the 1930s, as the European situation, worsened, the German refugees' rapport with the Hollywood community tightened, extending beyond the boundaries of the German-speaking community to include the growing antifascist circles of Los Angeles. In fact, all around them the entire Hollywood community had changed. The sound revolution had brought to the West Coast a new generation of film people from the theaters and the political and intellectual circles of New York. More to the left than the preceding Hollywood generation, what I have elsewhere called the Hollywood New Yorkers established a fruitful relationship with the European exiles which drew its strength from their shared commitment to antifascism and their common interest in the potential of Hollywood cinema.[73] Both the refugees and the American left, in fact, intended to engage Hollywood's mass-market cinema in the antifascist struggle. They had come to prefer it to avant-garde film and the traditional medium of the radical documentary, which, as Archibald MacLeish noted in 1937, was "apt to begin life in a smallish, radical or art theater and end in a lecture hall."[74]

On this basis, especially after 1936, the Hollywood community changed while antifascism shaped not only its films but also the social, political, and intellectual life of Los Angeles. At the center of the New antifascist Hollywood was the Hollywood Anti-Nazi League, the result of the efforts of two refugees: Prince Hubertus zu Löwenstein, an exponent of the old Catholic anti-Hitler Zentrum, and the communist Otto Katz—known also as Rudolf Breda or André Simon—a former assistant to the theater director Erwin Piscator.[75] Almost from the beginning, the émigrés and the New Yorkers formed the backbone of the League. Reporting on their trip to California in 1938–39, Erika and Klaus Mann described the Hollywood refugees as interested in two things, "films and politics."[76] Donald Ogden Stewart, the chairman of the League, recognized the strong participation of the Europeans in the organization. In his speech at the League's first anniversary party, Stewart jocularly referred to the heavily German audience as "Herren und Damen."[77] In one year the Hollywood Anti-Nazi League had become such a center of the refugee community that its fame had reached the East Coast, spurring Ludwig Roemer, the New York editor of the anti-Nazi *Die Clubszeitung des Deutschen Arbeiterclubs*, to send orchids to the editorial board, praising *Hollywood Now*, the League's publication, as a "splendid paper which I enjoyed very much."[78]

It is this intense collaboration that marks a new period in the history of the Hollywood émigrés, one that is hardly characterized by isolation and *Heimatlosigkeit*. In the 1960s, Fritz Lang told Peter Bogdanovich that as soon as he arrived in America, he felt the necessity to abandon all contact with Germany. This is only partly true, for his circle of close friends included exiles such as

Marlene Dietrich, Peter Lorre, and Lili Latté as well as American progressives such as the Los Angeles lawyer Charlie Katz, the Hollywood New Yorkers Dorothy Parker, Hy Kraft, and Humphrey Cobb—all active in the Hollywood Anti-Nazi League—and other members of the American radical intelligentsia such as Irving Lerner and Vera Caspary. Through the Hollywood New Yorkers the director got to know New York and its cultural circles. Through Hy Kraft, a New York radical then living in Hollywood, Lang met Irving Lerner and the filmmakers gravitating toward the progressive-minded Frontier Films.[79] By March 1937 the friendship between Lang and Lerner had become so intense that Lerner wrote Lang that his wife seemed "to be a little suspicious of our (ahem) relationship." By 1937 Lerner was advising the director on what to see on the New York stage and which books to buy. When Lerner visited Lang in Hollywood in 1938, Lang brought him on the set of *You and Me*, and Lerner, enthusiastic, wrote Jay Leyda that in Hollywood "there was certainly a great deal for us to learn."[80]

The cultural cross-fertilization between Lang and radical American culture is evident in the director's first Hollywood movie, *Fury*, the story of the attempted lynching of a man named Joe (Spencer Tracy) who is wrongly accused of kidnapping a little girl in a southern town. *Fury* offers evidence of the productive relationship between the central themes of Langian cinema—fate, violence, revenge—and ideas coming from the circles of the American left. With the overt anti-lynching message of *Fury*, Lang obviously meant to address politics, and American politics at that, albeit with a European inflection. The *Variety* reviewer noted the centrality of American themes to the film as he remarked with admiration that it was curious "that an Austrian director should so faithfully capture the nuances that are so inherently American and attuned to the native mentality."[81] In *Fury*, Lang revealed his European origins, and in particular his experience with the right-wing *Volk*-centered Nazi populism, by keeping his distance from the grassroots brand of populism that, as Warren Susman has shown, was typical of the American left in the 1930s.[82] In one scene, which was finally excised from the released version of the film, Joe passionately disagrees with a man (Ward Bond) who has mocked the American people as "sheep." "I suppose it was not the people who made this country what it is today?" Joe retorts. Yet by the end of the film he has changed his mind. Americans are too easily swayed by their undemocratic emotions. People are "sheep." In opposition to the "we, the people" invocations of the 1930s—as in both John Steinbeck's and John Ford's versions of *The Grapes of Wrath*, the master narrative of the Great Depression—Lang sees "the people" as dangerously close to turning into a "mob" ("Mob Rule" was the title of the first draft of the script).[83]

It is important to note that Lang was cautious in introducing this theme.

On the surface, the immediate subject of *Fury* is the denunciation of the lynching. The transformation of the people into a mob is instead left to the movement of the camera to represent. In the lynching scene, the point of view of the mob becomes that of the spectator, so the former becomes visually identified with the latter. Although contemporary film critics were generally oblivious to this, Lang thought that he had been quite explicit, as he explained the shot to Jimmie Vandiveer in the preapproved text of a 1936 radio interview: "I roll the camera forward as a man would walk and thus approach the jail. *The audience becomes the mob* and together we move along, up the streets, and finally directly up to the sheriff himself."[84]

Nor was Lang exceptional in his interest and involvement in American causes and circles. In her autobiography, Salka Viertel remembers the refugees beginning to concern themselves with American politics. In 1940 Billy Wilder, Fritz Lang, and Michael Curtiz endorsed the reelection of Franklin Delano Roosevelt.[85] Viertel herself ran one of the most famous of the political and literary salons in Los Angeles, at 165 Mabery Road in Santa Monica. By 1936, Donald Ogden Stewart noted in his autobiography, her salon had outgrown its refugee-only status and turned into what he calls "a rallying point for all rebels."[86]

IN 1931 THE communist film critic Harry Allan Potamkin had scolded the Hollywood Germans for failing to produce work in the studios in the social realist tradition of *Die Dreigroschenoper* (1931) by George Wilhelm Pabst. Instead they had dedicated themselves to the *papier mâché* of the Viennese waltz.[87] Yet the *papier mâché* sets which the Europeans were building had more to do with politics than Potamkin perceived. Judged from the "social realist" perspective of Potamkin, these films were bound to appear failures. Contemporary reality, however, did creep into the *papier mâché*. The intentionally unreal Vienna of *Champagne Waltz* and of Ernst Lubitsch's *The Merry Widow*, the Paris of William Thiele's *Lottery Lover*, of Mamoulian's *Love Me Tonight*, of Lubitsch's *Ninotchka* and *Angel*, the Sylvania of Lubitsch's *The Love Parade*, and the Tyrol of Joe May's *Music in the Air* all constructed the utopia of a Mitteleuropa devoid of Nazism, a "world of yesterday" (to quote the title of Stephan Zweig's autobiography) which fascism had destroyed. In the 1930s the international censors were more aware of the "hidden transcript" of these films than the New Yorkers. The Italian Fascist regime, for instance, considered *The Merry Widow* unfit for distribution in Italy because of the frivolousness with which the institution of monarchy was treated. Several scenes were to be expunged. How could the Italian people tolerate a monarch who packs his crown in his suitcase along with his underwear?[88]

But the most ambitious attempt of refugees and American-born antifascist Hollywoodians to transform the *papier mâché* into antifascist barriers was the series of "biopics" (biographical pictures) directed by William Dieterle for Warner Brothers. An actor-director at UFA, Dieterle had moved to Hollywood in 1929, and after twenty-two relatively uninteresting films was assigned to a minor project at Warner, *The Story of Louis Pasteur* (1936).[89] Dieterle chose as the subject of his next biopic Emile Zola, using a treatment developed by two refugees, Heinz Herald and Geza Herczeg, who had proposed it to Lubitsch, who in turn had sent them to Dieterle.[90] In the final version of *The Life of Emile Zola,* there is an almost palpable desire to go beyond the narrow limits that the studios' censorial apparatus imposed on Hollywood antifascist discourse. By making the "affaire Dreyfus" the center of the life of the French writer, the movie became an explicit attack against militarism and anti-Semitism. And when, on February 11, Jack Warner, a Polish-born Jew, ordered all references to Dreyfus's Jewish origin expunged from the dialogue, Dieterle and the writers made do.[91] While Major Henry (Robert Warwick) reads Dreyfus's file, Dieterle has the camera skillfully pan over the file, which identifies the captain as a "Jew."[92]

Even more explicit are the references to the issues of the day in one of Dieterle's subsequent biopics, *Juarez,* dedicated to Benito Juárez, the Mexican president whom Napoleon III tried to replace with Maximilian Hapsburg and his wife, Carlotta. The first draft of the film, by Aeneas McKenzie, was an innocuous celebration of Juárez, but when rewritten by John Huston and Wolfgang Reinhardt, the script changed dramatically. Commenting on McKenzie's treatment, Reinhardt, the son of the great Viennese stage director, wrote—in German—to producer Heinz Blanke that McKenzie had missed the point entirely. McKenzie had supplied "a historical tract but no film." The real point of the film was to highlight "the analogy between those times and the events of today in a dramatic, entertaining way." Reinhardt spoke of the necessity to make the film's message so clear that "every child must recognize that Napoleon with his Mexican intervention is none other than Mussolini and Hitler and their adventure in Spain."[93]

Yet although in *Juarez* the antifascist metaphor was only partially veiled, the refugees and Hollywood antifascists wanted more. There were among the refugees, Reinhardt wrote Henry Blanke, those who shared in the "attitude into which most Europeans in New York have fallen, which boils down to the sentence 'in [Hollywood] films only rubbish is to be found.'"[94] Until now, wrote the president of the Hollywood Anti-Nazi League, Donald Ogden Stewart, Hollywood cinema and *engagé* cinema had led separate lives. If the first lacked meaning, the second lacked an audience. Hollywood cinema, he urged, should now join "fact and fiction," political communication and entertainment, in a mass-marketable narrative of antifascism.[95]

With the New York premiere of *Confessions of a Nazi Spy* on April 28, 1939, the refugee community and the American-born Hollywood left scored an unquestionable success. For three years the Hollywood Anti-Nazi League had been demanding that Hollywood studios produce an openly anti-Nazi film, but with the exception of some small independent productions,[96] the studio executives had demurred. The principle that cinema should be essentially entertainment had been incorporated into the introduction of the voluntary Code of Moral Conduct of 1930, which had been made compulsory by the creation of the Production Code Administration (PCA) in 1934.[97] It did not displease most Hollywood executives that entertainment was also good business. Profits from the American market usually covered the costs of the film's production, distribution, and exhibition, while its revenues abroad provided the studios with a large part of their net profits. Producers were therefore aware that the loss of the German-dominated European markets would have been exceedingly painful. Not surprisingly, in November 1936, *Variety* reported that Fox studio executives were doing their best to prove the Aryan origins of the actor Jean Hersholt to ensure German distribution of *Country Doctor* (1936).[98] Likewise, in 1937 Universal had not shied away from ordering twenty-one cuts in the final version of *The Road Back* (1937), the film John Whale directed from the novel by Erich Maria Remarque. The Hollywood Anti-Nazi League had vehemently protested the cuts, and its official organ, *NOW*, had publicly accused the studio of having altered the end of the novel in order to "'glorify' Hitler," but Universal producers were not impressed by the argument.[99] Until 1938 the strategy of the League had been to castigate those producers who were ready to "to kiss the mat," while praising Walter Wanger, the producer of the pro-Loyalist *Blockade*, for making an "emotionally stirring" movie about the Spanish civil war.[100]

After 1938, however, the situation became more favorable. The League had become stronger. A 1943 FBI report, in fact, noted that in 1939, League "membership at the peak of its influence was approximately four thousand. Its influence spread to many times that number."[101] Furthermore, in October 1938, the trials against some German and German-American spies began in New York City. The final result of a two-year-long FBI investigation, the trials exposed the activities of a relatively widespread spy ring. The mastermind of the organization was Ignatz Griebl, a prominent member of the German-American Bund, who, with the help of the Gestapo, had persuaded a handful of German American citizens to pass classified information to the German government. One of the FBI agents assigned to the case, Leon G. Turrou, had sold the scoop to the *New York Post* for $25,000 before the case was actually complete. J. Edgar Hoover dismissed the agent "with prejudice," for breaking the "G-man oath" prohibiting agents from divulging the results of investigations. The state attorney in charge of the case, Lamar Hardy, enjoined the *Post* from publishing the exposé. As the trials began in federal court in New York, the story gained enough headlines for Warner Brothers to buy from Turrou the rights for a film to be made of his accounts (which the *Post* published after the end of the trial, which ran from December 4, 1938, to January 4, 1939). The studio also hired him as technical adviser for the film.[102]

No sooner did Warner announce the plan for the film than members of the League started petitioning Hal Wallis, the chief producer at Warner, for a part in the movie. Edward G. Robinson, a League member and one of Warner's top stars, openly hinted that his participation in the upcoming gangster film *Brother Orchid* was predicated on Wallis's willingness to let him do *Confessions*. "While on the subject of stories," he wrote to Wallis, "I want again to express a strong desire to appear in the International Spy Ring story you are going to do."[103] Similarly, Francis Lederer, a "passionately anti-German" Czech refugee and a member of the Anti-Nazi League on his way to relative stardom, asked Wallis to be cast in the film, and Marlene Dietrich begged Wallis for the modest and relatively unappealing role of a German hairdresser who works for the Gestapo. "Money," the star assured him, "is no object."[104]

The Hollywood network that mobilized most impressively to get an opportunity to work on the picture was that of the refugees. In 1941 Hedda Hopper remarked that "scores of actors, the great majority of them natives of Germany, clamored to have a role in the film."[105] In the end, the credits of *Confessions* bore evidence of such mobilization. Its stars, Robinson and Lederer, its director, the German-Ukrainian refugee Anatole Litvak, and both its screenwriters, John Wexley and Milton Krims, were active members of the League, while at least twelve of the other actors listed in the film's credits were anti-Nazi refugees.[106] Their impact on the film was bound to be felt.

Usually bypassed by critics, *Confessions* is one of the most intensely debated films of the 1930s—according to the critic Robert Warshow, along with *Grapes of Wrath* and the song "Ballad for the Americans," one of the models for the American *engagé* intelligentsia.[107] It was the product of collaboration between German and American anti-Nazis. The makers of *Confessions*, wrote the editor of the émigré magazine *Aufbau*, had succeeded in making what he termed "very strong anti-Nazi propaganda" and "America's first anti-Nazi film."[108] Reviewing the film, Manfred George noted that "while until now a marked intellectual, anti-Fascist tendency showed itself only in political rallies and in the production of marginal films, . . . Hollywood is now a more important center of the intellectual struggle against the dictatorships."[109] *New Masses* echoed this sentiment, praising the film profusely while highlighting its debt to the New York political and aesthetic avant-garde: "The fruitful experiments of men like Joris Ivens and Herbert Kline, and neglected bands like Frontier Films have at last reached Hollywood."[110]

That the film was even produced was in itself evidence of the strength of the new Hollywood community and of the alliance of Hollywood New Yorkers and Hollywood Europeans. Warner's producers had voiced their fears that too strong an anti-Nazi message would compromise the film's chances of receiving the Production Code seal of approval. Hal Wallis had repeatedly complained to Robert Lord that "we are using too many pictures of Hitler in our picture. . . . Let's watch this and keep it out of sets, as I am afraid we are heaping it on too thick." In particular, Wallis told Lord to dissuade Litvak from shooting a series of fade-ins and fade-outs, culminating in a swastika slowly filling the screen. The Nazi symbols, Wallis told his assistant, had to be used only "as they are necessary to the telling of the story and there is no obvious propaganda about them."[111] While the makers of *Confessions* did tone down the film's propaganda level, the refugees and Hollywood radicals got much of what they wanted. The film is unmistakably anti-Nazi, images of Hitler haunt the film from beginning to end, and the planned swastika fade-in/fade-out is also in the picture. In a glowing front-page review, the League's *NOW* stressed that the makers of *Confessions* had not only given the world an anti-Nazi film but also provided Hollywood with "a new technique" by downplaying the classic protagonist-driven narrative of the Hollywood film and "dramatiz[ing] the protest of the American people" rather than celebrating individual heroism.[112]

MANFRED GEORGE'S admiration extended to the community that produced the film. On his way back to New York after a long stay in Hollywood as a guest of Fritz Lang, George had written Katia Mann that he was going back east with "a heart made awfully heavy" by the idea of having to leave Hollywood behind. Looking back to the West Coast from New York, he saw the movie citadel as "a lost paradise," full of excitement, intellectual conversations, and the magic of movie making. "California is today a very progressive state. And Los Angeles is leading the way," George wrote in an essay for the *Deutsche Volksecho*.[113]

But if, by the end of the 1930s, many people in Hollywood were actively involved with the indigenous American left in the making of anti-Nazi films, and a sophisticated intellectual like George did not hesitate to call Hollywood a "paradise," whence the legend of Hollywood as an intellectual desert? And whence the emphasis on isolation and desperation? The characterizations of

loneliness and marginality that are so often associated with the Hollywood
Europeans are the result, I think, of three causes.

In the first place, this framework is due to the tendency to lump the Hollywood Europeans together with the rest of the German anti-Nazi *Emigranten,*
thus downplaying the specific status of film in the Euro-American modernist culture of the 1920s and 1930s. James T. Morrison has argued that high
modernism often rejected what it perceived as "the degradations of social
modernity" and built a "protective wedge" between degraded modernity and
modernist aesthetics. America and mass-marketed cinema, two quintessen-
tial features of modernity, did not escape its scorn.[114] But most of the "film
people," predominantly Jewish and deeply interested in film technology because of their profession, welcomed the liberating potential of Hollywood and
American modernity.[115]

Second, the presumption of marginality and isolation of the Hollywood
exiles is the result of what Andreas Huyssen has called the "anxiety of contamination" between high and low, modernism and mass culture. The roots of
this anxiety are perhaps to be found in the cold war period and in the general
reorientation of American liberalism's attitude toward mass culture effected
in that period. Unlike the liberals, the McCarthyist cold warriors had nothing
against mass culture or Hollywood per se. Once rid of the "reds" and the New
Dealers, Hollywood could go back to its business of producing all-American
entertainment. Eager to mark their differences from the witch-hunters,
though unable or unwilling to contain their onslaught on civil liberties, cold
war liberals often attacked the Hollywood Ten and their supporters not just
as Stalinists but as manufacturers of bad taste. Hollywood was the factory of
bad culture, and this was one of the reasons why it was not worth defending.
As this group established a certain degree of hegemony over the American
intelligentsia, Lewis Jacobs's *Rise of American Film* (1939), with its enthusiasm
for the possibilities of mass-market Hollywood productions, was cast aside. In
its place, American intellectuals read Adorno and Horkheimer's *Dialectic of
Enlightenment,* or, more often, one of its popularizations. In a flagrant demon-
stration of this attitude, in 1953 the Jewish liberal magazine *Commentary* argued that "the Jews who journeyed West to make movies might have remained
in New York to make dresses."[116] Because of this cultural framework, if a "real"
intellectual such as Fritz Lang or Wilhelm Murnau happened to settle in
Hollywood, his destiny could only have been one of isolation and desperation.

Third, the cold war also explains why so many of the Hollywood refugees
came to doubt Hollywood and became, in their own writings and autobiogra-
phies, extremely skeptical of mass culture. Alexander Stephan has published a
compendium of the many humiliations inflicted on the refugees by the FBI,

the Immigration and Naturalization Service, and the Office of Strategic Services. For many of the Hollywood Europeans, these mortifications intensified during the postwar HUAC investigations of the Hollywood film industry and the ensuing period of McCarthyism, when many refugees were blacklisted and tormented.[117] Certainly, for many of them, Hollywood lost much of its charm. The sociologist Donald Kent reports that only 1.3 percent of the "refugee intellectuals" went back to Europe at the end of the war.[118] But clearly this figure does not reflect the total experience of the Hollywood Europeans. Among the German-speaking directors, nineteen out of about sixty-nine—or 27 percent—left for Europe, though some later returned to California to work on specific productions.[119] The list of reverse migrants also includes Hollywood success stories such as Anatole Litvak, who settled in France after 1949; Fritz Lang, who went back to Germany in 1956; and, at the end of the 1950s, Douglas Sirk. William Dieterle himself returned to Germany in 1958. For many of the émigrés the postwar period was one of blacklists and bleak times. "Hollywood is bankrupt," wrote Dieterle to his fellow German director Ludwig Berger in 1948. "It is possible to produce films as mass products. But nobody, not even the Americans, will see them, because they are empty."[120]

Notes

1. See Anthony Heilbut, *Exiled in Paradise* (1983; reprint, Berkeley: University of California Press, 1996), 229–60; John Russell Taylor, *Strangers in Paradise* (New York: Holt, 1984), 142–71; John Baxter, *The Hollywood Exiles* (New York: Taplinger, 1976), esp. 161–79.

2. Wolfgang Gersch, "Antifaschistisches Engagement in Hollywood," in *Exil in den USA*, ed. Eike Middel (Frankfurt am Main: Röderberg Verlag, 1980), 417. Jan-Christopher Horak does not substantially disagree with this thesis, though he stresses that assimilation may even have predated immigration. In the majority of cases, the compromise did not cost these filmmakers much effort. Because of their social and ethnic origin in the Jewish middle class, Horak argues, Hollywood Germans were naturally sympathetic to Hollywood cinema's dominant values. Jan-Christopher Horak, *Anti-Nazi Filme der deutschsprachige Emigration von Hollywood* (Münster: Maks Publikationen, 1985), 381.

3. Heilbut, *Exiled in Paradise*.

4. On the Hollywood moguls, see Robert Sklar, *Moviemade America: A Cultural History of American Movies* (New York: Random House, 1975), 46; Larry May and Elaine Tyler May, "Why Jewish Movie Moguls? An Exploration in American Culture," *American Jewish History* 72, no. 1 (January 1982): 6–25. See also Neal Gabler, *An Empire of Their Own: How the Jews Invented Hollywood* (New York: Doubleday, 1988).

5. On the 1920s migration of European stars, see Graham Petrie, *Hollywood Destinies: European Directors in America, 1922–1931* (London: Routledge and Kegan Paul, 1985). See

also Salka Viertel, *The Kindness of Strangers* (New York: Holt, Rinehart, and Winston, 1969), 101.

6. Francis Koval, "Interview with William Dieterle," *Sight and Sound* 19 (July 1950): 107-9; Gene D. Phillips, "Conversation with Fred Zinnemann," *Focus on Film* no. 14 (Spring 1973): 21-32 passim.

7. Blaise Cendrars, *Hollywood la mecca del cinema* (1937), trans. Emanuela Stella (Rome: Lucarini, 1989), 49. My translation from the Italian.

8. Arnaldo Fraccaroli, *Hollywood: Paese d'avventura* (Milan: Treves, 1928), 10. All translations are my own unless otherwise indicated.

9. Cited in Hans Pensel, *Seastrom and Stiller in Hollywood* (New York: Vantage Press, 1969), 264.

10. Cedric Belfrage, "Teas Feature Social Life of Hollywood," *New York Herald Tribune*, August 7, 1927, Cedric Belfrage Papers, Tamiment Library, New York University, box 10, folder 27.

11. Kenneth Anger, *Hollywood Babylon* (1975; reprint, New York: Dell, 1981), 14.

12. On American nativism, see Anna Maria Martellone, ed., *La "questione" dell'immigrazione negli Stati Uniti* (Bologna: Il Mulino, 1980), 12-27. See also John Higham, *Strangers in the Land: Patterns of American Nativism, 1860–1925* (1955; reprint, New Brunswick, N.J.: Rutgers University Press, 1992).

13. Richard Koszarski, *The Man You Loved to Hate: Erich von Stroheim and Hollywood* (New York: Oxford University Press, 1983), 3.

14. Guido Fink, "Il crollo della case di cartapesta," *Cinema e Cinema* 6, nos. 18-19 (January–June 1979): 57-73.

15. See Harry Potamkin's critical assessment of the work done by the Hollywood Germans in the 1920s in "Die Dreigroschenoper," *Creative Art* (July 1931), reprinted in *The Compound Cinema: The Film Writings of Harry Alan Potamkin*, ed. Lewis Jacobs (New York: Teachers College Press, 1977), 490-92. See also Harry Potamkin, "Pabst and the Social Film," *Hound and Horn* (January 1933), reprinted ibid., 413.

16. See Molly Nolan, *Visions of Modernity* (New York: Oxford University Press, 1994).

17. Owen Gorin, "Das sensationelle Kalifornien," *Filmland* (March 1925): 17.

18. Ernst Lubitsch, "Wie ich Hollywood sehe," *Lichtbildbuhne*, July 21, 1927, 2.

19. Bertolt Brecht, *Gesammelte Werke*, 20 vols. (Frankfurt am Main: Suhrkamp, 1967), 20:10. Also partially cited in Anton Kaes, "Mass Culture and Modernity: Notes toward a Social History of Early American and German Cinema," in *America and the Germans*, 2 vols., ed. Frank Trommler and Joseph McVeigh (Philadelphia: University of Pennsylvania Press, 1985), 1:325.

20. Kaes, "Mass Culture and Modernity," 323. See Martin Jay, "Massenkultur und deutsche intellecktuelle Emigration: Der Fall Max Horkeimer und Siegfried Kracauer," in *Exil, Wissenschaft, Identität: Die Emigration deutscher Sozialwissenschaftler, 1933–1945*, ed. Ilja Srubar (Frankfurt am Main: Suhrkamp, 1988), 227-51.

21. On Murnau's *Sunrise*, see James Morrison, *Passport to Hollywood: Hollywood Films, European Directors* (Albany: SUNY Press, 1998), 33. In the modernist British magazine *Close Up*, Harry Potamkin called *Sunrise* "film's first realized form." See Harry M. Potam-

kin, "Phases of Unity: I," *Close-Up* (May 1929), reprinted in Jacobs, *The Compound Cinema*, 14–20.

22. Hermann Treuner, *Filmkunstler: Wir über uns selbst* (Berlin: Sybilla Verlag, 1928), 212. The modernity provided by urban culture was obviously no obstacle to happiness, either, in Murnau's first American film, *Sunrise*. In *Sunrise* the lure of the "woman of the city," along with the boredom of country life, threatens the marriage of "the man" (George O'Brien) and "his wife" (Janet Gaynor), but it is the sensual stimulation and excitement provided by their trip to the city that ultimately reconcile the couple and provide a happy ending which was not in the original novella by Hermann Sudermann, "Die Reise nach Tilsit."

23. Neil Sinyard and Adrian Turner, *Journey down Sunset Boulevard: The Films of Billy Wilder* (Ryde, Isle of Wight: BCW, 1979), 212.

24. Billy Wilder interviewed by Max Wilk, February 22, 1973. Tape in New York Public Library, Jewish Collection.

25. See Andreas Huyssen, *After the Great Divide: Modernism, Mass Culture, Postmodernism* (Bloomington: Indiana University Press, 1986).

26. Miriam Bratu Hansen, "Fallen Women, Rising Stars, New Horizons: Shangai Silent Film as Vernacular Modernism," *Film Quarterly* 54, no. 1 (Fall 2000): 10.

27. Frederick Kohner, *The Magician of Sunset Boulevard* (San Francisco: Morgan Press, 1977), 52–55.

28. Petrie, *Hollywood Destinies*, 1. See also Maria Hilchenbach, *Kino im Exil* (Munich: K. G. Saur, 1982), 128; Taylor, *Strangers in Paradise*, 9; Baxter, *The Hollywood Exiles*, 172–84. Heilbut, *Exiled in Paradise*, 229–60.

29. Carl Zuckmayer, *Als war's ein stuck von mir* (Frankfurt am Main: Fischer Verlag, 1969), 88.

30. Donald P. Kent, *The Refugee Intellectual* (New York: Columbia University Press, 1953), 217.

31. Gerald Pratley, *The Cinema of Otto Preminger* (New York: A. S. Barnes & Co., 1971), 37.

32. Preminger to Bruckner, April 23, 1936, in Norbert Grob, Rolf Aurich, and Wolfgang Jacobsen, *Otto Preminger* (Berlin: Stiftung Deutsche Kinemathek und Jovis Verlagsbüro, 1999), 7–8.

33. Lys Simonette and Kim H. Kowalke, eds., *Speak Low (When You Speak of Love)* (Berkeley: University of California Press, 1996), 71 (letter dated February 6, 1933), 115 (March 3–6, 1934), and 117 (March 8?, 1934).

34. On German producers in Paris (Max Glass, Hermann Millakowsky, Seymour Nebenzahl, Arnold Pressburger, Gregor Rabinovitsch, Eugene Tuscherer, and Erich Pommer), see Horak, *Anti-Nazi Filme*, 16–18.

35. Maurice Zolotow, *Billy Wilder in Hollywood* (New York: G. P. Putnam's Sons, 1977), 47–55.

36. See Alfred H. Barr, "Nationalism in German Films," *Hound and Horn* (January–March 1933): 278; Bernard Rosenberg and Harry Silverstein, eds., *The Real Tinsel* (New York: Macmillan, 1970), 333–50. In his biography of Fritz Lang, Pat Gilligan suggests

that Lang consciouly spread the rumor that Goebbels had offered him the directorship
of the German film industry. According to McGilligan, Lang left Germany because of
"hurt male pride" when his marriage to Thea von Harbou collapsed, and because he
worried about the consequence of his Jewish origins. Pat McGilligan, *Fritz Lang: The
Nature of the Beast* (New York: St. Martin's Press, 1997), 180–84. Lang probably exaggerated or even completely invented his meeting with Geobbels to create an antifascist
pedigree for himself. McGilligan's suggestion, however, entirely depoliticizes Lang's
choice to emigrate, which is a little surprising given the director's rapid engagement
with the American left once in Hollywood. Besides, it is worth noting that, as Mc-
Gilligan himself recognizes, the last German film Lang made before his exile, *Das
Testament von Dr. Mabuse*, had already been banned in Germany because of the parallel
Lang drew between Mabuse and Hitler. For the relationship between Lang and the
American left, see my *Hollywood Modernism* (Philadelphia: Temple University Press,
2001), esp. chap. 2.

37. Interview with Irene Kahn Atkins, in Henry Koster, *Henry Koster* (Metuchen, N.J.:
Scarecrow Press, 1987), 41.

38. See David Wyman, *Paper Walls: America and the Refugee Crisis, 1938–1941* (1968;
reprint, New York: Pantheon Books, 1985); idem, *The Abandonment of the Jews: America
and the Holocaust, 1941–1945* (New York: Pantheon Books, 1984).

39. *Variety*, February 12, 1936, 3.

40. Ibid.

41. Seventy-fifth Congr. House Committee on Immigration and Naturalization,
Hearings Concerning House Resolution 12325 "To restrict Admission of Alien Performing Artists to the U.S. for the Protection of Native Artists," February 18, 1937.

42. *Variety*, February 24, 1937, 31.

43. Seventy-fifth Congr. Hearings Concerning House Resolution 12325.

44. *Variety*, March 17, 1937, 2.

45. See Higham, *Strangers in the Land*.

46. *Anti-Nazi News*, January 20, 1937, 1.

47. After the Anschluss, together with Emanuel Celler (his opponent during the
hearings on the Alien Actors Bill), Dickstein "proposed that when the fiscal year 1938
ended on June 30, the U.S. combine all countries' unused quota allotments for that
year and make them available to refugees." Dickstein also supported the 1939 Wagner-
Rogers Bill, which was meant to allow twenty thousand German and Austrian children
into the United States beyond the quota. In January 1941 he proposed to turn Alaska
into "a refugee Haven." See Wyman, *Paper Walls*, 4, 79–92, 110–21. On Dickstein, see also
Dorothy Waring, *American Defender* (New York: Robert Speller, 1935).

48. *Variety*, November 17, 1937, 2, and December 1, 1937, 1.

49. On the economic situation of the studios in the 1930s, see Douglas Gomery, *The
Hollywood Studio System* (London: Macmillan, 1986), esp. 34, 102, 125.

50. *Aufbau*, June 1, 1939, 19.

51. *Hollywood Now*, June 19, 1939, 1–2.

52. Martin Dies, "The Reds in Hollywood," *Liberty*, February 17, 1940, 47. On Dies

and the refugees, see Saverio Giovacchini, "Fritz Lang, i 'Moguls' e altri 'recent citizens,'" in *Lo straniero interno*, ed. Enrico Pozzi (Florence: Ponte Alle Grazie, 1994), 172–73.

53. Gerald P. Nye, "War Propaganda: Our Madness Increases as Our Emergency Shrinks," *Vital Speeches of the Day*, September 15, 1941, 720–23.

54. *Chicago Tribune*, October 29, 1939, Scrapbook no. 3, Hedda Hopper Scrapbook Collection, Academy of Motion Picture Art and Sciences (hereafter AMPAS). After Pearl Harbor, the FBI scrutinized the refugees as enemy aliens. In 1944 Hopper noted that the "FBI wants to know about extras who insist upon speaking German on various sets. . . . It's a situation that's festering like a boil on the neck." Clipping, February 18, 1944, in Kohner Nachlass, Folder European Film Fund, Deutsche Kinemathek, Berlin.

55. *Aufbau*, October 19, 1940, 8; *New York Times*, September 22, 1940, 9:3.

56. *Variety*, October 9, 1940, 4.

57. *New York Times*, March 2, 1941, 9:5.

58. *Aufbau*, October 25, 1940, 9.

59. *Aufbau*, September 5, 1941, 14.

60. "I'm up to my hips—and he didn't use the word 'hips'—with German directors, I want you to come alone," Laemmle is supposed to have told Pasternak when he asked for a contract for Koster. Koster, *Henry Koster*, 41.

61. Lubitsch to Wallis, February 24, 1937, Personal Files, Correspondence, 1936–37, Wallis Papers, AMPAS.

62. Paul Weigel to Henry Blanke, n.d., *Zola* Production Files, Warner Brothers Archives, Doheny Library, University of Southern California (hereafter USC-WB).

63. Lang to Blanke, September 13, 1936, box 1, folder B, Lang Papers, American Film Institute, Los Angeles (hereafter AFI).

64. See Peter Bogdanovich, "Interview with Edgar G. Ulmer," in Todd McCarthy and Charles Flynn, *Kings of the Bs: Working within the Hollywood System* (New York: E. P. Dutton, 1975), 401–2; Douglas Sirk, *Sirk on Sirk: Interviews with Jon Halliday* (London: Secker and Warburg, 1971), 67. These efforts were not always successful. In 1946 director Curtis Bernhardt tried to employ cameraman Kurt Courant in his film *Possession*: "[Kurt Courant] was ideal for this film, so I persuaded Warner to let him shoot some tests with Miss [Joan] Crawford. She accepted him after she saw the tests. But the cameraman's union turned Courant down. Jack Warner was so impressed with Courant's test that he approached the union with this offer: to hire thirteen cameramen for his newsreel department if they would give him this one cameraman. And the union would not do it." Curtis Bernhardt, *Curtis Bernhardt: Interviews with Mary Kiersch* (Metuchen, N.J.: Scarecrow Press, 1986), 120.

65. Kohner cited in Helmut G. Asper, "Herzasthma des Exils," *Film-Dienst*, June 22, 1999, 43–45. On Kohner, see Frederik Kohner, *The Magician of Sunset Boulevard* (San Francisco: Morgan Press, 1977).

66. Lang to Katz, January 14, 1937, box 3, folder K, Lang Papers, AFI.

67. When the actor Albert Basserman asked EFF's treasurer Fred Keller for some help for a non-artist friend, Alfred Liebmann, Keller answered that the fund aided only artists, "especially actors, writers, composers," and advised Basserman to refer his friend

to the Jewish Joint Distribution Committee. Keller to Basserman, February 20, 1941, Kohner Nachlass, Folder European Film Fund, Deutsche Kinemathek, Berlin.

68. On the board of directors of the EFF sat Ernst Lubitsch, Charlotte Dieterle, Heinz Herald, Felix Jackson, Elizabeth Frank, and Paul Kohner. On the fund, see Giovacchini, *Hollywood Modernism*, 120–21. See also E. Bond Johnson, "Der Europen Film Fund in Hollywood," in *Deutsche Exillitteratur seit 1933*, 2 vols., ed. John M. Spalek and Joseph Strelka (Bern: A. Francke AG Verlag, 1976), 1:135–46; and Giovacchini, "Fritz Lang, i 'moguls' e altri 'recent citizens.'" An interesting primary source on the fund is Kohner, *Magician of Sunset Boulevard*.

69. Two documents in the Kohner Nachlass reveal the names and addresses of about six hundred refugees who were associated with the EFF either as donors or as beneficiaries. See list dated in pencil August 28, 1942, and "List of Loans Receivable," dated June 30, 1945, Kohner Nachlass, Folder European Film Fund, Deutsche Kinemathek, Berlin.

70. Kohner Nachlass, Folder European Film Fund, Deutsche Kinemathek, Berlin.

71. Keller to Robert S. Butts of Button, Herzog, and Butts, January 4, 1945, Kohner Nachlass, Folder European Film Fund, Deutsche Kinemathek, Berlin.

72. Ibid. See also Keller to Gerai, February 15, 1943, and Paul Kohner to Gerai, February 29, 1944, Kohner Nachlass, Folder European Film Fund, Deutsche Kinemathek, Berlin.

73. On the Hollywood New Yorkers, see my *Hollywood Modernism*.

74. MacLeish cited in Charles Wolfe, "The Poetics and Politics of Non-Fiction: Documentary Film," in *Grand Design*, ed. Tino Balio (New York: Scribner's, 1993), 355.

75. Hubertus zu Löwenstein, *Abenteurer der Freiheit* (Berlin: Ullstein, 1983), 164. Katz was the model for Kurt Müller, the anti-Nazi hero of *Watch on the Rhine* by Lillian Hellman. See Bernard F. Dick, *Hellman in Hollywood* (Rutherford, N.J.: Fairleigh Dickinson University Press, 1982), 86.

76. Erika and Klaus Mann, *Escape to Life* (Boston: Houghton Mifflin, 1939), 265.

77. *News of the World* (hereafter *NOW*), August 7, 1937, 1.

78. "NOW Gets Orchids from German Editor Who's Not a Nazi?" *NOW*, August 7, 1937, 7.

79. Lerner to Lang, March 1937, box 3, Folder Lerner, Lang Papers, AFI. On Frontier Films, see William Alexander, *Film on the Left: American Documentary Film from 1931 to 1942* (Princeton: Princeton University Press, 1981).

80. Lerner to Lang, March 1937, April 26, 1937, December 1937, and Lang to Lerner, December 22, 1937, box 3, folder Lerner, Lang Papers, AFI; Lerner to Leyda, February 1, 1938, Alphabetical Correspondence, Folder Lerner, Leyda Collection, Tamiment Library, New York University.

81. *Variety*, June 10, 1936, 18.

82. See Warren Susman, "The Culture of the Thirties," in *Culture as History* (New York: Pantheon Books, 1984), 178; Gary Gerstle, "The Protean Form of American Liberalism," *American Historical Review* 99 (October 1994): 1068; Michael Denning, *The Cultural Front* (New York: Verso, 1996), 123–36.

83. See "Mob Rule," script by Norman Krasna, Bartlett Cormack, and Fritz Lang, approved by Joseph L. Mankiewicz, dated February 10, 1936, with addition, Script Collection, AMPAS.

84. Transcript of *Evening Herald & Express Radio* interview with Fritz Lang by Jimmie Vandiveer, "Roving Reporter," June 16, 1936 (emphasis added), box 1, folder F, Lang Papers, AFI. American progressives were not aware of this little detour. Walter White of the NAACP wrote MGM "to express my profound appreciation" for the film. Walter White to MGM, May 28, 1936, box 1, folder F, Lang Papers, AFI. Lang's Hollywood leftist friends such as Humphrey Cobb praised the film for its "realism" (Humphrey Cobb to Fritz Lang, July 9, 1936, box 1, folder C, Lang Papers, AFI), and so did most of the intellectual, progressive magazines; see, for instance, *New Masses* (July 1936): 11.

85. *Aufbau*, October 25, 1940, 9.

86. Donald Ogden Stewart, *By a Stroke of Luck* (London: Paddington Press, 1975), 228.

87. Potamkin, "Die Dreigroschenoper." See also his "Pabst and the Social Film."

88. Joe Breen to the American Association of Motion Pictures Producers, October 31, 1935, *The Merry Widow* PCA File, Margaret Herrick Library, AMPAS.

89. On Dieterle, see Marta Mierendorff, *William Dieterle* (Berlin: Henschel Verlag, 1993).

90. See the essay by Heinrich Mann, "Zola," *Die weissen Blätter* 11 (1919): 1312–82, and the 1930 film by Weimer director and Hollywood refugee Richard Oswald, *Dreyfus* (Süd Film AG, 1930). On the Zola myth, see also Egbert Krispyn, *Anti-Nazi Writers in Exile* (Athens: University of Georgia Press, 1978), 48. See also *Zola* Story File, USC-WB.

91. Hal Wallis to Walter McEwen, February 11, 1937, *Zola* Story File, USC-WB.

92. Norman Reilly Raine, Heinz Herald, and Geza Herczeg, *The Life of Emile Zola*, final script (March 16, 1937), 51, Script Collection, AMPAS.

93. Reinhardt to Blanke, November 24, 1937, *Juarez* Picture File, USC-WB. My translation from the German. On the film, see also John Huston, *An Open Book* (New York: Knopf, 1980), 74.

94. Reinhardt to Blanke, November 2, 1938.

95. Donald Ogden Stewart, *Fighting Words* (New York: Harcourt & Brace, 1940), 5, 166.

96. See, for example, the film by Isobel Steele, *I Was a Captive of Nazi Germany* (Malvina Pictures Production, 1937), or Shepard Traube's *Hitler, Beast of Berlin* (Producers Releasing Corporation, 1934).

97. See Giuliana Muscio, ed., *Alle Porte di Hays* (Milan: Fabbri, 1991), 381–92.

98. See *Variety*, November 25, 1936, 13.

99. See *Variety*, June 9, 1937, 9.

100. *NOW*, June 25, 1938, 2; June 11, 1938, 3; May 30, 1937, 7. As for the 1938 film *Three Comrades*, *NOW* argued that "it is not any kind of version of Remarque's book. In fact, you can't, unless you've read the book tell which are the Nazis and which are their opponents." *NOW*, May 28, 1938, 3; see also Matthew Bernstein, *Walter Wanger: Hollywood Independent* (Berkeley: University of California Press, 1994).

101. Report of the Los Angeles Bureau of the FBI to Washington, D.C. (unnamed

recipient), February 18, 1943, 117, in *Communist Activity in the Entertainment Industry: FBI Surveillance Files on Hollywood, 1942–58*, ed. Daniel J. Leab (Bethesda, Md.: University Publishers of America, 1991), reel 1, microform edition.

102. *Newsweek*, July 9, 1938, 9. See also Leon G. Turrou, *The Nazi Conspiracy in America* (1939: reprint, Freeport, N.Y.: Books for Libraries Press, 1972).

103. Edward G. Robinson to Hal Wallis, October 20, 1938, Edward G. Robinson Papers, box 36, folder 20, USC-WB.

104. Hal Wallis, *Starmaker* (New York: Macmillan, 1980), 71; Ed Sullivan, "Hollywood," n.d., and *Herald Tribune* (Paris edition), February 15, 1939, *Confessions of a Nazi Spy* (hereafter *Confessions*) Clippings File, USC-WB.

105. *Los Angeles Times*, April 28, 1941, Scrapbook no. 5, Hedda Hopper Collection, AMPAS.

106. Among them William von Brinchen, Rudolf Amendt, Sig Rumann, Paul Lukas, Wolfgang Zilzer, Hans von Morhart, Hans von Twardowski, Willie Kaufman, Martin Kosleck, Hedwiga Reicher, Henry Victor, and Frederick Vogeding.

107. Robert Warshow, "The Culture of the Thirties," in *The Immediate Experience* (New York: Doubleday, 1962), 34.

108. *Aufbau*, May 1, 1939, 16.

109. Manfred George, "Was geht in Hollywood an," *Aufbau*, May 1, 1939, 6.

110. *New Masses*, May 9, 1939, 27–28.

111. Memo from Wallis to Lord, February 14, 1939, *Confessions* Picture File, USC-WB.

112. *NOW*, May 5, 1939, 1. For a complete analysis of this film, see my "Negotiated Confessions: The Making of *Confessions of a Nazi Spy*," in *Brave New Words. America in the '30s: Languages between Ideology and Experimentation*, ed. Maurizio Vaudagna and Bianca Tedeschini Lalli (Amsterdam: Amerika Instituut, 2000), 207–20.

113. Manfred George to Katia Mann, April 10, 1939, George Nachlass, Schiller National Museum, Deutsches Literaturarchiv, Marbach am Neckar; M.G. [Manfred George], "Die Politische Mission des Films: Der Nationale und der Anti-Nazi Film—Nur eine Mode? Einfluss der U.S.-Aussenpolitik," *Deutsche Volksecho*, April 29, 1939, Dieterle Nachlass, Folder "Juarez," Deutsche Kinemathek, Berlin.

114. Morrison, *Passport to Hollywood*, 17–18.

115. Jan-Christopher Horak calculates that only 5 percent of the Hollywood Germans were non-Jewish. See Jan-Christopher Horak, *Fluchtpunkt Hollywood* (Münster: Maks Publikationen, 1986), 38.

116. Morris Freedman, "New England and Hollywood," *Commentary* 16 (October 1953): 392. On the rise of the anti-Hollywood consensus, see Thom Andersen, "Red Hollywood," in *Literature and the Visual Arts in Contemporary Society*, ed. Suzanne Ferguson and Barbara Groseclose (Columbus: Ohio State University Press, 1985), 176–89. On the popularity of the *Dialektik* among American intellectuals of the 1950s, see Martin Jay, "The Frankfurt School in Exile," in *Permanent Exiles* (New York: Columbia University Press, 1986), 46.

117. Alexander Stephan, *Communazis* (1995; U.S. edition, New Haven: Yale University Press, 2000), 74.

118. Kent, *Refugee Intellectual*, 186.

119. Horak, *Fluchtpunkt Hollywood*; see also Giovacchini, "Fritz Lang, i 'moguls' e altri 'recent citizens,'" 180.

120. Dieterle to Berger, October 1948, Ludwig Berger Papers, Deutsche Akademie der Künste, Berlin.

"SECOND-CLASS REFUGEES"

Literary Exiles from Hitler's Germany and Their Translators

KRISHNA WINSTON

SOON AFTER Hitler came to power in January 1933, it became clear that the Nazis had a particular animosity toward writers who could be identified as Jewish, left wing, or critical of the regime. In May of that year students gleefully consigned many contemporary writers' works to public bonfires in Berlin and elsewhere, and even before that event some writers had discovered, either in the nick of time or too late, that their names were on the Gestapo's lists for the first wave of raids and arrests. Hitler's propaganda minister, Joseph Goebbels, came from a petty-bourgeois family in the Rhineland, and he had developed a fierce resentment of middle- and upper-class intellectuals during his university days, when he became bitterly aware of his own poverty and lack of social status.[1] And Hitler, an autodidact whose literary style liberal intellectuals had derided, knew from personal experience the power of the word and wanted to silence those he considered his enemies.

Many of the German and Austrian writers who reached America were what the Berlin *homme de lettres* Walter Mehring (1896–1981) described as "second-class refugees."[2] Whereas a "first-class refugee" such as Thomas Mann (1875–1955) found the means to rescue his books and even his desk so that he could set up his study in Princeton, and later in Santa Monica, as a near replica of his study back in Munich, the "second-class" literary refugees were not so fortunate. Although quite well or even very well known in Europe, they had not achieved the kind of recognition that would assure them a welcome in the United States. They had left behind their reputation, social status, and language, their familiar setting, and their worldly possessions, including their libraries, which represented the culture that had shaped them and to which they had contributed.[3]

If one reads the letters and diaries of Thomas Mann from the 1930s and 1940s, it becomes clear that despite his relatively fortunate material circumstances, he was by no means exempt from the sufferings of exile. Worry about the safety of others—his brother, his children, his friends and acquaintances—as well as anger at the Nazis and fear for his beloved Germany all took a toll on his health, and his sense of responsibility for his fellow intellectuals placed heavy burdens on him.[4] But in addition to his financial resources, Mann had a devoted translator, a faithful publisher, and an international audience, not only for the books he had written before leaving Europe but also for those he would write in exile. Americans were eager to hear what he had to say: he was constantly in demand for speeches, broadcasts, and statements. Mann became the ultimate authority on the question of determining which writers would be in particular danger as Hitler extended his control over Europe, and which ones merited support when they reached America.[5]

Even with Thomas Mann's backing, the writers whose reputations did not precede them to the United States found themselves in difficult circumstances once they arrived. These German writers read Latin and Greek and spoke French, but most of them lacked fluency in English.[6] Although they had personal stories to tell and insight into what was happening in Europe, no one was clamoring to hear them. They were sometimes faulted or mocked for their lack of adaptability, their self-pity, their appearance of arrogance. Staff members at relief agencies expressed incredulity at the refugees' reluctance to take jobs involving manual labor.[7] Compared with the circumstances of the exiles and refugees fleeing other political calamities of the twentieth century, and compared with the fate of the 6 million people or more whom Hitler killed, their lot might perhaps be considered fortunate: they escaped the extermination camps; they were not raped or mutilated; and although they often went hungry, they did not starve.[8] Nonetheless, the desperation they felt was genuine. The very basis of their existence and their self-respect was gone. It was as public intellectuals and masters of the word that they had attracted the attention—and hatred—of the Nazis. It was as figures who enjoyed a degree of recognition that many of them had found their way onto lists such as those of the Emergency Rescue Committee.[9] Small wonder, then, that writers already in their forties or older when they came to the United States clung to the belief that their emotional and intellectual survival depended on their finding publishers willing to take a chance on them. Those who were not completely broken by exile continued to write. They wrote in defiance of loneliness and poverty and, to paraphrase Hans Natonek (1892–1963), in search of themselves—of an identity that had once seemed relatively secure—and sometimes in search of a new identity.[10]

Located between the writer and the publisher in this situation was the translator. This essay depicts four of these three-way relationships, based on unpublished correspondence from the estate of my parents, Richard Winston (1917–1979) and Clara Winston (1921–1983). The Winstons began their career as a translating team in the late 1930s with the "second-class refugees," some of whom they met through Harry Slochower (1900–1988) of Brooklyn College. Richard Winston had studied German literature with Slochower from 1935 to 1939, and Clara Winston was a poet and fiction writer. Fiercely dedicated to the life of the mind, the Winstons were young and desperately poor when they first made the acquaintance of the refugees. Although much later they would translate the works of such prominent refugees as Thomas Mann, Erich Maria Remarque (1898–1970), and Carl Zuckmayer (1896–1977), it was the heart-rending and sometimes ludicrous struggles of the second-class refugees to find a voice in America—struggles in which they became implicated—that made an unforgettable impression on them. The Winstons left New York City in the early 1940s to live first in western Massachusetts and later in southern Vermont. Their personal and professional dealings with writers and publishers were thus conducted primarily through letters; the correspondence provides rich material on a career in cultural mediation that spanned forty years and on an aspect of the literary refugees' experience that deserves further exploration.

The writers discussed here—H. E. Jacob, Hans Sahl, Curt Riess, and Walter Mehring—were all Jewish, all of the same generation, all quite well known before they left Germany. They represent a wide range of personalities and talents caught up in similar circumstances, and their epistolary exchanges with their publishers and translators offer a wealth of insights into their re-sponses—some unique, some typical—to those circumstances and into their encounters with American culture.

Heinrich Eduard Jacob (1889–1967)

Heinrich Eduard Jacob, who always insisted that his Anglophile parents had given him the name Henry,[11] was interned in Dachau and Buchenwald for eleven months in 1938–39, after which he escaped to the United States by way of England. A writer of both fiction and nonfiction and a well-known play-wright and critic in Berlin, he already had a long list of publications when he came to America, including biographies of musicians and a history of coffee.[12] In the United States, Jacob, who became a citizen in 1945, chose to focus not on the experience of exile and not on himself but on cultural history—in the broadest sense. The Winstons first worked with him when they translated *Six Thousand Years of Bread*, published in 1944 by Doubleday. A few years later they translated his books on Emma Lazarus, author of the famous sonnet "The New Colossus" engraved on a plaque on the Statue of Liberty, and on Joseph Haydn.[13] Unfortunately, the Winstons' files do not contain any correspon-dence from the years before 1951. The first letter from Jacob discusses an un-published novel called "Babylon's Birthday," set in New York in 1909.[14] Jacob had recently offered a translated sample to three publishers, all of whom had expressed reservations about the plot. Now he asked the Winstons to translate another section, which he believed would put the publishers' doubts to rest, and he enclosed a check for $75 with the comment: "You know, Richard, that I am truly the very opposite of a well-heeled author. If I nonetheless dare to lay out such a sum for this purpose, it is because I have boundless faith in two things: my novel and its translator."[15]

This faith did not prevent him from chastising his translator a few days later for blunting some of his literary effects, and admonishing him, in a mixture of German and English, to "translate word for word and humorous effect for humorous effect, serious point for serious point and chuckling for chuckling."[16] Later letters document further attempts to place the novel, which was never to be published in the United States, and an effort to persuade Ben Huebsch, an editor at Viking, to reissue the English version of the history of coffee.[17] A letter written during this period shows how precarious Jacob's finances were: he could send his translator only $38, for illness had prevented him from writing for the German-language newspaper *Aufbau* and for the *New York Times*, and from completing an outline for a book on Liszt.[18] In another letter Jacob announces triumphantly that he has been asked by the *Saturday Review of Literature* to write book reviews. He describes his response thus: "Oh, yes, I *will*. . . . And that's the reason, my friend, why you'll hear from me again very soon."[19] What this hint implies becomes clear from the next letter, written in English, and apparently sent along with the text of Jacob's first piece for the *Saturday Review*, which he wanted back "not later than *Monday*, and it can't absolutely carry more than *500 words*."[20] Jacob wrote his reviews in German and had the Winstons translate them, for which they received a share of the proceeds.[21] In the same letter Jacob reports, with undisguised glee, that he has just received "the Mehring book"—*The Lost Library*—to review for the *Times*. He teases Richard Winston in English: "Funny thing it would be, if I would let the world know that you are a terribly bad translator. You would be helpless then—eh? But you know that I would never pull any punches on you." He comments that Mehring was speculating just the day before about who would do the *Times* review, and he insists on Winston's discretion: "Kein Wort über unsere dealings!" (Not a word about our dealings!).[22] Jacob concludes with an admonition that Winston should not expend all his "power of words" on another refugee, Curt Riess.

This letter reveals some of the competition that went on among the exiled writers and the possessiveness they felt toward their translator. It also shows the kind of pretense they felt it necessary to engage in to conceal their lack of mastery of English. Within the small world of the refugees living in New York, such intriguing could create an awkward situation for the translators: as his next letter shows, Jacob expected the Winstons to translate his review of the

Mehring book. In this letter Jacob faults the book for lacking any kind of plot or action, something he feels Anglo-American literary taste requires: "When we were children in Berlin, we learned that the English had no culture at all. They were tellers of rough tales. . . . But in the meantime I as well as Mehring became Americans. And we had to learn it the hard way . . . that without that technique, founded by Bret Harte and his generation, no story can be told." Jacob notes that in the review he has not criticized Mehring for his book's lack of "action" and "real tension" because "I am (and you are well aware of it, Dick) a gentle heart." He expresses sympathy for "the writer of today," who "is working in complete isolation."[23] As will become clear when Mehring's side of the story is told, the understanding and compassion a fellow refugee could extend did not, alas, carry the same weight for Mehring as recognition from an American reviewer.[24]

Some months later Jacob asked the Winstons to translate a letter to the editor of the *New York Times Book Review*, in which Jacob proposes that he be commissioned to write an article marking the tenth anniversary of the writer Stefan Zweig's suicide in Brazil. Jacob claims that his thirty-year friendship with Zweig puts him in a position to reveal factors in that writer's psychic makeup that would make his puzzling suicide comprehensible. In his cover note Jacob swears Richard Winston to deepest secrecy about this project, impressing upon him that he must not even mention Zweig's name in the next few months—"and you know *why*."[25] Such paranoid or conspiratorial behavior crops up often among the refugees, in part, no doubt, engendered by their experiences with the Gestapo in Germany and Austria. Those who had fled to France had also experienced the Vichy government's collaboration with the Nazis. The uncertain nature of the refugees' existence in wartime and early postwar America did nothing to allay their fearfulness. In his next letter Jacob bemoans the rejection of his Zweig proposal by the *Times*, ascribing it to the "market situation": no Zweig book, new or reissued, was currently available, a circumstance he found "a bit depressing." In the same letter he creates a further entanglement for Richard Winston, who four days earlier had been asked by Hiram Haydn, an editor at Bobbs-Merrill, to evaluate a novel by "H.E. Jacob, whom you will remember."[26] Jacob knows that Haydn will be sending the novel to "einem professional reader," someone "who would be neither a commie nor anti-commie nor a spinster, nor a sleep-walking Kafkaomane." Unsure how this unknown reader would react to the book, Jacob asks Winston to translate a synopsis of the important points of the book![27] Rather than allow Jacob to compromise his integrity, Winston reveals to the editor his long personal acquaintance with the author, acknowledging that it might interfere with his ability to be objective about the book; he then offers a remarkably balanced assessment of the work, at the end of which he has to ask the editor not to divulge the reader's identity to Jacob.[28]

Perhaps the most striking example of the conspiratorial tone in Jacob's correspondence can be found in a letter handwritten in English at the end of 1952:

> Dick, and I tell you this in full earnest, *all* our dealings have to remain a deep secret for the outside world. Even for these men of letters who might be in the same boat (with you as a navigator in publishing or even translating their English)—even for these men our dealings have to remain the most untouchable matter, not even to be *guessed* by them. . . . For, the world is buzzing with false friends—and even without them it is not so easy for good writers.

Yet the letter carries the good news that bookstore windows throughout the German-speaking countries are now displaying his books, and that he is writing reviews for German periodicals. This letter, significantly, is signed only "H."[29]

After 1952 the correspondence became sporadic. In the mid-1950s Jacob and his wife, Dora, returned to Europe, where they were almost constantly on the move, living in hotels for the most part; their return address always carried the notation "z.Zt." (at the time). Wherever they went, the Jacobs took with them a folder labeled "Propaganda," stuffed with newspaper clippings and correspondence with publishers.[30] Jacob continued to write, and boasted of the success he was achieving with his biographies of classical musicians and his cultural histories. The "fanfares" sounded "everywhere" in honor of his seventieth birthday came in for particular mention.[31] In the early 1960s the Winstons translated his biography of Mendelssohn.[32] They tried, without success, to interest a publisher in reissuing *Six Thousand Years of Bread* and also attempted to persuade Prentice-Hall to bring out Jacob's book on Mozart.[33] The correspondence continued until 1966, the year before Jacob's death, evidence of a long-lasting and durable friendship. But because of the Jacobs' peripatetic way of life, when word reached the Winstons, belatedly, of Jacob's death, they did not know where to find his widow.[34] Jacob's correspondence with the Winstons shows us a man who, despite his predilection for intrigue and his occasional self-absorbtion, also possessed great charm and resilience of spirit, as well as an unflagging capacity for work. Even under the most difficult of circumstances, including illness and lack of money, he continued to undertake the extensive research his works of fiction and nonfiction required. And despite his extraordinary productivity, he always paid close attention to questions of style, as his comments to the Winstons on the rhythm of his prose attest.[35]

Hans Sahl (1902–1993)

The correspondence between the poet, critic, and novelist Hans Sahl and the Winstons did not begin until 1958, when Sahl was looking for a translator for "poems, also a manuscript of a novel, and many essays that have appeared in Germany but not yet here."[36] Two years later Sahl resumed the correspondence, having just seen Walter Mehring and Erich Maria Remarque in Ascona (Switzerland) and been told by both of them that he should make every effort to get the Winstons to translate his novel.[37] From this correspondence we can see how much circumstances had changed for the refugees since the 1940s and early 1950s: Sahl had already found a publisher for his novel, and the Winstons' reputation was well established. They were so busy that, they replied, they would not be available for another eleven months.[38] But a sample translation done by another translator displeased Sahl, who himself had a long career translating plays into German.[39] Eventually the editor Julian Muller prevailed upon the Winstons to take on the translation, which they in fact delivered about seven months later.[40] Upon hearing rumors that they might do the book after all, Sahl wrote cordially in English to "THE ONE AND ONLY WINSTONS": "Please tell me when you intend to come to New York, so that I can receive you here with all the honors of visiting dignitaries. New York has to offer you: Sahl's home made chops and steaks, French cuisine, pretty girls, hard liquers. Man spricht Deutsch!"[41]

For all his cordiality, Sahl exhibited considerable anxiety even before he saw the translation. He wanted to visit the Winstons, who had not been able to come to New York, and make their acquaintance. He pictured them dissecting him at the dinner table—actually a surprisingly accurate image, for translators do gain intimate knowledge of their authors' idiosyncrasies and strengths from working so closely with their texts, and the Winstons often discussed translation matters, and authors, over meals.[42] Sahl's next letter, written after a visit of several days to his translators in Vermont, begins in English, referring jocularly to the Winstons' letter of invitation, which took up the tone of his initial invitation to them ("We could offer you some of the fried blubber and hardtack for which these arctic climes are famous"). He expresses gratitude for the discussions of "linguistic problems—please believe me when I say that I learned a lot about the difference between English and German style, more than I ever knew it existed (is that right, Clara, or are you going to change it?)." The prickliness implicit in the parenthetic remark manifests itself even more unmistakably in a postscript, written in German, in which Sahl complains that the Winstons have broken up a long sentence that he considers "very important for the entire book," thereby robbing it of "some of its punch."[43] In their reply, the Winstons point out that they broke up the sentence "precisely to keep its force, its 'punch.'"[44]

The Winstons must have confided to Julian Muller at Harcourt, Brace & World about the uncomfortable visit, for he responds, "The undersigned hereby deposes and states that he had no knowledge of any kind that an author thought about, inclined toward, made plans for, undertook transit for the purpose of, or actually did commit an invasion of the privacy of the translators engaged in the rightful pursuit of their profession."[45] This letter, like so many in the Winstons' correspondence, gives evidence of the warm relationships that developed between the translators and the editors or publishers, relationships that made it possible for the translators to intercede on occasion for their authors and also to receive backing when disputes with the authors arose.

The next few letters from Sahl to the Winstons are friendly, reporting on Sahl's impressions from a trip to Europe and expressing alarm about the international situation (it is the summer of 1961, just before and after the building of the Berlin Wall), and with the hyperalertness typical of the refugees, Sahl is fearful that a full-scale East-West confrontation is about to occur. One letter concludes:

> Dear translators, friends, fellow Americans, fellow pessimists and fellow victims of a merciless age. May I ask you in all modesty—what will become of us? Please add to your Vermont house a shelter for those whom you translated, so that we can translate each other in peace and security and untouched by fall-out (How nice it would be with H. E. Jacob, A. B. C. D. Sahl and the ghost of Thomas Mann, in a sort of underground-community devoted to good English and other occupational therapy).[46]

Although there is a sarcastic edge to Sahl's description of this underground community, his scenario in fact bears a strong resemblance to a Winston family fantasy, born of the protective feelings the translators developed for the "second-class" refugees. But the relationship with Sahl worsened after he received the completed translation. In one letter Richard Winston undertakes to explain why and how a translator may have to alter a detail in the original text in order to effect cultural transfer:

> You ask why we translate your milk warm from the cow into ice-cold milk. . . . Can't you see that the reason must have to do with the different responses of German and American readers? You present a man who is terribly hungry, longing for food. . . . Suddenly you ask this American reader to crave what he detests: *warm* milk, fresh from the cow. To the German, milk warm from the cow evokes feelings of pleasure; the American would only shudder.

Winston adds that he might keep the reference to warm milk

> if the object of the scene were to make the reader aware of the particular culture of the hungry man; if you wanted to bring the reader up short and remind him that a starving Arab dreams of fried locusts. . . . But . . . here Kobbe stands for general humanity, and there is no sense in slapping the reader in the face and reminding him that this man is a German . . . who likes his milk warm . . . unpasteurized—a wonder he lived long enough to get to Paris; he ought to have died of undulant fever long ago![47]

Later the editor would express his frustration with Sahl's insistence on being true to the German original at all costs; the conflict had apparently become so bitter that the editor gave the Winstons the option of not having their names appear on the translation. Yet in the same letter the editor expresses compassion for Sahl, who at the age of sixty had fathered a child with an incurable bone disease.[48]

After the book, *The Few and the Many*, appeared, the Winstons set aside their negative feelings about Sahl to write a letter to the *New York Times Book Review* defending the book, which the reviewer, Kay Boyle, had attacked.[49] And when Sahl complained that the publisher had failed to promote the book adequately—the kind of accusation often voiced by the refugees[50]—Richard Winston undertook to explain the realities of American publishing:

> He [the editor] and Harcourt Brace are as much victims of the system of American publishing as we are. Books can be suffocated to death even with the best of reviews; that has happened to Clara and me with our own books in the past, and with many translations. . . . Hans, please don't think I'm being the "hardboiled" and unfeeling American. . . . I speak out of discouragement and resignation; we've seen this happen so often to books of outstanding merit.[51]

Sahl remained unreconciled, and his relationship with the Winstons ended after their defense of his book and their attempts to moderate his expectations.

From this correspondence we can see that even after twenty years in America, Sahl had not shaken off his European assumptions, his understanding of the place of the writer in society. In Europe before the war, serious literature had mattered.[52] The economics of publishing, too, were very different from what the refugees had been accustomed to. In pre-Hitler Germany it was customary for publishers to provide regular, though modest, stipends to their authors—the twentieth-century equivalent of patronage. If writers supplemented these stipends with fees for reviews and articles, and perhaps some support from their families, they could maintain their café habit, go to the theater, and even afford the occasional holiday in Italy or on the French Riviera. Although they had all experienced the calamitous inflation of the early 1920s and then the depression, the writers had not been prepared for being both destitute and unrecognized. A number of organizations provided at least temporary support.[53] But the period between the refugees' arrival in the United States and the time when they began receiving restitution from the West German government was marked by unremitting anxiety about money.[54]

Curt Riess (1902–1993)

In his long lifetime Curt Riess wrote over one hundred books, covering an extraordinary range of subjects, from Joseph Goebbels to the actor Gustav Gründgens.[55] Unlike the other three writers discussed here, Riess was primarily a journalist. He came to the United States in 1934 as a correspondent for *Paris Soir*, and later returned to Europe as an American war correspondent, reporting in widely syndicated articles on Hitler's Germany, with a particular emphasis on espionage.[56] Riess thrived on intrigue, and had no hesitation about using others for his own ends. His acquaintance with the Winstons began in the late 1930s, when they translated his *Total Espionage*,[57] an account of the Nazis' spy system.

The first preserved letter in the Winstons' file is something of a bombshell: a copy of a letter from Richard Winston, written in 1946, in which he denounces the shoddiness of Riess's work, some of which, he alleges, verges on plagiarism, and characterizes Riess's relationship with him as increasingly "irksome and . . . exploitative." He calls attention to Riess's repeated promises of bonuses, "which have amounted, in all my collaboration with you, to exactly twenty-five dollars."[58] Apparently Riess's ego withstood this attack, and the relationship continued. The first letter from Riess in the file, dated 1947, finds him uncharacteristically gloomy: "How I managed to survive this year will remain a mystery to me, particularly on account of my illness, particularly on account of my inability to find any work." He says that he has nevertheless just completed his biography of Goebbels and has "plans to go to Europe and do many things. . . . I intend to write a novel dealing with life in Berlin after the 'liberation.'" He wants to know if the Winstons would be willing to work with him again, but he shows his usual lack of respect for the credit to which they were entitled as professionals: "My publisher feels that after I have written so many books in English . . . we cannot have the book translated 'officially.'"[59] In May 1951 Riess writes that he has sold a book and two articles, and wants to know what he would have to pay for having these, as well as several outlines, translated.[60] It is clear that he intends to pay for the translations himself;

indeed, many of the Winstons' early translations were paid for by the authors rather than the publishers. A subsequent letter brings outlines for articles on subjects such as "Twenty-four Hours in the Life of an American Spy in Germany," "The Comedy of Secret Service" (about spying in postwar Berlin), and "Adventures of a U.S. Agent behind the Iron Curtain."[61]

The letters that follow document a flurry of activity—books being turned out in a matter of months, articles being submitted, always under the greatest time pressure, which Riess tries to pass along to his translators. He implies that it is his projects that are keeping the Winstons afloat.[62] Occasionally he asks for their opinion of the material he is sending, but the questions are perfunctory.[63] In a letter written in 1953, the year he married the actress Heidemarie Hathayer, who had had a successful stage and screen career under the Nazis, Riess reveals the opportunism that obtained in his professional activity as well as in his personal life: "If the *Saturday Evening Post* is delighted with the book but objects to the ending, I'm happy to rewrite the last part. If there's a lot of money in a project, I can always come up with something."[64]

In 1958 Riess writes approvingly of the Winstons' plan to spend a good portion of the coming year in Zurich, where he and his wife have purchased a villa. He proposes a close collaboration: "My idea is to reconquer the American market. I think we should try to work out something together, that is, write a book together."[65] Two years later he writes: "I am here in New York and in hundreds of meetings. I have various things that should be of interest to you, primarily things of a financial nature."[66] That same year he asks, in English, for help with a matter he describes as "very important, very private. In order to get my German restitution, I must prove that at a certain time I was in very bad circumstances."[67] Five years later, despite the Winstons' annoyance with Riess's egotism, Richard Winston sent Riess's agent an outline of a novel that Riess had written under a pseudonym, with the comment: "I told him that no matter how busy I was, I would find time to do it, because I think it is far and away the best thing he has ever done. It provides insights into an aspect of the German phenomenon that few writers have examined . . . : the equivocal guilt and innocence of the great financiers and investors."[68]

After a gap of a few years, Riess discovered that Richard Winston was writing a biography of Thomas Mann and made an extraordinary suggestion:

> I would like to collaborate with you, without being named, more or less as your ghost writer. In the next few years I will have plenty of time, so I could come over and presumably live with you, since the children are out of the house now. Actually I wouldn't need to earn much money, or, to be precise any at all; it would be only my expenses and perhaps a bit of pocket money so I can buy myself a bottle of whiskey.[69]

Winston apparently did not respond to the offer,[70] but it is not difficult to imagine his reaction to being offered ghostwriting services by someone for whom he had performed the same service in the 1940s.

As Riess grew older, a sentimental tone crept into his letters. In 1976 he even ventured up to Vermont for a visit, and he invited the Winstons to stay with him in Switzerland "in case your dollars don't stretch far enough."[71] Although Riess was an inveterate opportunist and huckster, the connection between him and the Winstons endured for forty years; they were able to laugh at his self-importance, and grudgingly admired his ability to continue churning out books on any subject that he thought the market would bear.

Walter Mehring (1896–1981)

Walter Mehring was probably the most original writer among the four discussed here. A prominent member (and later historian) of the Berlin Dada group, he was known as the "Pupi-Dada," and in that capacity was photographed shortly after World War I with a bowler hat on his head and his neck sticking up through a chair whose seat had been removed.[72] Before the Nazi takeover he enjoyed a considerable reputation in Berlin for the chansons, poems, and skits he wrote for cabarets such as the famous "Schall und Rauch," for his essays and reviews, for a play, *The Merchant of Berlin* (1928), and many other works. Mehring embodied, more than the other writers discussed here, what the Nazis called a "rootless intellectual" (*heimatloser Geselle*). Exile became his literary topic long before he actually had to flee, and remained his lifelong preoccupation.[73] Together with Hans Natonek, Hertha Pauli (1909–1972), and Ernst Weiss (1882–1940), Mehring cabled Thomas Mann from France in early June 1940 asking him to help rescue the threatened writers.[74] This effort coincided with the establishment of the Emergency Rescue Committee.

Mehring met the Winstons in the early 1940s at Morning Star Farm in western Massachusetts, where they were living at the time, serving as farmhands in return for housing. Mehring was boarding at the farm, taking a break from the grim circumstances of his life in New York City. The first preserved letter of their correspondence, written in 1950, expresses Mehring's pleasure at having the Winstons translate *The Lost Library*, which he had begun writing during his time in the country. Like Sahl, Mehring had done translations, but his understanding of the art of translation complemented the Winstons'. In this first letter he quotes what he calls an "excellent definition" of translation that he has recently encountered: "A successful transmutation of thought and emotion from one language to another is both a technique, and, ultimately, a mystery. . . . [W]here German is general, the translator must often make his English specific."[75]

As installments of the translation reached him, Mehring made small suggestions, always delicately and humorously phrased. The letters contain repeated references to his wretched financial circumstances, for example: "I am wearing myself down, trying to come up with the bit of rent money through 'bit-parts.' It is too ridiculous—but we never have enough and are broke every weekend."[76]

When the book was completed, the editor at Bobbs-Merrill, Hiram Haydn, asked Jacques Barzun to vet the many literary references, then invited Richard Winston to come to New York for a final editing session. Haydn's letter reveals some of the reality of publishing the refugees, a reality that these writers seldom recognized: "I would like to suggest that you come down at our expense, but I am afraid the best we can do, in view of all the money already spent on this book and the likelihood of no very large sales, is to offer you a comfortable bed and peaceful surroundings."[77] Meanwhile, Mehring's agent, the refugee Barthold Fles (1902–1989), who also engaged in translation, editing, and publishing at various times, complained to Winston, "Frankly, I am somewhat annoyed—Walter hasn't even paid me my commission—neither on the first nor on the second payment—on the plea that he had debts."[78] When Mehring received the bound books, he quoted the jacket copy in a letter to the Winstons—"One hundred years from now, W. M.'s poems, essays, and novels will still be widely read"—and remarked, his signature humor barely concealing his anguish: "Paltry comfort! Transfer of authors' royalties into the hereafter remains highly problematic: 'Current Address Unknown: Addressee Presently Engaged in Transmigration of Souls.' . . . I would prefer a larger advance from our contemporaries." In this same letter Mehring reports that H. E. Jacob would write the *New York Times* review and wonders how much space Jacob will be given: "He is, like me, a 'second class refugee'—but for you and me it means a well-meaning reviewer, and for him some 30 dollars; so we all benefit!"[79]

Try as he might to put a good face on the matter, Mehring was dejected at being reviewed by a fellow refugee, and telephoned the Winstons "to hear a friendly voice." He apologizes in a subsequent letter for having spoken "rather incoherently" to Clara—Richard Winston was out in the barn milking the cow—and for "making so much fuss about [my book], as if it were the only important book you had to work on."[80] The Winstons' response, of which a draft in Clara's hand has been preserved, tries to put the question of the reviewer and the rewards of writing in perspective, suggesting that a reviewer who understands the milieu out of which the book comes is worth more than a stranger with a big name. "But I know—we all secretly long for the gesture of approbation from the Klamms of the Castle," they write, referring to Kafka's unfinished masterpiece. They urge Mehring to see the publication of the book

as the occasion for his debut and to recognize that expecting significant financial rewards would be unrealistic.[81] Understandably, Mehring responds with
sarcasm, but as usual it is rather gentle and self-mocking: "I am surprised to
learn from your letter that 'writing is unprofitable; especially the writing of
books.' Why didn't you tell me before. You would have spared me a lot of trouble."[82] A later letter brings word that Hannah Arendt and Kay Boyle have
praised the book, but that Bobbs-Merrill has allotted only a very small budget
to promotion—the common complaint. Mehring was starting another project,
however: "Sometimes I feel very enthusiastic with my new idea; sometimes depressed (when Marie Paul [his wife] comes back overworked and tired from her
job, while I was spending the whole day in great comfort at my writing table,
without earning a dime). Like every German, I pity my-self."[83]

As it turned out, The Lost Library was also reviewed (for the daily New York
Times) by Orville Prescott—the "objective" reviewer Mehring was hoping for.
The review calls The Lost Library "a sad and brilliant book," and presents Mehring as "a German author who has written twenty-four [books] . . . a man of
letters and a European intellectual . . . an exile who was pursued by his barba-
rous countrymen across much of Europe." Amid the praise, however, which
also applies to the translation, Prescott inserts these damning words: "This is
a profoundly European book, so European that parts of it will mean little to
American readers. There isn't much that even a well-read American can do but
blink and feel ignorant when he stumbles on such names as Josephin Peladan,
Oscar Panizza, Louise Labé, F. N. Marinetti, Barbey d'Aurevilly and Hugo
Ball."[84]

As an exchange of letters between Richard Winston and Hiram Haydn
indicates, the book did achieve a succès d'estime, which, however, did not
result in sales beyond the original printing of 5,500.[85] By November, Mehring
was deeply discouraged; Bobbs-Merrill would not be reprinting the book, there
were no copies in the bookstores, and he had fired his agent.[86] By February
1953, Mehring was feeling so desperate that he accepted a one-way ticket to
Zurich "bestowed on me through the courtesy of some moneyed well-wishers
(who decided it would be the best for me—a complete failure of a free lance
writer in a world of free enterprise—to try his luck in a backward continent."
He had some lectures and radio broadcasts lined up, and the German version
of The Lost Library was selling quite well.[87] This letter marks the end of the
preserved correspondence between Mehring and the Winstons. The rest of the
extant letters were written by his wife, the French painter Marie Paul. Shortly
after this trip, which he undertook alone, Mehring and his wife moved back
to Europe, where they lived very modestly, first in Zurich and later in Ascona.
During three visits of almost a year to Switzerland, the Winstons spent many
hours with the Mehrings. Walter would sit all day in cafés, drinking glass after

glass of white wine and doing some writing. He never had another book published in the United States, and the Winstons' efforts to interest publishers in
reissuing *The Lost Library* were politely rebuffed.[88] In Germany, Mehring was
gradually rediscovered. By the time of his death in 1981, a ten-volume edition
of his collected works had been undertaken by the Claassen publishing house,
edited by Christoph Buchwald, who in 1997 would be named managing director of the noted Suhrkamp publishing house.[89] On the hundredth anniversary
of Mehring's birth in 1996, the *Neue Zürcher Zeitung* devoted a long article to
him as the preeminent representative "of that era in German literary and
cultural history that extended from the end of Expressionism to exile and the
postwar period."[90]

THE WINSTONS' correspondence with these four literary exiles reveals four
very different personalities and temperaments, but also certain constants in
their response to their situation, chief among them an unflagging determination to assert themselves through the written word, even when they had little
prospect of being heard. Despite the unremitting anxiety and deprivation they
experienced during the Hitler period and its aftermath, these men lived very
long lives: only Jacob died in his seventies, while Mehring reached eighty-five
and both Riess and Sahl lived past ninety. They all survived long enough to
see at least some interest in their work and their life stories revive in the
German-speaking countries.[91] This initial sampling of four exiled writers' correspondence with their translators and editors suggests that much work remains to be done on these crucial three-way relationships.

Notes

1. See Ralf Georg Reuth, *Goebbels*, trans. Krishna Winston (New York: Harcourt
Brace, 1993), 19–39.

2. Unpublished letter from Walter Mehring to Richard and Clara Winston, June 19,
1951, collection of Krishna Winston. All unpublished letters referred to here come from
this collection; some are written in English, others in German. Translations are my
own. In 2004 the Winstons' professional correspondence and first editions of their
translations will be transferred to the Lilly Library at Indiana University, Bloomington,
for its collection on literary translation.

3. This idea provides the central conceit for Walter Mehring, *The Lost Library: The
Autobiography of a Culture*, trans. Richard and Clara Winston (Indianapolis: Bobbs-
Merrill, 1951). See also draft of a letter from H. E. Jacob to B. W. Huebsch on the back
of a letter from Jacob to Richard Winston, n.d. [March 21, 1951], in which Jacob refers
to having lost his library and most of his papers "during my concentration camp time
in Dachau and Buchenwald and my departure, which had to be undertaken in a great
rush."

4. See Thomas Mann, *Letters*, sel. and trans. Richard and Clara Winston (New York: Knopf, 1970), and *Diaries, 1918–1939*, trans. Richard and Clara Winston (New York: Abrams, 1982).

5. See Hans Natonek, *In Search of Myself*, trans. Barthold Fles, ed. Sugden Tilley (New York: Putnam's 1943), 57.

6. See Helmut Pfanner, *Exile in New York: German and Austrian Writers after 1933* (Detroit: Wayne State University Press, 1983), 95–96.

7. Sometimes they mocked themselves; see Natonek, *In Search*, 56, describing his visit to a relief agency for refugees the day after his arrival in New York: "I am meek. I am arrogant. Strong, yet weak. A prideful beggar. A Caliph of Bagdad in a coat of many patches."

8. Pfanner, *Exile*, quotes a letter from Leopold Heinemann, who apologizes for the misspellings in the letter and says that "from continued lack of food" he is "so weak that it takes all [his] energy to write at all" (72).

9. On the work of Varian Fry in rescuing these refugees, see Andy Marino, *American Pimpernel* (London: Arrow, 2000), 45–46. Two of the writers discussed in this essay, Walter Mehring and Hans Sahl, were rescued by Fry.

10. See Natonek, *In Search*.

11. This contention is confirmed by birth certificate no. 921, on file at the Berlin Standesamt (Bureau of Vital Statistics), 1/11; see *http://www.heinrich-eduard-jacob.de* under "Biographie."

12. H. E. Jacob, *Coffee: The Epic of a Commodity*, trans. Eden and Cedar Paul (London: Allen and Unwin, and New York: Viking, 1935).

13. H. E. Jacob: *The World of Emma Lazarus* (New York: Schocken, 1949); *Joseph Haydn: His Art, Times, and Glory* (New York: Rinehart, 1950).

14. H. E. Jacob to Richard Winston, March 10, 1951.

15. H. E. Jacob to Richard Winston, March 8, 1951.

16. H. E. Jacob to Richard Winston, March 10, 1951.

17. H. E. Jacob to Richard Winston, dated only "Frühlingsanfang" (beginning of spring, presumably March 21, 1951), with the letter to B. W. Huebsch on the back; H. E. Jacob, *Sage und Siegeszug des Kaffees* (Hamburg: Rowohlt, 1934).

18. H. E. Jacob to Richard Winston, April 23, 1951.

19. H. E. Jacob to Richard Winston, June 11, 1951.

20. H. E. Jacob to Richard Winston, June 20, 1951.

21. From an interview with Richard and Clara Winston conducted by Harry Zohn in the late 1970s. Tape in the possession of the author.

22. H. E. Jacob to Richard Winston, June 20, 1951.

23. H. E. Jacob to Richard Winston, June 27, 1951.

24. In the taped interview with Harry Zohn, the Winstons describe Jacob's review as damaging, a breach of the solidarity they felt the refugees owed one another. Hans Sahl, in *The Few and the Many*, trans. Richard and Clara Winston (New York: Harcourt, Brace & World, 1962), evokes the pervasive tensions and hostilities—political, professional, and personal—that beset refugee circles in New York.

25. H. E. Jacob to Richard Winston, November 3, 1951.

26. Hiram Haydn to Richard Winston, November 20, 1951.

27. H. E. Jacob to Richard Winston, November 24, 1951.

28. Richard Winston to Hiram Haydn, November 29, 1951 (carbon copy).

29. H. E. Jacob to Richard Winston, December 27, 1952.

30. I saw this folder during a visit to the Jacobs in Switzerland in 1960. A file of biographical documents and clippings listed among the holdings of the Akademie der Künste in Berlin may be this collection; see *http://www.adk.de/deutsch/verz_literatur_fst .html*.

31. H. E. Jacob to Richard Winston, April 13, 1960.

32. H. E. Jacob, *Felix Mendelssohn and His Times* (London: Barrie and Rockliff, and Englewood Cliffs, N.J.: Prentice-Hall, 1963).

33. See letter to Richard Winston from Clement Alexandre of Doubleday, October 24, 1960, and Richard Winston to Gladys Carr of Prentice-Hall, November 13, 1964 (carbon copy).

34. Richard Winston to Benjamin D. Webb, March 13, 1978 (carbon copy).

35. See, for example, H. E. Jacob to Richard Winston "written on the second Spring Day, a day under a blanket of snow" (March 22, 1951).

36. Hans Sahl to Richard Winston, September 11, 1958. Sahl had not succeeded in having books published in English; his only publication after his escape to the United States was a volume of poems, *Die hellen Nächte: Gedichte aus Frankreich* (New York: B. Fles Verlag, 1942). Nevertheless, Sahl stayed in the United States long after the other writers discussed here had returned to Europe—though not to reside in Germany. For statements by the many refugees who went back but refused to take up permanent residence in Germany, see Hermann Kesten, *Ich lebe nicht in der Bundesrepublik* (Munich: List, 1964).

37. Hans Sahl to Richard Winston, November 21, 1960.

38. Draft of Richard Winston to Hans Sahl, November 22, 1960.

39. Hans Sahl to Julian Muller of Harcourt Brace, November 27, 1960.

40. Julian Muller to Richard and Clara Winston, December 5, 1960 and September 14, 1961.

41. Hans Sahl to Richard and Clara Winston, February 13, 1961.

42. Hans Sahl to Richard and Clara Winston, May 19, 1961.

43. Hans Sahl to Richard and Clara Winston, May 30, 1961.

44. Draft of letter from Richard and Clara Winston to Hans Sahl, n.d. (June 1961).

45. Julian Muller to Richard Winston, June 12, 1961.

46. Hans Sahl to Richard and Clara Winston, September 14, 1961.

47. Richard Winston to Hans Sahl, October 6, 1961 (carbon copy).

48. Julian Muller to Richard Winston, May 9, 1962. The child died after three weeks. See Hans Sahl, *Das Exil im Exil* (Frankfurt: Luchterhand, 1991), 184.

49. Carbon of letter to the *New York Times Book Review* from Richard and Clara Winston, September 19, 1962.

50. Taped interview with Richard and Clara Winston by Harry Zohn. The Winstons

describe how the refugees often embarrassed them by appearing at the publishers' offices and demanding an audience with the sales staff. Walter Mehring would also go into bookstores and ask whether they had *"The Lost Library"* by Walter Mehring" (family reminiscence).

51. Draft of Richard Winston to Hans Sahl, n.d. (November 1962).

52. See Grete Weil, *My Sister, My Antigone*, trans. Krishna Winston (New York: Avon, 1984) 71, recalling the intellectual world of her youth: "There is no latest Thomas Mann anymore, no latest Gide or Mann book that one can keep track of, and not one that I absolutely must have the day it comes out."

53. See Natonek, *In Search,* 44–47.

54. See Pfanner, *Exile,* 68–83.

55. Curt Riess, *Joseph Goebbels: A Biography* (Garden City, N.Y.: Doubleday, 1948), and *Gustav Gründgens: Die klassische Biographie des grossen Künstlers* (Frankfurt am Main: Gutenberg, 1966).

56. Obituary by Wolfgang Saxon, *New York Times*, May 21, 1993, B8.

57. Published in 1941 by G. P. Putnam's Sons, New York. The extent of the Winstons' collaboration with Riess is difficult to determine because their names are omitted from many of the works to which they contributed, either as translators or as ghostwriters.

58. Richard Winston to Curt Riess, June 14, 1946 (carbon copy).

59. Curt Riess to Richard Winston, November 28, 1947.

60. Curt Riess to Richard Winston, May 23, 1951.

61. Enclosure with letter from Curt Riess to Richard Winston, June 6, 1951.

62. Curt Riess to Richard Winston, June 24, October 1, and November 11, 1951, and January 8, 1952.

63. E.g., Curt Riess to Richard Winston, July 13, 1953.

64. Curt Riess to Richard Winston, July 30, 1953.

65. Curt Riess to Richard Winston, October 12, 1958.

66. Curt Riess to Richard Winston, January 9, 1960.

67. Curt Riess to Richard Winston, November 22, 1960.

68. Richard Winston to Max Wilkinson, May 6, 1965 (carbon copy).

69. Curt Riess to Richard Winston, October 26, 1973.

70. Curt Riess to Richard Winston, April 28, 1976.

71. Curt Riess to Richard Winston, November 22, 1976 and February 5, 1979.

72. See Walter Mehring, *Berlin Dada* (Zurich: Schifferli, 1959), plate 6.

73. See Krishna Winston, "Idee und Sprache des Exils bei Walter Mehring" (honors thesis, Smith College, 1965).

74. Marino, *American Pimpernel,* 45–46. Weiss committed suicide before he could be rescued.

75. Walter Mehring to Richard and Clara Winston, [illegible] 22, 1950.

76. Walter Mehring to Richard and Clara Winston, January 16, 1951.

77. Hiram Haydn to Richard Winston, February 9, 1951.

78. Barthold Fles to Richard Winston, February 14, 1951.

79. Walter Mehring to Richard and Clara Winston, June 19, 1951.

80. Walter Mehring to Richard and Clara Winston, June 25, 1951.

81. Draft of Richard and Clara Winston to Walter Mehring, n.d. (June 1951).

82. Walter Mehring to Richard and Clara Winston, June 29, 1951.

83. Walter Mehring to Richard and Clara Winston, July 11, 1951.

84. Orville Prescott, "Books of the Times," *New York Times*, August 8, 1952.

85. Draft of Richard Winston to Hiram Haydn, August 28, 1951; Haydn to Winston, September 5, 1951.

86. Walter Mehring to Richard Winston, November 16, 1951; Barthold Fles to Winston, September 27, 1951.

87. Walter Mehring to Richard and Clara Winston, February 10, 1953.

88. Letters to Richard Winston from Fred Jordan of Grove Press, March 30, 1958, and Morris Philipson of Random House, June 6, 1961.

89. "Feuilleton," *Süddeutsche Zeitung*, November 13, 1997. Buchwald left Suhrkamp in 2000.

90. *Neue Zürcher Zeitung*, April 29, 1996, 23.

91. The durability and value of Jacob's works of cultural history can be seen from the reissue of his books *Six Thousand Years of Bread* (New York: Lyons and Burford, 1997) and *Coffee: The Epic of a Commodity* (Short Hills, N.J.: Burford, 1998). Jacob is the only one of the writers discussed here for whom a Web site has been established: *http://www.heinrich-eduard-jacob.de*. Hans Sahl's collected works, *Gesammelte Werke*, ed. Klaus Schöffling (Zurich: Ammann, 1983), including his memoirs, were published in eight volumes almost ten years before his death. Riess continued publishing without interruption until the year before his death. He wrote his memoirs, *Das war ein Leben! Erinnerungen* (Munich: Langen Müller, 1986), in which he says not a word about his translators or any difficulties he might have experienced in exile. His next-to-last work was a tribute to his wife, *Die Frau mit den hundert Gesichtern: Requiem für Heidemarie Hatheyer* (Düsseldorf: Droste, 1991). In 1981 Mehring's eighty-fifth birthday was celebrated in Zurich; see Eugen Züst, *Feier zum 85. Geburtstag von Walter Mehring, in Anweenheit des Jubilars* (Zurich, 1981). In December of that same year, the Predigerkirche in Zurich became the site of a memorial service; see Eugen Züst, *Gedenkfeier für Walter Mehring* (Zurich, 1981). The first book-length study of Mehring appeared two years after his death: Frank Hellberg, *Walter Mehring: Schriftsteller zwischen Kabarett und Avantgarde* (Bonn: Bouvier, 1983).

IV

CODA

The exile is a stranger even to his grave.

<small>ANTRANIK ZAROUKIAN</small>

TO BE AN exile is to have a special status and to represent a
unique social type. One is different from all but those who
share the same fate of having been forced to flee and seek
refuge on a foreign shore. The dispossessed are sometimes
disoriented, often dependent, and ever conscious of their
foreignness. For those who are refugees, that persistent
awareness of difference is something that colors thoughts,
feelings, and interactions with others throughout the life
course. Understandably, many see it as a curse. But for some
refugees, estrangement and marginality may be turned into a
paradoxical advantage: heightening awareness of many things
others take for granted; providing distance for more objective
assessments of social realities; serving as a vehicle for both
introspection and social commentary. In skilled hands, the
"outsider within" status of the articulate refugee provides
others with a vicarious sort of insight into a realm that is
otherwise difficult to comprehend: the social, political,
psychological, and personal meaning of exile.

A stunning example of this—and a reprise of the principal
leitmotif of this volume, is provided by the thoughtful
recollections of two Cuban refugees, a father, Rubén D. Rumbaut,
a psychiatrist and poet, and his son, Rubén G. Rumbaut, a
sociologist and specialist on immigration and refugee issues.
Rubén G. is also a member of a special group he labels "the one
and a half generation," that is, the children of exiles who arrive in
their country of asylum already aware of their estate, members of
an uprooted cohort but still young enough to be socialized (or
resocialized) where they are resettled.

The contribution of the Rumbauts that follows is in three
parts: commentaries by each dating back some twenty-five years

and then a reexamination of their personal and professional thoughts, written in the form of a dialogue between them. The entire selection is a fitting coda to our examination of some aspects of the anatomy of exile, and it ends with a coda of its own.

Self and Circumstance

Journeys and Visions of Exile

RUBÉN D. RUMBAUT AND RUBÉN G. RUMBAUT

FOREWORD

Rubén G. Rumbaut

"I AM MY self and my circumstance," wrote José Ortega y Gasset, the Spanish philosopher, on the eve of World War I, in his *Meditations on Quixote*.[1] The self in exile, and the circumstances of exile, are as varied as human character and human history. Forced uprooting from one's homeland and community—*coerced homelessness*—may be the common crisis that confronts all exiles and refugees, but such groups are affected by, perceive, and react to their changed and changing circumstances in different ways. Exile is not a uniform journey but many different journeys, and "it" cannot be grasped by a single vision, but requires many—reflecting the different vantages and framings of different selves, and indeed of the same self over time, in circumstances that never stay the same. The meaning of exile, and of home, varies—not least as a function of age and generation, of biography and history, of self and circumstance.

Over a quarter of a century ago, in May 1976, my father and I, a psychiatrist and a sociologist, teamed together to offer our reflections and perspectives on the experience of exile. Under a common title, "Two Generational Perspectives on the Experience of Exile," we each presented a short paper on this theme at the annual meeting of the American Society of Adolescent Psychiatry; these follow, unedited, and constitute the first half of this chapter.[2] In December 2000 we collaborated again at the invitation of Peter Rose, adjusting and updating our respective visions and journeys with the passage of time. Those reflections, which were presented at a national symposium, "The Anatomy of Exile," at Smith College, constitute the second half of this chapter.

Back then, at the ASAP meetings, my father's paper offered a personal account, describing how we came from Cuba into exile in July 1960, a family of seven—he had turned thirty-eight the week before, and I was on the eve of my twelfth birthday—clueless as to the journeys that awaited us all in the years to come. But there we were, in 1976, just blocks from the place in Miami where we had first landed—he was by then fifty-three, I was twenty-seven—speaking in a language neither of us had spoken when we arrived, trying to make sense of the profoundly affecting experience we shared in common. He spoke as a survivor of "four shocks"—including "exile shock," a concept he coined to distinguish it from other phenomena. I spoke from the vantage of the "one-and-a-half" generation, the term I coined to distinguish between the first-generation adult protagonists (literally, "first actors") of the decision to go into exile, and the generation of their children, who as deuteragonists ("second actors") tend to be free of the impulse for self-justification that drives their parents' exilic vision.

And here we were, in 2000—he was now seventy-eight, having lived more than half his life in the United States, and I was about the same age as he was back in 1976—trying to do so again, older and wiser, to some ineluctable extent trapped by history and character, by time and self and circumstance, but still drawn to the experience of *el exilio*, to that "big bang" that so long ago set us off in a journey whose destination, besides the grave, remains as uncertain now as it was then. To be sure, our remarks on that occasion were not intended to encompass or summarize, even in a nutshell, the years of clinical work, empirical research, and scholarly reflection that had occupied and preoccupied each of us in efforts to understand the varieties of contemporary immigrants and refugees and their modes of adaptation. Instead, taken together, this chapter consists of a selective set of reflections, spanning a quarter century of changing circumstances, of two selves, two journeys, two visions, two voices, two generational perspectives on the experience of exile—but one solidary collaboration, now as then.

I. FOUR SHOCKS: A PERSONAL ACCOUNT
Rubén D. Rumbaut

        I came to this country in July 1960. I was then in my late thirties, a physician, a psychiatrist. My family accompanied me: my wife and our five children, consisting of three boys (ages eleven, ten, and nine) and two girls (ages seven and five). A sixth child, a girl, was born later, in 1963.

We came directly from Havana to Miami, to a small hotel on the beach. We had never expected expatriation, not even in our bleakest moments, and were not really prepared for it. On leaving Cuba we were hopeful that our absence was going to be rather short, perhaps two or three years. We tried to protect the children from the pains and agonies of the decision and preparations for leaving, our fears of the unknown, and the prospect of a separation from the homeland. We waited until the school year was over and left during vacation time. Therefore, they spent the initial weeks of exile enjoying sea, sand, and sun.

The events of 1961 [the Bay of Pigs invasion and its aftermath] persuaded us that our stay was going to be prolonged. In consequence, we applied ourselves to learning English, and I prepared myself for taking the ECFMG [Foreign Medical Graduates] examination. On passing the exam, I accepted a psychiatric position at a Veterans Hospital in Albuquerque, New Mexico, where we resided for almost five years. To fulfill the requirements of the Board of Psychiatry and Neurology, I then went to the Menninger School of Psychiatry in Topeka. Lastly, we moved to Houston, where I received my board certification. Since then I have been involved in academic and hospital psychiatry.

In these sixteen years of residence in the United States, we have lived in Florida, New Mexico, Kansas, and Texas. Our children have passed through kindergarten, primary and secondary school, college and university, not only in the four states already mentioned but also in Missouri, Massachusetts, California, and Washington, D.C. Three have married native-born Americans. My wife, in addition to taking excellent care of the home, the children, and the frequent moves, worked during part of the process. We have now a native-born American child and grandchild. Difficulties, hard work, long studies, competition, adversities, and acculturation under pressure have not been alien to any member of the family.

Exile in this country is not a new historical experience for the Cubans. During the first Independence War (1868–78) and again on the occasion of the second and final Independence War (1895–98), Cubans came here by the thousands. Popular resistance against Machado in the thirties and Batista in the fifties brought Cuban exiles to these shores once again. Nothing, however, can compare with the massive exodus since Castro took power in January 1959. Of the approximately 7 million people who populated the island then, 1 million have gone into exile, the great majority of them to the USA.

Among the early exiles were fifteen thousand Cuban children who were sent ahead by their parents when the revolution turned toward a totalitarian path. The U.S. and Cuban governments permitted children under sixteen to come here under waivers of visa, while their parents were required to possess visas. Unfortunately, intervening events made it extremely difficult for the adults to get them. As a result, hundreds upon hundreds of those "Operation Peter Pan" children had to be placed with relatives or friends, in foster homes, or in institutions (including orphanages) scattered across 110 American cities. Some of those children, raised in poor homes in Cuba, ended in rich foster homes here, while some had the reverse experience. A percentage of these children were deliberately discouraged from speaking Spanish, while other children, confused and angry at what they interpreted as a "desertion" by their parents, suppressed or repressed the knowledge of their native language. In any case, those children who were not accompanied by parents obviously underwent a

different psychological experience than those who were. Some were reunited
with their parents in a matter of months, while some remained separated for
a long period of time. Some never saw their parents again.[3]

For my wife and me, the decision to leave a dearly loved country entailed
an agony that lasted for months. New decisions and personal trials followed,
in never-ending succession. The ideological struggle consumes part of the time
and energies of any refugee; the survival struggle another part; the duties
toward family, job, and the host society yet another part. One feels torn between diverse moral and ideological imperatives. Several dilemmas ensue: Resettlement? Change of professions, specialties, fields, and goals? Retraining?
Private, hospital, or academic practice? Board certification? Other important
decisions need to be made: Should one increase income by multiple simultaneous means, or study and prepare again for the future after having seen one
"future" evaporate before one's very eyes, or simply work hard in one's profession and hope for the best? Lastly, in what way should we proceed with the
children's education?

In addition to our private struggles, we had to fight against other odds. We
came to this country on the threshold of marked social, cultural, and political
upheavals. For example, our exile paralleled in time the Vietnam War. We have
witnessed the assassination of one president and of his brother (a presidential
candidate), the murder of a Nobel Prize–winner, the resignation of another
president and a vice president, and the attempted assassination and crippling
of another presidential candidate. All this in the face of the senseless violence,
the campus unrest, the city riots, the flower children, the drug epidemic, and
the profound changes in social mores, sex roles, sexual values, religious beliefs,
and lifestyles. Finally, our exile has coincided with a period of world turbu-
lence and with an extraordinary turning point in history.[4]

FOR LACK of a better concept, I will attempt to describe the impact of all
these things with the worn-out word "shock." I believe we have gone through
four of them: "cultural shock," "exile shock," "future shock," and "generational shock."

In the process of going from the Cuban culture into the American culture,
we found a series of similarities and dissimilarities. It was pleasant to deal with
the former and difficult to cope with the latter. The Cuban pace was slower,
less competitive, with less emphasis on unrelenting work and more on leisure;
families were more patriarchal and close-knit, children were more protected
and watched, and premarital virginity of women was highly esteemed. Inter-
personal relationships tended to be warmer, noisier, more expressive, and less
formal. Individualistic trends were strong. The Cubans are (according to Erna

Ferguson, an American author) "the fastest talkers in the world." Quick, clever, and long-winded, conversation, humor, gestures, music, dance, politics, journalism, oratory, and sports flourish among them. Lack of foresight and careful planning, superficiality and frivolity were considered national defects. Despite strong Spanish and Catholic traditions, religious adherence was rather nominal. Devoted churchgoers in Cuba were always less than 10 percent of the population. People, traditionally Christian, nevertheless had moral guidelines more hedonistic than puritanical and more permissive than strict. Parents and children treated each other with a familiarity and informality far different than in Spain and even other Ibero-American countries, although independence from parental influence and marriage were habitually achieved later than in the United States. We found it more difficult to adapt to the "rat race"—"rush, rush, rush," "bigger is better," "time is money," "mind your own business," "follow the arrow," "get to the point," "go through channels," and "always be on time." We found it disconcerting that the religious concept "in God we trust" appears printed not on religious medals but on all the coins and the paper money, as if the faith—just in case—ought to be backed by the omnipotent American dollar. We found alien aspects of food, climate, distance, mobility, family separation and fragmentation, early departure of the children from the family, unrestricted freedom for girls, and what seemed to us too much routine, scheduling, and predictability of numerous aspects of daily life.

The process of transculturation has been more difficult, above all, for the women. It was also harder for the black Cubans than for the white Cubans, for the older than for the younger, and for the nonprofessional and less educated than for the professional and better educated. The children fared better. Their cerebral cortex, as Wilder Penfield postulated,[5] is still "uncommitted" before adolescence; thus, they learn new languages without difficulties and without an accent. Paraphrasing the concept with literary license, I would also speak of their "uncommitted heart." In contradistinction, the hearts of the adults are already committed to their native soil, and so the land cannot be left behind without tearing apart some of the invisible fibers of the heart.

On the positive side, we found the same basic background: a Judeo-Christian, Greek-Roman historical tradition; same alphabet, grammar, schooling, sciences, and arts; similar encompassing Western culture and fundamental values. In addition to geographical proximity and historical ties, all these similarities made many things easier than they would have been otherwise. The "cultural shock" existed but in itself was not of major proportions.

"Exile shock" is a different thing. It entails much more than simply moving from one culture to another. The refugee is the reluctant immigrant, a person who has lost his homeland against his will, and whose bridges are burned behind him. He cannot return at will. The length of his expatriation, the separation from relatives and friends, and the change of the political situation in his country are not in his hands. Even communication with his compatriots does not rest in his hands. This complex, multidetermined feeling of loss, helplessness, hopelessness, frustration, rage, and sadness is the essence of the exile experience, and, as such, is different from the "culture shock" just described and from the slow adaptation of a voluntary immigrant to the chosen new land of his dreams.

Periodically the media refer to the Cubans' "success story" in the United States. I will not argue with that evaluation, but I will add a note of caution. Success derives from exemplary performance but says little about how people feel inside. Sadness and depression derive from experiences of loss, uprootedness, uncertainty, conflicting loyalties, and isolation, and frequently represent the silent inner price that has to be paid for the outer, acclaimed victory. Parallel to almost every public "success story" of an adult Cuban refugee, there is a private "boat and raft" story of escape, tears, blood, sweat, and toil which have left deep-seated psychological scars.

"Future shock" is defined as the shattering stress and disorientation that can be induced in individuals by subjecting them to too much change in too short a time: a reaction to vertiginous change.[6] The pace of communication, transportation, information, and reproduction has accelerated so much, and human events are accumulating with such speed, that the future appears to be coming toward us with the velocity of a meteor. There is almost no way to prepare for it reasonably and calmly, or to assimilate adequately the changes already upon us in the present. This phenomenon is worldwide and fairly recent. It has been incubating for years, to be sure, but has only been perceived, recognized, and labeled during the decade of the sixties—the same decade that saw the beginnings of the Cuban exile as well as the turmoil within American society.

Margaret Mead, with her comprehensive, telescopic view of mankind's evolution, has made a diagnosis that implies another more profound and unique kind of shock. In her book *Culture and Commitment: A Study of the Generation Gap*, she describes what I am labeling here "generational shock." In her opinion, until today mankind has evolved through two main types of cultures: the *postfigurative* ones, in which children learn principally from their forebears, and the *cofigurative* ones, in which both children and adults learn from their peers. We are now entering a period, new in history, in which we, the adults, will have to learn from our children: a *prefigurative* culture. We have at this moment, simultaneously available for the first time, examples of the way men have lived at every period of the last fifty thousand years. In almost poetic tones she affirms:

> Today, nowhere in the world are there elders who know what the children know, no matter how remote and simple the societies in which the children live. In the past there were always some elders who knew more than any children, in terms of their experience of having grown up within a cultural system. Today there are none. It is not only that parents are no longer guides, but that there are no guides, whether one seeks them in one's own country or abroad.

Lastly, talking about our generation, she gives us these thought-provoking statements:

> No generation has ever known, experienced, and incorporated such rapid changes. . . . They know more about change than any other generation has ever known and so stand, over, against, and vastly alienated, from the young, who by the very nature of their position, have had to reject their elders' past. . . . We have to realize that no other generation will ever experience what we have experienced. In this sense we must recognize that we have no descendants, as our children have no forebears. At this breaking point between two radically different and closely related groups, both are inevitably very lonely, as we face each other knowing that they will never experience what we have experienced, and that we can never experience what they have experienced.[7]

And so, here I am, survivor of four different kinds of "shocks," giving you my generational perspective of the experience of exile in the 1960s, and sharing this tribune with my eldest son. The eleven-year-old youngster who, from this very street, looked with inquiring eyes at the USA on the day of our arrival is now a sociologist working on his Ph.D. thesis, and still inquiring. In the style of the times, I just did my thing for the audience, and now he is going to do his thing. In so doing, we both hope that we are being useful to you while demonstrating how, despite all the "shocks" and all the "gaps," two generations still can work smoothly together for a common, worthwhile goal.

II. THE ONE-AND-A-HALF GENERATION: CRISIS, COMMITMENT, AND IDENTITY
Rubén G. Rumbaut

The experience of exile is an increasingly frequent phenomenon in a rapidly changing world that at once determines and is determined by it. While the fact of forced uprootedness from one's community—*coerced homelessness*—is the common crisis that confronts all refugee groups, whatever the diversity of their situation, such groups are affected by, perceive, and manage their changed circumstances in different ways. Any phenomenology of exile can give only a tentative and incomplete rendering of an experience that, like any other relation of self and social circumstance, needs to be placed in its larger historical, political, and economic context if it is to be adequately understood. Here I can sketch only some general themes of the experience of Cuban exile groups in the United States in the 1960s, focusing on the relation between the parent generation and a youth that reached adulthood in exile, a youth in transition in reference both to the new society and to its ethnic origins.

I follow the usage of the concept of "youth" as a stage of life intervening as a "psychosocial moratorium" between the stages of precocious adolescence and mature adulthood.[8] The possibility of this type of moratorium prior to full absorption into the labor force is a recent historical phenomenon, made institutionally possible for other than elite youth by the lengthening of the formal educational process in developed industrial societies. And I focus on children of Cuban exiles who were born in Cuba but have come of age in the United States—what I would label the "one-and-a-half" generation rather than the "second" generation of children born here—for whom the notion of being in "exile" from a Cuban homeland (though not necessarily a Cuban heritage) may apply neither by definition nor by self-conception.

This discussion is necessarily limited and selective; in particular, I make no mention here of the Cuban Revolution of 1959, nor of the complex of motives that led large sectors of Cuban society to emigrate. Instead, from a personal perspective, I will suggest some observations on the themes of exile, youth, and identity formation in the context of the general cultural crisis of the United States in the last decade.

Some Elements of the Experience of Exile

The experience of exile can be conceived as a dialectic of loss and reconstruction, entailing a prolonged inner agony (from the Greek *agonia*, "a struggle or contest for victory," and *agonistes*, "actor"), marked by a persistent conflict of loyalties and manifesting identifiable coping patterns in the expatriate's response to severe stress. Psychosocially, it involves an arduous process of dislocation and relocation, uprootedness and new growth, anomie and adaptation. In the process of acting to reconstruct a meaningful social world in a new country, the exile is challenged to resolve dual crises: a "crisis of loss" (coming to terms with the past) and a "crisis of load" (coming to terms with the present and immediate future).

On the one hand, exiles are by definition "losers" in sociopolitical conflicts. They lose or are separated from home and homeland, family and friends, work and social status, material possessions, and meaningful sources of identity and self-validation. Refugees from war-torn contexts in particular are also often traumatized by violent events prior to and during flight, including life-threatening experiences and the death of significant others. On the other hand, the exile is at the same time overloaded with compelling pressures to survive, find shelter and work, learn a different language, and adjust to a radically changed environment, often amid conditions of poverty, prejudice, minority status, pervasive uncertainty, and "culture shock."[9] The magnitude of the "shock" and the ability to cope with it, in turn, depend on the *social distance* traveled from place of origin to place of destination.

In the Cuban case, the arduousness has been mitigated by a variety of factors: (1) the resources of the exiles as a group, including their comparatively high level of education and occupational experience and technical skills, their familiarity with U.S. society, and their ideological congruence with dominant U.S. political values; (2) the creation of a network of ethnic communities, the most salient example of which is the teeming colony of "Little Havana" in Miami, which permits the maintenance of a vigorous sense of collective identity and ethnic consciousness; and (3) the organized reception accorded the refugees by American public and private agencies, which facilitated their entry and subsequent resettlement.[10] Indeed, structurally the Cuban emigration to the United States has been aptly described as a "golden exile,"[11] and one that contrasts sharply, particularly in social class origins and rapid economic advancement, with previous mass migrations of the nineteenth and twentieth centuries.

If exile exerts inordinate psychological pressures and dilemmas, the relation of the exile to the host culture is also in part characterized by what has been called the "objectivity" and the "doubtful loyalty" of the stranger.[12] Unlike the native, who typically takes for granted the assumptions of his or her culture, the stranger brings a more critical if estranged vantage to the new situation, a vantage that combines at once elements of distance and nearness, indifference and involvement. The exile as stranger is not bound "to worship the idols of the tribe";[13] although a commitment is retained to one's own, he or she is not bound by the customary commitments, conventions, and prejudices of the host society. As a marginal person, the exile surveys and questions the new set of life circumstances with an attitude of social and cultural skepticism. "Culture shock" interrupts the normal flow of everyday life and reveals the relativity and precariousness of conventional social arrangements. Thus it is one of the ironies of exile that, despite the practical and psychological problems it inflicts, the very condition of uprootedness, in forcing the individual to reconstruct his or her life with a newfound and vivid awareness that it is far less guaranteed than it seems, can potentially free him or her to transcend the accepted constraints that bind native members to their group.

To be sure, the meaning of exile is interpreted variously by expatriates occupying different generational and socioeconomic locations. For example, the Cuban case is seen ideologically by expatriate groups as fundamentally a political exile, a political and moral decision to renounce not one's homeland but the policies of a revolutionary regime (although more recent expatriates appear to be less "pushed out" by political conditions than "pulled out" by hopes of economic self-advancement). To the parent generation, as the protagonists (from the Greek *protos* and *agonistes*, meaning "first actors") in the decision to leave, going into exile is a crucial act of self-definition and represents a profound loss and a profound commitment. Their response typically demands a prolonged mourning of that loss and a vigorous justification of that decision; a tendency to idealize both the status quo ante and the society that offers asylum; a bitter resistance to interpretations that denigrate the meaning of their commitment and threaten ego integrity; a sense of the provisionality of their exile and a lingering wish to return to the homeland under new political circumstances.

But to the generation of their children, deuteragonists (from *deuteros* and *agonistes*, "second actors") in this drama, exile carries a different scheme of relevances and represents less a personal loss than a discontinuity with one's origins, less a personal commitment than an inherited circumstance. Their adaptive response, sometimes in reaction to perceptions of ethnic discrimination in the host society, may lead to a firm sense of ethnic pride as a source of meaning and identity, but it is essentially freed of the impulse to justify and protect the parents' worldview; it demands solidarity with the family's common predicament and its perception of a shared crisis rather than with the particular ideological allegiances of the parent generation; and for the generation of youth, the problems of forging new beginnings lack the intense affective significance that this process carries for the adult protagonists, who lived the original agony of opting for exile and who are defined by its consequences.

In short, the relations of parent and youth generations in exile reflect their differing vantages and modes of response and adaptation, and include elements of cohesion and continuity as well as conflict and discontinuity—which are shaped in turn by a set of factors, ranging from their age at arrival to their pace of acculturation, and to the political, economic, social, and cultural contexts of their exodus and resettlement. To understand the *inter*generational and *intra*generational experience of exile requires a look at the politics of commitment as well as at the psychology of adaptation.

Some Elements of the Experience of Youth

Clearly, any understanding of youth in exile requires a prior understanding of the phenomenon of youth generally. Let me turn, then, to a consideration of some elements of the experience of youth, particularly the problem of ego identity. The abundant energy and vitality of youth are no doubt what led a wry George Bernard Shaw to remark that youth is too good a thing to be left to the young. Youth involves a process of self-discovery and experimentation in significant areas of social life: the sexual and the political, the cultural and the economic, the educational and the occupational. Youth as a stage of life involves both a developmental and a social transition, a sojourn for values and identity which is both prolonged and made more problematic in continually changing modern capitalist societies characterized by an instability of values and identity.

The question of identity, which frames what Erikson has called the "crisis" of youth,[14] is not exhausted by the psychological dynamics of one's native origins and childhood identifications nor by the structure of one's social circumstances. Certainly the process called "self" is shaped by the concrete interplay of one's character and society and is ultimately confirmed by others, but it is not merely the product or reflection of a fixed reality. Ego identity is also the creative and ongoing expression of one's choices and commitments, of one's *praxis* in the world. Indeed, the coherence of any sense of identity and personal wholeness is achieved largely through commitment.[15] The circumstance of exile—one that is to some extent paralleled within the United States by conditions of rapid change and mobility in a society increasingly eroding a sense of community—presents the youth with a more ambiguous framework of obstacles, opportunities, and often obsolete models within which one must commit oneself to a style of "fidelity"[16] that constitutes an active expression of identity. Put differently, among the chief tasks of identity formation is "the development of an 'ideology,' that is, of a philosophy of life, a basic outlook on the world which can orient one's actions in adult life,"[17] a task made more difficult in the context of present-day U.S. society.

For a generation of youth in exile, the formative dialogue is with their "psycho-historical actuality,"[18] that is, with their context, one shared primarily with American peers who form their actual network of relationships and affiliations, rather than within Cuban enclaves which are no longer central to their lives. For certain sectors of this "one-and-a-half" generation of youth, particularly student groups, it was the general crisis of the United States in the 1960s that presented the context for ideological commitment and identity formation, a context sustained by the development of a youth counterculture and in which youth movements themselves became a principal agency of change and challenge to established arrangements. Generational conflict was sharpened and accelerated by this period of profound societal conflict: a period of raised social consciousness and struggle for ideals of social justice; of radicalization and resistance, revolt and repression, polarization and delegitimation of national authority, which tore the bonds of generation and community; of confrontation with the contradictions of American society, developing first through an identification with a growing civil rights movement and finally expanding to a general critique of American institutions, both nationally (where the focus was on issues of racism and inequality) and internationally (where the focus was on issues of imperialism and war).[19] It was, whatever the nature of our response to it, a period of flux and upheaval which has indelibly affected us all.

I have been referring to "parent" and "youth" generations in a broad and somewhat indiscriminate way. Like any other social category, the concept of "generations" becomes elusive on close inspection: a "generation" (like a "social class" or an "ethnic group") is formed by the nature of the bonds that unite its members, by their consciousness of and participation in a common condition, by their mode of collective response to their historical actuality.[20] There is, of course, considerable diversity within generational units. Still, I think the following generalization applies: if the parent generation in exile was defined by the events of the Cuban Revolution of the 1950s and its aftermath—if that was the decisive crisis of their experience—then, and with not a little irony, the Vietnam War of the past decade defined significant segments of the youth generation; that, more than their own inherited exile, was the decisive crisis of their experience. And yet, despite the nature of generational conflict precipitated by these events, it is precisely the *shared* circumstance of exile—however differently is has defined and been defined by parent and youth generations, and however differently it has shaped ideology and identity—which remains a singular bond between them, a continuing source of generational solidarity, enrichment, and mutual confirmation.

Finally, with respect to the issue of youth in transition and its relevance to this audience, these considerations contain some implications for contemporary psychiatry and social science, and here it may be well to conclude with the following observation by Erik Erikson:

> Our understanding of these processes is not furthered by the "clinical" reduction of [youth] phenomena to their infantile antecedents and to an underlying dichotomy of drive and conscience. [Youth's] development comprises a new set of identification processes, both with significant persons and with ideological forces, which give importance to individual life by relating it to a living commu-

nity and to ongoing history, and by counterpointing the newly won individual identity with some communal solidarity.[21]

Youth act in the world, and are not merely acted upon (or "act out"); they determined their world and are not simply determined by "heredity" or "environment"; they create new realities and are not just an echo of their surroundings. A psychiatry or social science that becomes little more than a technique for a general adjustment is impoverished and misses the promise of its profession: to lend a radical sagacity to human problems within their irreducible historical actuality.

III. LOT'S WIFE: LOOKING BACK AT HOME AND EXILE
Rubén D. Rumbaut

At the annual meeting of the American Society for Adolescent Psychiatry, held in Miami Beach in May 1976, my eldest son and I presented papers on the theme of "Two Generational Perspectives on the Experience of Exile." Today, a quarter century later, in an unexpected and extraordinary opportunity, we were invited again, this time by Peter Rose and Smith College, to touch on the same subjects. The occasion is so rare in history that we did not hesitate to accept immediately. So here we are, repeating the immortal phrase of Friar Luis de León, spoken several centuries ago, when he was returned to his chair at the University of Salamanca after many years of prison, censorship, and strict vigilance by the Inquisition: "Como decíamos ayer . . ." (As we were just saying . . .).

My first contact with the idea of exile came early on, in my childhood, when my parents brought home a set of books they thought would be good for my education—about twenty volumes, entitled *Tesoro de la Juventud* (Treasury for Youth), made up of encyclopedic essays and stories on all sorts of topics, all illustrated. One was about the effect of Beethoven's music on its listeners. Another showed the deck of a ship full of people about to leave their homeland, coming from Europe to the United States. The image stayed engraved in my mind as an example of the effect on people of that uprooting experience— of the painful separation from the homeland, and of the sadness on the faces of the people as they left all that behind. Ever since, that idea, that concept, has been present in my mind, in my subconscious, though I never suspected that one day I would become one of those people. I am sure those early memories inform something of the substance of "A Psalm for Refugees: Lot's Wife"—a poem I would write several decades later to portray the image of the disobeying wife who looked back at her homeland as more faithful to it than those who moved on and never looked back, as an object of honor and not of calumny, as a symbol of fidelity and not of disparagement—and even seep into my experience of exile itself.

To my previous report and personal account of 1976 I would now add several chapters. During these last twenty-five years I have suffered important losses: my dear beloved wife in 1997, after fifty years of companionship and engagement and marriage; recent losses of a son-in-law and a daughter-in-law, of my home in Houston, and my recent move to San Marcos, Texas, earlier this year. It is a miracle of sorts that I am still physically able to dictate these notes from my new home in Texas. My medical history during the last decade has included diseases, accidents, and surgeries. I had a triple bypass heart operation, a gall bladder extirpation, two cataract operations; and I have also suffered since 1997 from a gait disorder, exhaustively explored by clinicians and neurologists without satisfactory diagnosis or treatment, to the exclusion of all the usual suspects, from Lou Gehrig's disease to Parkinson's, brain or spinal tumors, infarcts and organic sequelae. (In view of all this mystery I have decided to call it the Rumbaut syndrome, because every physician has the right to call an unexplained syndrome by his own name, especially when he suffers from it and no one has come out with a definite conclusion.) At any rate, I'm suffering it now from the neck down and need a tripod to walk, but from the neck up I feel OK. I think, I read, I watch TV every day, I write, I have good memory, I hear very well, I see satisfactorily since the cataract operation, and all my senses are in fine shape.

In my case the length of my exile has now extended for forty years. The four shocks that I described in 1976 still stand, though some diluted and attenuated by the passage of time, others modified: culture shock, future shock, generational shock, and exile shock. For instance, culture shock diminishes with acculturation and a positive reception in the new country. Future shock, in contrast, increases with the pace of technological and social change. Generation gaps may be maintained, though in different ways, depending on and varying with the person. There have been different distances and gaps between different generations and waves of Cubans who have come here over the past four decades. There are some in the second generation (children born in the United States who are not "in exile," by definition) who want to retain some attachment to Cuba and to travel there, and there are some exiles who would condemn them for their attitude and perspective. Much depends on how you manage "home," and not making things worse by rejecting those you love because they do not share your exact ideology.

Exile shock, however, is maintained because the possibility of return remains unavailing and the sense of loss remains raw, if hidden. The unconscious is not able to perceive the passage of time. The experience of exile is a trauma that leaves a scar—it never disappears. The initial impact is traumatic, but it scarifies, and that remains as a permanent mark. I continue to *feel* in exile. I never desired it or imagined it; I did not come here for the American Dream but because of the Cuban Nightmare. Once here I had to make my way again, and represent my homeland in what I do here. One's homeland is not an "imagined community" (that's what Benedict Anderson imagines);[22] rather, homeland is a remembered community, remembered via a shared history—a history that for forty years I have remembered and shared in exile.

Exile is a defining fate; you don't just take it off like you would a pair of shoes. It involves going though the searing agony of loss—"encarnando el fenómeno" (living it in the flesh)—quite unlike the vantage of distant observers, "-ologists" of various disciplines and subjects. From the point of view of dispassionate observers, the claim can be made that a person ceases to be an "exile" when that person has become a citizen of a new country, learned its language and customs, and so on. But to an exile, you cannot take the label away; it is seen as a cross and as a term of honor. For some (not all, since some others do fundamentally adapt to new circumstances), the essence of that trauma persists, and they will die feeling it. In that sense exile is a subjective variable.

In the United States people received us well; I never felt discriminated against, rejected, or excluded. But while I am very grateful for that reception, and although I have a different citizenship and am regulated by the laws and norms of the new society, I have not become transformed as a person. And while I have always maintained a hope of return, I've been disabused of the idea (almost as wishful thinking) by the death of my wife and of so many colleagues and friends who were never able to return.

If I have a message or lesson to be drawn from my experience, it is that life—including everything that occurs in one's life, even exile—should be contemplated with the conviction that it changes with the passage of time: not because of time per se but because during those passing years events are happening, leaving an imprint, changing the circumstances of one's self. If you act with that conviction, you can react flexibly—but some exiles react inflexibly, having drawn a line in the sand and refused to accept the malleability of life, of human possibilities. One does not control the future; the future is not a function of one's wishful thinking.

Whether you like it or not, in the Cuban case the inflexible exile reacts wholly around Fidel Castro (that is, around the object of one's anger and hatred, the perceived cause of one's loss). Some end up distancing themselves from "reality" as they become more and more wedded to conspiratorial collective imaginings and irrationalities. "Cuba" continues to exist in its landscape, its beaches, its royal palm trees, and many other distinguishing features. But in exile one need not convert oneself into a member of the geriatric militias of Miami who rigidly and wishfully believe that they are the guardians of the historic exile. One needs to be realistic and not fixed, not inflexible, not filled with wishful thinking. The image of clay—as a flexible, malleable, modifiable medium—is apt here. As an image it suggests that experiences and human relationships modeled in clay are not immutable, but that as events occur and people react differently, it leaves a modified outcome. In that sense it serves as an image that better reflects reality; it is also symbolic of earth, land, vitality, fertility, life source. The history of this exile will be written neither in marble nor in sand but in clay.

More and more I observe my existence now as if through a rearview mirror instead of the windshield. This is a condition of aging and it happens to everybody, whether an exile or not. The passing of the years muffles all events and modifies each pain, each smile, each tear, each day and each night. For my observations and comments I have to rely much more on my son's eyes and ears. Despite all the shocks and the gaps and the years, we have managed to share our thoughts productively and to collaborate smoothly together for a common worthwhile goal.

IV. LOT'S CHILDREN: THE POST-EXILE GENERATION
Rubén G. Rumbaut

Several years ago David Rieff penned a perceptive portrayal of *el exilio* in *The Exile: Cuba in the Heart of Miami*.[23] He depicted the many facets of *el tema*, the main topic of conversation in Cuban Miami, a catchall phrase that described everything relating to "the exile." He wrote of men and women who lived and breathed *el tema*, who loved their lost homeland—indeed, who felt their love of Cuba as a "sacred illness," the bedrock of the exiles' cohesion—and who "were horrified by the existence of a younger generation so far along in their indifference to Cuba that they were loath even to acknowledge its existence." The wound that was exile was for them, Rieff observed, "unstanchable" after more than three decades, reflecting "the sense of lives, and homes, and youth, all gone forever . . . and the inexpressible, desolate sense of all exiles the world over share at being at ease and at home nowhere on earth."[24] Aptly, the book opens with this epigraph from Czeslaw Milosz: "It is possible that there is no other memory than the memory of wounds."

"Fresh starts" in the United States were for immigrants, motivated to get ahead; exile was about looking back, and remembering. In Cuban Miami—a mere forty-five-minute flight from a Havana that might as well have been light years away—the exiles "continued to live, metaphorically at least, with their bags packed and a strong fantasy alive in their hearts of what they would do in Cuba and for Cuba when, at last, they were finally able to return." Yet these "argonauts of nostalgia" were blind to the possibility that their own *cubania*, their sense of Cubanness and their roots in a lost past, might be purely generational, that it might stop with them and not extend to their Americanized children, who were thoroughly at home in Miami. Assimilation and exile did not mix. To assimilate was to accept that the exile was over, and, on a political level, that Fidel Castro had won, that all had been for naught. "The paradox was that the more comfortable they felt [in Miami], the more the wound of exile would be stanched, and the more their defining pain went away, the less they would be able to consider themselves to be exiles."[25]

Generational shifts in frames of reference are apparent to any Cuban American parent, even in Miami. In *Life on the Hyphen*, the Cuban American writer Gustavo Pérez Firmat, a "1.5er" who came with his parents into exile in Miami at the age of eleven, observed that his U.S.-born, Miami-raised children could no more be "saved" from their Americanness than his parents could be "saved" from their Cubanness; for his children, Cuba was "an endearing fiction, as ethereal as the smoke from their grandfather's cigars (which are not even Cuban but Dominican)"; and even for himself he would now envision a return to Cuba as a form of second exile, increasingly alien with the passage of time.[26] How accurate are those portrayals by Rieff and Pérez Firmat, an outsider and an insider to the group, and what are their implications for our understanding of the Cuban diaspora?

The end of the twentieth century may well have seen the end of an era of the Cuban diaspora. Inexorably, a new generation of largely U.S.-born and U.S.-oriented Cuban Americans has been replacing the generations who defined the meaning of being Cuban in exile. The signs of transition are everywhere, from the daily obituaries in Miami newspapers[27] to glossy new magazines like *Generation ñ*, devoted to exploring "life on the hyphen" for the young cohorts now coming of age in "Havana USA." Whether these *pinos nuevos*, in José Martí's famous metaphor of a century ago,[28] will be able to sustain a Cuban identity and an attachment to the Cuban nation is an open question.

Consider these related questions: If the future of Cuba as a nation lies with its children, then who are those children? Who "is" Cuba? Do the children of the diaspora belong to it, and do they identify with it? Do they feel that sense of belonging and of attachment to *la patria*—to the "father-land," "motherland," "home-land"—that suffuses their parents' national self?[29] Where is "home" for this post-exile generation (the U.S.-born children of the exiles)?[30] How is the post-exile generation likely to act and react to changes in Cuba? As time passes and events unfold, as they will, however unpredictably, will they call Cuba home? Or will they become only curious visitors, genealogical tourists, largely indifferent both to the manifold possibilities of national reconciliation and to the intransigent "vertical" position maintained by some sectors in exile of utter opposition to the regime in power—a politics not only of vindication but of vengeance as well?

The future of Cuba as a nation has a rendezvous with demographic destiny coming up shortly. Fidel Castro is in his mid-seventies; most Cubans on the island today were born well after the triumph of the revolution in 1959. The main protagonists of the tragic drama of revolution and exile are aging and passing on. In the not too distant future, they will make their exits from history—stage left or stage right, with a bang or with a whimper, some with great personal dignity, undiminished by their circumstances, but exits nonetheless. They will pass into the collective memory of Cuban history. And when the wall of bitter enmity between Cubans, on the island and in the diaspora, dissolves at last in the new century, the question of what it means to be Cuban in America will become all the more consequential. What bridges will form then, and who will cross them?

The Case of the 400,000 Missing Cubans

New national-level evidence bearing on this question suggests that a Cuban identity in the United States is rapidly eroding, especially as a result of intermarriage and dispersal outside the dense ethnic enclave in South Florida. An analysis of data collected in the late 1990s by the annual Current Population Surveys of the U.S. Census Bureau, which (unlike the decennial censuses since 1970) now asks questions about parents' country of birth, is illuminating in this regard. For decades official statistics on ethnic and racial identity have relied entirely on self-reports (on what persons say they are). I measured "Cuban identity" in two ways: a *subjective* identity (if the respondent self-identified as Cuban in the Hispanic question of the CPS), and an *objective* identity (if the respondent either was born in Cuba or had one or both parents born in Cuba). By the latter method, I estimated a Cuban-origin population (of persons born in Cuba or with at least one Cuban-born parent) of 1.6 million living in the United States as of 1997. But by the subjective identity method, which is the one used in reporting official data, there were only 1.2 million Cubans in the country at that time, a figure entirely in line with the 1990 (and now 2000) census counts. I dubbed this "the case of the 400,000 missing Cubans"—the substantial 25 percent who no longer identified as Cuban and who were fading into the twilight of ethnicity.

What happened to their identity? Of the "missing" 400,000, only 11 percent were born in Cuba, only 14 percent had two Cuban-born parents, and 80 percent lived outside the the primary enclave in South Florida. By contrast, of the 1.2 million who *did* identify as Cuban, over two-thirds were Cuban-born, four out of five (78 percent) had two Cuban parents, and a whopping three out of five (59 percent) were concentrated in metropolitan Miami alone, where they were more likely to sustain a Cuban identity into the second generation. Generation, parentage, intermarriage, and location were thus the main predictors of identity—and of identity loss. The 1990 census had counted almost 1.1 million (self-reported) Cubans in the United States. Of these, about 750,000 were born in Cuba, mostly exiles who came after 1959, and their median age was fifty. In sharp contrast, the median age of the approximately 300,000 born in the United States was only fifteen—and of that post-exile generation, 80 percent were under thirty, born after 1959. Census data on married persons also showed that 25 percent of Cubans in the United States were married to non-Hispanics—a figure that did not include the significant number of Cubans married to non-Cuban Hispanics. Those rates of intermarriage have increased over the past decade, raising still more questions about the meaning and construction of identity among their children.

Growing up in Cuban Miami

What do we know of the young people growing up in Cuban Miami? The best available evidence comes from the Children of Immigrants Longitudinal Study (CILS), the largest survey of its kind to date in the United States. The study has followed a sample of over 5,200 youths representing 77 different nationalities in South Florida and Southern California, from junior high in 1991–92 (when most were fourteen or fifteen years old) to the end of senior high school in 1995–96.[31] The sample was evenly divided by sex and nativity (half were foreign-born, half were born in the United States to foreign-born parents). Since Miami was one of the two sites in CILS, it is not surprising that children of Cuban origin represent the largest single ethnic group in the study. Over 1,200 of the CILS respondents surveyed in 1992 had at least one parent born in Cuba; in most cases both parents were Cuban-born (77 percent), but the children themselves were mostly U.S.-born (71 percent).

The study confirms that without exception, children of immigrants and refugees learn to speak English proficiently and come to prefer it to their mother tongue. While a foreign language was spoken in 93 percent of these households, 73 percent of all the children already preferred to speak English in 1992, and that proportion swelled to 88 percent by 1995–96. In these respects, Cubans did not represent an exceptional case in comparison with the other groups in the study. Even in Cuban Miami, English-language proficiency and preference for English was high and increased over time. By 1995–96, about 95 percent of the Cuban respondents preferred to speak English—suggestive of their rapid Americanization despite their location in "Havana USA." Still, the Cubans significantly surpassed all other groups in the proportion who remained fluent bilinguals; this was especially evident among those enrolled in bilingual private schools, the majority (55 percent) of whom were fluent in both Spanish and English by the end of high school (compared to 42 percent of Cubans in public schools).

CILS respondents where asked to indicate, in an open-ended question, how they identified themselves. Of all the groups in the study, the Cuban respondents were the *least* likely to identify by national origin—that is, as "Cuban." This was true in both the 1992 baseline survey and the 1995–96 follow-up, and among those in private school (only 3 percent to 6 percent thought of themselves as Cuban) and in public school (only 17 percent self-identified as Cuban); the small proportion who did tended to be Cuban-born. In the first survey the Cubans were among the groups with the highest percentage identifying as plain "American," though those numbers plummeted by the follow-up survey. Instead, the Cubans in private school shifted increasingly in favor of a hyphenated "Cuban-American" identity over time (from 58 percent to 71 percent), while the Cubans in public school were more likely to have adopted the pan-ethnic label of "Hispanic" (increasing from 8 percent to 32 percent). When they were first interviewed in 1992, relatively few thought of themselves as "Hispanics"—unlike most other Latin Americans—but by 1995–96, that identification with a racial-ethnic minority group had made great strides: 30 percent of all respondents with Cuban parents identified that way. In terms of identity, the process of "becoming American" for these youths is taking a bifurcated path, with the more socioeconomically advantaged and ambitious adopting a more mainstream hyphenated identity (a bilingual "life on the hyphen"), while others internalize a minority group identity.

CILS respondents were also asked to indicate if they had ever felt discriminated against, and whether they expected that they would be discriminated against no matter how much education they achieved. Tellingly, Cubans in Miami (whether in private or public schools) were the group *least* likely to report experiencing or expecting discrimination, even less than white respondents from Europe and Canada. That finding is noteworthy, and points to the protective nature of the dense Cuban enclave in which they have been raised—and to the fact that they are the only group to form a majority in the city where they have settled.

This sense of security from outside discrimination shows in other ways. Psychologically, Cuban-origin youth in Miami were found to have self-esteem scores well above average and the lowest level of depressive symptoms of any group in the study. Of all groups in CILS, the Cubans (in both public and private schools) watched more television and put in the least effort on homework, and in this unflattering respect they came across as perhaps the most assimilated of the 1.5- and second-generation groups. Finally, CILS respondents were also asked to agree or disagree with the statement that "the U.S. is the best country in which to live." Of all the groups, Cubans were most likely to agree with that statement, and by decisive margins. Furthermore, the percentages increased over time, so that by 1995–96, more than 80 percent of all the Cuban respondents agreed with the statement.

"Becoming American" takes different forms, has different meanings, and is reached by different paths. But the process is one in which all children of immigrants and refugees are inexorably engaged—forming a new national self and defining an identity for themselves, which is to say, a meaningful place in the society that is "home" to them. In the latest survey we asked them which place felt most like "home": the United States, their or their parents' homeland, both, or neither. The overwhelming majority—nine out of ten—said that the United States was "home," while minuscule proportions (just over 1 percent) indicated that either their country of origin or neither felt most like home. The rest, fewer than one in ten, indicated that "both countries" felt like home to them. Even in Miami, the heart of the Cuban community, they are coming of age in an American crucible, one not capable of sustaining intergenerationally a deeply felt sense of belonging to a Cuban nation. In the generational movement from exiles to ethnics, a hyphenated "Cuban-American" ethnicity is likely to flourish, especially in Miami. Yet even there it will most probably be absorbed into the vast American mainstream: a post-exile generation that will see itself mostly and natively as American, with or without the hyphen, and that will see Cuba nostalgically as origin but not as destiny, as the past and even the wished-for future of their *criollo* parents, but not as their own. This, in any case, is what present signs and trends seem strongly to suggest.

But who knows what the law of unintended consequences has in store for Cuba and for Cubans, in and out of the island, and what surprises await all of us yet? Our children, and grandchildren, may still surprise us themselves. Theirs, after all, will be the last word. But unlike their parents in exile, inces-

santly remembering and looking back home as in the metaphorical story of
Lot's wife, for Lot's children there is no similar memory of wounds, no phan-
tom pain, over a homeland that was never lost in the first place.

CODA
Rubén D. Rumbaut

A Psalm for Refugees: Lot's Wife

In that way:
  your neck
turned toward the past;
  your hair
loose, long, in disarray and gray;
  your eyes
absolutely fixed in the flames;
  your flesh
braised by burning ashes;
  your feet
covered by creeping lava;
  your whole body
made into salt, stone, and coal, and diamond;
  not wanting
any distraction, any consolation;
  ignoring
the present and the future, and all images
different from that perennial, radiant image
which fuses into itself
the cradle with the grave,
the home with the old land,
and the unforgettable
presence of persons, places, times, and circumstances;
that total, vivid, never-passing image
where all the things we were, and had, and loved,
forever lie . . .

  Statue of the exile,
tall trunk, deep root, firm rock, and living water;
biblical pillar; tireless, sharp spur;
dry pain without asylum or respite;

dark silhouette against the red bright fire;
sentinel, solitary, and ever-watching;
infinite witness of the human history
erect between destruction and expulsion.

You, the one who defied
the orders of departing and forgetting;
the most loyal, most faithful,
most tenacious
beyond fear, beyond death;
of all your ancient people
only you have remained:
single survivor since the day you died
among corpses that chose—they thought—to live.

I do not know
if your city sinned more than other cities;
I do not know
if the extermination was predestined;
I do not know
the cause of so much darkness, so much pain.
But from the catastrophe and the exodus
(when all the ashes cooled
and all the noises ceased
and the last sandal wore slowly away)
I know that you persist
the same forever;
you, heroine
victorious over death, space, and time,
sculptured in the flower of the mountain
with your profile of salt and mute defiance,
a longing gesture in the extended hand
while eternally looking at your land.

Notes

1. José Ortega y Gasset (1914). The original text reads, "Yo soy yo y mi circunstancia, y si no la salvo a ella, no me salvo yo." For an English language edition, see José Ortega y Gasset, *Meditations on Quixote*, trans. Evelyn Rugg, intro. Diego Marín (Urbana: University of Illinois Press, 2000), 1:322.

2. The two papers were presented on May 8, 1976, at the annual meeting of the American Society for Adolescent Psychiatry, Miami Beach. They are reproduced here in their original form. The theme of the ASAP meetings was "Youth in Transition: Developmental, Clinical, and Cultural Aspects."

3. Cuban Refugee Center, *Cuba's Children in Exile* (Washington, D.C.: U.S. Government Printing Office, 1967).

4. Rubén D. Rumbaut and Rubén G. Rumbaut, "The Family in Exile: Cuban Expatriates in the United States," *American Journal of Psychiatry* 133, no. 4 (April 1976): 395-99.

5. Wilder Penfield, "Conditioning the Uncommitted Cortex for Language Learning," *Brain: A Journal of Neurology* 88 (November 1965): 787-98.

6. Alvin Toffler, *Future Shock* (New York: Random House, 1970).

7. Margaret Mead, *Culture and Commitment: A Study of the Generation Gap* (Garden City, N.Y.: National History Press, 1970), 60-61.

8. Erik H. Erikson, *Identity: Youth and Crisis* (New York: W. W. Norton, 1968), 156-58.

9. A. C. Garza-Guerrero, "Culture Shock: Its Mourning and the Vicissitudes of Identity," *Journal of the American Psychoanalytic Association* 22 (1974): 408-29. See also Everett V. Stonequist, *The Marginal Man: A Study in Personality and Culture Conflict* (New York: Russell & Russell, 1937).

10. Rumbaut and Rumbaut, "Family in Exile."

11. Alejandro Portes, "Dilemmas of a Golden Exile: Integration of Cuban Refugee Families in Milwaukee," *American Sociological Review* 34 (1969): 505-18.

12. Georg Simmel, "The Stranger," in *The Sociology of Georg Simmel*, ed. and trans. Kurt H. Wolff (New York: Free Press, 1967), 402-8.

13. Alfred Schutz, "The Stranger: An Essay in Social Psychology," in *Collected Papers* (The Hague: Martinus Nijhoff, 1964), 2:91-105.

14. Erikson, *Identity*.

15. Kenneth Keniston, *The Uncommitted: Alienated Youth in American Society* (New York: Dell, 1965), 163.

16. Erik H. Erikson, "Youth: Fidelity and Diversity," in *The Challenge of Youth*, ed. Erik H. Erikson (Garden City, N.Y.: Anchor Books, 1965), 1-28. See also Erik H. Erikson, "Human Strength and the Cycle of Generations," in *Insight and Responsibility* (New York: W. W. Norton, 1964), 125.

17. Kenneth Keniston, "Social Change and Youth in America," in Erikson, *The Challenge of Youth*, 212.

18. Erik H. Erikson, "Psychological Reality and Historical Actuality," in *Insight and Responsibility*, 161-215.

19. Richard Flacks, *Youth and Social Change* (Chicago: Markham Publishing, 1971). See also Kenneth Keniston, *Young Radicals: Notes on Committed Youth* (New York: Harcourt, Brace & World, 1968).

20. Karl Mannheim, "The Problem of Generations" (1928), in *Essays on the Sociology of Knowledge*, ed. Paul Kecskemeti (New York: Oxford University Press, 1952), 276-322.

21. Erikson, "Youth: Fidelity and Diversity," 23. See also Erik H. Erikson, "Identity and Uprootedness in Our Time," in *Insight and Responsibility*, 83–107.

22. Benedict Anderson, *Imagined Communities: Reflections on the Origin and Spread of Nationalism* (New York: Verso, 1991).

23. David Rieff, *The Exile: Cuba in the Heart of Miami* (New York: Simon & Schuster, 1993).

24. Ibid., 22, 63, 102, 146.

25. Ibid., 27, 30, 60, 158.

26. Gustavo Pérez Firmat, *Life on the Hyphen: The Cuban-American Way* (Austin: University of Texas Press, 1994), 5.

27. Census data and life table analyses suggest that probably 100,000 Cubans who came in the early 1960s had died in exile by the year 2000, as had as many as 150,000 of the older Cubans who were airlifted during 1965–74. By 2010 the generational transition is likely to be virtually complete.

28. Martí, the quintessence of Cuban patriotism, was the Cuban-born son of Spanish immigrants who spent most of his adult life in exile in the United States, a struggle that deepened rather than weakened his sense of Cuban identity.

29. A woman in a camp in Croatia captured in a vivid metaphor the war-torn refugees' sense of loss of homeland: "They're like people who have lost a limb. Amputees. They can still feel their homeland, even though it's gone. It tingles. Subconsciously they know everything was destroyed, but as long as they're in camp they can dream it's still there." Christopher Merrill, *The Old Bridge: The Third Balkan War and the Age of the Refugee* (Minneapolis: Milkweed Editions, 1995), 36.

30. I call it a "post-exile" generation because to speak of a second generation in exile is an oxymoron: in Spanish, the word for "exile" is *destierro* (literally, "without one's homeland"), but for the second-generation children of the exiles, the land of their birth is the United States, most often the Florida peninsula, where two-thirds of the Cuban-origin population of the United States is concentrated.

31. See Rubén G. Rumbaut and Alejandro Portes, eds., *Ethnicities: Children of Immigrants in America* (Berkeley and New York: University of California Press and Russell Sage Foundation, 2001); and Alejandro Portes and Rubén G. Rumbaut, *Legacies: The Story of the Immigrant Second Generation* (Berkeley and New York: University of California Press and Russell Sage Foundation, 2001). The CILS study was still ongoing, with a third wave of interviews being carried out in 2001–2 when the respondents were in their mid-twenties.

Notes on Contributors

Deirdre Bonifaz, a writer, was born in New York and grew up in the hill town of West Whately, Massachusetts. She attended Bennington College, studied at the Sorbonne, and worked at the MIT Center for International Studies before her marriage to Cristobal Bonifaz, from Quito, Ecuador. Together they moved to the Sudan. What she witnessed in Asmara and in Khartoum turned her into an activist. At various times she worked for Head Start and the U.S. Committee for UNICEF. She is writing a book about her maternal grandmother, Bertha Goldberg, who died in 1945. At the time, refugees from World War II were staying with her parents, Blanche and Jimmy Cooney, on Morning Star Farm in West Whately.

Lâle Aka Burk, a native of Turkey, is senior lecturer in the Department of Biological Sciences at Smith College. She is a graduate of Roberts College in Istanbul and has a Ph.D. from the University of Massachusetts. Although most of her studies and publications are in the area of natural products and organic chemistry, her recent research has been focused on refugee professors from Nazi Germany who, invited to Turkey to participate in Atatürk's reforms, had a remarkable effect on the development of higher education in Turkey.

Polina Dimova, a native of Bulgaria, graduated from Smith College in 2002. She was a fellow of the "Anatomy of Exile" project in her senior year. She is currently a Ph.D. candidate in comparative literature at the University of California, Berkeley, where she works on English, German, and Russian literature and offers a reading-and-composition course on exile, displacement, and the literary imagination.

Donna Robinson Divine, professor of government at Smith College, also holds the Morningstar Family Chair in Jewish Studies. A graduate of Brandeis University with a Ph.D. from Columbia University, she is the author of books and articles on various aspects of Israeli and Arab politics and history and is currently engaged in research on Zionist culture and politics in Palestine during the period of British rule (1918–1948).

Saverio Giovacchini, a native of Florence, studied at the University of Florence and Smith College before entering NYU, where he received a Ph.D. in American history. He recently spent a year as a fellow at the Warren Center in American History at Harvard before becoming associate professor of history and media studies at the University of Maryland. He is the author of the prizewinning book *Hollywood Modernism*, a volume that closely examines the impact of refugee filmmakers.

Ruth Gruber, a scholar, journalist, and photographer, was born in 1911 and received a Ph.D. from the University of Cologne in 1931, at the age of twenty. Recipient of a Lifetime Achievement Award given by her peers in the American Society of Journalists and Authors, she is the author of numerous books, including *Raquela, Exodus 1947: The Ship That Launched a Nation*, and *Haven: The Unknown Story of 1,000 World War II Refugees*.

Gertraud E. G. Gutzmann was born in East Pomerania, received her secondary education in East Germany and her Ph.D. from the University of Massachusetts. A professor of German studies at Smith College, she has over the past quarter century taught a wide range of courses, including those on twentieth-century German-speaking women writers and women in the Third Reich. Her scholarly interests include nineteenth-century literature and twentieth-century politics and literature, particularly artistic responses to the experience of exile (1933–1947).

Charles Killinger is Patricia Havill Whalen Professor of History at Valencia Community College and adjunct professor of Italian history at the University of Central Florida. He has a Ph.D. from Florida State University. A specialist in the study of fascism and reactions to it, his books include *Rebel in Two Worlds: Gaetano Savemini in Italy and America* and *A History of Italy*.

Karen Koehler holds a Ph.D. from Princeton University and is associate professor of art and architectural history at Hampshire College and lecturer in American studies at Mount Holyoke College. She has served as a lecturer in the Department of the History of Art at Yale University and as a visiting lecturer in American studies and art history at Smith College. She is currently teaching a course on exile and completing work on a book on the emigration of the German architect and former Bauhaus director Walter Gropius.

Orm Øverland has taught American literature and American studies at the University of Bergen in his native Norway since 1970 and has frequently served as a visiting professor and resident scholar at American and Canadian universities. Among his many books are *The Western Home: A Literary History of Norwegian America* and *Immigrant Minds, American Identities*. He has a Ph.D. from Yale University.

Thalia Pandiri is professor of classics and comparative literature at Smith College and editor in chief of *Metamorphoses*, a journal of literary translation. She holds a Ph.D. from Columbia University.

Peter I. Rose, the organizing fellow of the Kahn Institute project "The Anatomy of Exile" and editor of *The Dispossessed*, is a senior fellow of the Kahn Institute and Sophia Smith Professor Emeritus at Smith College, and a specialist in the study of race, ethnicity, immigration, and refugee policy. His books include *They and We*, *The Subject Is Race*, *Strangers in Their Midst*, *Americans from Africa*, *Mainstream and Margins*, *Working with Refugees*, *Tempest-Tost*, and *Guest Appearances and Other Travels in Time and Space*. He received a Ph.D. from Cornell University in 1959.

Rubén D. Rumbaut, a writer, poet, and physician, was born in Cienfuegos, Cuba, and graduated from Havana School of Medicine and the Havana School of Journalism. He was exiled to the United States in 1960 and practiced psychiatry in this country for many years. Dr. Rumbaut died in 2003.

Rubén G. Rumbaut was born and raised in Havana and received his Ph.D. in sociology from Brandeis University. A professor of sociology at the University of California, Irvine, he is a leading authority on immigration and refugee movements and is coauthor, with Alejandro Portes, of many books on the subject, including *Latin Journey*, *Immigrant America*, and the award-winning *Legacies*.

Richard Preston Unsworth is a senior fellow at the Kahn Liberal Arts Institute at Smith College. He received a B.D. from Yale Divinity School and a Th.M. from Harvard Divinity School. His multifaceted career has included serving as dean of the Tuck School at Dartmouth College, president and headmaster of Northfield–Mount Hermon School and of the Berkshire School, and longtime chaplain at Smith College, where he also taught in the Department of Religion. He is writing a biography of the French pacifist André Trocmé.

Krishna Winston, professor of German at Wesleyan University, is currently conducting research on a number of exiled German writers and their translators and publishers. She has a Ph.D. from Yale University. The daughter of Richard and Clara Winston, prominently mentioned in her essay, she is a distinguished translator of many German authors including Siegfried Lenz, Christoph Heim, Eve Heller, Rainer Werner Fassbinder, Peter Handke, and Günter Grass.

Index